WHO OWNS THE NEWS?

WHO OWNS
THE NEWS?

A HISTORY OF COPYRIGHT

Will Slauter

STANFORD UNIVERSITY PRESS
Stanford, California

Stanford University Press
Stanford, California

Printed in the United States of America
on acid-free, archival-quality paper

Library of Congress Cataloging-in-Publication Data

Names: Slauter, Will, author.
Title: Who owns the news? : a history of copyright / Will Slauter.
Description: Stanford, California : Stanford University Press, 2019. |
Includes bibliographical references and index.
Identifiers: LCCN 2018035343 (print) | LCCN 2018038154 (ebook) |
ISBN 9781503607729 (e-book) | ISBN 9781503604889
(cloth : alk. paper) | ISBN 9781503607712 (pbk. : alk. paper)
Subjects: LCSH: Copyright—News articles—United States—History. |
Copyright—News articles—Great Britain—History. | Journalism—
United States—History. | Journalism—Great Britain—History. | Press
law—United States—History. | Press law—Great Britain—History.
Classification: LCC Z652.N4 (ebook) | LCC Z652.N4 S57 2018 (print) |
DDC 364.16/620973—dc23
LC record available at https://lccn.loc.gov/2018035343

Typeset by Motto Publishing Services in 10/15 Sabon

Cover design by Christian Fuenfhausen

For Guillaume

Contents

Acknowledgments

The research and writing of this book was supported by generous fellowships from the National Endowment for the Humanities, the American Antiquarian Society, the John W. Kluge Center of the Library of Congress, the New York Public Library, and the Library Company of Philadelphia. The staff of all these institutions did so much to facilitate my research and make my time in the archives stimulating and productive. I also received travel funds and other support from Florida State University, the Centre de recherches historiques (EA 1571) at Univerité Paris 8—Saint Denis, and the Laboratoire de recherches sur les cultures anglophones (LARCA, UMR 8225) at Université Paris Diderot. Appointment as a member of the Institut univeritaire de France in 2015 provided the time and resources necessary to bring the book to completion.

This project began in the spring of 2009 at the Columbia Society of Fellows in the Humanities. While at Columbia, I benefited from exchanges with colleagues in the Graduate School of Journalism, including Lucas Graves, Nicholas Lemann, Michael Schudson, and Andie Tucher. Columbia's Heyman Center for the Humanities, and especially Eileen Gillooly, continued to support my work by inviting me back to speak in 2012 and cosponsoring a workshop of the International Society for the History and Theory of Intellectual Property (ISHTIP) held in Paris in 2013. My book owes much to the interdisciplinary scholars who make up the ISHTIP community. I presented an overview of the project at the 2010 ISHTIP workshop in Washington, DC, and the final chapter was part of the 2017 workshop in Toronto. In between, I benefited from years of stimulating discussion and advice from ISHTIP regulars, including Sara Bannerman, Jose Bellido, Michael Birnhack, Kathy Bowrey, Gabriel Galvez-Behar, Eva Hemmungs Wirtén, Fiona Macmillan, Jessica Silbey, Simon Stern, Eva E. Subotnik, and Julian Thomas. I am particularly indebted to Martha Woodmansee for her intellectual guidance and comments on my work, and to Lionel Bently for reading drafts and suggesting new avenues to consider. H. Tomás Gómez-Arostegui was generous with his comments by email and over the phone, and Peter Jaszi provided crucial advice and encouragement.

Robert Darnton and Anthony Grafton, who mentored me as a history PhD student at Princeton, have continued to be sources of inspiration and guidance. Discussing the project over a coffee in Paris, Sarah Maza suggested, "You could call it *Who Owns the News?*"; I never let go of that idea. In the field of journalism history, I have learned much from exchanges with Joseph M. Adelman, the late James L. Baughman, Victoria E. M. Gardner, Brooke Kroeger, David Paul Nord, and Jeffrey Pasley. I owe special thanks to the historians, literary scholars, book historians, and legal scholars who have commented on draft chapters and oral presentations related to this book. These include Isabella Alexander, Gene Allen, Thomas Augst, Fabrice Bensimon, Oren Bracha, Robert Brauneis, Trevor Cook, Richard Danbury, Ian Gadd, Ellen Gruber Garvey, Andrew Hobbs, Leon Jackson, Richard R. John, John McCusker, Claire Parfait, Stephan Pigeon, Joad Raymond, Megan Richardson, Jonathan Silberstein-Loeb, Rebecca Spang, Michael Stamm, Simon Stern, and Heidi J. S. Tworek. Michael Winship read several chapters when they were in a messy state and helped me to improve them. Molly O'Hagan Hardy combined intellectual rigor and good humor as we talked through the central issues in this book, and her comments on the manuscript were a tremendous help. I was fortunate that my time as a Kluge Fellow at the Library of Congress overlapped with Zvi Rosen's tenure as the Kaminstein Scholar in Residence at the US Copyright Office; he taught me much about historical copyright records.

At Université Paris 8 and at Université Paris Diderot, I have been lucky to enjoy the support of numerous colleagues, and although I can't thank them all properly here, I want to mention those who commented on draft chapters or presentations: François Brunet, Emmanuelle de Champs, Ariane Fennetaux, Mark Meigs, Alice Monter, Stéphanie Prévost, Cécile Roudeau, Ann Thomson, and Sophie Vasset. Robert Mankin and Marie-Jeanne Rossignol organized a conference at Institut Charles V in 2009 at which I gave the first public presentation of this project. Robert passed away in 2017 and is sorely missed in our department. I will never forget how he helped me to transition to the French university system. Claire Parfait welcomed me into the fold of French scholars interested in history of the book and has been an endless source of advice. I am also grateful to Juliette Bourdin, Erica Gilles, Lynn S. Meskill, Isabelle Olivero, Allan Potofsky, and Yael Sternhell for all of their help with the intellectual and practical aspects of writing this book.

I was fortunate to receive several invitations to present my work and receive valuable feedback. These include the Séminaire franco-britannique d'histoire, Université Paris IV-Sorbonne (2013), the Oxford Intellectual Property Research Seminar, hosted by Dev Gangjee (2014); the Cambridge Modern Cultural History Seminar, led by Lawrence Klein and Peter Mandler (2014); the Managing the News in Early Modern Europe conference, convened by Michiel van Groesen and Helmer Helmers in Amsterdam (2014); the Edward S. and Melinda Sadar Lecture in Writing in the Disciplines, Case Western Reserve University (2015); the Toronto Centre for the Book, hosted by Thomas Keymer and Simon Stern (2016); the Open University Book History seminar, hosted by Edmund King and Shafquat Towheed (2017); the EUI workshop on authorship, organized by John-Erik Hansson, Matilda Greig, and Mikko Samuli Toivanen (2017); and the Rise of the Newspaper conference at the Huntington Library, organized by Rachel Scarborough King and William Warner (2017). I also want to thank participants in the 2017 workshop on copyright and nineteenth-century periodicals held at Université Paris Diderot: M. H. Beals, Lionel Bently, Laurel Brake, Elena Cooper, Aileen Fyfe, Paul Fyfe, Julie McDougall-Waters, Noah Moxham, James Mussell, and Thomas Vranken.

For archival assistance at the New York Public Library, I want to thank Thomas Lannon, Tal Nadan, and Weatherly Stephan; at the AP Archives, Valerie Komor and Francesca Pitaro; at the Library Company of Philadelphia, James N. Green, Connie King, and Erika Piola. At the American Antiquarian Society (AAS), thanks to Daniel Boudreau, Andrew Bourque, Paul Erickson, Dennis Laurie, and Kimberly Pelkey for their help locating materials and answering my questions, and thanks to

Vincent Golden for sharing his expertise on nineteenth-century newspapers. At the Library of Congress, I owe thanks to Travis Hensley, Janice Hyde, and Mary Lou Reker of the Kluge Center, and to Theo Christov for so many stimulating conversations. In the US Copyright Office Public Records Room, I owe thanks to Angela Hightower and Pat Rigsby. Isaac Warden provided valuable research assistance at the Library of Congress. Back in Paris, LARCA's brilliant Jean-Marie Boeglin facilitated research trips and conferences.

At Stanford University Press, I want to thank my editor Margo Irvin for believing in this project and providing crucial advice, and to thank Nora Spiegel for managing the production process. I am grateful to the four anonymous reviewers who invested in my work and provided suggestions for improvement. Chapter 2 is a significantly revised and expanded version of an article that first appeared as "Upright Piracy: Understanding the Lack of Copyright for Journalism in Eighteenth-Century Britain" (*Book History* 16 [2013], 34–61. Copyright © The Society for the History of Authorship, Reading and Publishing. Reprinted with permission by Johns Hopkins University Press).

The advice, encouragement, and stimulating conversation of close friends and family members have saved me repeatedly, and I hope to thank them all in person. But I do want to record my gratitude to family members on both sides of the Atlantic. Mom; Dad and Nida; Eric, George, and Nora; Ryan, Abby, and Lorelei; Lucie, Bernard, Marie-Hélène, Ann-Lore, Andrew, and Léon—thank you for everything that you add to the world. Finally, to Guillaume: your patience, advice, and encouragement have made it possible for me to write this book. Your incomparable sense of humor has enriched my life in countless other ways. This book is dedicated to you.

WHO OWNS THE NEWS?

Introduction

NEWS IS INTRACTABLE. It has always been difficult to define and nearly impossible to control. For centuries, publishers have sought ways to make news exclusive. Some have even claimed it was a form of property. But such attempts have repeatedly encountered resistance on political and cultural grounds.

In 1733, a London paper called the *Grub-Street Journal* was accused of "piracy." The offense? Each week's issue contained a digest of news compiled from eight to ten other London papers. The editor would read these papers looking for different accounts of the same event and then reproduce short excerpts one after the other, always indicating the source. The *Grub-Street Journal* was a satirical paper, and its news digest poked fun at contemporary politicians and news writers. But it also had a serious purpose. By juxtaposing different versions of the same story, the *Journal* exposed the errors and contradictions that filled the press. (See figures 1 and 2.) When accused of unfair dealing, the *Journal*'s editor defended himself on the grounds of public utility. He wrote, "Our method of comparing the articles of one paper with those of another is not only not piratical, but extremely useful, and even necessary to put a stop to the currency of false news."[1]

Almost three hundred years later, in the first decade of the twenty-first century, a new kind of news aggregation—this time powered by computer algorithms that pulled articles from across the web—threatened a newspaper industry in crisis. Publishers and press agencies complained about internet aggregators and media-monitoring services that reproduced headlines and short snippets of news without permission.[2] Some initiated lawsuits in order to negotiate licensing deals with technology firms such as Google and Yahoo; others lobbied for legislative changes that would better protect news organizations against unauthorized use of their content.[3] Much had changed since the eighteenth

> ### DOMESTIC NEWS.
>
> C. *Daily Courant.*   DA. *Daily Advertiser.*
> P. *Daily Post-Boy.*   SJ. *St. James's Evening Post.*
> DP. *Daily Post.*   WE. *White-hall Evening Post.*
> DJ. *Daily Journal.*   LE. *London Evening Post.*
>
> THURSDAY, *Aug.* 1. Yesterday their majesties, &c.
> hunted a buck in Richmond New Park, for the first
> time, &c. *P. DA.* —— A stag. *DP.* —— A hind. *DJ.*
> —— Which afforded some hours diversion. *P.* ——
> Very good diversion near two hours. *DP. DA.* ——
> Excellent sport. *DJ.* —— It lasted little more than an
> hour: the dogs, having eaten in the night a whole dead
> horse, were nor keen enough to afford much diversion.
> *LE.* —— *These contradictions are* good diversion *to the*
> *reader.*

FIGURE 1. The *Grub-Street Journal* reproduced short phrases from several newspapers one after the other, revealing humorous contradictions in the reporting of a single event (August 8, 1734). Courtesy of the Beinecke Rare Book and Manuscript Library, Yale University.

> On sunday Mr. Longley, a Cornfactor at the White-
> hart Inn in Southwark (who about 6 weeks ago marry'd
> the Widow who kept the Pine-apple, a noted eating house,
> the corner of S. Martin's-court in Castle-street) died, un-
> der violent suspicions of being poison'd, his body having
> swell'd that it burst. *DJ.* He dy'd on tuesday morning:
> There had been great differences between them ever since
> the unhappy marriage: it is reported, that she was much
> vex'd to find his circumstances not so agreeable; and he
> was uneasy to find that she kept company with ano-
> ther man, whom he found one night in her chamber: she
> then said she would give him a pill for it; and accordingly
> sent a servant for some poison, and under some pretence
> gave it him in a cup, immediately after which he fell in-
> to violent disorders, and in a little time died. *DP.* ——
> On thursday night between 11 and 12 the Coroner's in-
> quest brought in their verdict *Wilful murder.* Some of
> the poison dregs, lodg'd in the body, were given to a
> dog, which expir'd as soon as he eat it. Dorothy Long-
> ley is in custody in the New Jail in Southwark. *P.*

FIGURE 2. An example of how the editor aggregated sentences from three named sources (the *Daily Journal*, *Daily Post*, and *Post Boy*) to provide readers with a more complete account (September 9, 1731). Courtesy of the Beinecke Rare Book and Manuscript Library, Yale University.

century. New technologies, new business strategies, and new cultural practices had transformed how news was disseminated. Professional journalism, which had not existed in the days of the *Grub-Street Journal*, was in crisis as newspapers drastically reduced staff or closed entirely.[4] The context was different, and the political stakes were higher, but websites accused of theft or free riding could have done worse than to echo the *Grub-Street Journal*'s claim that juxtaposing short extracts of news was useful to the public. Yet in a world in which it was possible to copy and retransmit texts instantly, how would news organizations recoup their investments in reporting the news?

Of course, copyright law has changed significantly in the last three hundred years. In the 1730s, the statute in Great Britain explicitly protected books but did not mention newspapers, journals, or magazines. The editor of the *Grub-Street Journal* suggested that some newspaper material, such as original poems and essays, should be treated as literary property, but he thought that news was different. He wrote that "no man can assume to himself a Property by employing persons to collect a heap of trivial, ridiculous, and false paragraphs of news, and then publishing them daily to the world."[5] By the mid-nineteenth century, major changes in the business of news led newspaper publishers and agencies in Great Britain and the United States to begin to think of news in more proprietary terms. In both countries, special legislation to protect news for a short period of time was proposed on different occasions in the nineteenth and early twentieth centuries. Proponents argued that collecting and distributing news was expensive and that copyright would provide the necessary incentive to furnish the public with timely access to quality journalism. Critics objected that copyright was inappropriate for news. While some claimed that news lacked the qualities associated with literary authorship, others worried that copyright could restrict the flow of information of public concern.

By the early twentieth century, copyright was available for newspapers—the twists and turns that led to this development will be explored in the chapters that follow—but the idea of exclusive rights in the factual details of news remained controversial. Thanks in part to legal disputes over news, courts had begun to distinguish between facts and expressions, insisting that only the latter could be protected by copyright. During World War I, this limitation led the Associated Press (AP) to turn away from copyright in hopes of finding another means of protecting the factual details of news. In a case that the AP brought against one of its competitors, the US Supreme Court in 1918 ruled that news should be regarded as *"quasi* property." Although the AP could not restrict how members of the public used news after it was published, the organization had a right to stop competitors from copying *or rewriting* AP news for as long as it had commercial value.[6] This ruling gave rise to the misappropriation doctrine, also known as the "hot news" doctrine, which has been invoked in lawsuits against websites that republished news and stock recommendations online. Despite dramatic changes in the technology, economics, and culture of news since 1918, the hot news doctrine has even figured in policy discussions about how to protect journalism in the digital age.[7]

In the chapters that follow, the historical developments that I just outlined will be given the context they need to be properly understood. But even taken out of context, these examples reveal that debates about copying—how copying affects the ability of news organizations to function and how copying affects public access to news—are not new. The consequences of treating news as a kind of property have been discussed numerous times in the past. But such debates tend to fizzle out and be forgotten the next time the issue comes up—hence the need for a historical approach. The purpose of this book is to understand the recurring struggle to balance the interests of rival publishers and the public good in relation to long-term shifts in publishing and the law.

A HISTORICAL APPROACH

This book covers developments in Great Britain and the United States.[8] Examining related issues in other countries would no doubt reveal how different policy decisions and publishing strategies led to different outcomes in those places.[9] The choice to focus on Britain and the United States was motivated by the fact that when it comes to copyright law, these countries share a common heritage that differs from the authors' rights tradition that developed in continental Europe.[10] In some respects, the history of journalism in Britain and America is also linked.[11] And yet the timing and rationale of attempts to establish legal protection for news differed in the two countries. These differences reveal that new communications technologies—from the electric telegraph to the internet—cannot by themselves explain when and why people have lobbied for new legislation or gone to court to stop others from copying. News publishers have always worked within a larger political economy determined by government regulations, industry practices, and institutional arrangements, such as partnerships and joint ventures.[12] The different policy decisions and business strategies that developed in Britain and America help to explain why certain kinds of copying came to be seen as problematic at distinct moments in time.

Complaints about piracy (more on this term shortly) and discussions about whether news can be the subject of some kind of property right go back much further than the introduction of the telegraph in the mid-nineteenth century. In the sixteenth and seventeenth centuries, printers and booksellers who dealt in news already struggled with how to reach readers faster than their competitors and how to prevent the sorts of copying that would undermine their investments. This book therefore begins with a chapter on the sixteenth and seventeenth centuries, a period when the publication of news was regulated through a combination of censorship and royal privileges. This combination made it possible to have exclusive rights over news, but it also restricted the sorts of news that could be published. The breakdown of press licensing at the end of the seventeenth century and the creation of the first copyright statutes in the eighteenth century were important changes in public policy that had profound effects on the publication of news. Over the course of the eighteenth and nineteenth centuries, new attitudes toward authorship and convictions about the benefits of allowing information to circulate made the idea of legally enforced monopolies on news seem less and less defensible. Yet changes in the business of news also made certain kinds of exclusivity desirable for publishers, press associations, and agencies. In many ways, we still live with this tension today.

WHAT DOES IT MEAN TO OWN NEWS?

Admittedly, there are many ways to answer the question of who owns the news. This book is not primarily concerned with who controls the assets of major news outlets (who owns the media?) or the growing power that advertisers and technology firms have over the kinds of information available to the public. These questions are certainly important, and they rightly receive attention from scholars and journalists.[13] The focus here, though, is on attempts to control news by treating it as a form of intangible property. At the heart of the story is the evolving relationship between news publishing and copyright law, but it is important to note at the outset that copyright is not the only weapon in the battle over who owns the news. As the following chapters will show, writers, editors, and publishers have adopted a range of strategies to exert control over the news they collected or produced. They have requested and sometimes obtained state-sanctioned monopolies, formed cartels that turned potential "pirates" into partners, changed their times of publication to reduce the chance of being copied, set traps—such as deliberately publishing false news—to catch "thieves," and used the press to publicly embarrass those who did not play by the rules they sought to impose.

These and other strategies, including recourse to copyright law, could be seen as responses to a problem inherent to news as a commercial product. News is what economists call a nonrivalrous good. Unlike food or fuel, one person's consumption of news does not reduce the quantity available for others. Even if all the copies of a newspaper are sold, more can be printed, and at an extremely low marginal cost. Fixed costs for the production of news are high because they include salaries, travel expenses, equipment, and other overhead. Marginal costs—the cost of printing another copy of a newspaper, for example—have always been low, and now they approach zero. Publishers of news have tended to charge for access to it, thereby trying to exclude those who do not pay. But news has never been totally excludable. Long before networked computers made it possible to instantly copy and transmit words, photographs, and videos, people were able to share news by talking about it, transcribing it into letters, or passing around newspapers. And in the absence of some law or agreement to the contrary, it has always been possible to republish news collected or produced by a competitor. For these reasons, news resembles what is known as a public good. In economic terms, public goods are nonrivalrous and nonexcludable. They cannot be depleted, and they can be enjoyed by people who do not pay. Public goods are often seen as providing benefits to the community as a whole, not just to the individuals who would choose to pay for them. Indeed, they often have to be subsidized because individuals will not pay enough to cover their costs. Street lighting and fire departments are good examples: local taxpayers contribute to their upkeep, but anybody visiting the town can benefit from them. News is more complicated; it is nonrivalrous but also partly excludable. Publishers can restrict access by placing articles behind a paywall, but some subscribers will share them with nonsubscribers, and the details of the news will quickly be relayed in multiple ways.[14]

Copyright law can be viewed as a mechanism for dealing with the public-goods problem as it affects not just news publications but all sorts of literary, artistic, and scientific works. By granting certain exclusive rights (especially the sole right to produce and sell copies of the work), the state creates boundaries where none naturally exist, thereby providing authors and publishers with an incentive to create new works.[15] But the fact that published news is nonrivalrous and can be reproduced at zero marginal cost does not mean that the problem of piracy is a universal and unchanging one. Historical context matters. The kinds of activities denounced as piracy and the strategies used to combat them have varied by time and place. The arguments for and against treating news as a species of property have also developed over time. Understanding this history means grappling with several terms—starting with *property*—that have been central to discussions of rights in news but have meant different things to different people. The other words that constitute moving targets in our story are *piracy, copyright,* and *news* itself. For all of these terms, it is important to pay attention to how people have used them in different contexts and the goals that they have sought to accomplish.

METAPHORS OF OWNERSHIP:
PROPERTY AND PIRACY

Property has long been the single most important metaphor underpinning legal rights to writings and other works of the mind.[16] In the case of land, property has often been understood as a set of rights enjoyed by the owner, including the right to use and dispose of the land (such as by selling it) and the right to exclude others from the land. A corollary of the right to exclude is the right to license others to use the land and to set the terms of their use. When applied to writings, property might entail the right to exclude others from performing some actions but not others. For example, in eighteenth-century Britain, the copyright statute gave authors and their assignees the sole right to print, import, and sell copies of their books, but it did not allow them to prevent others from making translations, abridgments, and other adaptations. Over time, the duration of the copyright term has expanded, but so has the list of exclusive rights enjoyed by the individuals or corporations that the law recognizes as the copyright owners.[17]

But copyright law is not the only basis on which authors and publishers have made property claims. In various contexts, they have developed trade customs or referred to the common law in an effort to secure rights that were not recognized by the copyright statutes. The notion of a property right resulting from one's labor, formulated most famously by John Locke at the end of the seventeenth century, was seized and elaborated on by those who sought to defend a property right based on the mental labor of authors.[18] As we shall see, publishers of news in a variety of formats developed variations of this argument, stressing the need to *protect* (another persistent metaphor) the labor and investment that went into collecting and distributing news, regardless of whether such a property right was actually recognized by the law.

The property metaphor was apparent in many of the terms that authors and publishers used to denounce violations of their supposed rights, including *invasion* and *trespass* (by analogy to property in land), *theft* and *robbery* (property in moveable goods), and *piracy* (a ship's cargo).[19] Beginning in the mid-seventeenth century, as Adrian Johns has shown, the word *piracy* was used by printers and booksellers to denounce various activities that transgressed the shared norms of their community. The appeal of the metaphor depended not only on the idea of theft but also on the image of seagoing pirates as outlaws who threatened the social and political order.[20] The term *piracy* has in fact been used to refer to a range of practices, not all of which were illegal at the time. For most of the nineteenth century, for example, American law did not recognize copyright for authors who were not citizens or residents of the United States. It was therefore perfectly legal for American publishers to issue reprints of British novels without permission. But from the perspective of British authors and publishers, unauthorized editions were unfair and immoral. They were piracies.[21] Interestingly, American publishers who issued these reprints also developed their own customs, known as courtesies of the trade, to avoid ruinous competition with each other. They created rules to determine who had the exclusive rights over individual novels and even the future works of a particular British author. Publishers who violated these customary rights by printing a book claimed by someone else were denounced as pirates, even though according to American law the work was in the public domain.[22]

The example of transatlantic reprinting shows that what counted as piracy depended not only on the geography of copyright jurisdictions but also on publishing strategies and evolving notions of right and wrong.[23] Similar factors were at play in the realm of news. The word *piracy* was more or less common depending on the period, and it was used to refer to a range of unwelcome actions, from the appropriation or imitation of a title to verbatim copying and paraphrasing of individual articles. In most cases, the practices being denounced were not explicitly prohibited by law, but they seemed unjust or dishonorable to those making the accusation. In the case of news, attitudes toward copying—whether it was seen as harmful, innocuous, or even beneficial—generally depended on who was copying, how soon they were doing it, whether they cited the source, and where they were located in relation to one's own customers. Much depended on the frequency of publication and the geographic territory in which publishers sought their customers. For example, a daily newspaper might not have minded being copied by a weekly journal, since it had already profited from being first to announce the news. But a morning paper might have objected to copying by evening papers in the same city. Meanwhile, a paper in one city might have accepted being copied by papers in another city if properly credited as the source of the news, unless, of course, they were in direct competition for readers and advertisers. These spatial and temporal boundaries were always somewhat elastic, and they were stretched in various ways as a result of new forms of publication (such as evening papers and magazines), new modes of business organization (especially press associations and agencies), and new means of transporting newspapers or relaying individual stories (the railroad, telegraph, radio, and the internet). News publications have always been situated in time and space in relation to other publications and to communications technology providers, from the post office and telegraph companies to social media platforms. Whether copying is perceived as harmful depends on these relationships.

HOW TO WRITE THE HISTORY OF COPYRIGHT

Like *property* and *piracy*, *copyright* is a term whose meaning has depended on the context and the goals of the person using it. One reason for this is that the purpose and scope of copyright have often been subject to debate. Another reason is that writers, publishers, and readers do not always understand copyright in the same terms as do lawyers or judges. The premise of this book is that the history of copyright should be a history of how copyright was understood and used by individuals in the past. My approach is inspired by interdisciplinary scholarship that has stressed how individual authors and publishers navigated questions of copyright as well as studies of "copyright pioneers" who campaigned for new laws or went to court in an attempt to obtain recognition of new rights.[24] I reconstruct the history of legislation and case law related to copyright for news publications, but I also insist on the need to study legal developments in relation to changes in publishing practice. In that respect, my book is indebted to several generations of scholarship in the field known as history of the book. Historians and literary scholars working in this field have revealed that it is impossible to understand the early history of copyright without studying the organizational structure of the book trade. They have also shown that printers and publishers often ignored copyright or developed trade customs to regulate their businesses.[25] But most histories of publishing that discuss copyright focus on books, and news publications followed a different trajectory. Copyright law was designed for books, and the different formats in which news was published and the different business models developed around news challenged existing frameworks in many ways.

As I attempt to weave together the history of law and the history of publishing practice, I accept that the relationship between the two is not always clear. Sometimes a statute or court ruling led to changes in the way news publishers operated; other times, shifts in publishing inspired discussions of the law or attempts to change it. Many times, however, it is impossible to identify a relationship. But by considering law and publishing practice together, I hope to provide a clear explanation of developments while acknowledging the ambiguity and uncertainty that shaped how individuals understood and made use of copyright. Copyright registration records, an underutilized resource, are studied alongside court cases, other archival evidence, and the news publications themselves to determine when and where individuals have sought out copyright protection, with what motivations, and to what effect. Attempts to assert copyright or other kinds of property rights in news were sometimes driven by the will of an individual or group to establish a new legal principle; in other cases, they reflected the desire to stop a particular rival. Sometimes the arguments used to justify exclusive rights had a close relationship to the practices of publishers or press agencies; other times, there was a gap between rhetoric and reality. That does not make it any less important, however, to study the rhetoric.

WHAT IS NEWS?

Efforts to protect news by legal means have been repeatedly hindered by the difficulty of defining news. What is it we are trying to protect, against whom, and for how long?[26] Even for industry insiders, the definition of news has often seemed elusive. Prompted by an inquiry from the trade journal *Editor & Publisher* in 1932, a number of figures in the New York newspaper world volunteered their definitions of news. But none seemed satisfactory to the person making the inquiry or to the respondents themselves. Julian S. Mason of the *New York Evening Post* highlighted the subjective experience of individuals, suggesting that "news is something which you can hardly bear to wait to tell somebody else." Frank M. O'Brien of the *Sun* said that to qualify for news, something had to be not previously published and within the bounds of what was considered suitable for a newspaper. Arthur Hays Sulzberger of the *New York Times* proposed that "what's new is news," but he considered this definition imperfect. Kent Cooper, general manager of the AP, supposedly boasted, "The Associated Press report is my definition of the word *news*."[27]

Historians and sociologists have suggested that news is culturally constructed: news is not what happened but stories about what happened, and these stories are shaped by professional norms and literary conventions as well as the tastes of the public and the concerns of advertisers.[28] Although the history of journalism has usually been written in a national framework, a strand of recent scholarship has highlighted the transnational circulation of news. Stressing the importance of exchanges and networks, these studies have suggested that news is as much about the process by which people learn of events as it is about the content. In fact, the two cannot be easily separated.[29] Journalism scholars have sometimes distinguished between *events* occurring in the world, *sources* of information about those events, and the *news* that is produced from these sources. But in many instances the distinctions become blurred and it is difficult to tell the difference between the event, the source, the information, and the news.[30]

The difficulty defining news became apparent whenever people attempted to claim exclusive rights over it. Many of the disputes covered in this book centered on the struggle to protect breaking news, usually in the form of short, factual accounts of what happened. In these cases, publishers and press agencies struggled to define the news as something distinct from the occurrence. It may seem obvious that there is a difference between the fact that something occurred and a verbal or visual representation of it, but attempts to obtain exclusive rights over news often encountered the objection that nobody could own *the news*. It was often unclear what each side meant by *the news*; it was difficult to distinguish between the expression and the fact.

Rather than imposing a definition of news, I accept that news has always been difficult to define, and in the course of the book I highlight how disputes over ownership rights have often led to new definitions. For example, in response to efforts to pass a special copyright law for news in the United States in 1884, opponents circulated a petition arguing that news was not eligible for copyright because it was not the product of "creative and inventive talent." The petition asked, "What is news?" It answered that news was "the statement of facts, the history of current events. Can anyone create or invent a fact or event? If he cannot create or invent a fact or event, how can he copyright it?"[31] The active resistance to the 1884 legislation, which is further explored in chapter 6, provides an example of how attempts to protect news led writers, judges, politicians, and others to advance arguments about the purpose and acceptable boundaries of copyright. Another example of this process can be found in an American court case from 1828 involving the unauthorized republication of market news. In this case, which is fully analyzed in chapter 4, the attempt to use copyright to protect commercial and financial information led the judge to articulate a principle that would be followed for decades to come: copyright was meant to promote works that made a lasting contribution to learning.[32] Disputes over news also helped to shape legal doctrine with respect to the scope of copyright protection. One of the earliest court rulings to distinguish between protected expressions and unprotected facts was an 1892 case in Britain involving the copying of news paragraphs. And a 1900 dispute over whether newspaper accounts of public speeches could be protected created an important precedent by emphasizing the reporter's labor and skill as the basis for copyright, thereby setting a low threshold for originality in British copyright law.[33] These and other cases explored in this book show how studying the sometimes tense relationship between news and copyright law sheds light on the history of both. Copyright might have developed differently without the legislative proposals, debates, and court cases involving news. Meanwhile, efforts to use the law to protect news led to debates about what news was and how best to promote public access to it.

With these goals in mind, the following chapters are organized roughly in chronological order, but they do not all share the same emphasis. Some offer a narrative of change over a relatively long period (chapters 1, 2, 5, and 6), whereas others focus on a more restricted era to explore the attitudes and practices of newspaper editors (chapter 3) or analyze a single court case and its significance (chapters 4 and 7). Three of the chapters focus on Britain and four on the United States; the epilogue considers recent developments and ongoing issues in both countries. Since this is an overview covering more than four hundred years, I necessarily made choices about what to highlight. Readers familiar with journalism history may be struck by the absence of certain personalities or events that usually feature in accounts of the development of journalism. Those who are well versed in copyright law might note that the focus on news decenters certain legislative or judicial developments in favor of others. But it is hoped that the choices made here provide a new way of thinking about the history of news publishing and the history of copyright by studying them together.

Owning News in an Age of Censorship and Monopoly

THE DESIRE TO LEARN WHAT'S NEW is deeply rooted in most societies, and attempts to make money catering to this desire have a long history. By the sixteenth century, a commercial market for news was already developing in England and throughout Europe. Information about politics and trade flowed through the letters of diplomats and merchants, and individuals known as "intelligencers" made a business supplying elite clients with handwritten newsletters that detailed the latest developments in other cities and countries. Meanwhile, printers and booksellers experimented with how to convey news of battles, natural disasters, and strange occurrences to a wider range of paying customers. Over the course of the seventeenth century, the expansion of postal routes and courier services across Europe made it possible to expect more regular updates from other places, creating new opportunities to sell news. Relying on reports that arrived in the mail, publishers began to issue news in weekly periodicals that sought to maintain the interest of readers from one issue to the next.[1]

Early news entrepreneurs had to figure out how to distribute their publications fast enough to make a profit before rival publications appeared. Compilers of handwritten newsletters and printers regularly reproduced reports first published by their counterparts in other cities. Such copying generally raised few objections if the individuals involved were not competing for the same customers. But in cases in which they saw each other as rivals, copying was more of a threat. Of course, the potential for unauthorized copies to harm the sale of original works was common to all genres, not just news. In England the desire of printers and booksellers to avoid ruinous competition with one another was an important motivation for creating a single state-sanctioned guild known as the Stationers' Company, which was incorporated by royal charter in 1557.[2] In order to protect their investments, members of the Stationers'

Company developed shared customs to determine who had the right to print and sell a given book. They referred to rights in *copies* and spoke of the need to uphold the "propriety of copies," a phrase that evoked notions of proper conduct as well as of property rights (the words *propriety* and *property* were nearly synonymous at that time). In this context, the word *copy* not only referred to the physical manuscript being printed (a connotation that persists in the idea of an author's "fair copy"), it also designated the intangible work—text and all—over which stationers claimed exclusive rights.[3] The Stationers' Company policed its members and sanctioned those who printed or sold a copy belonging to another. By the late seventeenth century, the term *piracy* was being used to describe such offenses, but accusations of printing someone else's copy go back much further. What qualified as a violation of trade propriety and what was later branded as piracy depended on what was taken but also on the relationships of those involved.[4] Producers of news in the sixteenth and seventeenth centuries complained about verbatim reprinting, but they also objected to the reuse of titles or the creation of rival publications reporting the same event, even if none of the words were copied. These complaints resulted from the desire to enforce some degree of *exclusivity* in order to make news profitable.

But the creation of exclusive rights in news publications also depended on the interests of government. Whereas members of the Stationers' Company worried about protecting their investments, political and religious authorities sought to control the flow of news and impose limits on public discussion. Admittedly, not all news was treated as a commercial product. Much of it was exchanged orally or in writing among relatives and friends or within networks of trade and political patronage. Such nonmonetary exchanges were crucial to the way news traveled and acquired significance for people, but they have been examined elsewhere.[5] The focus here will be on printed news sold for a profit; it was in this context that publishers used a combination of legal and commercial strategies to try to make news exclusive. And it was in the realm of print that the monarchy, Parliament, and the City of London showed the most interest in controlling news.

Given how difficult it was to stop the flow of news entirely, the authorities tended to favor the same strategies that they employed to regulate printing in general: they used *licensing* (requiring approval before publication) and awarded *privileges* (assigning exclusive rights to a work or a whole category of publications). In practice, it remained difficult to stop others from copying, but when it came to the laws and customs governing printing, there was no distinction between news and other genres. Printers and booksellers claimed exclusive rights in broadsides, pamphlets, and periodicals conveying news. Special privileges were awarded for publications reporting commerce, public health, and criminal trials. And during many years, one or two individuals had a monopoly on political news. At the end of the seventeenth century, when the regime of licensing broke down permanently and new attitudes toward the circulation of information began to develop, it became much harder to monopolize coverage of an event or claim the exclusive right to publish a particular version of the news.

This chapter thus introduces a paradox: before the development of modern copyright beginning in the early eighteenth century, it was easier to claim exclusive rights in news than it would be subsequently. The first British copyright law, known as the Statute of Anne, went into effect in 1710. Although some of its provisions were based on customs established by the Stationers' Company, it also included new rules and concepts that broke with the past.[6] Significantly, the protection offered by the Statute of Anne was entirely divorced from state censorship and the practices of the guild. One no longer had to submit a manuscript to a censor before publication or be a member of the Stationers' Company to set up a press or sell printed works, including news. And beginning with the Statute of Anne, the law recognized authors as the first owners of their writings. What is less well understood is how this transition from an early-modern regime of licensing and guild customs to a modern regime of statutory copyright affected the publication of news. One of my contentions is that the end of licensing, combined with the particular ways copyright was interpreted and used in the decades after 1710, was crucial to the growth of newspapers. But to appreciate the extent to which the eighteenth century marked a turning point, it is necessary to examine what came before.

Rather than attempting to provide a comprehensive account of censorship and publishing practices in the sixteenth and seventeenth centuries, this chapter highlights the variety of early news publications and explains how they fit into the nexus of licensing, privileges, and trade customs that governed the world of printing. Contemporaries used many different words to describe news and the distinct forms in which it appeared, including *tidings, relations, occurrences, corantos, diurnals, newsbooks*, and *proceedings*. By contrast, the word *newspaper* began to be used only toward the end of the seventeenth century, a reminder that the newspaper's rise to prominence amid the tremendous variety of early news publications was not inevitable.[7] Indeed, the success of a particular kind of newspaper in the English-speaking world would depend on a series of interrelated changes in government regulations, publishing practices, and attitudes toward the circulation of information that began in the late seventeenth and early eighteenth centuries.

NEWS AND THE REGULATION OF PRINT

During the sixteenth and seventeenth centuries, ordinary people did not enjoy freedom of speech or the right to be informed of foreign or domestic policy decisions. The circulation of news in manuscript was more tolerated than was printed news, because its audience was more restricted. Diplomats, royal advisors, and members of Parliament exchanged information and leaked sensitive details in order to achieve political ends. Unauthorized accounts of trials and parliamentary proceedings circulated in newsletters and other manuscript publications sold to a well-connected clientele. Wider discussion of "affairs of state" was seen as an invasion of the *arcana imperii*, the secret realm of knowledge reserved for the monarch and his counselors.[8] As one study put it, "News of State was the property of the State. The public had no recognized right to political information."[9] Of course, information was porous, and people found ways to talk about events and policies when they gathered at markets, taverns, and churches.[10] But that does not change the fact that they did not have any recognized right to learn about or discuss political news.

The monarchy and the Stationers' Company each had an interest in regulating who printed what. The commercial objectives of the company and the political objectives of the monarchy together shaped how censorship worked in this period.[11] It is hazardous to generalize, because the extent to which the available mechanisms of control were applied depended on the context. But during the sixteenth and seventeenth centuries, there were two primary methods that the monarchy and the Stationers' Company relied on to govern printing: licensing and privileges.

Obtaining the authorization of a government licensor before publication was required beginning in the reign of Henry VIII (r. 1509–1547), when religious controversies related to the Protestant Reformation led to more official scrutiny of what was being printed. Censorship was not systematic. Much depended on the political circumstances and the zeal of the licensors, and there were too few of them to peruse all works before publication.[12] But that did not mean that censorship was ineffective. The fact that the government sometimes prosecuted individuals for failing to obtain a license or for the more serious offenses of seditious libel and treason necessarily had a chilling effect on writers. Printers tended to operate on the assumption that they needed to seek a licensor's approval for works that dealt with sensitive subjects.[13]

Printers also needed some way to stop competitors from issuing identical or substantially similar works, so they sought out privileges. Their motivations were similar to those of inventors and manufacturers who requested the exclusive right to exploit an invention or engage in a particular trade. Such privileges, usually awarded through letters patent, amounted to commercial monopolies for a specified number of years. The first one granted to a printer dates to around 1510, when Richard Pynson received the exclusive right, for two years, to print the first statute of Henry VIII's reign. By granting such privileges, monarchs could not only reward individuals through patronage but also promote the uniformity of important works (such as the Bible) by concentrating production in the hands of trusted individuals. The need for revenue was also a factor, since printers were willing to pay for privileges. Each monarch appointed an official king's (or queen's) printer, who had the exclusive right to print proclamations, injunctions, and other works issued by royal authority. Monarchs also granted privileges that covered whole classes of works, such as lawbooks or grammar books. Obtaining a privilege did not necessarily eliminate the problem of piracy, and there were rival claimants on occasion. But a patent holder whose rights were infringed could seek relief from the royal courts.[14]

Printers and booksellers realized that they could protect their interests even more effectively if they followed the example of other crafts and formed a single officially sanctioned guild. They succeeded in 1557, when Queen Mary I (r. 1553–1558) granted a royal charter of incorporation to the Stationers' Company. This charter, which was confirmed by subsequent monarchs, gave the Stationers' Company the right to keep apprentices, search workshops to ensure standards, and protect the trade from outsiders. Only members of the Stationers' Company were allowed to maintain presses or use them, and these presses had to be located in London. Exceptions were recognized for the University of Cambridge and the University of Oxford, which already had their own privileges for printing. The Stationers' Company thus enjoyed an almost complete monopoly on printing and bookselling.[15] Crucially, the monarchy also gave the company the powers needed to enforce this monopoly. The company's officers had the right to search the premises of all printers and booksellers in the kingdom, seize anything that violated any statute or proclamation, and imprison anyone who operated an illegal press. Subsequent royal decrees increased these powers of search and seizure, which were ostensibly justified by the government's need to suppress "seditious" and "blasphemous" works.[16] Most of the searches that the Stationers' Company performed, however, were not for works that the authorities had already deemed dangerous but for pirated editions— works that violated a member's exclusive rights.[17]

RIGHTS IN COPIES

Within the Stationers' Company, the justification for recognizing exclusive rights in printed works was the shared desire to avoid the kind of reprinting that would make it impossible to recoup investments, creating disorder in the trade. The stationers developed the custom, which was later recognized by royal decrees and Acts of Parliament, that the first member to enter a title in the company's "entry book of copies" (often referred to as the register) had the exclusive right to print and sell that work. By the early seventeenth century, such rights were treated as perpetual; they could be bought, inherited, or divided among several stationers and remain valuable assets for generations. Both printers and booksellers could own "copies," but eventually the booksellers became dominant. The booksellers took on some of the functions of modern publishers by financing the printing of works and coordinating their distribution, often by partnering with other booksellers.[18]

Before a work could be published, it had to be shown to one of the wardens of the Stationers' Company, who checked to make sure that it did not infringe the rights of other members. This internal check by company wardens was distinct from the process of licensing by royal officials. Indeed, some of the entries in the register indicate that the company's permission to publish was contingent on the stationer seeking approval from a licensor. But not all works that were authorized by the company were entered in the register. Entry required paying a separate fee to the clerk in addition to the fee paid to the warden for authorization. Stationers had to decide whether entry in the register was worth the cost, with the result that many titles were not entered.[19]

The register served as a record of rights to print and sell books and other publications, and it was consulted whenever disputes arose. These disputes were handled by the Stationers' Company's governing body, which was known as the Court of Assistants because it was made up of senior members called assistants. Company rules specified that a stationer whose rights were infringed by a fellow stationer had to seek relief here before turning to the royal courts. The goal was to resolve controversies internally and avoid publicity. If the accused party denied the charge, mediators would be appointed to investigate the evidence on both sides and propose a solution. In cases involving something other than wholesale reprinting, the mediators had to examine the works to determine whether the substance of the first work had been incorporated into the second. On some occasions, they judged epitomes, abridgments, and even translations to be violations of another member's copy.[20]

Individual stationers tended to respect the decisions of the Court of Assistants. Authors were not part of the Stationers' Company and played little or no role in the vast majority of disputes brought before the Court of Assistants. In most cases, once an author gave or sold a manuscript to a stationer, it was the latter who owned the copy.[21] The company was small enough—between twenty and thirty master printers depending on the period, plus journeymen and apprentices—that members knew and watched over each other. In the rare cases in which the Court of Assistants' decision was not respected, members could appeal to the royal courts to uphold their exclusive rights and declare the infringing work to be illegal. The authority that gave legal sanction to the company's printing privileges varied over time, and there were periods when political circumstances left the stationers without external protection, but for most of this period, the privileges recorded in the register were recognized by royal decrees or parliamentary legislation.[22] And when it came to printing rights, there was no distinction between news and other genres of publication: if a work was registered, it necessarily belonged to someone.

OWNING NEWS IN BALLADS AND PAMPHLETS

It is important to remember that printed news existed in a range of forms and that the newspaper was not the dominant mode of selling news until the eighteenth century. Newspapers are ongoing publications that have a stable, recognizable title and are issued at regular intervals. In that sense, they are periodicals.[23] Publishing news in periodical form is artificial, since most events of public concern do not occur on a predictable schedule. Adherence to weekly or daily periodicity creates the obligation to go to press regardless of whether something interesting occurs. News received after an issue is printed must be held until the following day or week. In addition to the need for a steady supply of news, periodicals require an effective means of distributing each issue to customers. Both of these tasks depend on a reliable postal service, which was only beginning to develop in the early seventeenth century. In addition, periodicals involve a regular production schedule in a fixed location, making it easier for the authorities to monitor them. Taken together, these factors help to explain why most printed news during the sixteenth and seventeenth centuries did not appear in periodicals but in stand-alone publications, especially broadsides and pamphlets.[24]

Broadsides featured words, and sometimes images, printed on one side of a sheet so that they could be posted to a wall or post for public viewing. Official broadsides, such as royal proclamations and Acts of Parliament, were not to be reproduced by anyone but the designated patent holders. Unofficial broadsides, however, were an important commercial venture for stationers. Hawked on the street for a half penny or penny each, the most popular titles sold thousands of copies.[25] Many of these broadsides contained news, in prose or in verse, accompanied by woodcut illustrations. Ballad writers put topical material—such as a fire or the execution of a criminal—to verse, but rather than providing a straightforward narrative, they tended to exploit the event to teach a moral lesson. A natural disaster or birth deformity, for example, could be presented as evidence of a community being punished for its sins and an opportunity for moral improvement. Of course, not all ballads could be considered news, but many focused on recent events, including crimes, natural disasters, and battles. It has been estimated that one-third of the approximately ten thousand broadside ballads that have survived from the seventeenth century dealt with politics in some way.[26]

Singing was one of the most popular ways of engaging with news and political commentary in this period. Even those who could not read or afford to purchase printed works could still learn what was going on by listening to ballads or by joining in the collective musical experience. The flexibility of the medium was what made it so powerful: new tales could quickly be set to familiar tunes, and singers could modify the details of the stories as they transmitted them.[27] Ballads were inherently collaborative, making authorship hard to pin down, but the stationers who specialized in them tended to pay a onetime fee to a writer, after which point the stationers owned the copy.[28] Ballads made up a majority of the works entered in the Stationers' Company register in the late sixteenth and early seventeenth centuries. All printed works were supposed to be registered, but it has been estimated that only half of surviving ballads were.[29] For those ballads that were registered, cases of piracy could be brought before the Court of Assistants, which tended to order the infringer to stop printing the work and to pay fines or damages to the registered owner.[30]

But entry in the register was not the only method that stationers used to protect against piracy. In 1612, the Stationers' Company restricted the printing of ballads to five members, ostensibly to hinder the production of unlicensed and offensive works. The company canceled this restriction in 1620, but a de facto monopoly was soon created by a group of six stationers who formed a partnership. By sharing ownership in a large stock of popular ballads, the partners avoided competition with each other. Meanwhile, by working together to distribute these ballads quickly, they made it harder for pirated editions to flourish. The existence of such partnerships helps to explain why the number of complaints involving ballads brought before the Court of Assistants declined during the second half of the seventeenth century.[31]

Besides ballads and other broadsides, the other main format for printed news was the prose pamphlet. Pamphlets consisted of one or more sheets of paper folded and stitched together to make a small book. A common length for news pamphlets was twenty-four pages. Many of them focused on foreign affairs, not only because domestic news was more closely monitored but also because English readers were interested in events on the continent. Because discussion of "affairs of state" was restricted, pamphlets on English events tended to focus on accidents, crimes, and executions. Not all news pamphlets were entered in the Stationers' Register. Some stationers anticipated that their works would not pass censorship and published them with a false imprint (naming someone other than the actual printer) or no imprint at all. Others wanted to avoid paying the fee required for entering a work in the register.[32] But those pamphlets that were registered were recognized as property in the same way as other printed works.[33]

The title page from one of them is shown in figure 3. This "true relation"—a common name for news publications in this period—recounted how a gentleman named John Barterham (elsewhere spelled Bartram), after losing a lawsuit in the Court of Chancery, killed the judicial official who ruled against him, only to take his own life a few days later. News of these events would have spread orally before the ac-

FIGURE 3. This pamphlet published in 1617 was entered in the Stationers' Company register as the property of the bookseller Lawrence Lisle, who appears on the title page as "L. L." Used with permission of the Folger Shakespeare Library. (STC 24435).

count could be printed. The goal of the pamphlet, which has a semi-official character, was to counteract rumors, erode public sympathy for Bartram, and use his story to offer a moral and political lesson. The message was that a gentleman who thinks he has been mistreated by the courts should petition the king for relief, not take justice into his own hands, let alone commit the cowardly and sinful act of suicide.[34] The pamphlet may have had propagandistic aims, but the right to print and sell it was nonetheless the property of the bookseller Lawrence Lisle, who entered the title in the Stationers' Register (he appears on the title page as L. L.).[35]

The woodcut illustration in figure 3 raises other questions. Ballads and news pamphlets often featured such woodcuts, but most were stock images rather than specific likenesses of the people and places in the news. In many cases, the choice of illustration depended on the woodblocks that were available, although some illustrations were commissioned directly for the purpose and thus more closely reflected the events being reported. Reprinting a pamphlet registered by another stationer was clearly a violation of his "copy," but there is less evidence of how stationers viewed the reuse of illustrations as part of another work. It was common for nearly identical images to appear on multiple pamphlets and broadsides, even those produced years apart. Sometimes this resulted from carving a new block of wood in imitation of an existing image, but other times it reflected the fact that printers shared a stock of woodblocks or that they had purchased or inherited the stock of other printers.[36]

The Stationers' Register shows that printers and booksellers sometimes tried to corner the market on news of a particular event. In 1597, a stationer registered a pamphlet about a recent battle, and his entry claimed that he reserved the exclusive right to "any ballad that shall be made thereof."[37] A similar technique was to enter a generalized title in an attempt to block others from issuing similar works. The clerk of the Stationers' Company had power over the form of entries and could make informal agreements with members, such as promising to refuse future applications to register works on the same topic. Some stationers would produce a ballad and pamphlet on the same event and enter both titles simultaneously. The double entry made it more difficult for other stationers to register their own accounts of the same event, unless they were careful to use a different title and a substantially different text. Even then, they risked friction with fellow stationers.[38]

The distinction between owning a particular version of an event and having a monopoly on all accounts of that event was not always clear. In 1602, two stationers sought to protect recent news of English victories over Spanish forces and Irish rebels by entering "All the newes out of Ireland with the Yeildinge up of Chinsale [Kinsale] &c." They soon accused another stationer of infringing their rights, and the Court of Assistants found in their favor, ordering the other man to pay ten shillings for violating their "claime to the Irish newes."[39] The source of this news was a letter from a soldier in Ireland to a friend in London. The defendant may have thought that any stationer had the right to publish such news, but the Court of Assistants ruled otherwise.[40]

CONTROLLING NEWS OF
COMMERCE AND URBAN HEALTH

Recording a title in the Stationers' Company register was not the only way to claim exclusive rights in printed works during this period. Privileges were also granted by the monarch in the form of letters patent. One did not need to be a member of the Stationers' Company to receive a patent (although stationers also obtained them), and the rights could extend beyond a specific title to encompass a whole category of publications. In the realm of news, one category in which this mattered from an early date was the price current. Price currents were essentially lists of prices at which goods were being traded. They were generally produced weekly and sold by subscription to the merchant community. Following the first price currents in Antwerp (1540) and Amsterdam (1585), London had one by 1601.[41]

For most of the seventeenth century, patent holders had a monopoly on this form of publication. In 1634, a broker named John Day obtained a patent from Charles I (r. 1625–1649) to publish "weekly bills of the several rates of prices of all commodities."[42] The patent was initially for fourteen years, but Day succeeded in having it renewed and then transferred to a former apprentice named Humphrey Brome in 1655. In addition to dealing with successive governments during the turbulent period of the English Civil War (1642–1651) and the Commonwealth and Protectorate (1649–1660), Day and Brome also had to curry the favor of the lord mayor and aldermen of London, who had an interest in ensuring that the prices being published were accurate. After the restoration of the monarchy in 1660, Brome applied for and received new letters patent from Charles II (r. 1660–1685). The new patent gave Brome a monopoly on price currents for thirty-one years along with the right to assign the grant to others. After changing hands a couple of times, the patent became the property of a wealthy merchant and loyal servant of Charles II named Robert Wooley. He issued the price current from around 1671 until his death in 1696.[43]

Another form of market news protected by patents was the bills of entry, which listed the types and quantities of merchandise entered in the custom house books. By the early seventeenth century, merchants and shopkeepers were procuring handwritten copies of these entries from custom house clerks, and eventually someone thought to make a business out of printing them. In 1619, two members of the royal household, Alexander Foster and Richard Greene, purchased from King James I (r. 1603–1625) the office of Clerk of the Bills, giving them the sole right to issue these publications. The patent was an important incentive, as it was with price currents, because of the limited clientele for such publications—a few hundred copies sold to merchants, government offices, and coffeehouses. In 1660, Charles II gave this monopoly to the merchant Andrew King to reward him for his commitment to the monarchy during the English Civil War. After King's death, some rogue clerks passed their information on to printers, who issued unauthorized bills of entry. King's executors sought assistance from the crown, and Charles II wrote personally to the commissioners of the customs to prohibit this practice and honor the patent. King's heirs held the patent until 1722, when a man named Thomas Lewis took it over. The Lewis family controlled the patent for the rest of the eighteenth century. It gave them the exclusive right to publish the entries of every custom house in England and Wales. The clerks in various ports resented this monopoly; they wanted to be able to collect fees from individual merchants making inquiries.[44]

Beyond the realm of commerce, the London bills of mortality provide another example of a regularly issued periodical protected by patent. The bills of mortality provided weekly updates on births and deaths in the metropolis. Over time, they came to be printed on two sides of a sheet. One side listed the number of burials and plague burials by parish and provided aggregate totals for christenings and burials. The other side offered a breakdown of deaths by cause (see figures 4 and 5). The weekly tallies of christenings and burials were compiled by the clerk of each local parish church. The causes of death were determined by individuals known as "searchers," typically elderly women who lacked medical training but did their best to ascertain what had happened. Initially the bills of mortality were intended for government use. The City of London made an agreement with the parish clerks, who received an annual subsidy in exchange for weekly reports. But the figures found their way into the letters of merchants, and manuscript copies of the bills began to circulate. During the plague epidemic of 1603–1604, John Windet, the official printer for the City of London, began issuing printed bills to the general public. From this point on, the bills could be purchased by annual subscription for four shillings a year or purchased individually for a penny each, the same price as a typical ballad.[45]

During the epidemic of 1603–1604, Windet took extraordinary steps to get the bills out to customers quickly and reduce the temptation of other printers to issue pirated editions. To speed up production, he kept as much type standing as possible and operated two presses simultaneously, enabling him to print twice as fast.[46] He had to do this because other stationers infringed his patent as printer of the City of London in an attempt to profit from demand for the bills. The first to do so was Felix Kyngston in 1603. Windet complained to the Stationers' Company, which recognized Windet's rights and ordered Kyngston to pay a ten-shilling fine.[47] A few years later, Windet complained about another unauthorized version of the bills, and the company ordered the offending printer to pay twenty shillings.[48]

Over time, the parish clerks asserted greater control over the production and sale of the weekly bills. Royal charters granted by James I and Charles I recognized that the Worshipful Company of Parish Clerks had the obligation to deliver weekly bills of mortality to the king and lord mayor as well as the exclusive right to sell the bills to the public. In 1625, another outbreak of plague renewed interest in the bills, and the

FIGURE 4. London bill of mortality for the week of August 22–29, 1665 (recto), showing the number of burials and plague burials by parish. Reproduced by permission of The Bodleian Library, University of Oxford. (Arch. Ad35).

London 36 — From the of 22 August to the 29. — **1665**

Parish	Bur.	Plag.	Parish	Bur.	Plag.	Parish	Bur.	Plag.
St Alban Woodstreet	16	12	St George Botolphlane			St Martin Ludgate	9	6
Alhallows Barking	25	21	St Gregory by St Pauls	32	25	St Martin Organs	10	9
Alhallows Breadstreet	2		St Hellens	7	6	St Martin Outwitch	5	4
Alhallows Great	21	10	St James Dukes place	9	6	St Martin Vintrey	23	22
Alhallows Honylane	1	1	St James Garlicchithe	6	4	St Matthew Fridaystreet	1	1
Alhallows Lesse	11	9	St John Baptist	6	5	St Maudlin Milkstreet	2	
Alhallows Lumbardstreet	8	7	St John Evangelist			St Maudlin Oldfishstreet	6	7
Alhallows Staining	7	5	St John Zachary	1	1	St Michael Bassishaw	19	18
Alhallows the Wall	44	40	St Katharine Coleman	9	5	St Michael Cornhill	3	
St Alphage	38	22	St Katharine Creechurch	8	5	St Michael Crookedlane	6	5
St Andrew Hubbard	1		St Lawrence Jewry	12	8	St Michael Queenhithe	18	11
St Andrew Undershaft	18	14	St Lawrence Pountney	18	9	St Michael Queen		
St Andrew Wardrobe	35	29	St Leonard Eastcheap			St Michael Royal	14	11
St Ann Aldersgate	21	13	St Leonard Fosterlane	34	30	St Michael Woodstreet	2	6
St Ann Blackfryers	41	31	St Magnus Parish	4	4	St Mildred Breadstreet	2	2
St Antholins Parish	4	2	St Margaret Lothbury	1		St Mildred Poultrey	1	
St Austins Parish	3	3	St Margaret Moses	3	3	St Nicholas Acons	4	1
St Bartholomew Exchange	4	3	St Margaret Newfishstreet	2	1	St Nicholas Coleabby	5	3
St Bennet Fynck	2	2	St Margaret Pattons	1		St Nicholas Olaves	6	6
St Bennet Gracechurch	1	1	St Mary Abchurch	5	4	St Olave Hartstreet	9	6
St Bennet Paulswharf	41	29	St Mary Aldermanbury	11	7	St Olave Jewry	8	4
St Bennet Sherehog			St Mary Aldermary	8	6	St Olave Silverstreet	23	17
St Bennet Billingsgate	2	2	St Mary le Bow	6	4	St Pancras Soperlane	2	2
Christ Church	43	37	St Mary Bothaw	5		St Peter Cheap	5	
St Christophers			St Mary Colechurch	1		St Peter Cornhill	4	1
St Clement Eastcheap	1	1	St Mary Hill	2	1	St Peter Paulswharf	10	7
St Dionis Backchurch	3	2	St Mary Mounthaw	5	3	St Peter Poor	1	
St Dunstan East	9	5	St Mary Sommerset	22	18	St Steven Colemanstreet	36	29
St Edmund Lumbardstr	2	1	St Mary Staining	5	4	St Steven Walbrook	1	
St Ethelborough	23	18	St Mary Woolchurch	1		St Swithin	4	2
St Faith	1		St Mary Woolnoth	2	1	St Thomas Apostle	12	10
St Foster	14	13	St Martin Iremongerlane	2		Trinity Parish	4	3
St Gabriel Fenchurch								

Christned in the 97 Parishes within the Walls—29   Buried—933   Plague—700

Parish	Bur.	Plag.	Parish	Bur.	Plag.	Parish	Bur.	Plag.
St Andrew Holborn	399	380	St Botolph Aldgate	374	346	Saviours Southwark	310	261
St Bartholomew Great	72	65	St Botolph Bishopsgate	316	280	S. Sepulchres Parish	447	336
St Bartholomew Lesse	12	8	St Dunstan West	53	42	St Thomas Southwark	27	22
St Bridget	181	152	St George Southwark	147	120	Trinity Minories	5	4
Bridewell Precinct	12	9	St Giles Cripplegate	842	605	At the Pesthouse	9	9
St Botolph Aldersgate	91	80	St Olave Southwark	321	209			

Christned in the 16 Parishes without the Walls—61   Buried, and at the Pesthouse—3627   Plague—2928

Parish	Bur.	Plag.	Parish	Bur.	Plag.	Parish	Bur.	Plag.
St Giles in the fields	170	146	Lambeth Parish	25	17	St Mary Islington	69	65
Hackney Parish	10	7	St Leonard Shoreditch	280	238	St Mary Whitechappel	496	462
St James Clerkenwel	143	122	St Magdalen Bermondsey	108	78	Rotherith Parish	7	2
St Katharine Tower	87	71	St Mary Newington	121	104	Stepney Parish	530	442

Christned in the 12 out Parishes in Middlesex and Surry—58   Buried—2045   Plague—1759

Parish	Bur.	Plag.	Parish	Bur.	Plag.	Parish	Bur.	Plag.
St Clement Danes	110	82	St Martin in the fields	387	287	St Margaret Westminster	345	309
St Paul Covent Garden	24	21	St Mary Savoy	25	16	Whereof at the Pesthouse	8	

Christned in the 5 Parishes in the City and Liberties of Westminster—21   Buried—891   Plague—715

FIGURE 5. London bill of mortality for August 22–29, 1665 (verso), with a breakdown of the different causes of death as determined by parish searchers. Reproduced by permission of The Bodleian Library, University of Oxford. (Arch. Ad35).

The Diseases and Casualties this Week.

Cause	No.	Cause	No.
Abortive	6	Meagrome	1
Aged	52	Plague	6102
Bleeding	1	Planet	3
Cancer	2	Purples	2
Childbed	40	Quinsie	3
Chrisomes	19	Rickets	23
Collick	1	Rising of the Lights	18
Consumption	145	Scowring	3
Convulsion	93	Scurvy	3
Dropsie	34	Spotted Feaver	156
Feaver	383	Stilborn	10
Flox and Small-pox	1	Stone	1
Flux	1	Stopping of the stomach	7
Gangrene	1	Strangury	1
Gowt	1	Suddenly	2
Grief	4	Surfeit	99
Griping in the Guts	65	Teeth	133
Jaundies	4	Thrush	3
Imposthume	13	Timpany	1
Infants	17	Tissick	3
Killd by a fall from a horse at Alhallows Lumbardstreet	1	Ulcer	4
Kingsevil	3	Winde	4
		Wormes	23

Christned { Males — 87, Females — 82, In all — 169 }   Buried { Males — 3811, Females — 3685, In all — 7496 }   Plague — 6102

Increased in the Burials this Week — 1928

Parishes clear of the Plague — 17   Parishes Infected — 113

The Assize of Bread set forth by Order of the Lord Maior and Court of Aldermen, A penny Wheaten Loaf to contain Nine Ounces and a half, and three half-penny White Loaves the like weight.

clerks obtained authorization to install a press in their company hall. They were no longer bound to use the official printer of the City, but they had to pay the Stationers' Company a bond guaranteeing that they would not use the press for anything other than the bills.[49] The clerks now had exclusive rights over a weekly publication that was a best seller in times of epidemic but which required tremendous coordination to produce and distribute quickly.

Others were eager to enter the fray. In 1635, two gentlemen, Alexander May and Thomas Matthew, obtained a patent to produce a more detailed version of the bills of mortality. Whereas the bills being issued by the clerks listed only the names of each parish, May and Matthew promised to organize information according to "streets, lanes and frequent places of concourse," arranged in sixteen columns. The patent required the parish clerks to supply May and Matthew with all the information they collected by a specified time each week. The clerks could use the same information to produce their own bills as before, but they were not allowed to imitate the new format developed by May and Matthew.[50] For reasons that remain unclear, May and Matthew never issued any bills—at least none have been found—but the threat of this rivalry seems to have spurred the parish clerks into action, because the earliest extant weekly bills from the clerks' own press are from 1635.[51] For approximately the next two centuries, the Worshipful Company of Parish Clerks managed this weekly publication, and the coordination required to produce reliable information often proved challenging. Surviving records of the company reveal how officers repeatedly fined clerks who failed to send in timely and complete reports. They also had to worry about counterfeit bills, which confused the public and discredited the company. Individual clerks were given an allotment to sell in their own parishes, but some tried to make extra money by selling outside their areas. Company officers responded by ordering everyone to respect the designated day and time of publication and to remain within their respective parishes.[52]

The bills of mortality were one product among many hawked on the streets of London, and the clerks had to compete with the peddlers, chapmen, and ballad sellers already working their districts. During the plague epidemic of 1665–1666, the Worshipful Company of Parish Clerks ordered its members not to give itinerant vendors any copies to sell. The goal was to protect the sales territories of individual parish clerks. Further orders in 1695 specified that all arrangements with third-party distributors such as booksellers and peddlers had to be approved by the officers and done for "the common Profit and Benefit of the Company."[53] In 1695, the company's troubles in this area were only beginning. Over the course of the eighteenth century, the weekly bills of mortality would face a declining subscriber base. Part of this decline may be explained by the lack of plague epidemics in England after 1666. But the bills also suffered from the way newspapers and magazines in the eighteenth century extracted information from the bills, making it harder for them to survive as separate publications. The publishers of price currents faced similar challenges. The declining effectiveness of royal patents for these kinds of publications went hand in hand with changes in the business and culture of news that are discussed in chapter 2.

CORANTOS AND THE STRUGGLE
TO CONTROL FOREIGN NEWS

Given that so-called affairs of state were seen as the prerogative of the monarch and that patents were granted for periodicals such as price currents and bills of mortality, it is not surprising that individuals also sought out privileges for periodicals reporting news of politics and diplomacy. The first petition for such a patent seems to have been made around 1621. At that time, English readers were eager for reports of the Thirty Years' War (1618–1648), and James I was concerned about criticisms of his policy toward that war. A pair of writers known as intelligencers, who had experience supplying manuscript newsletters to elite clients, now sought the exclusive right to print a weekly publication devoted to foreign affairs. They argued that such a publication would enable the monarch to counteract false news and rumors and that regular installments of official news would contribute to political and religious harmony. The petition even suggested that it might be harmful to deny news to English people at a time when it was being made available in various places around Europe. In these places, according to the petition, "the ploughman and artisan" were able to learn about the world's affairs through printed "occurrences." Why should the English be denied the same, they asked?[54]

The request was not honored. James I was more interested in stopping the flow of news from Europe than in encouraging discussion of foreign affairs by ploughmen and artisans. In fact, the king issued two proclamations warning people not to write or speak of "causes of State and secrets of Empire, either at home, or abroad."[55] Despite the threat of punishment, several stationers began to specialize in news publications, and some even tried to issue a weekly periodical. In doing so, they imitated and translated from the *corantos* that were cropping up in cities across Europe to report news of the Thirty Years' War.[56] These publications were called corantos because they provided a current of news from various places, bringing readers up-to-date (what the French still call *au courant*) on events. James I tried to cut off the supply of news by banning the importation of corantos from the Netherlands, but this strategy proved ineffective. So, in the fall of 1621, he appointed a licensor named George Cottington to approve all news before publication.[57]

With the licensor in place, the tone of news publications changed. Few now dared criticize the king's policies. But Cottington did authorize a series of corantos put out by the stationers Nicholas Bourne and Thomas Archer. The consistency of the title (each issue began "A Currant of news dated . . .") signaled the desire to build a following by promising regular installments of news. When additional reports arrived after an issue had gone to press, the partners might decide to release them separately under a title such as *An extraordinarie Currant of newes Dated at Vienna the 18th of May 1622*. In this title, the word *extraordinary* probably referred to the special express service that carried the news (in opposition to the so-called ordinary post), but it also provides an early example of what would later be called "extras." Soon two other stationers, Nathaniel Newbery and William Sheffard, began issuing a weekly publication, which was also called *A Currant of newes*, and in August another stationer named Nathaniel Butter began producing *The certaine newes of this week* (with slight variations of the title going forward).[58] Although they still referred to them as "currants," the London stationers were no longer imitating the format of the Dutch corantos. Instead, they produced twenty-four-page quarto pamphlets, a format that tripled the number of words that could be printed each week.[59]

Authorization by the licensor and entry in the Stationers' Register entitled these printers and booksellers to claim exclusive rights in their publications, but it did not alleviate the ruinous effects of competing with each other for the attention of readers. Recognizing this fact, a group of five stationers soon formed a consortium to jointly produce a single news periodical.[60] Weekly publication was the goal, but delays in obtaining news from across the English Channel made this impossible to achieve. The partners also ran into trouble when they republished a newsworthy document registered by another stationer. The work in question was an edict of the king of France, and it was claimed as the property of Nathaniel Newbery. The Court of Assistants ordered the consortium partners to pay Newbery forty shillings in damages "for printing his Copie."[61] The fact that the text was an official document issued by a foreign ruler did not lessen Newbery's ownership rights in the eyes of the Stationers' Company's officers. As far as they were concerned, a document of this sort could be treated as exclusive regardless of its source or its potential interest to the public.

But stationers knew that registration alone could not guarantee protection against piracy. As with ballads, creating partnerships enabled coranto publishers to spread risk and satisfy demand before pirates or imitators got to work. Indeed, Newbery may have made peace with members of the consortium, because his name appeared alongside theirs in a later issue of their periodical.[62] Each coranto put out by this group was numbered, enabling readers to recognize them as part of a series. Moreover, between 1622 and 1624, a single man, Thomas Gainsford, acted as the editor, giving the publication a distinctive narrative style that contributed to its appeal. But success was short-lived. Gainsford died in 1624, and disagreements led the partners to break up the same year.[63]

Butter and Bourne continued to collaborate, but they remained on a tight leash. After England went to war with France in 1627, Charles I was irritated by reports in the weekly corantos. A multilingual former diplomat named Georg Rudolf Weckherlin was appointed to license all news publications. His job was to ensure that accounts reflected well on English interests. But some stationers bypassed censorship, leading the king to write personally to the Stationers' Company and remind them to obtain approval for all news. In 1632, a complaint by the Spanish ambassador about a report in one of the corantos provided a pretext for the Privy Council to ban the printing of all news until further notice.[64]

Butter and Bourne appealed to the king. They promised that if they had the exclusive right to print news, they would avoid reports that might offend the king or his allies. Like the earlier petition by the two intelligencers around 1621, Butter and Bourne argued that weekly newssheets represented a financial benefit for them and, if handled properly, could be useful to the kingdom.[65] Charles I referred the matter to his secretaries of state, who dragged their feet. It is possible that they sought to encourage other offers so as to sell the patent to the highest bidder. More likely, neither Charles nor his secretaries of state were convinced of the utility of having an official government organ along the lines of the French *Gazette*, which was established in 1631.[66]

Butter and Bourne finally obtained a patent giving them the sole right to publish foreign news in 1638. They also wanted to report domestic news, but this was refused. Still, they now had the exclusive right to translate news first published abroad, a potentially lucrative monopoly. Granted for twenty-one years in exchange for an annual contribution to the repair of St. Paul's Cathedral, the patent represented an effort to control the flow of news by entrusting it to two individuals who promised not to publish anything that might offend the monarchy, the church, foreign princes, or ambassadors.[67] In return, Butter and Bourne could count on the Privy Council to enforce their patent against infringement. But they still had to submit each issue to a licensor. Butter and Bourne later explained to readers that the changes requested by the licensor made them wary of publishing what they knew to be partial and incomplete reports.[68]

In any case, by the time Butter and Bourne received their patent in 1638, people's attention had shifted from European affairs to struggles closer to home, namely Scottish resistance to Charles I's religious policies and the growing rift between the king and Parliament. Although these developments received some treatment in manuscript publications available to a restricted elite, Butter and Bourne were not allowed to report on them. Still, the conflicts that ultimately led to the outbreak of the English Civil War in 1642 undermined royal authority over printing, opening the way to a sudden increase in short, anonymous publications, many of which contained news and political commentary. In the 1630s, an average of five hundred to seven hundred printed works appeared each year; in 1641, the number shot up to two thousand.[69]

THE ENGLISH CIVIL WAR IN NEWS

The English Civil War was an important period in the development of political journalism. In the early 1640s, much of the activity focused on covering Parliament. Scriveners operating in stalls near Westminster Hall gathered rumors and solicited details from members of Parliament (MPs) in order to prepare manuscript reports of proceedings. Some of them began producing manuscript publications known as diurnals, which aggregated each day's proceedings into a weekly digest for sale to the public. Soon, printers were issuing newsbooks that copied from and eventually replaced the manuscript diurnals. These publications were called newsbooks because they were eight- or sixteen-page pamphlets, and some of them had continuous pagination from one issue to the next, enabling readers to bind successive issues together as books. Whereas a manuscript diurnal might cost one shilling and sixpence, many newsbooks sold for a penny (one-eighteenth the price). The printed newsbook was not merely a substitute for the manuscript diurnal; it expanded access to political news beyond the closed world of MPs and their friends to members of the public.[70]

By January 1642, there were at least eight different newsbooks available in London. For the scriveners who saw their work being appropriated, a logical response was to partner with a printer. The most well-known of these was Samuel Pecke, who edited *A Perfect Diurnall of the Passages in Parliament* for more than a decade, working with different printers and publishers along the way. Pecke and his fellow editors were mostly anonymous, and the titles of their publications were similar.

Each claimed to be the "truest" or "most perfect" diurnal.[71] In the race to attract readers, stationers frequently copied the title and format of an existing publication without necessarily copying its text. These were what bibliographers refer to as counterfeit editions, because they were designed to usurp the readership of an existing publication. In 1642, Humphrey Blunden published a newsbook entitled *Continuation of the True Diurnall of Passages in Parliament*. Another publisher issued a counterfeit with the same title but different text, and this was in turn counterfeited by a third individual. Pecke's *A Perfect Diurnall* was imitated by several newsbooks, including one published by Robert Wood, in the summer of 1642. Wood's imitation was then imitated by other printers who used variations of his name, including Robert Woody and Robert Woodner. The use of the genuine publisher's name in a counterfeit edition would not work for long, because if a customer went to the shop of the person named on the title page, he would find the genuine edition rather than the counterfeit. It seems likely that such counterfeits were sold by hawkers to unsuspecting customers on the streets.[72]

Verbatim reprinting of an entire newsbook was a different threat, but one that publishers largely figured out how to circumvent. Reaching the public in advance of rivals was key. After the type was set (a time-consuming process), two men would work together to operate a wooden press. They could produce an average of roughly 250 impressions (on one side of each sheet) in an hour before turning over the stack of paper and repeating the process on the other side.[73] To speed up production, a publisher could arrange for two or more presses to be used simultaneously, each working with its own set of type. Surviving issues of Pecke's *A Perfect Diurnall* from 1642–1643 suggest that two different printing shops carried out the work on behalf of the publisher. The use of two presses to make a single work (what bibliographers call double typesettings) meant that not all copies were visually identical, and sometimes one of the printers introduced errors. Figures 6 and 7 show two different typesettings of *A Perfect Diurnall* for the week of March 7–14, 1642. The news is the same, but the issue is labeled number 7 in one typesetting and number 9 in the other. The one labeled number 9 also includes the name of the publisher, whereas the other does not. Because

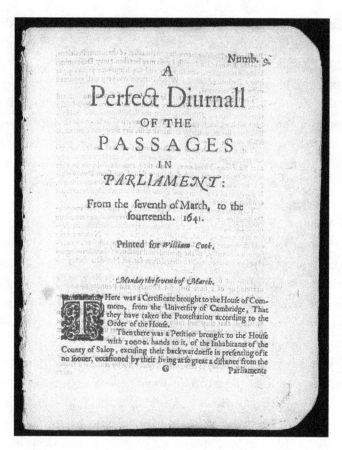

FIGURES 6 AND 7. Two typesettings of the newsbook *A Perfect Diurnall* for March 7–14, 1642. (The year on the title page is 1641 following the Old Style English calendar in which the new year began on March 25.) In order to speed up production, the manuscript was given to two printing shops, leading to differences in layout and typography and the introduction of errors. Above, the issue is labeled number 9 and William Cook is named as the publisher. Opposite, the same text is presented as number 7 and Cook's name is missing. Courtesy of the Beinecke Rare Book and Manuscript Library, Yale University.

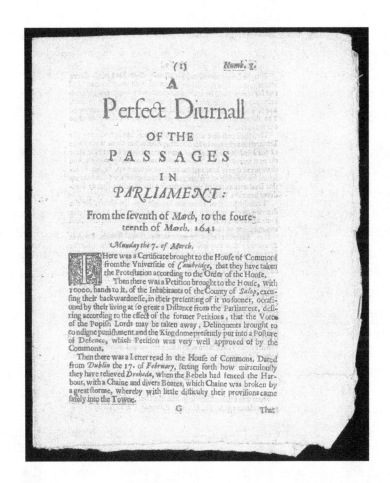

they were produced in different shops, the layout and typography are also not identical.[74]

The use of double typesettings does not necessarily mean that publishers sought to double the number of copies, but it does show their desire to meet demand quickly. This strategy effectively made piracy less profitable. There is some evidence of unauthorized reprints of newsbooks in the early 1640s, but it does not seem to have been widespread, because by the time a copyist set the type and printed his own version, the news would have been considered stale. Publishers who noticed that they were unable to meet demand one week could adjust their capacity by arranging for a double typesetting the following week. Unauthorized reprints in other cities could represent an attractive opportunity if the original printing was not available in a sufficient number of copies. But for most of the 1640s, London publishers seem to have found effective ways of distributing their authorized versions to provincial towns by coordinating with country booksellers and peddlers, making it harder for pirated versions to flourish.[75]

DISPUTING TITLES

For the publishers of newsbooks, the most valuable property was the title itself. On both the royalist and parliamentarian sides of the English Civil War, the producers of newsbooks engaged in sophisticated forms of counterfeiting, imitation, and usurpation. Sometimes the goal was to make money by passing off one publication as another; other times the point was to supplant a rival and occupy a particular ideological position reflected in the title.[76] Disputes over titles could also result from shifting alliances among writers and publishers. But was it possible to have the exclusive right to a title?

This question was at the center of a bitter dispute in 1648. John Dillingham, a writer, and Robert White, a printer, each claimed the exclusive right to publish a newsbook called the *Moderate Intelligencer*. The feud began when Gilbert Mabbott, the official licensor of newsbooks appointed by Parliament, stopped authorizing Dillingham's publication on the grounds that it had contained a remark that offended several MPs. Mabbott, who was among those pushing to bring Charles I to trial, had political motives for silencing Dillingham, who was indeed more moderate. Although Mabbott denied a license to Dillingham, he allowed White to publish a version of the *Moderate Intelligencer* composed by another writer, who may have been Mabbott himself (he was known to be writing for newsbooks while acting as licensor). Dillingham complained to the House of Lords, urging them to recognize his right to a title he had been using for three years. The Lords responded by ordering Mabbott to authorize Dillingham's *Moderate Intelligencer* (and nobody else's) unless Mabbott could produce a good reason for doing otherwise. Mabbott pointed to a seemingly pro-royalist and antiparliamentarian passage that had appeared in Dillingham's newsbook and accused Dillingham of failing to obtain a license for the issue that contained this offensive passage.[77]

The printer White also petitioned the Lords, arguing that he owned the title because it was entered under his name in the Stationers' Register. White provided a certificate from the Stationers' Company clerk as proof of his ownership, and he urged the Lords to respect "the custom and ancient privileges" of the company. The stationers' privileges were based on the assumption that once an author sold or gave a manuscript to a stationer, it belonged to the latter. Newsbooks were different because they involved an ongoing collaboration between writers and stationers. Still, White claimed that entry in the register gave him exclusive rights, regardless of whether he wrote the text or hired someone to do it.[78]

Ultimately, the Lords granted the title to Dillingham. Their reasons were probably political. Mabbott (who seemed to be working with White) was in favor of bringing the king to trial, whereas most of the Lords were in favor of reconciliation. Dillingham found a new printer, Robert Leybourne, and assured readers that the version printed by Leybourne was the only genuine *Moderate Intelligencer*. White didn't give up right away, but the Lords soon ordered him to stop.[79] He then removed the word *Intelligencer* from his title, which became simply *The Moderate*. Although this title continued to irritate Dillingham for a while, White also made changes that ultimately made it easier for readers to distinguish between the two publications. He switched his day of publication from Thursday to Tuesday, enabling *The Moderate* to leave London in the Tuesday post and thereby attract readers in the provinces. Moreover, he turned *The Moderate* into a radical publication. Editorial choices about which reports to publish and how to frame them made it increasingly difficult to confuse *The Moderate* with the *Moderate Intelligencer*.[80]

The fortunes of individual newsbooks rose and fell with the political situation, but the genre as a whole flourished until 1649, a year in which about fifty different titles appeared at one time or another. After the execution of Charles I and the creation of the Commonwealth in

1649, Parliament set up a new licensing system. Parliament authorized two newsbooks, one focusing on political and military news and the other covering Parliament itself, although a few unlicensed publications also appeared.[81] Licensing was more strictly enforced after 1655, when Oliver Cromwell and the Council of State gave a monopoly on news publications to Marchamont Nedham. A few years earlier Nedham had been an outspoken proponent of republicanism and a critic of censorship; now he was working with Cromwell's regime and profiting from a monopoly position. His two periodicals, the *Publick Intelligencer* and *Mercurius Politicus*, were the only regular sources of printed news. Still, Nedham had a relatively free hand, and his publications cannot be dismissed as propaganda. *Mercurius Politicus* contained a mix of news, editorial commentary, quotations from foreign publications, and letters from correspondents, which were sometimes invented or embellished by Nedham. Given the context of censorship and state-sanctioned monopoly, one might expect a bland publication that avoided controversy. In fact, *Politicus* was varied and multivocal and sought-after by readers. Nedham's monopoly position and his editorial strategy resulted in a highly profitable enterprise.[82]

OFFICIAL NEWSPAPERS

The idea of an official monopoly on political news was not new, but beginning with Cromwell's Protectorate in the 1650s, successive governments made greater use of this strategy. Charles II was restored to the throne in 1660, and his secretaries of state were given licensing authority over news. They initially gave a monopoly to Henry Muddiman, a news writer who had supported the royalists during the English Civil War. Muddiman's connections to Joseph Williamson, an undersecretary of state, gave him access to the diplomatic correspondence of the monarchy and the privilege of sending letters postage-free. Muddiman used these advantages to develop an extensive network of correspondents who provided him with news. He printed some and saved the rest for handwritten newsletters sent to a more restricted clientele. Muddiman had about one hundred subscribers who paid five pounds a year for their weekly newsletters, which came to roughly two shillings per week, or twenty-four times the price of a printed paper that sold for a penny.[83]

Muddiman continued his newsletter business but lost his monopoly on printed news in 1663 when Charles II granted Roger L'Estrange, a zealous licensor, the exclusive right to print and sell "all Narratives or relacions [sic] not exceeding two sheets of Paper & all Advertisements, Mercuries, Diurnalls & books of Publick Intelligence."[84] But Williamson, the undersecretary of state, soon found a way to replace L'Estrange's newspapers with an official publication under direct government control. In exchange for compensation, L'Estrange agreed to end his two news publications early in 1666, although he retained the exclusive right to print separate advertisements, probably as a reward for his service. Williamson's official newspaper began as the *Oxford Gazette* in November 1665 (the court was in exile there while the plague ravaged London) and changed its name to the *London Gazette* in February 1666. The *Gazette* consisted mostly of short bulletins of foreign news along with official notices of government appointments, bankruptcies, and the like.[85]

Williamson hired an editor for the *Gazette*, but like Muddiman, he kept the best news for his own subscription newsletter business. The newsletters were sent out to paying subscribers and others who received them in exchange for providing news. Local postmasters were expected to summarize information and rumors they found in the letters under their care. Williamson returned the favor by sending them free copies of the *Gazette* that they could sell to local customers. Postmasters also distributed copies to inns, taverns, and coffeehouses. In this way, the post office was both a means for the monarchy to disseminate its official version of events and a powerful apparatus for collecting intelligence.[86]

The legal basis for the licensing of news publications and all other printed works was the Printing Act of 1662. This law confirmed the Stationers' Company's monopoly, limited the number of presses, and restricted printing to London. All works were required to be authorized by a royal censor and entered in the Stationers' Company register.[87] For Parliament, the goal was to ensure that all printed works, regardless of their form, were subject to licensing. For the Stationers' Company, the goal was to protect rights in copies of all kinds, including pamphlets, ballads, and other ephemeral works. Although individual stationers could obtain authorization to print news in pamphlets or broadsides, it was not possible to obtain a license to issue a newspaper (the word was beginning to be used around this time) since that would have violated the monopoly of the *London Gazette*.[88] This monopoly was broken temporarily, however, on occasions when Parliament allowed the Printing Act to lapse. The act had to be renewed periodically, and Parliament failed to do this on two occasions. The first time was in 1679 during the controversy over whether to exclude Charles II's brother James from the throne on the grounds that he was Catholic. This controversy saw an outpouring of unlicensed anti-Catholic pamphlets and newspapers. MPs who supported exclusion may have deliberately stalled renewal of the Printing Act in order to encourage these anti-Catholic writings.[89]

For Charles II, the newspapers were particularly bothersome because they were ongoing and attracted a following. Since he could not rely on licensing, the king needed another way to suppress them. He solicited the advice of sympathetic judges, who determined that the king could use his royal prerogative to ban any publication he deemed a danger to public peace. Charles II immediately issued a proclamation prohibiting the publication of news without his prior authorization.[90] The proclamation was used to prosecute writers, printers, and publishers of newspapers. At one of these trials in 1680, Sir George Jeffreys, the Recorder of London, opened the prosecution by summarizing the current judicial consensus as follows: "No person whatsoever could expose to the public knowledge anything that concerned the affairs of the public, without license from the king."[91] But the claim that licensing was the prerogative of the monarch alarmed a number of MPs, who suggested that the king was usurping Parliament's role in regulating the press. By the end of 1680, probably with the encouragement of these MPs, several printers again began issuing newspapers. Although the government continued to assert the royal prerogative in an attempt to suppress newspapers, it also adopted a new strategy of responding to and refuting its critics. Roger L'Estrange defended the monarchy in a periodical called the *Observator in Question and Answer* (1681–1687). After James II (r. 1685–1688) became king in 1685, Parliament renewed the Printing Act. This was used to eliminate unlicensed publications, leaving the *London Gazette* and L'Estrange's *Observator* as the only political newspapers.[92]

In the area of crime reporting, the City of London granted two important monopolies beginning in the early 1680s. Stationers had been issuing broadsides and pamphlets devoted to trials and executions, but these appeared irregularly, focused only on certain trials, and were often incomplete or contradictory. The City sought to impose order by authorizing two official serials, the *Proceedings of Old Bailey* and the *Account of the Ordinary of Newgate*. Old Bailey was the trial venue for major crimes in London, Westminster, and Middlesex. It was where some of the most sensational trials took place. Newgate was London's largest prison, and its chaplain, or "ordinary," was able to report on the behavior and dying words of executed criminals. The *Proceedings* and the *Account* were published under the authority of the City of London beginning in 1684. The City contracted with printers who paid an annual fee in exchange for the exclusive right to print and sell these publications. These privileges were valuable because they meant that nobody else could publish the trials at Old Bailey or reproduce the titillating accounts of criminals awaiting execution at Newgate.[93]

As James II struggled to keep a grip on power in the late 1680s, a number of unlicensed pamphlets and broadsides appeared, but putting out a regular newspaper remained too risky. When the king fled in December 1688, four unofficial newspapers were set up, but they did not last long because the new monarchs, William III and Mary II (who ruled together from 1689 until Mary's death in 1694) sought to limit ongoing discussion of political developments. The public was warned that news had to be authorized before publication and that all individuals involved in unlicensed publications—writers, printers, and hawkers—would be prosecuted. The Bill of Rights of 1689 did not guarantee freedom of the press, and the *London Gazette* remained the only authorized newspaper. The House of Commons allowed the publication of its votes, which appeared in an officially supervised publication, but other accounts of Parliament remained a breach of privilege. The notion that the Glorious Revolution ushered in an era of press freedom is quickly dispelled by the fact that there were seventeen trials for unlicensed printing between 1689 and 1695.[94]

THE BREAKDOWN OF LICENSING

Nevertheless, the 1690s represented an important period of growth for news publications, especially periodicals covering commerce and finance. The increased circulation of information in print was related to the expansion of overseas trade, the creation of the Bank of England, and the growth of joint-stock companies.[95] Periodicals were ideally suited to reporting on trade and finance because members of the business community needed regular updates about the prices of stocks and commodities, the arrival and departure of ships, and the importation and exportation of goods. Price currents and bills of entry had existed in London since the beginning of the seventeenth century and were protected by patents, making it all the more feasible for the publishers to make money selling information. With the increase in trade toward the end of the century, the demand for regular updates of market news increased, making it possible for other publications to thrive even without the benefit of a patent. Beginning in the 1690s, merchants could subscribe not only to commodity price currents and bills of entry but also to stock and exchange currents, which listed the prices of stocks and the rates at which foreign bills of exchange traded locally, and marine lists, which catalogued the arrival and departure of ships in various ports.[96] There were also weekly periodicals, such as John Houghton's *Collection for the Improvement of Husbandry and Trade* (1692–1703), that offered a variety of information and commentary on commerce, manufacturing, and agriculture.[97]

The 1690s also witnessed a major decline in support for press licensing. Some MPs began to associate licensing with arbitrary rule and undesirable monopolies. With the emergence of political factions at the end of the seventeenth century—the Whigs and the Tories—it became apparent that censorship could be used as a political weapon by the party in power. The trade restrictions at the heart of the Printing Act also became increasingly unpopular. That law limited printing and bookselling to London and restricted the number of presses and master printers. Meanwhile, it confirmed the monopoly of the Stationers' Company and the printing rights that its members enjoyed by virtue of entering a title in the Stationers' Register. Since a handful of members owned the most profitable works, the company was also vulnerable to criticism from within. Indeed, when the Printing Act came up for renewal in 1693, several printers and booksellers complained to the House of Commons about how licensing enabled a few stationers to dominate whole categories of works under the pretext of preventing seditious publications. Parliament did renew the act, but only for one year and to the end of the next session. By the time it came up for renewal again in 1695, the philosopher John Locke had prepared a written critique of licensing that highlighted the dangers of both censorship and trade monopolies. The MP Edward Clarke used Locke's remarks to campaign against renewal. Clarke sponsored two bills that would have reduced the power of the Stationers' Company and either eliminated or diluted licensing, but neither of these bills made it out of committee before the end of the session. The result was that the Printing Act lapsed in 1695, and no new regulations replaced it.[98]

After 1695, the Stationers' Company no longer had an official monopoly on printing or any way to enforce rights in copies against nonmembers. Although the term *piracy* had been used since the mid-seventeenth century, it became much more common after 1695 because of the disorder that followed the lapse of the Printing Act. The Court of Assistants continued to sanction stationers who printed other members' copies, but the problem surpassed the company's capacity to control it, and the situation was exacerbated by deaths and bankruptcies that weakened company leadership. In this context, the term *piracy* was used to refer to a range of practices that violated long-standing customs, regardless of whether they were illegal. Activities denounced as piracy included not only verbatim reprintings of entire books but also unauthorized abridgments and close imitations of existing works.[99] In the years after 1695, the Stationers' Company repeatedly petitioned Parliament for new regulations that would protect its members' rights and, they claimed, help prevent the spread of seditious and blasphemous works. But many MPs had come to question the effectiveness of licensing and were sympathetic to complaints about the company's monopoly. While agreeing that some form of press regulation was needed, Parliament could not settle on a solution. A dozen bills were proposed in the fifteen years following the lapse of the Printing Act in 1695, but none passed.[100]

THE GROWTH OF NEWSPAPERS

After 1695, the newspaper and periodical press grew rapidly. One no longer had to obtain the authorization of a licensor or the Stationers' Company to print something, and the number and location of presses were no longer restricted. In London alone, the number of printing houses grew from forty-five in 1695 to about seventy just ten years later.[101] Censorship still existed after publication in the form of prosecutions for seditious libel, which was understood to include any public statement encouraging contempt or ridicule of the government or its officials. Despite the end of licensing in 1695, no law guaranteed freedom of the press in the British Isles. Moreover, it remained illegal to report parliamentary proceedings. The Lords and Commons still considered it a breach of privilege to publish the debates or identify individual members by name. They insisted on these privileges until the 1770s.[102] Those who wanted to follow Parliament closely had to seek out handwritten newsletters; the compilers of these newsletters tried to strike a balance between serving their elite customers and avoiding trouble with Parliament.[103]

Still, there is no doubt that 1695 marked a major turning point in terms of the number and variety of news periodicals available to the public. In May 1695, at least five new newspapers were started in London, and several more appeared in the months ahead. Although many of these titles did not survive very long, three triweekly newspapers became successful and lasted into the 1730s: the *Flying Post*, the *Post Boy*, and the *Post Man*. The reference to the post in all of these titles made clear that newspapers depended on regular mail delivery (now three times a week to and from London) to obtain news and distribute it to customers.[104] But the lapse of the Printing Act also meant that printers could now set up in other towns. By 1705 there were newspapers in Norwich, Bristol, and Exeter, and by 1720 there were over twenty newspapers in towns outside of London.[105] The same went for ballads: many of the presses set up after 1695 turned out the occasional ballad, meaning that the trade was no longer concentrated in the hands of a few London stationers as it had been for most of the seventeenth century.[106]

As newspapers and other periodicals proliferated, the question arose whether they might be treated as property. The Stationers' Company had long recognized exclusive rights in all sorts of printed works, not just books. In keeping with that tradition, one of the bills considered by Parliament after 1695 would have recognized "the property or sole right of printing" for books, pamphlets, portraits, and "papers."[107] Meanwhile, a number of political leaders thought that the publication of news should be subject to licensing, even if other forms of print were not. In response to some objectionable articles in one newspaper in 1697, the House of Commons briefly considered a "Bill to prevent the Writing, Printing, and Publishing any News without License."[108] No such law was passed, although Parliament continued to consider various measures, and in 1702, Queen Anne (r. 1702–1714) issued a proclamation in an attempt to restrain the publication of "false news" and "irreligious and seditious papers and libels."[109] Press licensing also had proponents in Parliament, but the issue remained too controversial to obtain a consensus.

The Stationers' Company therefore lobbied for a law that would protect the "property of books and copies" in the absence of licensing.[110] In this context, a stationer named John How urged for the need to protect newspapers and pamphlets as well as the more learned and weighty tomes usually highlighted in the company's pleas for legislation. "There is no civiliz'd State, or City in the World," How wrote in 1709, "where such an extensive Liberty is allow'd to any People as in this, where News, and all other sorts of Papers, are suffer'd to be *pirated*, and cry'd about the Streets by a parcel of *Vagabond Hawkers*, to the great Prejudice and Ruin of the just Proprietors of such Papers."[111] How recommended that Parliament pass a law protecting property rights in all forms of print; he variously mentioned books, pamphlets, papers, maps, charts, and pictures, always adding "&c." to signal that his list was not exhaustive. He thought the statute should explicitly prohibit copying any *part* of a work and that it should be illegal to make "epitomes" or abridgments without permission. According to How, even the reuse or imitation of an existing title should be against the law.[112]

These recommendations were not followed. In early 1710, Parliament passed what has become known as the first copyright statute, although the word *copyright* did not actually appear in the text. While employing the vocabulary of *rights in copies* developed by the Stationers' Company, the full title of the new law also announced a new justification for these rights. It was called "An Act for the Encouragement of Learning, by Vesting the Copies of Printed Books in the Authors or Purchasors of Such Copies, during the Times Therein Mentioned." It provided authors and "proprietors"—namely printers or booksellers who financed a publication—with the exclusive right to print and sell their books for a limited period of time.[113] The statute did not mention newspapers or other periodicals. Whether this was an oversight or a deliberate attempt to restrict the subject matter of copyright remains open to debate. But it was a departure from previous press regulations and the long-standing customs of the Stationers' Company, which had recognized exclusive rights over a wide range of works, including news publications. The significance of this change for the publishers and readers of news is explored in the next chapter.

CHAPTER 2

Toward a Culture of Copying
in Eighteenth-Century Britain

IN THE SEVENTEENTH CENTURY, the publication of news in the British Isles was regulated through licensing and printing privileges. Similar arrangements continued in most European countries during the eighteenth century. The publisher of a gazette or journal generally had a monopoly in the territory governed by the prince or council that had granted the privilege.[1] In Britain, by contrast, the lapse of the Printing Act in 1695 put an end to press licensing and the monopoly of the Stationers' Company. Yet the extent to which 1695 marked a turning point in publishing remains a matter of debate. At the time, Parliament's failure to renew licensing was not celebrated as ushering in an era of press freedom. Censorship still existed in the form of prosecutions for seditious libel, and book publishing continued to be dominated by a small number of London stationers.[2] With respect to newspapers, however, there is no doubt that 1695 was a turning point. One no longer had to obtain the authorization of a licenser or the Stationers' Company to issue a newspaper, and the number and location of presses was no longer regulated. But the end of licensing also made it much more difficult to claim exclusive rights in accounts of recent events. Now that anyone could publish a newspaper or weekly journal, was there any way to stop rivals from issuing cheap reprints, let alone copying individual articles for use in their own publications? Would an unregulated press be undermined by rampant piracy?

In 1710, the Act for the Encouragement of Learning (also known as the Statute of Anne) provided authors and their assignees with the sole right to print and sell their works for a limited period of time. By recognizing authors as the original owners of their writings and by granting them exclusive rights without the need for prior authorization, the Statute of Anne represented a major shift in public policy. Learning was to be encouraged by allowing authors to publish what they wanted and by protecting the investments that printers and booksellers made in their works.[3] The Stationers' Register remained the official record of literary property, but the company's clerk was now required to allow everyone (regardless of membership in the company) to consult the register to see which works were protected and to enter their own titles in exchange for a fee. In line with the goal of encouraging learning, the statute also required the deposit of nine copies of each work for the use of designated libraries. Protection was limited to twenty-one years for existing works and fourteen years for works published after the statute went into force. If the author was still alive at the end of the fourteen-year term, then the monopoly was extended for an additional fourteen years.[4] The Statute of Anne thus announced the end of the perpetual privileges of the Stationers' Company and the beginning of a limited-term copyright available to everyone.

But there was a difference between what the statute said and how publishing worked. Although the new law contained a number of provisions that might have revolutionized the book trade, printers and booksellers tended to proceed with business as usual for several decades after 1710. Some did not register their works under the Statute of Anne at all; others ignored the deposit requirements and the term limits of the statute. The major London booksellers continued to buy and sell copyrights (the word became more common starting in the 1730s) on the assumption that they were perpetual, and they developed commercial strategies for enforcing their claims.[5] When challenged in court, these booksellers argued that authors enjoyed a common-law property in their writings that was akin to property in land—it could be purchased and inherited but could not simply cease to exist after a certain number of years. Their opponents insisted that there was no perpetual property in published works. Instead, Parliament granted authors and their assignees a temporary monopoly, and after this expired, everyone was free to reprint the work. These arguments were developed in connection with a series of court cases between the 1740s and 1770s known as the "battle of the booksellers." It was only in 1774 that the House of Lords, which served as the highest court of appeal, settled the matter by ruling that everyone had the right to reproduce works whose terms of protection under the Statute of Anne had expired.[6]

Beyond these disagreements over the origin and duration of rights in published writings, there was uncertainty about what kinds of works qualified for copyright. The preamble to the Statute of Anne mentioned "books and other writings," but subsequent clauses referred only to books, and the stated rationale of the legislation was to encourage "learned men to compose and write useful books."[7] The reference to "useful books" could be read as a sign that Parliament meant to limit the types of works eligible for protection, but there is no evidence to prove that this was the intention.[8] The more important question is how contemporaries interpreted and made use of the law. Because the statute referred mainly to books and most court cases centered on books, it has sometimes been assumed that newspapers and other periodicals were simply not eligible for copyright.[9] Such an assumption ignores the extent to which the boundaries of copyright law—both the range of works eligible for protection and the scope of that protection—were subject to debate at the time. It is also important to note that attitudes and practices changed over the course of the eighteenth century.[10] In 1710, it was far from obvious that newspapers were excluded from protection under the Statute of Anne. In fact, in the years after 1710, a number of writers and publishers claimed exclusive rights in various publications containing news and commentary on current affairs. By the end of the century, however, such claims were almost nonexistent. This chapter describes this shift, which was crucial to the subsequent growth of newspapers and their role in public debate. The culture of copying that developed in the eighteenth century did not result directly from the language of the Statute of Anne or from court decisions. Rather, it depended on changes in publishing practice that ultimately made copyright seem inappropriate for newspapers. Over the course of the eighteenth century, a particular kind of newspaper—sold by subscription, supported by advertisements, and containing a wide range of material—came to dominate English-language journalism. The editors and publishers of these newspapers recognized that copying enabled news to spread and facilitated commentary on reports issued by rivals. They could have claimed copyright, but doing so would have been counterproductive given the way news publishing worked at the time.

EARLY COPYRIGHT ENTRIES

When the Statute of Anne went into effect in 1710, it did not seem irrelevant or inapplicable to writers and publishers involved in news publications. One way to gauge the works that contemporaries sought to protect is to examine the titles they entered in the Stationers' Register. The register cannot be treated as a complete record of literary property, however, because failure to register a work did not mean that it automatically entered the public domain. One had to register in order to sue for the statutory remedies—namely the forfeiture of unauthorized copies and payment of financial penalties. These remedies could be sought from the law courts of the King's Bench, the Common Pleas, or the Exchequer.[11] But in practice, most literary property disputes were brought before the Court of Chancery, a court of equity in which plaintiffs could obtain an injunction to stop defendants from printing or selling unauthorized copies. Members of the trade found that injunctions provided a simpler and more effective remedy than suing for the penalties offered by the Statute of Anne. And as early as 1716, the Court of Chancery rejected the claim that if a work was not registered then it could be freely reprinted by anyone.[12] Savvy publishers, especially those who sought legal counsel, would have realized that they did not need to register a work in order to obtain an injunction as long as they could show that they had secured rights from the author. But there were many reasons why a given work might not be registered, from ignorance and indifference to concern with the cost of library deposit and doubts about the effectiveness of the statute in combatting piracy. In any case, a work's absence from the register cannot be interpreted as a forfeiture of copyright, and it would be wrong to treat the register as an exhaustive record of literary property.[13]

For our purposes, the register does provide clues about the kinds of works for which individuals actively sought the protection of the Statute of Anne. In the years immediately following 1710, people entered all sorts of nonbook publications, including broadsides, pamphlets, papers, maps, and copper plates (used to produce engravings). Stationers had long entered a variety of works, so it is not surprising that some of them continued to do so after 1710. And as had been the case in the seventeenth century, the titles entered represented a range of genres and subjects, from dictionaries and stage plays to reports of speeches and accounts of battles. Stand-alone news publications, in the form of broadsides and pamphlets, were actually among the first works registered in 1710. These included official addresses presented to the Queen by townships and counties; reports of speeches, trials, and executions; and pamphlets dealing with current political and religious questions.[14]

One of the most sensational political affairs of the period, and one that led to the first infringement suit under the Statute of Anne, was the trial of the Tory preacher Henry Sacheverell for "high crimes and misdemeanors." The controversy centered on Sacheverell's "Fifth of November" sermon, which criticized the Protestant settlement and questioned the religious convictions of some of Queen Anne's ministers. The printed version of this sermon may have sold as many as a hundred thousand copies.[15] Demand for accounts of Sacheverell's trial was therefore expected to be high. A number of broadsides and pamphlets related to the trial were registered under the Statute of Anne, but there was also an official version protected by parliamentary privilege. The resulting struggle showed that it was possible to enforce a copyright in a trial report but also that it was becoming increasingly difficult to monopolize coverage of an event, even in cases in which Parliament had assigned exclusive rights to a printer.

A SENSATIONAL TRIAL

Before the Sacheverell trial opened, the House of Commons passed a resolution forbidding any publication that reproduced statements by MPs and witnesses without the permission of the Commons. Moreover, the lord chancellor, who oversaw the trial in the House of Lords, appointed Jacob Tonson official printer of the trial; nobody else was allowed to publish an account of it. Tonson was one of the most powerful book publishers of his time, and he had connections to the Whig leadership that put Sacheverell on trial. He and his nephew were also the official printers of the *London Gazette* and the *Votes of the House of Commons*. There was some speculation at the time about whether Tonson paid for the Lords' privilege or whether he received it as a favor from the lord chancellor. Either way, Tonson did not rely exclusively on the order of the House of Lords. He also entered his work under the Statute of Anne.[16]

Granting Tonson a privilege may have been an attempt by the Whig leadership to shut down debate about the trial, but this strategy did not work. Tories produced their own versions, which were also registered under the Statute of Anne. The bookseller and newspaper editor Abel Roper was the first to do so. In fact, Roper attempted to pass off his work as the official version by placing Tonson's name on the title page rather than his own. Infuriated, Tonson published newspaper notices denouncing Roper's edition as "spurious" and "imperfect."[17] He also complained to the House of Lords, which had Roper arrested for breach of privilege. But Roper was released upon paying a bond, and there is no record of a trial. In the end, Tonson was unable to stop Roper from selling his book, which satisfied the market for a Tory version and benefited from the publicity that Roper gave it in his newspaper, the *Post Boy*.[18]

Another unauthorized account of the Sacheverell trial was issued by John Baker, who also entered his title under the Statute of Anne. The fact that he was able to do so signaled that an important shift had occurred. Before the Statute of Anne went into effect in 1710, the Stationers' Company had complete control over the register. Following company custom, the clerk would verify that a work did not violate any existing rights before entering it in the register, and members found ways to block rival works on the same topic.[19] The Statute of Anne opened registration to everyone, including someone like Baker who was not a stationer and had no scruples about provoking Tonson, who was one of the company's most senior members. In addition, the law specified that the clerk could be fined if he refused to enter a title, making it impossible for authors or publishers to stop others from entering works with similar titles.[20] Still, it is important to remember that registration was merely a *claim* of ownership; the validity of the claim had to be determined by a judge if and when a lawsuit was brought.

Advertisements for Baker's version of the trial boasted that it was more "complete" than any existing version and promised a money-back guarantee for any reader who was unsatisfied. It was more complete because Baker included material from the existing accounts by both Tonson and Roper. Since it was obvious that Baker had copied from his version, Tonson sought an injunction from the Court of Chancery, citing his rights by virtue of the order of the House of Lords and the Statute of Anne. He obtained a preliminary injunction and issued advertisements reminding all members of the trade to respect the court's order. Leaving nothing to chance, he also published his own cheaper octavo edition of the trial. Baker responded by hiring a solicitor to challenge the Court of Chancery's jurisdiction over the case, but he never pressed for a hearing, so the injunction stood. Tonson soon released his cheaper edition, and it seems that Baker stopped advertising his.[21]

Tonson's success in obtaining an injunction against Baker showed that it was possible to protect a report of a sensational trial, whereas his inability to hinder Roper's edition revealed that it was not possible to monopolize coverage of a trial, even with an order of the House of Lords.[22] That Roper was able to continue selling his unauthorized version may reflect the fact that he had an effective distribution system. But Tonson's was even more effective. As was common practice in the book trade, Tonson protected his literary property by colluding with other booksellers who formed associations known as congers. Members of a conger would purchase copies of books being published by other members and agree to respect a set retail price, thereby avoiding competition and guaranteeing wider distribution of one another's books. To further bind their interests, they divided the copyrights for certain works into shares. Each shareholder had an interest in seeing that these books were distributed quickly, thereby making it harder for pirate editions to succeed. The congers further discouraged piracy by agreeing to cut off the supply of books to any retailers who dealt in unauthorized reprints, a threat of retaliation that could have a powerful effect. A classic study of the English book trade referred to the protection afforded by such collusive activities as de facto copyright—a proprietary claim that was effective because it was respected by members of the trade, regardless of its legal basis.[23]

Although newspapers and other periodicals were not mentioned in the Statute of Anne, some of them were registered. In the 1710s, at least twenty-four different periodicals were entered, including essay-based journals such as the *Spectator* and the *Guardian*, two of the triweekly newspapers (the *Flying Post* and the *Post Man*), and a semiweekly price current.[24] Whereas some owners entered periodicals in batches of dozens or even hundreds of issues at a time, others entered the title once, specifying that it was "to be continued weekly." If the registration fee of sixpence and the deposit requirement of nine copies had been enforced for every issue of a periodical, then the cost probably would have dissuaded publishers from registering journals and newspapers. But since the statute contained no explicit provisions for periodicals, it was unclear whether each issue had to be registered separately. The fact that some writers and publishers entered the titles of periodicals despite this uncertainty shows that they sought to maintain some kind of exclusivity over them.

One motivation was to protect the rights to republish periodicals in book form. The *Tatler* (1709–1711) by Richard Steele and especially the *Spectator* (1711–1712) by Steele and Joseph Addison are examples of periodicals that were reissued in collected volumes and widely read throughout the eighteenth century. The *Tatler* contained a mix of news paragraphs, short essays of contemporary interest, and advertisements. At the end of 1709, one of the most notorious literary pirates of the age, Henry Hills Jr., reprinted the first one hundred issues of the *Tatler* and bound them into a single volume. His idea was to profit from interest in the *Tatler* by repackaging it in book form, but he did not ask anyone's permission to do this. The printer John Nutt, acting on Steele's behalf, rushed to enter the *Tatler* in the Stationers' Register, claiming "property" over the text in every conceivable publishing format—folio, octavo, duodecimo, "and all other Volumes whatsoever."[25] Nutt also printed newspaper notices denouncing Hills's edition as shabby and imperfect and promising imminent delivery of a neat and correct edition. Hills retreated, but his actions had spurred a publishing innovation: the reissue of successful periodicals in book form.[26] The *Spectator*, which succeeded the *Tatler*, contained lively essays on social, cultural, and economic topics. It was entered in the Stationers' Register in batches as it was published, and the right to republish the collected issues remained valuable for decades.[27]

In the case of newspapers, the main factor motivating registration during the 1710s was the general climate of competition that followed the passage of the Stamp Act in 1712. The Stamp Act required newspapers printed on a half sheet of paper to pay a duty of a half penny per copy; those printed on a whole sheet owed a full penny per copy. But the statute failed to specify what qualified as a newspaper (and was therefore subject to the tax), and it contained no provision for newspapers printed on more than a full sheet of paper.[28] Consequently, some printers increased the length of their publications and registered them as pamphlets instead of newspapers, thereby paying the much lower duty of two shillings per sheet on one copy of a pamphlet instead of a penny for every copy of a newspaper. Others, in clear violation of the law, evaded the tax by printing their publications on unstamped paper. Those who paid the duty had to raise their prices, and they resented the unstamped papers that undersold them. Although printers and booksellers sometimes used the word *piracy* in this context, they did not complain about the unauthorized copying of individual articles so much as the price cutting of the "pirate printers," which harmed their sales.[29]

Many newspapers and weekly journals were launched in the 1710s, and most of them imitated existing publications. Such imitation often began with the title, much to the chagrin of those who thought titles should be exclusive. In 1714, Robert Mawson issued a paper called the *Weekly Journal*, and within a year he was complaining of "two Pirating Printers [who] have published each a Sham Weekly Journal, at the Price of a Penny, . . . a bare Collection from the other Papers."[30] John Applebee was one of these printers. Although he started his publication nine months after Mawson, Applebee was actually the first to register his title under the Statute of Anne. He also appealed to the public by renaming his paper the *Original Weekly Journal*. Mawson registered a "postscript" and a "supplement" to his own paper, suggesting that he sought to protect these particular articles from being copied. But he also made a more comprehensive entry, claiming ownership of "the Weekly Journal, from January 1st 1714 to August the 27 inclusive 1715."[31] Alas, this entry did not discourage others from printing similar publications with the same title, and eventually Mawson gave up his *Weekly Journal* to start a new publication with an equally generic name: the *News Letter*. Mawson announced sarcastically that any "Pirating Printer, or Peddling Bookseller" who asked for his charity would receive his full consent "to Print *Weekly-Journals*, rather than They shall hang Themselves for want of other Employ."[32]

Readers were warned about unscrupulous printers who tried to pass off their publications as somebody else's. Francis Clifton of the *Oxford Post* denounced James Read for doing this in 1718. "I'm credibly inform'd," Clifton wrote, "this Grand Pirate Printer designs to invade my Right, by Printing and publishing a Paper by the Name of the Oxford Post." According to Clifton, Read tried to deceive readers by attaching Clifton's initials to the paper and using "the same Figure at the Frontispiece." Clifton urged customers to verify "that my Name be Right Spelled and at full length, at the Bottom of the first and last Page, for if one Letter thereof differs from this Present Paper, you may assure your selves the whole is spurious."[33] The fact that printers occasionally made errors while setting the type provided one way to distinguish the copy from the original. Given the prevalence of imitations and counterfeits during this period, printers asked readers to pay attention to such details.

TOWARD A CULTURE OF COPYING

Writers and publishers concerned about the republication of individual articles faced greater obstacles than those worried about counterfeit editions or the appropriation of titles. Admittedly, the problem of partial copying affected many genres besides newspapers. Reference books, for example, were often compiled from existing works. Although compilations such as dictionaries and encyclopedias were seen as eligible for literary property, other compilers did not tend to respect rights to individual components of the work. Ephraim Chambers's *Cyclopaedia,* first published in 1728, was one of the most valuable copyrights in Britain by midcentury. Although Chambers presented himself as the "author" of the *Cyclopaedia* because he arranged and presented existing materials in a new way, he did not claim any credit for the parts that made up the whole. As he put it, "The Book is not mine, 'tis every body's, the mix'd Issue of a thousand Loins. . . . If ever you wrote any thing your self, 'tis possible there is something in it of yours."[34] Chambers and other compilers of encyclopedias had a complex position on the question of literary property. They defended their right to excerpt and abridge existing works in order to create a new compilation that made knowledge accessible to the public. But they also argued that their careful selection and arrangement of material justified copyright protection. In this way, they claimed a property in their own compilations while legitimizing their reuse of existing works.[35]

Recent research on the history of encyclopedias has borrowed the zoological term *stigmergy* to describe publications that rely on the contributions of individuals who do not necessarily know that they are all contributing to the same work, much as wasps and termites create their homes by modifying and adding to structures made by their predecessors and peers.[36] The value of newspapers was obviously more time sensitive than was that of encyclopedias. Nonetheless, early newspapers could also be considered stigmergic collaborations in the sense that they drew on a range of existing sources. Contributors to a newspaper or weekly journal did not necessarily know who else was contributing to the same publication or which other articles the printer-editor would select and arrange on the page alongside their own. Periodicals were similar to encyclopedias in that those who produced them needed to be able to reuse parts of existing works while protecting themselves against the kind of wholesale reprinting that created cheaper substitutes for their products. It was for this reason that some publishers of journals, newspapers, and price currents entered their titles under the Statute of Anne.

Attempts to protect individual newspaper articles were much more rare, although in 1710 the writer John De Fonvive did register several issues of his newspaper, the *Post Man,* in an attempt to stop others from republishing successive installments of "The Preamble to the State of the War of the Dutch."[37] This text was actually an official document presented to the States General of the Netherlands; presumably it had been translated especially for the *Post Man.* In any case, De Fonvive's entries make clear that he was trying to profit as much as possible from contemporary interest in this document rather than to claim exclusivity over everything in his newspaper. A few proprietors entered individual issues of newspapers, no doubt to protect valuable articles, but the practice remained extremely rare.[38]

A more common strategy for deterring a rival from copying individual items was to change one's day or time of publication. It was more difficult to prevent weekly papers from recycling material from the dailies or to stop evening papers from pilfering morning ones. The *Evening Post,* established in 1709, timed its publication to be ready to leave London with the evening mail for the countryside. Far from disguising its reliance on the morning papers, the *Evening Post* claimed to be providing a valuable service to its customers. A banner at the top of the page proclaimed, "This Paper comes out every Post Night at Six a Clock" and "contains the Substance of all the other News, with fresh Advices."[39] The model of the *Evening Post* was to be followed by numerous evening papers in the years and decades to come. Printing late in the day enabled them to republish material from the morning papers while adding postscripts with late-breaking news.

In the late 1710s, a clever solution to the problem of evening papers copying from morning ones was proposed by the writer John Toland in a policy memorandum that he prepared for one of his political patrons. Toland noticed that evening papers copied most of their news from the morning papers, adding "some fresher passages, commonly made up of scandal and sedition."[40] According to Toland, before the advent of the evening papers individuals in London would read morning papers and then forward them to friends and family in the countryside, thereby contributing to post office revenue while promoting the circulation of the relatively tame morning papers. Now the evening papers were cutting into the sales of the morning papers while spreading more scandalous writings. Toland also claimed that the evening papers' reliance on copying led the official *London Gazette* to stall publication "till late at night, for fear of being pirated (to use the Bookseller's language) by these evening posts." This delay in publication could further divert attention away from the *Gazette* and toward the evening papers. Toland's memorandum recommended tightening regulations for newspapers in order to better serve the interests of government while preserving "the property of the subject." He was referring to the rights of the proprietors of morning newspapers. Toland described the evening papers as "a crying injustice against the authors and proprietors of the other papers, who, being at great pains and expense both for domestic and foreign intelligence, are thus robb'd of the fruit of their industry by those pirates copying their papers in the evening, without further trouble or charge."[41]

The idea that individuals had a right to the fruits of their labor can be traced back to John Locke's influential account of the origins of property, first published in 1690. Locke argued that property resulted from the natural rights of individuals over their bodily labor. By cultivating land that was not already claimed, individuals "mixed" their labor with the land, thereby appropriating it. The same went for fruit gathered on land held in common: picking the fruit made it one's own.[42] Locke's basic idea was to prove enormously influential in many subsequent arguments about literary property, not least in the middle decades of the eighteenth century, when London booksellers fought a series of court battles in an effort to establish that authors enjoyed a common-law right to their mental labors that could not be restricted by the Statute of Anne.[43] In his policy memorandum, Toland applied a very similar idea to the collection of news, arguing that the "pains" and "expense" involved in gathering "intelligence" justified the exclusive right to profit from that intelligence. Toland was assembling as many arguments as possible to support the idea of new regulations for newspapers, and he seems to have thought it wise for the government to appeal to the rights of "authors and proprietors" in this context. His idea was that stricter regulations could increase government revenue and limit the spread of scandalous writings while protecting compliant publishers against "injustice." In order to achieve these goals, Toland recommended closing the loopholes in the Stamp Act and prohibiting afternoon and evening newspapers altogether. To hinder piracy and encourage more respectable morning publications, he thought all news should have to be published before 10:00 a.m.[44]

The Stamp Act was revised in 1725, partly as a result of lobbying by the owners of stamped papers, who were tired of the unstamped papers underselling them. The loophole related to the number of sheets was closed, but Toland's suggestion about prohibiting afternoon and evening publication was not adopted. Stamped evening papers flourished, and despite the clearer language of the Stamp Act, unstamped papers also continued to appear. Eventually, the government, with the blessing of the stamped papers, suppressed the unstamped papers by going after the hawkers who distributed them. A 1743 law specified fines and imprisonment for anyone selling unstamped papers, and vigorous enforcement quickly put such papers out of business.[45]

Like the owners of evening papers, printers in towns outside of London also made a business out of copying. By incorporating reports from newspapers based in London and other regions of the country, provincial newspapers offered a digest of news, saving readers the expense of further subscriptions and postage. A newspaper printed closer to home also had the advantage of including news and advertisements of local interest. By the early 1720s, there were over twenty provincial papers, many of them on the main post roads leading out from London. Most made little claim to being original. Some of them even disowned the material they reprinted by naming their sources and stating that they were not responsible for the accuracy of reports.[46] Others emphasized that a weekly publication schedule gave them time to filter out some of the rumors and contradictions that characterized daily and triweekly papers in London. Travel times were decreasing thanks to better roads and faster horse-and-carriage services, but the fact that provincial papers appeared only once a week meant that there was bound to be a lag of at least a day, and often more, between the first publication of news in

London and its republication elsewhere. In this context, London propri-etors had little reason to complain about the way newspapers in other places excerpted and digested their news.[47] Over the course of the nine-teenth century, as discussed in chapter 5, the dynamic between the Lon-don press and provincial newspapers changed significantly, leading to more direct competition for readers and more concern about piracy.

But in the eighteenth century, cultural and economic factors worked against the idea of literary property in newspaper articles. Anonym-ity was widespread. In addition to paragraphs and essays translated or copied from other publications, newspapers contained anonymous and pseudonymous letters submitted by readers and reports attributed to unnamed but "honorable" individuals (merchants and military offi-cers were common sources). The propensity not to indicate the author of each text stemmed in part from the heterogeneous nature of news-papers, but there were also political and cultural reasons for it. Some writers sought to avoid prosecution for seditious libel, while others sim-ply wanted to avoid being personally associated with a particular point of view. Anonymity facilitated debate at a time when many writers cel-ebrated the ability to assume a depersonalized voice in discussions of public affairs, and to claim to speak on behalf of the public rather than in their own names.[48]

The business organization of the London press also discouraged the idea of treating newspaper articles as exclusive. By 1730, it became common for the ownership of newspapers and weekly journals to be di-vided into shares. Joint ownership by eight to twelve shareholders, and sometimes more, spread the financial risk of publication and provided the partners with a sideline revenue stream in the form of dividends. Crucially, it also gave them an advertising channel for their other prod-ucts. Booksellers dominated the lists of shareholders, a fact that helps to explain the large number of advertisements for books in eighteenth-century newspapers. Other shareholders included theater managers, auctioneers, and sometimes the principal writer or editor of the publica-tion. A successful newspaper could hope to sell between two thousand and three thousand copies, sometimes more, but profitability depended on advertising, and shareholders had a responsibility to attract paid notices.[49] The amount of space devoted to ads in eighteenth-century newspapers represented a major change from the seventeenth century, when relatively few ads appeared. In England's first daily newspaper, the *Daily Courant* (1702–1735), ads took up one-half and sometimes as much as two-thirds of each four-page issue. The *Daily Post* (1719–1746) and the *Daily Advertiser* (1731–1798) devoted as much as three-quarters of their space to ads, including most of the first page, and after 1730 the majority of daily newspapers used the word *advertiser* in their titles.[50] The shareholders handed daily operations over to printers and editors, who scanned other papers looking for paragraphs and essays to reprint, especially material that they could use to mock or criticize their competitors. Such one-upmanship was a feature of the London press, and as long as their papers were doing well financially, proprietors had little reason to complain about the copying of individual articles. Indeed, they knew that their own papers relied on copying.

THE ARRIVAL OF MAGAZINES

After the 1710s, few newspaper proprietors entered their titles under the Statute of Anne, and entries for periodicals as a whole fell from twenty-four in the 1710s to three in the 1720s and none in the 1730s.[51] This decline in registrations could be due to a number of factors. Some printers and booksellers may have realized that failure to register did not hinder the ability to obtain an injunction against unauthorized reprints.[52] Others may have decided to avoid the trouble and cost of registering and depositing works for which protection was uncertain. Many probably did not think copyright was necessary. But the drop-off in entries should not be interpreted as proof that nobody was interested in the question of literary property for newspapers and other periodicals. In fact, during the 1730s there was a brief but significant debate on the subject.

The context for this discussion was the appearance of the first successful monthly magazines. The *Gentleman's Magazine*, established by Edward Cave in 1731, contained a digest of news and essays from newspapers and weekly journals. Although in later years Cave would increase the amount of original material that appeared in his magazine, in the 1730s he borrowed heavily from other publications.[53] An engrav-

FIGURE 8. The engraving that appeared on the title page of the *Gentleman's Magazine* (this example from April 1732), with the titles of newspapers and weekly journals buttressing Edward Cave's printing shop at St. John's Gate. Source: Hathi Trust (original from Princeton University, digitized by Google).

ing that appeared on the title page of each issue illustrated how Cave built on existing publications to create a new work (see figure 8). The image was of St. John's Gate, the office of the *Gentleman's Magazine*. Buttressing the gate on both sides were the titles of the newspapers and weekly journals the magazine drew on. Far from hiding his reliance on other publications, Cave used their titles to attract customers.

The success of Cave's venture led a group of booksellers to found the rival *London Magazine* in 1732. The new magazine ridiculed its predecessor while imitating it in almost every respect. The *London Magazine* was divided into two parts, just like the *Gentleman's Magazine*, and included the same kind of material. Its subtitle, *Gentleman's Monthly Intelligencer*, also echoed Cave's publication, whose full title was *Gentleman's Magazine; or, Monthly Intelligencer*. Cave responded by advising readers not to be deceived by this imitation and urging them not to support a project that was "supplanting an Author in his whole Plan, Design, and even Title."[54] The owners of the London Magazine responded by publicly accusing Cave of piracy. They wrote, "Your Assurance, we think, is very extraordinary, in reflecting upon us for compiling a Book of this Kind from the Public Papers, in several of which we have a Property, when you have not the least Share in any one of them; which makes your Work little better than a downright Piracy."[55]

The proprietors of the London Magazine were claiming that they had a right to reprint excerpts from the weekly papers because they had an ownership stake in some of them.[56] Their claim obscured the complexity of group ownership. These men did not have shares, let alone complete ownership, of all the publications from which they copied, and they did not ask permission to reprint material from papers owned by others. Neither side mentioned the Statute of Anne or registration in Stationers' Hall. The debate centered on trade customs rather than statutory copyright. The proprietors of the London Magazine claimed that as booksellers who owned shares in several weekly papers they had rights that Cave, as a mere printer, did not. Cave responded by pointing out that one of the partners in the London Magazine, Charles Ackers, was also a printer. Sticking to their original argument, the partners insisted that "Mr Ackers (tho' a Printer, as well as Mr Cave) is qualified for being a Proprietor, by being a Partner of the Weekly Register; which Mr Cave is not; therefore every Essay, or Poem, which is taken from thence, is his Right, and Mr Cave is the Supplanter."[57] Cave rejected this idea that "half a dozen Men have a Right to publish Abridgements." He had just as much "Right to the publick Papers" as anyone else.[58]

Cave also offered a positive argument: his careful selection and arrangement of previously published material provided a service to the public.[59] Cave suggested that the property should reside not in the individual texts that made up a given issue but in the periodical's overall design. What was unfair, according to Cave, was the close imitation of his plan, design, and title. Cave was indeed the first to use the word magazine in the title of a monthly periodical. But the proprietors of the London Magazine insisted that nobody could have exclusive rights to a title, let alone a whole category of publication. Everyone was free to publish a newspaper or magazine, and the public would decide which ones to favor.[60]

A literary weekly called the *Grub-Street Journal* became involved in this dispute by publishing many of the rival notices by Cave and the proprietors of the *London Magazine*. Two of the shareholders of the *London Magazine* were also partners in the *Grub-Street Journal*, which helps to explain why the *Journal* largely took their side in the controversy.[61] The *Journal's* editor, Richard Russel, agreed that it was wrong to republish someone else's writings without permission, and suggested that the Statute of Anne was inadequate because it did not protect against the kind of "piracy" being committed by the *Gentleman's Magazine*.[62] Cave responded by accusing the *Grub-Street Journal* of pirating material from the daily and weekly papers. Russel then defended himself on the grounds of public utility. "Our method of comparing the articles of one paper with those of another," he wrote, "is not only not piratical, but extremely useful, and even necessary to put a stop to the currency of false news."[63] Weekly journals had long contained excerpts from the daily papers, but individual paragraphs often contradicted one another, and since the journals rarely indicated their sources, readers had no way to determine the authenticity of reports. The *Grub-Street Journal*, by contrast, printed reports on a particular subject one after the other, always indicating the name of the newspaper that had originally published them. This format enabled readers to compare multiple versions of the same event or combine details from several sources into a composite account (see figures 1 and 2 in the introduction).[64]

The idea of labeling sources was not new. In the seventeenth century, some corantos and newsbooks had done so, and when the *Daily Courant* began publication in 1702, it promised to indicate sources so that "the Publick, seeing from what Country a piece of News comes with the Allowance of that Government, may be better able to Judge of the Credibility and Fairness of the Relation."[65] The goal was to earn the trust of readers rather than to give credit to the newspaper that had first published a report. Other newspapers also promised to copy "faithfully" and label their sources, but few made good on practices of citation, and acknowledgment remained irregular well into the nineteenth century. The *Grub-Street Journal* was unique in consistently labeling each snippet of news, although a few other contemporary papers imitated this practice briefly.[66]

Russel defended his conscientious method of compiling news against charges of both plagiarism and piracy. He defined *plagiarism* as "the surreptitious taking of passages out of any author's compositions without naming him" and *piracy* as "the invasion of another's property by reprinting his copies to his detriment." Russel claimed that he could not be accused of plagiarism because the author of each article was named, but in fact only the title of the publication was given. As for the charge of piracy, he maintained that there was no such thing as a property in news. He wrote, "No man can assume to himself a Property by employing persons to collect a heap of trivial, ridiculous, and false paragraphs of news; and then publishing them daily to the world."[67] For Russel, the people involved (casual employees rather than authors), the work process ("collecting" rather than writing), and the final product (trivial, ridiculous, and false) all worked against the idea of a literary property in news.

The same standards did not necessarily apply to poems and essays appearing in weekly journals. An anonymous piece in the *Grub-Street Journal*, written by Russel or someone else, complained about the propensity of newspapers and magazines "to take out of our *Journal* Poetical Pieces especially, and to reprint them as their own, without the least acknowledgment from whence they had them: this we take to be plagiary, piracy, or literary theft, in the properest sense."[68] In this case, the writer did not clearly distinguish between piracy and plagiarism. These terms were often conflated during the eighteenth century, and to some extent they continue to generate confusion.[69] Was the contributor to the *Grub-Street Journal* upset that the poems had been reprinted or that the *Journal* had not received credit for them? The example he provided suggests that it was the failure to acknowledge the source that constituted the "literary theft." He explained that the *Post Boy* had copied a poem from the *Grub-Street Journal*, which had printed it at the author's request. But rather than credit the *Journal*, the *Post Boy* placed the poem under an Ireland dateline, thereby concealing its true origin. The example highlighted a major cultural obstacle that stood in the way of establishing shared protocols of citation during this period: in some circumstances editors and printers concealed their sources in order to make a piece appear original. In other cases, they made it look as though the text had come from some other place (such as by putting it under an Ireland dateline) when in fact it had been produced locally.

Not all eighteenth-century printers and editors agreed with Russel that newspaper paragraphs should be open to copying. After all, not all paragraphs were alike. In 1737, the writer of a weekly paper called *Common Sense* claimed that his contributors

now and then make some little Remarks upon Events that happen in the World, which they choose to throw out by Way of Paragraphs rather than introduce them into their Essay; and which they observe are constantly stolen by the *London Evening Post*, without any acknowledgement from whence he has them;—We hereby order the said *London Evening Post* to keep to his own province of stealing silly paragraphs of Domestic News wherever he can pick them up, not meddle upon any pretense whatever with Things which are onely [*sic*] designed for *Common Sense*.—If they go on to commit these Depredations they shall hear of It in a Manner that will do them no Service.[70]

The writer distinguished not between paragraphs and essays, as the *Grub-Street Journal* had done, but between two different types of paragraphs: (1) news items that could be found in numerous papers and (2) paragraphs written especially for *Common Sense*. Yet the writer did not explain how a reader or an editor of a competing publication could know the difference.

A MISSED OPPORTUNITY?

In the 1730s, attempts to replace the Statute of Anne with a new law offered an opportunity to clarify the question of literary property for newspapers and periodicals. In 1737, a contributor to the *Grub-Street Journal* referred to a bill being proposed by booksellers and expressed the wish that it were "drawn much fuller than I hear it is; that so the *Grub-Street Journal* might be secured to its Proprietors, free from the depredations of the *Magaziners*."[71] This writer suggested that contributions to weekly journals should be treated as the property of a journal's owners rather than of the writers themselves, leaving numerous questions unanswered. Would each paragraph, letter, or article need to be entered in the Stationers' Register? Would news reports be protected as well as poems and essays? The writer did not specify, and nobody else seems to have stepped forward with a more concrete proposal. Another contributor to the *Grub-Street Journal* dismissed the whole idea of literary property for periodicals, highlighting the "sensible pleasure" enjoyed by authors who saw their writings copied from the weekly journals into the magazines.[72] Some editors, like Russel, wanted their publication mentioned whenever material was copied from it. But Russel also believed that poems and essays appearing in periodicals should be treated as literary property, and he was frustrated that there was no way to stop Cave. By reproducing texts "verbatim and at full length" without mentioning their source, Cave was passing off the work of others as his own, "as stolen linen, handkerchiefs, &c. are rendered the fitter for sale, by taking out the mark of the owner's name."[73]

The *Grub-Street Journal* ended publication in 1737, and Russel and his partners blamed Cave for ruining their paper along with several other weeklies. They estimated that each monthly issue of the *Gentleman's Magazine* contained material from about ten different weekly papers and that the owners of these papers spent a combined total of twenty guineas in "Copy-money" each month. This amount would correspond to an average rate of half a guinea for a leading article in each week's issue.[74] Some newspapers and journals had writers on salary, but most paid for occasional submissions, such as a leading article, while depending on unpaid correspondents and copied material to fill the remaining space.[75] In terms of production costs, payments for occasional contributions paled in comparison to the sums advanced to cover the stamp duty. Monthly magazines were exempt from the stamp duty, but weekly journals were not. Russel and his partners denounced this as another unfair advantage enjoyed by Cave and his imitators. While "pillaging" material from the weekly papers, the magazines reduced the sale of the latter, causing their combined circulation to fall by thousands of copies a week.[76] Looking back on the early years of the *Gentleman's Magazine,* Russel expressed surprise that such a "mean undertaking" had been encouraged by readers and that London booksellers made no effort to stop it. Instead, the partners of the *London Magazine* imitated Cave by creating a "piratical pamphlet" of their own. Russel regretted that booksellers did not adhere to a moral code that would have prevented them from pillaging one another's works. "Had such notions of right and wrong generally prevailed," he wrote, "the *Gentleman's Magazine* had either never appeared at all, or had at least been soon forced to disappear."[77]

Although newspaper and magazine writings were not mentioned in the Statute of Anne, Russel argued that they were a form of literary property. As was common during the period, he began with the Lockean premise that individuals had a property in the fruits of their labor. "A person who composes any thing in writing intended for the benefit of others," Russel wrote, "has a right to some advantage by way of grateful return from them, for that product of the labour of his mind, as well as for the product of any bodily labour. This original right he may transfer by gift, or for some valuable consideration, to any person, who from thenceforth becomes the sole proprietor of that production." Russel thought that most booksellers did not respect the natural rights of authors and that the statutes should be revised. "Unless the Bill now depending put an effectual stop to it, the chief business of Book-selling will consist in the execution of piratical projects, to the great disadvantage of the fair trader, as well as of the Public."[78] Russel was referring to a copyright-reform bill proposed by London booksellers in 1737, the main objective of which was to extend the duration of protection to the lifetime of the author plus eleven years. The bill also contained some proposals that might have affected newspapers and magazines. One clause gave authors or their assignees the sole right to authorize abridgments and translations, provided that they did so within three years of publication. If they did not exercise this right within three years, then anyone would be free to produce an abridgment or translation. The bill also provided for copyright in "any Book, Pamphlet, or Writing." The reference to "any . . . writing" might have provided an opening for newspaper and magazine contributions, although these were not explicitly mentioned. In any case, the extension of the copyright term was too controversial, and the bill did not make it past the House of Lords.[79]

The Statute of Anne did not explicitly prohibit others from making abridgments of protected works, a fact that Cave and other magazine publishers exploited. Yet Cave was sued in 1739 for republishing parts of a book of sermons in the *Gentleman's Magazine*. He defended himself by noting that excerpts of books had often appeared in periodicals without causing complaint and that these excerpts encouraged sales by whetting readers' appetites. According to Cave, "It was not in the meaning or intention of the said Act of Parliament to restrain any Person from Extracting any Passage or Passages out of the Works of any Author." He suggested that such a restriction would be "greatly prejudicial to the spreading of knowledge and learning."[80] Although Cave lost this particular case, another court decision in 1741 created the important precedent that some abridgments could be considered new works—and therefore not an infringement of copyright—as long as they showed the "invention, learning, and judgment" of the person who prepared them. Simply shortening a work to create a substitute for the original was a clear violation of the Statute of Anne, but other abridgments would have to be judged on a case-by-case basis to determine whether they were "fair" and therefore permitted by the statute.[81]

After midcentury, some magazine publishers began to show interest in protecting contributions that they paid for. An important context for this was the Seven Years' War (1756–1763), when demand for news fueled rivalries among publishers. In 1757 and 1758, the *Monitor*, a weekly that featured commentary on the war and criticism of the current administration, frequently contained a notice that it was entered at Stationers' Hall, "and whoever presumes to *Print* or *Publish* it, or any Part thereof shall be prosecuted, as the Law directs."[82] This competitive climate also led the proprietors of the *London Magazine* to register successive monthly issues for copyright in 1759.[83] After a few months they stopped registering, presumably because in the meantime, the lead proprietor, Richard Baldwin, had obtained a royal license (the first step in securing a patent). The license granted Baldwin explicit rights beyond those offered by the Statute of Anne, including the sole right to abridge and translate items that first appeared in the magazine. Baldwin claimed to have undertaken "great expense in paying Authors for their Labours in writing and compiling" pieces for the magazine, and he was particularly interested in protecting an ongoing series titled "An Impartial and Succinct History of the Origin and Progress of the Present War."[84] This series included several maps and charts that had been reproduced without permission in other periodicals. Baldwin had the royal license printed and distributed copies of it in hopes of dissuading rivals from pillaging his magazine. Ten years later, the *London Magazine* entered a few monthly issues under the Statute of Anne, and the language of the entries indicates that the goal was to protect biographical pieces on William Shakespeare, the actor David Garrick, and others.[85] Publishers were thus beginning to claim literary property in individual contributions to periodicals. By the end of the eighteenth century, some magazines were being registered for copyright, but newspapers were not.[86]

THE RISE OF THE COMMERCIAL ADVERTISER

One reason for the lack of interest in copyright among newspaper publishers is the rise to prominence of a particular kind of newspaper that bundled together a range of material supported by advertisements. In the first two decades of the eighteenth century, the triweekly newspapers had focused on short bulletins of military and diplomatic news, leaving room for essay-based periodicals such as Addison and Steele's *Spectator* to treat various topics in more detail. But over time a new sort of newspaper, which for lack of a better term might be called the commercial advertiser, came to dominate English-language journalism. These papers contained not just news paragraphs and advertisements but also essays, letters to the printer, excerpts from pamphlets, price lists, shipping news, and more. The mix of content in the commercial advertisers gave them a broad appeal that made it more difficult for separate essay-based publications and specialized periodicals such as price currents, marine lists, and bills of mortality to compete for readers and advertisers. The *Public Advertiser* (1752–1794), *Gazetteer and New Daily Advertiser*

(1764–1796), and *Morning Chronicle* (1769–1865) are successful examples of this kind of newspaper. Although papers outside London tended to be owned by a local printer rather than by a group of shareholders, they also depended on a combination of subscription sales and advertising to become profitable. And like the London newspapers, they used a mix of original submissions and copied material to fill their columns.[87]

Newspapers copied almost all nonlocal news from publications based in other cities. The official *London Gazette* still existed, but its function was now different. Rather than having a monopoly on news, as it did in the late seventeenth century, the *Gazette* now provided official government notices and a steady stream of foreign news that could be easily republished and commented on by other newspapers. As newspapers traveled through the post, printers and editors seized on material that could be republished for their local readers. The basic nugget of news was the paragraph, a textual unit that could be easily detached from one source and inserted into another.[88] When it came to labeling the source of reports, some printers and editors were more careful than others, but few hid the fact that they were copying. In towns outside London, where newspapers were published weekly, printers prided themselves on carefully selecting news from London dailies and triweeklies along with reports first published by their counterparts in other regions of the country.[89]

Over time the paragraph became a journalistic genre in itself. The writer for *Common Sense* had complained in 1737 about other papers unfairly copying his original paragraphs, but for most writers and politicians, it was the fact that paragraphs were easy to reproduce that made them effective tools of persuasion. By the 1760s, writers across the political spectrum were exploiting the paragraph as a weapon in the battle for public opinion. Rival editors warned readers about the existence of "paragraph writers" who were ready to take up the pen to defend any cause for pay. John Campbell, a writer employed by prime minister Lord Bute to counter the arguments of the radical John Wilkes and his supporters, described the process this way: "I have . . . very carefully watched all the Inflammatory Paragraphs that have appeared in the Papers and have encountered them by other Paragraphs, better founded as well as of a better tendency."[90]

Given the commercial and political influences that fed into the press, editors frequently mocked one another's claims of impartiality and truthfulness. In this context, the notion of copyright for news was floated, but only as a joke. In a satire on the conventions of London journalism, one newspaper offered excerpts from a fictional publication called "The Lying Intelligencer" in which the owner promised the "freshest, most important, and best authenticated lies, both foreign and domestic." The liar also warned other newspapers that his work had been entered at Stationers' Hall and that "whoever pirates the copy, by printing the whole in their Papers, shall be prosecuted with the utmost rigour of the law. If they only pilfer particular passages, I shall rely upon the public taste, to distinguish between my high-zested lies, and their flat insipid truths."[91]

Although copyright for newspaper articles seemed absurd to some, the desire to spread a political message as widely as possible was not necessarily incompatible with the goal of profiting from demand for popular letters or essays appearing in newspapers. In the 1760s, a couple of individual issues of the controversial *North Briton* were registered for copyright, and notices warned that whoever reprinted these papers would be prosecuted.[92] Presumably, the publisher sought to capitalize on demand for back issues. Others claimed copyright in accounts of recent events published in pamphlet form. Advertisements for pamphlets reporting crimes, trials, or political controversies thus sometimes warned potential "pirates" that they would be prosecuted to the full extent of the law. Some of the notices claimed that reproducing "any part" of the pamphlet was illegal, although such claims never seem to have been tested in court.[93] Sensational crimes could inspire multiple accounts, leading their publishers to issue dueling advertisements that combined copyright notices with warnings against "spurious" versions.[94] In the case of newspaper essays that were popular enough to be reissued in pamphlet form, publishers might enter the title of the series after it had been published in the newspaper but before it was reissued

as a pamphlet. Such was the case with the Junius letters, a series of political essays that boosted the circulation of the *Public Advertiser* from
1769 to 1772. The printer-proprietor of that paper, Henry Sampson
Woodfall, registered the Junius letters for copyright in 1772 before re-
issuing them in book form.[95] Registration should not be taken as proof
of a valid copyright, since that had to be determined by the courts. But
the registration records do indicate that publishers sometimes asserted
the exclusive right to republish selected essays or letters commissioned
for their newspapers.

On the whole, however, newspapers copied freely from each other,
and this made economic sense. Although business records for eighteenth-
century newspapers are rare, the *Public Advertiser*'s accounts for the
1760s have survived. They indicate that occasional expenses for collecting news and paying writers were marginal compared to outlays for paper, printing labor, and stamp and advertising duties.[96] In fact, the high
costs of taxation and newspaper production during this period were in
some ways offset by the negligible amount spent on reporting. Even editors at newspapers within London, who we might think of as competing for readers, were not generally concerned about the copying of individual news items. They tended to treat news as a shared resource that
could be reused and adapted at will.

One area in which publishers began to invest in original reporting
in the late eighteenth century was coverage of Parliament. Since the seventeenth century, both Houses of Parliament had insisted that it was a
breach of privilege for anyone to report the debates or identify speakers by name. Details nonetheless leaked out in handwritten newsletters,
and magazines contained occasional reports beginning in the 1730s.
But a major breakthrough occurred in 1771, when the House of Commons summoned several printers and newspaper editors for violating its
standing orders against publication. John Wilkes, now an alderman of
London, mobilized constables and helped some of the printers resist ar-
rest, thereby challenging the authority of the House of Commons. Although some MPs claimed that newspaper accounts should be prohibited because they tended to misrepresent what was said, others defended
the right of the public to be informed. Once it became clear that Wilkes

had the upper hand, the Commons dropped the charges against the printers, giving them tacit permission to publish. The House of Lords followed suit a few years later in 1774.[97]

Some of the daily and triweekly newspapers invested in sending reporters to cover Parliament, but their versions were not treated as exclusive. Newspapers that did not send reporters cobbled together accounts from those that did. An editor's choices about which speakers to highlight and how to introduce them revealed a paper's political orientation. In fact, the text of the speeches themselves often varied depending on the newspaper one read. Some speakers submitted manuscripts of their speeches to the press or worked with reporters to prepare an authorized version, but no reporter claimed to be providing a verbatim transcript of the debates. William Woodfall, a respected writer for the *Morning Chronicle*, described his typical account as "a mere skeleton of the arguments urged upon the occasion" and warned readers not to expect "the exact phraseology used by the speakers."[98] The printed accounts were shaped by the memories, literary imaginations, and political convictions of reporters. These accounts then traveled from one newspaper to another, undergoing alterations at the hands of editors who adapted them to fit their own columns and conform to the political leanings of their papers.[99] In this context, the freedom with which editors appropriated and modified reports could be seen to have facilitated commentary and plurality of coverage.

OLD MONOPOLIES BREAKING DOWN

Specialized periodicals reporting on commerce and finance showed more interest in maintaining exclusivity, no doubt because these publications had fewer subscribers and were not generally supported by advertisements. The bills of entry, which listed the goods entered in the custom houses and were of interest to merchants, had been governed by royal patent during the seventeenth century. This continued to be the case in the eighteenth century, but it became increasingly difficult to enforce the monopoly. In the 1760s, a man named Richard Robinson contracted with the patent holder to have the right to publish bills of entry for the port of Liverpool. But his subscriptions declined as local newspapers began reporting the same information, either by copying from his official publication or by obtaining it from the local custom house in violation of the patent. The patent holder intervened in an attempt to protect his and Robinson's rights, but this proved to be ineffective. Although rights to the bills of entry for all ports in England and Wales technically remained in the hands of patent holders, newspaper editors in Liverpool and elsewhere increasingly treated such information as open to copying.[100]

Price currents, another type of business newspaper, had also been monopolized by patent holders for most of the seventeenth century, but there was more competition in this field starting in the 1690s. As the stock exchange developed, a broker named John Castaing saw the opportunity for a periodical that focused on stock quotations rather than on commodity prices. The result was the *Course of the Exchange*, which was published by Castaing and his descendants from the 1690s until the 1770s. They faced several rivals during this time. Between 1714 and 1722, another broker named John Freke issued a publication that looked similar, contained much the same information, and was published on the same days of the week. In addition, Freke's version cost ten shillings per year instead of twelve, obliging Castaing's son John Jr. to lower his own price.[101] Freke also registered his price current under the Statute of Anne, the first publisher of a business paper to do so.[102] Eventually Freke put his own name on the masthead, suggesting that he was not trying to pass off his publication as Castaing's but simply to profit from growing interest in stocks during the period leading up to the South Sea Bubble of 1720. His publication only lasted two years after the bubble burst.[103]

In the late 1730s, the Castaings faced another rival who copied both their information and their title. *The London Course of the Exchange*, issued by Francis Viouja and Benjamin Cole, looked so similar to the original that it fooled some contemporaries and subsequent librarians; a copy was even found amid a run of the genuine publication in the Bank of England's files.[104] The pirated edition lasted for about three years, after which Castaing's family again dominated the field until later in the century, when stockbrokers created a more formal organization. By

1786, the *Course of the Exchange* was being published by a broker appointed by the members of the Stock Exchange. What began as the initiative of a private broker thus became more formally linked to the institution of the Stock Exchange.[105]

The single most important provider of financial and commercial information during the eighteenth century was the Lloyd's association of insurance brokers. The organization began as a coffeehouse operated by Edward Lloyd at the end of the seventeenth century. All coffeehouses were important sites for the discussion of news, but over time Lloyd's developed systematic arrangements for the collection, storing, and publication of information. The insurance underwriters who made up the association had agents in the ports. They kept track of arriving and departing ships and their cargoes and recorded any reports relayed by the captain or crew. These reports were sent to the master of Lloyd's Coffee House, who sifted through them and copied selected information into a reference book that could be consulted in the coffeehouse. The master also chose some of the reports for publication in a twice-weekly paper called *Lloyd's List*. The roots of this publication stretch back to the 1690s, and a version of it exists online today.[106]

The news-gathering efforts of Lloyd's benefited the press as a whole, because other newspapers often copied from *Lloyd's List*. But on some occasions the association tried to claim exclusive rights. In the 1750s, Lloyd's sent an early version of a cease-and-desist letter to several provincial newspapers, threatening a lawsuit if they continued to copy from *Lloyd's List*. A Manchester paper that received this notice informed readers that it would discontinue ship news "until we are thoroughly inform'd of the Legality or Illegality thereof."[107] Although Lloyd's may have been able to intimidate an editor here and there, prevailing practices among newspapers meant that the organization was fighting a losing battle. The total number of subscribers to *Lloyd's List* would have been significantly lower than that of many political newspapers of the day—a few hundred rather than a couple thousand—so losing even a small number of subscribers could hurt. Lloyd's information was frequently copied by newspapers, but merchants and brokers who wanted the freshest information possible would still have taken a subscription, and it is possible that the publication was subsidized by member fees or other activities of the Lloyd's association.[108]

Specialized periodicals that had enjoyed monopoly positions in the seventeenth century suffered from the proliferation of newspapers and magazines during the eighteenth century. One of these was the bills of mortality, which had been protected by privileges from the crown and the City of London since the early seventeenth century. Over time the attention of readers was diverted from the bills to an increasing number and variety of publications devoted to current events. The reliability of the information contained in the bills, especially the causes of death as determined by parish searchers, was also criticized. In 1819, the physician George Man Burrows observed that when "there were few other channels of information, these weekly bills excited considerable interest, and were a source of profit to the Company [of Parish Clerks]."[109] But now the bills were far from profitable, and many of the clerks lacked the motivation or resources to provide accurate and timely returns. When the head clerk appeared before Parliament in 1833, he admitted that the Company of Parish Clerks depended on its annual subsidy from the City to keep the operation going and that the company was ready to relinquish its privilege over the bills.[110] Following the Civil Registration Act of 1836, the bills of mortality were superseded by the weekly reports of births and deaths issued by the office of the Registrar General.[111]

In the area of crime news, the two serials that had received privileges from the City of London in 1683—the *Ordinary of Newgate's Account* and the *Proceedings of Old Bailey*—also faced increasing competition from unofficial pamphlets, broadsides, and newspapers that reported on crimes and trials. By the 1770s, the *Account* no longer existed as a serial, although the chaplain of Newgate Prison (known as the ordinary) occasionally exploited interest in notorious criminals by issuing pamphlets containing their confessions.[112] The *Proceedings* lasted much longer—eventually becoming known as the *Sessions Papers*—but only because the City of London agreed to fund it. By the late eighteenth century, the idea of accurate trial reports subsidized by the government had replaced the older model of a monopoly given to an individual patent holder who assumed the risk of publication in exchange for exclusivity.[113] By taking over responsibility for the *Sessions Papers*, the City recognized that a reliable and trustworthy record benefited the wider community, not just the individuals who chose to purchase a copy. It was an early example of treating a certain kind of reporting as a *public good* in both the civic and economic senses of the term.

A RIGHT TO NEWS?

Apart from the economic and cultural factors that encouraged newspapers to copy from each other, it is tempting to ask whether copying was also defended on political grounds. After all, news was no longer subject to prepublication censorship, and the proprietary rights that existed in the seventeenth century had been closely linked to licensing. Did eighteenth-century writers or publishers articulate a public right to news and political commentary in order to justify the exclusion of newspaper articles from copyright? Was copyright for news somehow seen as being at odds with press freedom?

Most discussions of freedom of the press in the eighteenth century concerned the right to publish free from prior authorization. Such a freedom was not announced in the Bill of Rights of 1689 or subsequent legislation; it merely resulted from the 1695 lapse of the Printing Act. But over time writers developed positive arguments about the need to monitor and criticize the government in order to reveal corruption and abuse. As the century progressed, political leaders also discussed the rights of ordinary people to hold and express opinions. Whereas some lauded the benefits of disseminating knowledge to the wider population, others feared the social and political consequences of broader discussions of politics and diplomacy.[114] The question of public access also came up in debates about literary property for books. During the middle decades of the century, as London booksellers argued that the duration of copyright should be extended, opponents of this idea invoked the figure of the ordinary reader whose access to knowledge and literature was hindered by the high prices that copyright enabled booksellers to charge. Even those who believed that copyright benefitted society by providing an incentive to authors insisted that this benefit was contingent on limiting the duration of the monopoly. They suggested that after the copyright in a book expired, competition would lead to cheap editions of previously expensive works.[115]

These issues were at the heart of the so-called battle of the booksellers, which culminated in *Donaldson v. Beckett* (1774).[116] In this case, the Scottish bookseller Alexander Donaldson and his brother John defended their right to reprint works whose terms of protection under the Statute of Anne had expired. They were opposed by London booksellers who argued that authors enjoyed a common-law property in their writings that superseded the terms of the statute. The Donaldsons stressed the "public utility" of limiting the duration of copyright. They argued that "the Common Law has ever regarded *public Utility*, the Mother of *Justice* and of *Equity*. *Public Utility* requires that the Productions of the Mind should be diffused as wide as possible, and therefore the *Common Law* could not, upon any Principles consistent with itself, abridge the Right of multiplying copies."[117] In the end, the House of Lords sided with the Donaldsons, affirming that anyone was allowed to republish works whose statutory copyright had expired.

Interestingly, the question of public access to news and political commentary was broached during the debate that preceded the vote in the House of Lords. One of the lords who spoke was Thomas Howard, Earl of Effingham. He worried that strong copyright protection could be used to restrict the circulation of writings that criticized a minister of state or other public official. Specifically, he imagined the publication of a pamphlet that described "some very unconstitutional and despotic measure . . . and that the minister bought up the impression and copyright, thereby choaking [*sic*] the channel of public information, and securing in his closet the secret which might prevent the loss of freedom to the subject."[118] Effingham's speech has been pointed to as evidence that some contemporaries were concerned that copyright potentially restricted freedom of the press—copyright could be used as a form of censorship.[119] But Effingham's fear centered on criticisms of public officials rather than on news or information per se, and he referred to an account that first appeared in a pamphlet rather than in a newspaper. Most discussions of copyright in the late eighteenth century did not consider newspaper writings, probably because by that time no publishers were claiming copyright in their newspapers. The idea that copyright could restrict the flow of information of public concern would be more clearly articulated beginning in the mid-nineteenth century, when the campaign to end the stamp duty and other "taxes on knowledge" led the owners of established newspapers to lobby for a special copyright in news reports (see chapter 5). But in the late eighteenth century, there was no need to provide such a counterargument, because the business and culture of news publishing worked against the very idea of exclusivity.

PUBLISHING PRACTICE AND THE LAW

The Statute of Anne's references to "useful books" and the "encouragement of learning" could be interpreted as signs that Parliament sought to restrict the kinds of works eligible for literary property. But the statute was ambiguous, and this ambiguity created a space for writers, printers, and booksellers to work out shared norms and practices. Initially, some newspapers and weekly journals were registered for copyright, and the exclusive right to reprint a successful periodical such as the *Spectator* could be valuable. But after the debate in the 1730s involving magazines and weekly journals, there was very little discussion of copyright for newspaper and magazine writings for the rest of the century. Most proprietors of newspapers did not enter their works under the Statute of Anne or otherwise claim exclusive rights in news. Those who specialized in financial and commercial information did attempt to stop others from copying, but with little success. A few magazine publishers sought to protect maps and other features that they paid for. But newspaper editors would not have dreamed of prohibiting the copying of individual paragraphs, essays, or letters, because that would have made it much harder to fill their own columns. Newspapers were interdependent, and editors treated individual articles as shared resources.

The lack of copyright for newspaper writings should not be seen as a failure of eighteenth-century publishers to "catch up" by acquiring the kind of protection already available for books. Rather, the underlying economics and dominant cultural practices of eighteenth-century journalism worked against the very idea of treating news as property.

The free republication of newspaper articles would not have thrived for so long if writers, publishers, and readers had not derived benefits from it. Republication went hand in hand with anonymity and disguised authorship. Some planted stories or mislabeled sources in an attempt to advance political or financial goals, while others cherished the ability to assume a depersonalized voice in debates about culture, society, and government.[120] As Richard Russel of the *Grub-Street Journal* recognized back in the 1730s, copying not only enabled news to spread—it also facilitated commentary and analysis.

CHAPTER 3

Scissors Editors:
Cutting and Pasting in Early America

IN 1790, A PHILADELPHIA READER mocked Benjamin Franklin Bache, the grandson of Benjamin Franklin and printer of the *General Advertiser*, for the way he reproduced material from other newspapers.[1] In a letter that Bache nonetheless chose to publish in his newspaper, the reader described what he saw when he visited the printing shop. Bache had an inkstand on his desk and a pen behind his ear, but he did not need either, because he relied on his scissors instead:

> There was a great heap of newspapers laying on the table, and on the floor all about you, and you had in your hand a large pair of taylors' [*sic*] shears, and there you cut out of other papers as much as you thought would fill yours. The young man would come down and ask for more copy. How much more[?] About half a column. You tumbled over the papers and measured it off to him in half a minute. And that's the way you make money, and then you grumble and tell us how difficult it is for one to be a Printer.[2]

The idea that a printer might choose which articles to republish based on their length was not absurd. Each issue of a newspaper contained the same number of pages and columns to fill. Printers selected, arranged, and modified material from a range of sources to fill this space. Using scissors to cut out existing texts made sense from the standpoint of printers (more on this later), but it also opened them up to mockery. The reader that was just quoted portrayed Bache as a failed artisan rather than as a writer; he used the instrument of another trade—the tailor's shears—to appropriate the work of other printers.

Descriptions of newspaper editors with scissors became more common around 1800, in Britain as well as the United States.[3] Whereas some portrayed copying as lazy or immoral, others celebrated the capacity of editors to select and republish material from other publications. The fact that they drew attention to copying—and the use of scissors in particular—suggested that attitudes toward the authorship and ownership of newspaper texts were changing at the very moment that the volume of recirculated material was increasing. In the United States, this copying was actually encouraged by postal policy. Although copying was important to British newspapers—and would continue to be so during the nineteenth century—specific policy choices and cultural practices in the United States created a decentralized news environment that encouraged the active exchange of news among publishers.[4] This chapter shifts the focus from Britain to the United States during the early-republic and antebellum eras to explore how newspaper printers and editors dealt with questions of copying.

During and immediately following the American Revolution, political leaders frequently noted the importance of newspapers in a democratic society. They championed newspapers as crucial vectors of information about politics and commerce. The way to encourage the circulation of news to all parts of the country, they decided, was to charge extremely low postage for newspapers sent to subscribers and to allow printers to exchange newspapers with each other through the mails for free.[5] The Post Office Act of 1792, which enacted these principles into law, needs to be understood as a counterpart to the Copyright Act of 1790. The latter explicitly protected "maps, charts, and books," reflecting the fact that Congress sought to promote learning in the new nation.[6] In setting up the new post office, legislators sought to facilitate access to information of more immediate political and commercial interest. There is no evidence to prove that lawmakers considered including newspapers in the copyright statute and then decided not to, but there is every reason to believe that granting copyright to newspapers would not have made sense to them. Copying was what enabled news to spread, and postal policy in the early American republic encouraged printers to exchange newspapers in order to obtain news from other places and republish it for their local readers.

Although those familiar with early American newspapers have long recognized that copying was common, digital tools have made it possible to study the phenomenon on a new scale. By using computer algorithms to locate similar strings of text across collections of digitized newspapers, scholars have begun to track the movement of newspaper articles and identify which ones were most often reprinted.[7] A study of changing attitudes toward copying is a necessary complement to such computational analysis. The infrastructure and rate schedule of the post office clearly encouraged the exchange of news, but that does not mean that copying was unproblematic. In fact, newspaper editors and publishers showed a growing sensitivity toward copying. They did not yet seek copyright protection, but they did try to develop shared customs to regulate the way copied material was handled. After 1800, as the printing and editorial functions of newspapers started to separate, a number of editors began to express concern about the need to acknowledge one's sources and to give credit to the first newspaper that published something. These requests for credit—and related accusations of "pilfering" news—also depended on changes in business practice. In the 1820s and 1830s, increased investments in news gathering led some publishers to cut off the supply of news to exchange partners that did not provide sufficient credit. Some went so far as to set traps for copyists by feeding them fake news. Meanwhile, newspapers in large cities in the Northeast—and especially New York—worked to attract paying readers in neighboring towns and the surrounding countryside, cutting into the readership of smaller papers that relied extensively on copying. By the 1840s, editors in various locations were complaining more frequently about copying. They attempted to impose new protocols of citation and acknowledgment, but they remained uninterested in copyright law.[8] Editors sought ways to keep the news flowing while receiving the kind of credit that could boost the reputations—and circulations—of their newspapers.

CUTTING AND PASTING

The practice of using scissors and paste to help prepare a work for the press is almost as old as printing itself. From at least the sixteenth century, compilers of encyclopedias and other reference works found that cutting out passages from existing works and pasting them on paper was faster than transcribing by hand and avoided introducing errors of transcription.[9] Using a printed copy also facilitated the work of preparing a text for the press. With manuscripts, the handwriting had to be deciphered, and the number of words and lines had to be counted to determine how much space the text would take up in the printed version. Working from printed copy, an editor could more easily estimate how much text would fit, and the compositor setting the type could work faster and with fewer mistakes.[10]

The compilers of eighteenth-century encyclopedias continued to rely on scissors. The editor of the first edition of the *Encyclopaedia Britannica* (1768–1771) supposedly joked that he had "made a Dictionary of Arts and Sciences with a *pair of scissors.*"[11] The need to save time and avoid errors of transcription was equally true of newspapers. Most early American newspapers were small family businesses, but even for larger printing shops in major cities, it would have been practical to work from existing material whenever possible. It made no sense to copy a text by hand if one could cut out paragraphs or use a pen to mark which ones should be reproduced along with any changes desired by the editor.[12]

Some of the early American newspapers that have survived were the exchange copies that printers and editors used as sources. Among the massive newspaper holdings of the American Antiquarian Society (AAS) in Worcester, Massachusetts, are the exchange copies kept by Isaiah Thomas, printer of the *Massachusetts Spy* newspaper and founder of the AAS. Many of Thomas's volumes contain marks surrounding the paragraphs, letters, and essays that he chose to republish. Thomas's files reveal that he occasionally cut out a paragraph or column of text. More commonly, he marked the selected material with a pen and kept the newspaper whole. This practice is consistent with Thomas's interest in preserving printed works, but it also seems likely that a printer would be less likely to save newspapers that had lots of holes in them. Still, there are enough cutouts in the exchange papers preserved at the AAS and other libraries to confirm that early newspaper printers clipped articles to save time.[13]

Exchange copies provide concrete evidence of how printers and editors worked. In many cases, they had to rely on intermediate sources, making it difficult for them—let alone their readers—to know how the chain of copying might have altered the news. For example, if a Boston newspaper reprinted material from a London newspaper, the Boston printer might indicate the full title, but more often he simply referred to "a London paper" or put the news under a London dateline. When another American newspaper used the Boston paper as a source for London news, it almost never acknowledged this fact. If an article already contained a credit line such as "From the Public Advertiser," a printer would have to decide whether to include or omit this line when reprinting the article.

Thomas's files provide examples. In 1782, his *Massachusetts Spy* contained a letter signed "Cincinnatus" and labeled "From the Freeman's Journal." The reader might assume that Thomas had copied this letter directly from the *Freeman's Journal* in Philadelphia. But Thomas's exchange files reveal that he copied the letter and accompanying credit line from the *New Jersey Journal*.[14] Mail delivery was unreliable, and printers had to do their best with whatever sources arrived. Thomas also altered credit lines. The *New Jersey Journal* had labeled one article "From the St. James's Chronicle," but Thomas crossed off that title and wrote, "From a late London Paper."[15] Whatever Thomas's reasons for doing this—he may have been attempting to simplify things for the reader, or he may have sought to distance himself from the *St. James's Chronicle* for some reason—his alteration affected the chain of evidence. Thomas's newspaper files show that he was generally a careful editor who avoided printing doubtful news and warned readers about unconfirmed reports. In the summer of 1781, for example, Thomas chose to republish a paragraph from the *New Jersey Journal* reporting a French naval victory against British forces in the Caribbean. He modified this article by adding the phrase, "This account wants confirmation." He also instructed the typesetter to hold this paragraph until the rest of the week's news was set in type. Thomas was hoping to receive subsequent reports that would confirm or contradict the paragraph from the *New Jersey Journal*. The fact that the paragraph ultimately appeared in the *Massachusetts Spy*, accompanied by Thomas's warning, suggests that no further reports arrived before the paper went to press.[16]

POSTAL EXCHANGE

Although copying from other publications had long been the primary means of obtaining nonlocal news, the Post Office Act of 1792 guaranteed that printers and editors could count on access to a wider range of news delivered on a more predictable schedule. The law contained two provisions that enabled the newspaper press to grow and flourish in nineteenth-century America. First, it specified very low postage for newspapers compared to private letters. Subscribers paid one cent for newspapers that traveled up to 100 miles and one and a half cents for those that traveled farther. Whereas the typical four-page newspaper could be sent 450 miles (and any distance beyond that) for one and a half cents, a letter written on four sheets of paper would cost one dollar to travel the same distance. These rates meant that sending personal correspondence through the mail was too expensive for most people.[17] As a result, the two main functions of the post office from 1792 until the late 1840s (when postage rates for letters were lowered) were handling business correspondence and distributing newspapers. The rate structures ensured that the former subsidized the latter. The total number of newspapers sent through the mail grew from nearly two million a year in 1800 to six million in 1820, sixteen million in 1830, and thirty-nine million in 1840. These figures do not represent the total circulation of newspapers, though, since in addition to the post office, customers received newspapers through private carriers, street vendors, and directly from the printer. Yet newspapers clearly made up the bulk of the mail handled by the post office while contributing only a fraction of its revenue.[18]

The fact that there were two zones for newspaper postage was a compromise. Proponents of a uniform postal rate argued that the government should encourage the circulation of news to all parts of the country. Proponents of graduated postage insisted that a flat rate would benefit newspapers in large cities at the expense of those in rural areas. If there was no difference in postage, then readers in the countryside or other cities might prefer to subscribe directly to a few newspapers in New York and Philadelphia, making it harder for small local newspapers to survive. There was no sense that papers in small towns might maintain an advantage by reporting local news. Papers outside the major cities were published weekly, so most readers would learn the latest news orally before it could be printed. Apart from advertisements and the occasional editorial, people turned to their local newspaper for news from other cities. Legislators who opposed uniform postage celebrated the role of local printer-editors in selecting and commenting on news from other places, not least reports from Washington and the state capitals. Similar arguments would be aired each time the post office considered reforming its policy with respect to newspapers.[19]

The second crucial feature of the 1792 act was that it charged no fee for newspapers exchanged among printers. The idea was not entirely new. During the colonial period, a number of local postmasters—a position often held by printers—had encouraged postriders not to charge for newspapers sent from one printer to another. But the free exchange of newspapers during the colonial era was hampered by the limited development of the post roads and by the fact that printers who served as postmasters sometimes refused to carry their rivals' papers.[20] The 1792 act sought to transform this ad hoc privilege into a right for all printers, regardless of their political connections. Printers were permitted to send a copy of their newspapers to as many other printers as desired, free of postage. This policy amounted to a government subsidy of the news-gathering efforts of newspapers around the country. It had profound implications for the way newspapers functioned and the kinds of material they made available to readers.[21]

Printers and editors worked hard to build up their exchange lists, but there were many reasons why a request to exchange papers might be refused. Some editors did not want to exchange with papers of different political leanings; others did not have time to read additional papers or sought to avoid the cost of producing more copies to be sent out in exchange (for some papers, exchange copies may have amounted to 10 percent of the print run). Larger, more established newspapers could afford to discriminate. Many editors saw exchanges as a means of disseminating their views and attracting additional subscribers. For that to work, the source had to be properly credited, so it is not surprising that failure to credit could provide grounds for ending an exchange relationship. In choosing what to print, editors often had this wider exchange network in mind. They sought not only material that would please their own readers but also items that would be of interest to editors in other places.[22] Maintaining a reciprocal relationship could require significant effort. One printer in Burlington, Vermont, became so annoyed at the neglect of one of his exchange partners that he wrote on the masthead of his outgoing newspaper: "Damn you send me a paper!"[23]

Compiling news from exchange papers could be a labor-intensive process. Hezekiah Niles, who founded the Baltimore-based *Weekly Register* in 1811 and edited it for twenty-five years, sought to create the nation's leading digest of domestic and foreign news. Niles carefully selected the papers he wanted to receive, rejecting those that he thought would not be useful. Still, he spent up to three days per week reading through exchange papers to decide which accounts to republish. Niles insisted that writing editorials was much less difficult than assembling an interesting digest of news from around the country. As he put it, "To attempt to cull 'the wheat from the chaff' of the multitudinous reports, surmises and conjectures; to glean the substance of ten thousand columns of what is called *news*; to retain *all* the useful and necessary facts, and reject the vast body of matter which appears to have been made for no other purpose than to *fill up* the newspapers—requires much patience, perseverance and care."[24]

ASKING TO BE COPIED

Niles's *Weekly Register* embodied the ideal of an impartial digest of news, but the exchange system also allowed for highly partisan material to circulate. Indeed, the ideal of impartiality announced in many newspapers was often honored in the breach. Whereas some editors actively exploited postal networks to disseminate political views, others claimed to be neutral but still reprinted highly partisan material. The openness of the system and the culture of anonymity enabled politicians and editors to create a series of articles that looked as though they were written by different individuals, giving the impression of a broad consensus on a particular topic; an experienced editor, however, could identify the articles as coming from the same source. Niles referred to such deceptive practices as the "manufacture" of public opinion.[25] His frustration with the way exchanges were exploited for political purposes reveals that the system had both benefits and risks. The free exchange among printers ensured that readers had access to news from around the country, but it also enabled the spread of false and biased information. A newspaper could have a limited subscriber base and still be influential if its reports and editorial matter were reprinted in other places. Yet it remained difficult for women and minorities to get into print.[26]

In order to disseminate news, editorials, and political essays, editors sometimes literally asked to be copied. In 1831 a paper based in Wilkes-Barre, Pennsylvania, politely asked the New York *Courier and Enquirer* to reprint a letter advocating the construction of a railroad from New York to the Pennsylvania coal fields. As was typical, the request was made publicly, in the pages of the Wilkes-Barre newspaper, which was sent in exchange for the *Courier and Enquirer*.[27] Printing the request rather than sending a letter reduced the cost (printers' exchanges were free, whereas letter postage was expensive) but it also had an important social function. Published requests offered an opportunity to publicly praise the influence, integrity, or other qualities of one's exchange partners. Such praise was an important part of establishing exchange relationships.[28]

Political controversies also motivated editors to explicitly ask that certain articles be republished. In 1830, the *Georgia Journal* reacted to unfavorable reports about that state's treatment of Native Americans by asking, "Will the National Journal, the New York Journal of Commerce, and Daily Advertiser, the Boston Courier, and their coworkers, republish the following statement, as a slight atonement for the almost innumerable slanders against Georgia, which they have heretofore given currency to?" The *Georgia Journal* wanted to publicize the fact that a white man had been convicted of robbery against a Cherokee person in order to show that the Georgia courts were more evenhanded than was often claimed.[29] Thanks to digital newspaper databases, it is now possible to identify some of the newspapers that chose to reprint the article in question, but physical copies in libraries reveal even more about the work of scissors editors.[30] For example, the copy of the *Georgia Journal* held by the AAS was the exchange copy sent to the *National Journal* in Washington, and it has a hole where the article "Georgia and the Indians" used to be. That's because the Washington editor clipped the article and gave it to the typographers for inclusion in an upcoming issue. He also added this note to introduce the article: "We readily comply with the request of the Milledgeville [Georgia] Journal to republish the following article. We have no desire to be unjust to Georgia, and, as far as this article can be considered evidence that she is not disposed to be unjust to the Indians, she is welcome to the benefit of its circulation."[31] Like the example of the *Courier and Enquirer* noted earlier, this one reveals how editors read each other's papers, responded to criticism, and asked for help in circulating their views. In order to encourage their counterparts to honor these requests, they often included headnotes that appealed to their fellow editors' sense of honor or justice. The response of the *National Journal* indicated the extent to which getting an article republished and having "the benefit of its circulation" depended on the convictions of the editors involved.

Free postal exchange was the foundation of the early American press, enabling news and political opinion to spread, but it created burdens for the post office. As the country expanded westward after the War of 1812, the costs of printers' exchanges came under scrutiny, especially when the post office was running a deficit. In 1822 and again in 1825, bills before Congress proposed to limit each printer to a maximum of fifty free exchange papers, after which they would have to pay for postage. On both occasions the clause was struck from the bill. By the 1820s this privilege had become a cornerstone of the American press that senators and representatives actively defended.[32] In the 1830s, Postmaster General Amos Kendall suggested a new approach to relieving the growing burden of exchange papers. Kendall estimated that the nation's newspaper network had expanded from about 150 titles along the eastern seaboard in 1792 to between 1,300 and 1,500 titles spread over a much wider geographic area in 1838. His estimates seem to have been low but not wildly so.[33] Kendall claimed that many newspapers were exchanging with five hundred to six hundred others but that only a hundred or so could possibly be useful. He proposed limiting exchanges to smaller digests of news called slips, containing up to two columns of text. The slips could be cut from a newspaper's regular edition or printed especially for the purpose. The post office had opened a horse-express service on a few select routes in 1837, and Kendall reported that on these lines the slips had already proven their usefulness. He thought that using slips on all mail routes would alleviate the post office while reducing the work of editors, who would no longer have to sift through bulky newspapers to locate the content that was unique to each one.[34] Congress did not act on either suggestion, and the full subsidy for printers' exchanges continued until it was eliminated as part of a general abolition of franking in 1873. Even then, the policy did not disappear without a fight by newspaper publishers and politicians who defended the utility of free exchanges and sought in vain to have them reinstated.[35]

CHANGING ATTITUDES

The openness of the exchange system also raised the question of whether copied material should be acknowledged. Attitudes toward copying were evolving during this period. Writers were beginning to laud originality rather than imitation as the ideal form of authorship, and the use of quotation marks was becoming more common in printed texts.[36] These changes were reflected in the newspapers. In 1799, a contributor to a Providence, Rhode Island, paper announced, "I shall be acquitted of plagiarism, when my readers remember my prodigal use of inverted commas, and my care to give credit for borrowed thought and expression."[37] A few years earlier, a reader of the *National Gazette*, based in Philadelphia, criticized newspaper printers and editors who tried to excuse plagiarism by referring to it as "borrowing" or "culling." He cited a recent example in which legislative debates had been copied without acknowledgment from another newspaper. Although the "brethren of the type" might think that such material was free for the taking, this reader insisted that it was "rank plagiarism." He suspected that most editors did not like to admit how much they copied or to draw attention to the talents of their peers. He hoped that they would be more honest in the future.[38]

Some newspaper editors also began to express frustration at not receiving credit for original material appearing in their papers. William Coleman, the editor of the *New York Evening Post*, was among the first to articulate the notion of unfair competition in journalism. In 1805 Coleman explained that he felt a sense of injustice whenever he saw "an article, belonging to ourselves, appropriated by another, and given to the world as his own." Coleman suggested that all authors were entitled to whatever "advantage" may result from their labors. "The advantage belonging to newspaper editorial writing is to multiply subscribers," he wrote, and when "a man takes his scissors and cuts out my article and gives it to the world as his own, he derives an unfair advantage from my productions, and multiplies his subscribers at my expense." According to Coleman, the common practice of using datelines rather than citing newspaper titles contributed to this problem. He complained about "certain type setting gentlemen who contrive to avoid offending against the letter of plagiarism" by republishing articles under the heading "New York" or "Boston" rather than naming the specific paper from which they had copied. "As these scissor-authors very well know, the reader very rarely stops to take any notice of the place or date, and therefore, while by this contrivance they deprive the owner of the privilege of complaining, they in fact secure the whole credit and advantage of the article to themselves."[39]

The kinds of datelines that Coleman disliked had existed from the earliest manuscript newsletters and printed corantos, which organized news by geographic provenance rather than by subject or perceived importance. Although some newspapers used more precise labels, such as "From the London Evening Post," most simply placed the copied paragraphs under a London dateline. These conventions did not satisfy Coleman, who saw himself as a writer rather than a compiler. The focus of his complaint was the "advertising papers." To have a successful advertising paper, according to Coleman, all one needed was enough skill to set the type and enough education to read the proofs. As he put it, "Whoever can do this, and has a competent share of discernment to find out what will please his readers, and is attentive to procure it by the help of a pair of shears, may enrich himself at pleasure."[40]

William Duane of the Philadelphia *Aurora* cited this argument with approval in an editorial titled "Scissors Editors."[41] Duane and Coleman represented a new generation of editors who developed closer connections to political parties; they also had stronger editorial voices than most of their predecessors. Beginning around 1800 in the United States, it was possible to envision political editing as a career. Republicans and Federalists needed mouthpieces at the local, state, and national levels, and this created opportunities for young men of the artisan and middling classes. Running a newspaper provided a way for them to make a living while realizing their political ambitions. Although these editors copied many of the news reports that they published, they also contributed original essays in which their own views—and those of their political patrons—came to the fore.[42] This nascent sense of an editorial voice helps to explain why Coleman and Duane were especially sensitive to copying.

Duane and Coleman shared this attitude despite being in opposing political camps. The *Aurora* was started by Benjamin Franklin Bache as the *General Advertiser* in 1790 but quickly became an outspoken Republican newspaper and was renamed the *Aurora* in 1794. The *New York Evening Post* was a Federalist paper started by Alexander Hamilton and his associates in 1801 with Coleman as the first editor. Coleman and Duane often exchanged harsh words, but they agreed about the injustice of republishing articles without credit. As Duane put it, "Although we differ with the Evening Post in politics, we have a fellow feeling respecting pence."[43] In fact, Coleman was well paid, but his salary depended on political patronage rather than on subscriptions. Duane's *Aurora* was an influential Republican organ but did not enjoy the same amount of financial support. Duane, like most newspaper publishers of the period, struggled with debt. Subscribers were often slow to pay and some never paid at all, making it all the more frustrating to lose some to a rival paper.[44] Duane claimed to have lost six hundred subscribers in five years thanks to the growth of country newspapers that reprinted extracts from the *Aurora*.[45] The loss of six hundred subscribers would have been significant at a time when many newspapers struggled to even achieve that number.

Although Duane described unacknowledged copying as "pilfering"
or "robbery," he also implied that these offenses could be avoided by
giving credit to the *Aurora*. Credit—a word with both ethical and financial connotations—became central to discussions of journalistic
practice in the nineteenth century. Eighteenth-century newspapers had
also used the word, but mainly to refer to the trustworthiness (or credibility) of the news rather than as an acknowledgment (or reward) due
to its author. For example, in 1787, a South Carolina newspaper introduced an item this way: "We extract the following anecdote of the
present king of Prussia, from a German newspaper of the first credit."[46]
For Coleman, Duane, and other nineteenth-century editors who complained about unacknowledged copying, getting credit was about securing a just reward for their labor. They criticized editors who reprinted
material that was, in Duane's words, "collected by labour and expense,
by the employment of ability" and then passed off as their own. Duane
accused his political opponents of setting out to destroy the *Aurora*, in
part by stealing material from it. He cited the example of a rival editor
who claimed to have attended the impeachment of judges in Lancaster,
Pennsylvania, when the editor had, in fact, copied the account verbatim
from the *Aurora*. Duane referred to this kind of reprinting as "downright robbery." He used the term *pilfering* for lesser offenses, such as
when rivals placed copied articles under a Philadelphia dateline instead
of explicitly crediting the *Aurora*. "In this way," Duane wrote, "instead
of adequate support being extended to the Evening Post or to the Aurora, the substance of each is taken to gain support for other papers,
and thus the wasps batten on the fruits of the bees' industry."[47]

By describing copying without credit as "pilfering" and "robbery,"
these editors treated newspaper writings as akin to property in mov-
able goods rather than in land, which was difficult to steal (although
it could be invaded or trespassed on). The metaphor of theft was common in complaints about the reprinting of books as well. Before 1891,
when American copyright law changed, it was perfectly legal for American publishers to reprint works by foreign authors without their permission. Yet such reprinting was regularly denounced as "robbery" and
"piracy."[48] But while authors and book publishers lobbied for changes

to copyright law that would actually make this so-called piracy illegal, newspaper publishers did not show any such interest in copyright. In fact, Duane, Coleman, and other newspaper editors made only partial use of the rhetoric of property in the early nineteenth century. Although they described the right to profit from their labor, they did not demand the right to exclude others from using their news or editorials. They also did not envision requiring permission or payment to reproduce newspaper material. As Benjamin Russell of the Boston *Columbian Centinel* explained, no publisher was "willing to pay money for information, which they receive in their exchange papers."[49] By participating in the exchange system, editors willingly made their news and editorials available to other newspapers, including rivals. But some of them were beginning to seek a degree of control over how their writings were used by insisting on the need for credit.

"KNIGHTS OF THE SCISSORS"

The exchange system at the heart of early American journalism involved a tension. On the one hand, exchange facilitated the circulation of news and gave editors an active role in selecting material for their readers. On the other hand, it frustrated those who disliked seeing their words used without acknowledgment. This tension helps to explain why the image of scissors could be used to celebrate the virtues of conscientious editing and to denounce practices that seemed lazy or unfair. Printers of weeklies in small towns and rural areas, which were referred to as "country papers," tended to celebrate the value of careful selection over the lure of original articles. Andie Tucher, a leading specialist of American journalism during this period, put it this way: "In a country paper, originality did *not* count, and the publication of novel or local fare was often taken as a sign of editorial desperation, a last resort when the mail carrying more important tidings was late."[50] But reliance on scissors was also associated with editors that were too busy or unskilled to do their own writing—especially if they were of a rival political camp. In 1807, the editor of the Poughkeepsie *Barometer* was described as an "old Gentleman . . . mournfully engaged in cutting out paragraphs with his scissors, sending them to his compositors, laying them before his

EDITOR.

FIGURE 9. A depiction of a scissors editor from a collection of nineteenth-century comic valentines (c. 1840–1900). Courtesy of the American Antiquarian Society.

daily diminishing patrons as something new, and incurring a certainty of expense with a dwindled and uncertain income."[51]

Few editors would have denied that scissors were basic tools of the trade. Joseph T. Buckingham, printer and editor of the *New England Galaxy* in Boston, offered a playful description of his editorial process. Buckingham operated a daily and a weekly paper. To keep up with the news, he had to work through seventy or eighty exchange papers each morning.

We seated ourselves at the aforesaid table, on which were scissors, paste-dish, pen and ink, the indispensable implements of our profession, to commence our

ordinary labour. . . . Having cast our eye over the New York Gazette, and the
Daily Advertiser, (our invariable standard for news from that city) and clipped
out a few paragraphs, the Washington papers were next put in requisition. An
article in the National Journal, or the National Intelligencer, we undertook
to *remanufacture* (giving the Journal, or the Intelligencer credit for the *raw
material*).[52]

The need to give credit was more frequently discussed in the 1810s
and 1820s. Some worried that not giving credit caused confusion for
readers, who were left to assume that unattributed reports had been prepared by their local editor.[53] Others complained that not mentioning the
source robbed the first newspaper of its reputation. Buckingham was
particularly concerned about credit for "original communications" and
described the "misery" of seeing his work reprinted without acknowledgment. He surmised that "there are some, who never having possessed
any property of this description, know nothing of the feelings of ownership; and others who have, from custom, become hardened in this species of robbery."[54] The example that Buckingham cited in this instance
was not so much a case of unacknowledged copying as one of mistaken
attribution. The *City of Washington Gazette* reproduced a poem and
credited the *New York Evening Post*, which in turn credited the "Dedham (Eng.) Gazette." But as Buckingham pointed out, the poem had
originally appeared in his *New England Galaxy* and was from there
copied into the *Dedham Gazette,* which was based in Massachusetts,
not England.[55] For Buckingham, careless citational practices only made
it easier for "editorial thieves and pickpockets" to "live by the labours of
the industrious." Observing that "this crime is growing every day more
common," he suggested the need to make "a catalogue of these *knights
of the scissors*" in an effort to shame editors into changing their ways.[56]

As the number of newspapers grew, so did the number of editors,
not to mention the need for special scissors adapted to what the Pittsfield, Massachusetts, *Sun* called "the sinewy digitals of the makers of
items and paragraphs."[57] Personifications of scissors became common.[58]
The editor of a Chillicothe, Ohio, paper thus lamented the loss of a
trusted companion with a knack for finding good articles:

Never were scissors so keen at a paragraph—they had an instinct which surely led them to single out just what was spicy and interesting. . . . For five years— five long, adventurous years—did they do good service—always ready, un-complaining, unwearied!—and then such a model for scissors!—such a clear pleasant ring they had, as the fresh paper parted before them! We shall never "cotton" to the cold steel, let it come in whatever shape it may, as we did to our long tried "assistant"![59]

Many editors saw their most important role as selecting the best mate-rial for republication. In this context, according to another Ohio edi-tor in 1854, "scissors and paste contribute a vast amount to the pleasure and profit of the million newspaper readers of our country, and should at least be entitled to their degree of praise."[60] But scissors could also be blamed for all that was bad in the world of newspapers. According to some editors, an overreliance on scissors encouraged the spread of erro-neous and biased statements, as though human agency was of negligi-ble importance.[61]

It is important to remember that editors could modify the material they republished. In an article titled "How to Make Old Things New," the New York *Commercial Advertiser* described in 1826 how news-paper articles often underwent "more transformations than the locust, or the butterfly, from the chrysalis state to the end of their existence." While some editors rewrote paragraphs, inflecting them with their own views, others condensed, combined, and reworked material "so that by the time [an article] has travelled back to its original parent, he has lost all knowledge of its identity." The results could be ugly. "Sometimes our knight of the scissors clips off the head of a paragraph, and sticks on an-other which he fancies more becoming, while another, for the same rea-son, dismembers the tail, and still another, deprives it of its body."[62]

Certain kinds of newspaper material, according to the editor of the *Commercial Advertiser* just quoted, were particularly likely to "travel a wide circuit, before they return to us," sometimes at an interval of months or years.[63] These included wise sayings, humorous stories, and strange anecdotes that still appealed to people years after they were first published. Recent studies that use computer algorithms to identify reprinted texts reveal the extent to which this was true. An early finding of the ongoing Viral Texts project led by Ryan Cordell at Northeastern University was that informational pieces such as lists, tables, recipes, scientific reports, and trivia columns were among the most frequently reprinted items in their corpus of nineteenth-century newspapers. Lists of facts and anecdotes were reprinted hundreds of times, and because they were less time sensitive than news, they could be put in a drawer or box for later use. Cordell found that the most frequently reprinted items tended to be "concise, quotable, and widely relatable texts that would have been easy to recontextualize for different newspapers and new audiences—and that could easily be made to fit different locations on the newspaper page, as editors and their compositors might need."[64]

The comments of contemporary editors confirm that they kept clippings of less time-sensitive items for later use. A Boston editor described his own practice in the mid-1840s:

In the absence of anything like news, and the want of a topic of sufficient interest to induce us to write upon it, we yesterday tumbled over a heap of old clippings upon our table, which had gradually increased in bulk from day to day, as our eye and our scissors chanced to light upon a paragraph that pleased us—a sort of unarranged scrap-book—and we have selected from the pile a few items which we lay before our reader as food for thought.[65]

The image of an "unarranged scrap-book" acknowledged that newspaper editors were aware of the wider culture of scrapbooking in nineteenth-century America. They knew that some readers would clip and save selected articles and discard the rest of the paper. Similarly, editors perused the exchange papers they received looking not only for news but also for less time-sensitive material that readers enjoyed and reused. The need to fill the available space was a constant preoccupation for many printers, but it is important to remember that newspapers contained a lot besides news. Poems, stories, anecdotes, and lists were an important part of the attraction of newspapers.[66]

The memoirs of editors and descriptions of newspaper offices from the period reveal more about how clipping fit into the editorial and printing process. The author of an 1855 biography of Horace Greeley, editor of the *New York Tribune*, described his visit to the offices of that paper. A night reader looked over exchange papers "with scissors ready for any paragraph of news that catches his eye." Once an editor approved clippings or original articles for publication, he sent these slips of paper up to the composing room, where they were put on hooks according to the font in which they were to be set. Compositors worked by pulling a "take" from the hook, setting it in type, and then returning for another one. The foreman gave editors a list of articles already in type and those waiting to be set, and the editors marked those that had to be printed immediately and those what would keep for another day. The editors also indicated the order in which individual items should appear in the paper.[67] In his 1875 memoirs, the newspaper man A. F. Hill described the editorial process in more detail, giving examples of how he reworked paragraphs, sometimes performing significant alterations or summarizing them in his own words. Hill insisted on the importance of the scissors, but his memoirs also revealed the extent to which editors could alter the material they reproduced.[68]

STRUGGLING WITH CREDIT

The question of what kinds of newspaper material deserved credit was a matter of debate. When the *Federal Republican* accused the *Baltimore Patriot* of not giving the "usual credit" to ship news taken from its pages in 1821, the *Patriot* claimed that "it is not 'usual' to give 'credit' for scraps of ship news." But since the *Federal Republican* had complained about uncredited articles, the *Baltimore Patriot* decided to take a closer look at that paper, only to find that it had copied "whole columns" of congressional proceedings from the *National Intelligencer* and state legislative reports from the *Maryland Gazette*. In these cases, credit should have been given, for it was not only "usual" but also "just and fair" to do so.[69] The editor of the *Connecticut Herald*, for his part, insisted that ship news was also worthy of credit. He called on editors to always identify the original source of ship news rather than to cite a derivative version.[70]

Beyond acknowledging the work of others, another reason for citing sources was to be able to hold individuals accountable for false or erroneous reports. A New Jersey paper in 1822 suggested that acknowl-edging the source of each item would create a situation in which "ev-ery one becomes responsible for the veracity of what he publishes, as the author can at once be detected, if he gives to the public what is incor-rect."[71] Such an aspiration was difficult to achieve in practice. Postal de-lays were common; editors and printers had to rely on whatever news-papers arrived, and since these did not always cite their sources, it was easy to credit the wrong paper by accident.[72] Before the telephone or the internet, fact-checking nonlocal news required comparing as many printed sources as possible, looking for details that agreed. When multi-ple accounts were not available, editors had to decide which newspapers to trust based on past experience. The *Vermont Chronicle* provided this example in 1833:

EAST INDIES. The account of a "dreadful conspiracy," in our paper last week, is confirmed, excepting the date, which should have been some where about 1772, instead of 1832. We found it in the N.Y. Commercial Advertiser, the Edi-tor of which says he "cut it out of an English paper with [his] own scissors" and that the English Editors did not consider it as a hoax. It was copied by Poulson and some other respectable Editors, whose example, after some hesitation, we thought it safe to follow,—especially as the article exhibited internal evidence of being no fiction.[73]

The Vermont editor was fully aware of the pitfalls of relying on other newspapers, but he also had strategies for determining the authenticity of reports. His explanation for why he printed the story shows that he was a conscientious editor who looked for internal evidence that raised red flags. It also reveals how the exchange system involved editors in webs of trust and credibility.

Citing the source publication provided a way of denying responsibil-ity, but there was always the risk that giving credit might be interpreted as an endorsement. In the 1820s, the editor of the *Baltimore Patriot* at-tempted to solve this problem by distinguishing between *credit*, which he called "a technical printer's phrase" for citing sources, and *approba-tion*, which signaled approval of the views expressed. He wrote, "For even [the editor of a rival newspaper] cannot expect, that one half of his statements should be *credited*, or that he could gain any credit by making them." Still, this rival deserved to have his paper named whenever an extract was taken, for "this is the common practice."[74] Labeling the source of copied paragraphs or simply lumping them together under the heading "Exchange Paper" provided a way of denying responsibility for reports. Conversely, paragraphs or essays that were not otherwise attributed might now be understood as having been prepared locally. As the *New Bedford Mercury* explained in 1824, "We shall uniformly give credit for every article we extract from other papers, and our readers will consider all pieces in this journal not thus accredited as editorial."[75]

By the 1840s, a number of editors insisted that credit was required for all material that was paid for or contributed by a member of staff. But not everyone agreed on this point. Whereas some editors tried to enforce the "common practice" of giving credit, others claimed pride in seeing their material reappear elsewhere, even without acknowledgment. In response to one newspaper's complaint about "cribbing," the Philadelphia *Public Ledger* explained that "all creation cribs from us, but we never mind it. We can scarcely pick up a paper, and not find some stray 'emanation,' without a mark to show where it came from. We always take these things as compliments."[76] The Philadelphia-based *National Gazette*, for its part, claimed that editors were under no obligation to give credit for most of the news appearing in newspapers. Nevertheless, the same paper complained when its commercial report was copied, citing the "labor" and "expenditure" required to collect the information. The editor suggested that nobody should be allowed to copy such information, with or without acknowledgment.[77] The New York *Journal of Commerce* insisted that this approach was misguided, announcing: "We hold that any paragraph or article, whether it be news or editorial remarks, or a communication, or review of the market, or any thing else, which originates in one paper, may be honorably copied into another, by giving credit for the same." The Philadelphia *North American* endorsed this view. According to both papers, there was no basis for distinguishing between market news and other kinds of articles. As the editor of the *Journal of Commerce* put it, "Whether it is obtained by means of newsboats, or correspondence, or mere industry in collecting the facts, or good-will on the part of a friend, or by accident, so as to speak, it is fairly the property of the paper which obtained it." Although he used the word *property*, the editor did not envision newspapers being able to prohibit others from republishing their original material. He claimed that editors had the right to republish any material they wanted, so long as they credited the source. The word *property* thus occupied a somewhat awkward place in a discussion that centered more on what the *Journal of Commerce* called the "matter of editorial courtesy, or rights."[78]

During the early-to-mid-nineteenth century, newspaper editors who demanded credit for copied material were not imagining bylines for individual reporters or editors but rather an acknowledgment of the newspaper that first published something. Although editors sometimes signed their editorials or displayed their names on the masthead, individual contributors rarely received credit. And despite a growing interest in the question of acknowledgment, newspaper editors still had no mutually agreed-upon rules of citation. Some placed the title of a source newspaper in italics at the foot of a paragraph; others placed it in all caps at the head of a column. Many preferred to mention the source in the opening line of the news. Although plenty of paragraphs and essays remained unattributed, an increasing number of them were marked off as belonging to one newspaper or another. Phrases such as "From our Correspondent" or "For the [title of newspaper]" began appearing in major metropolitan papers in the 1830s and became more common in the following decades. Bylines that gave the full names of contributors rather than using initials or pseudonyms could be found in newspapers and magazines by the 1840s but were largely reserved for fiction, poetry, and the occasional piece of history or biography. In the case of news articles, author bylines were extremely rare before the 1890s, when the first trade journals campaigned to increase the pay and respect accorded to journalists. The process was a gradual one, and bylines for individual reporters did not become widespread until the late twentieth century.[79]

MOCKERY AND RETALIATION

Before the appearance of the first professional journals in the 1880s and the first journalism schools in the early twentieth century, newspaper editors attempted to establish shared norms by policing each other in the columns of their newspapers.[80] One tactic for punishing newspapers that failed to credit was to temporarily interrupt their access to news. New York papers catering to merchants adopted this tactic in the 1820s and 1830s as they invested more heavily in gathering European news from incoming ships. On one occasion in 1831, the *Albany Argus* expressed surprise that it had not received the usual "slip" from the New York–based *Courier and Enquirer* following the arrival of a ship carrying interesting news. Some of the larger publishers were beginning to issue such slips in order to exchange breaking news more efficiently; slips could be sent in advance of the regular edition, and they featured the special reports collected by the newspaper that issued them.[81] On this occasion, the *Courier* explained that it had deliberately withheld its slip from the *Albany Argus* because of the Albany editor's failure to credit news taken from the *Courier*. They hoped that this retaliation would serve as a warning to others.[82]

The context for the *Courier's* retaliation was increasing competition for the latest European news. In the mid-1820s, several morning newspapers in New York organized an association to pool their resources and share the costs of collecting foreign news.[83] The *Courier* eventually became frustrated by the arrangements and decided to break off from the group, purchasing its own boats and hiring its own agents to meet incoming ships.[84] Although some papers argued for the need to cooperate rather than compete over the collection of such news, the *Courier* claimed the opposite, declaring, "We like competition; it is the life of business, and as for the 'ruinous competition' of which the *Commercial* [another newspaper] speaks, it is not a matter in which the public are interested. If early news is worth having, it will be furnished by editors, and cheerfully paid for by those who receive it. . . . We know the feelings of our merchants on this subject; they want and will have the news, cost what it may."[85]

But the expense involved in news gathering also led the *Courier's* proprietors to bait ungrateful copyists with false news. There may have been earlier examples, but the following one would be cited in the memoirs of newspapermen as an example of the kind of retaliation that accompanied the race for breaking news in this period.[86] On October 31, 1831, the *Courier* correctly reported that Warsaw had fallen to Russian forces on the night of September 7–8, ending the Polish-Russian War of 1830–1831 (also known as the November Uprising). The news had taken almost two months to cross Europe to Britain and then travel by ship to America, but the *Courier* was the first New York paper to have it. The *Courier* relied on the report in a British newspaper that was handed to them by a passenger on a recently arrived ship.[87] After other newspapers copied this report without any credit to the *Courier*, that paper's editors decided to set a trap. Early the next morning they sent a bogus version of their morning edition to the offices of competitors. This version claimed that the previous day's news about Warsaw was unfounded and that the Polish people had actually triumphed. It even included reports attributed to London and Paris newspapers—but which were actually fabricated by the *Courier*'s editors—celebrating the Polish victory.[88] The *Courier* also intentionally inserted an error into the otherwise accurate news displayed on its outdoor bulletin board. At this time, New York publishers were beginning to announce late-breaking news by painting it in large letters on boards outside their offices. The bulletins enticed readers to buy the most recent edition and, in the process, made reading the news a public experience in which crowds gathered to learn the latest updates.[89] The editors of the *Courier* knew that other newspapers took news from these bulletins. When they announced the fall of Warsaw on the board, they lied about the date it happened. Any newspaper that included the erroneous date must have copied.[90]

The *Courier* claimed that several editors stopped their presses to announce the triumph of the Poles, only to realize later that the news was fake.[91] The lead proprietor of the *Courier*, James Watson Webb, tried to get his rivals who made up the association of morning papers to admit to being duped and to publicly acknowledge that they were in "the daily practice of obtaining possession at an early hour in the morning of a copy of the Courier and Enquirer, and *cribbing* therefrom the latest Foreign Intelligence."[92] According to Webb, what his rivals did amounted to fraud: they obtained news that had been collected by others and then passed it off as their own. The *Journal of Commerce*, a member of the association and one of the papers that Webb claimed to have fooled, responded by publishing affidavits from press employees certifying that they had never set the bogus news in type. The *Journal* also reproduced a series of paragraphs from nine different newspapers condemning the *Courier*'s actions and blaming Webb and his partners for willingly disseminating false news.[93]

Apart from the fact that few editors seem to have been fooled, the *Courier*'s hoax backfired. Several newspapers claimed that the *Courier*'s forgery was a far worse offense than "pirating" or "cribbing" news. The *Courier*'s rivals amplified the criticism in an attempt to erode public confidence in that paper. One of these critics claimed that in perpetrating the hoax, the *Courier* was attempting to "extort acknowledgments" that were "unknown to the conventional regulations of courtesy heretofore existing among the profession."[94] The suggestion was that the *Courier*'s owners were overly jealous and were trying to impose new journalistic customs unilaterally. After midcentury, as discussed in chapter 6, the model preferred by the morning association—cooperation rather than competition—would transform American journalism and lead to an entirely different approach to maintaining the exclusivity of news. In the meantime, though, the *Courier* was not alone in calling for credit or in using hoaxes to try to catch ungrateful copyists.[95]

In the 1840s, newspapers around the country referred more often to the financial resources and labor they invested in gathering news. In addition to publicly shaming newspapers that copied without credit, they threatened to cut them off as exchange partners.[96] Within New York, intense competition for breaking news led publishers to adopt more proprietary rhetoric. In 1840, for example, James Gordon Bennett of the *New York Herald* arranged for a reporter to cover a speech by Daniel Webster on Long Island. Bennett also paid an express service to carry the transcript back to New York. "The Special Express cost us some money," Bennett wrote, "and we are certainly entitled to the benefit of our enterprise and expenditure, without being at the mercy of plunderers and pilferers, without acknowledgment." Bennett tried to publicly embarrass news "pickpockets"—singling them out by name in print—

and informed his readers that he sometimes felt compelled to delay publication of the *Herald* to avoid being scooped.[97]

The frequency with which editors discussed the need for credit led
some to respond with parody. In 1841, the *Baltimore Sun* mocked editors who took this question too seriously, especially given the vogue for
hoaxes and humbugs in antebellum America. Penny papers in the 1830s
used fake news stories to boost circulation. The most famous example was the so-called moon hoax that appeared in Benjamin Day's New
York *Sun* in 1835. It consisted of a series of articles reporting that Sir
John Herschel's telescope revealed life on the moon.[98] The articles were
written by Richard Adams Locke, who, after working for Day, founded
a paper called the *New Era*, which contained further scientific hoaxes.
The editor of the *Baltimore Sun* used Locke's notoriety to make fun of
editors' concerns about credit:

CREDIT WHERE DUE.—The unexpected news from the Moon, given in the
Sun of yesterday morning, and which was received at a very late hour on the
night previous, together with the strange fashion of the Lunatarian type on
which it was printed, may have made some confusion among the types [i.e.,
typesetters] of the Sun. The consequence of this was, that *Richard Adams
Locke* was despoiled of the credit due him for his wonderful discoveries in Lu-
nataria, made in 1835.[99]

CREDIT VERSUS COPYRIGHT

When the Philadelphia printer and publisher Mathew Carey sat down
to write his autobiography in the 1830s, he looked back on the beginning of his career and noted that "the printers had then more scruples
about pirating on each other, than some of them have at present."[100]
Carey was referring to reports of legislative debates that he had prepared for his newspaper, the *Pennsylvania Herald,* starting in 1785.
These may not have been copied at first because they were unauthorized, and their success was not yet proven. Carey exaggerated the extent to which the practices of newspaper editors had changed since the
1780s, but his comment nonetheless registered a shift in attitudes toward copying. Newspaper copying was not new in the 1830s, but it was

more frequently remarked on than it had been fifty years earlier. Frequent descriptions of "scissors editors" and "knights of the scissors" revealed a new sensitivity to the act of copying at the heart of the early American press. Whereas some associated scissors with lazy or immoral editors, others personified the editorial shears to highlight a process of selection and republication that benefited readers.

This heightened awareness of clipping reflected changing attitudes as well as important shifts in the business of news. After 1800, a generation of politically active editors saw themselves as writers rather than compilers; they began to articulate a notion of unfair competition in journalism. Beginning in the 1820s, rivalries between big-city dailies and country weeklies also led to complaints about copying. In the 1830s, increased investments in news gathering and competition over street sales led to more extreme attempts to impose new editorial norms by cutting off news from exchange partners or baiting rivals with false news. With few exceptions, newspaper editors who complained about unacknowledged copying did not use the term *plagiarism*; they referred to a failure to give *credit*. The word choice was significant because they were interested in the ethical and financial connotations of credit. Editors sought to establish shared protocols of citation and acknowledgment that could boost the reputation of their papers while encouraging the circulation of their writings.[101] They did not want to end the exchange system; they wanted it to continue on specific terms. Editors understood that newspapers were mutually dependent. As a newspaper in Fremont, Ohio, put it in 1854, "A general 'reciprocity treaty' seems to prevail among the different newspapers over our country, so that each may assist the other in collecting intelligence and together circulate the vast amount of news, of politics and literature, that circulates through the thousand columns of the periodical press over the land."[102] With this in mind, editors sought ways to keep the news circulating while giving credit to the newspaper that had first published it.

The shifts in attitudes toward copying described here preceded the major technological and commercial transformations that would radically alter the business of news beginning around midcentury—the spread of the telegraph and the creation of the first press associations.

As discussed in chapter 6, these changes would eventually lead to a view among some newspaper publishers that copying should be governed by law rather than by cultural norms or editorial courtesy. But in the first half of the century, most American newspaper publishers showed no interest in copyright. The same could not be said for the owners of specialized periodicals catering to the business community, namely price currents and shipping lists. Such publications were registered for American copyright as early as 1791, and in 1828, they were at the center of one of the earliest reported copyright trials in the United States. We now turn to that case and to the larger question of what kinds of works were eligible for copyright in nineteenth-century America.

CHAPTER 4

Market News and the Limits of Copyright in Nineteenth-Century America

COULD NEWS PUBLICATIONS be protected by copyright in nineteenth-century America? Like Britain, the United States initially took what might be called a closed-list approach to copyright: the statute enumerated specific categories of copyrightable works. By contrast, in an open-list approach, the law states a general principle and then gives illustrative examples not meant to be exhaustive.[1] The Copyright Act of 1790, like the British Statute of Anne, was called "An Act for the Encouragement of Learning," and many of its provisions were copied directly from the British statute. But whereas the latter had referred only to books (with one vague reference to "other writings"), the American law explicitly protected "maps, charts, and books."[2] Over the course of the nineteenth century, amendments and revisions to the law brought in new subject matter (prints, stage plays, photographs, and so on), and in 1909 the United States moved to an open-list approach in which copyright subsisted in "all the writings of an author."[3]

One reason for the closed-list approach in the nineteenth century was that legislation tended to be a reaction to requests by interest groups that lobbied for new laws. Legislatures did not begin with the idea of drafting a general intellectual property law that would apply to all works of the mind. The idea of intellectual property as a separate branch of law did not even exist until the late nineteenth century. Instead, copyright, patent, and trademark legislation was drafted in response to lobbying by creators and publishers, who sought protection as a result of changes in the organization of their trades, the introduction of new technologies, the development of new business strategies, and so on.[4] This continues to be the case today. Furthermore, the way that copyright law is applied and understood depends on litigation, which can have quite specific roots, such as the rivalry between two firms or the desire of an individual or company to establish a new principle in their industry.

For genres or forms of publication that were not explicitly mentioned in the Copyright Act of 1790, judges had to determine whether they fit into established categories. But copyright litigation was exceptional. Judicial ambiguity was slow to be resolved, and this created space for authors and publishers to develop—and dispute—customs of the trade. Such ambiguity was particularly pronounced for most types of news publications. Yet some were registered for copyright. These included pamphlets reporting crimes, trials, and executions; lithographs representing dramatic events, especially fires and steamboat accidents; and market news appearing in price currents.[5] The validity of such copyright claims remained largely untested in the courts. But the question of whether commercial and financial news could be owned was at the heart of one of the earliest reported copyright cases in America, *Clayton v. Stone* (1828).[6]

In that case, the owners of the *Shipping and Commercial List, and New York Price Current* sued the owners of a New York newspaper called the *Commercial Advertiser*. The *Shipping and Commercial List* catered to the business community; it contained updates on the prices of commodities and stocks, listed the arrival and departure of ships and their cargoes, and offered commentary on market trends for various goods. Despite the specialized nature of this publication, *Clayton v. Stone* has usually been understood as creating a broader precedent that newspapers were not eligible for copyright. The headnotes for the decision as reported in an 1856 compilation of circuit court cases, which were later copied into West Publishing's *Federal Cases* (the source still cited today), suggest that one of the main findings of the court was that "a newspaper or price-current is not such a publication as falls under the protection of the copyright law."[7] The judge's decision was also cited with approval by the US Supreme Court in *Baker v. Selden* (1879), which raised the prominence of *Clayton v. Stone*, leading it to be cited in later cases.[8] In 1900, a federal court cited *Clayton* and went on to suggest that "there can be no general copyright of a newspaper composed in large part of matter not entitled to protection."[9] That finding was invalidated by the Copyright Act of 1909, which listed newspapers as eligible subject matter and specified that a single registration for each issue of a newspaper sufficed to protect all of its copyrightable components.[10] But publishers, lawyers, and judges continued to disagree about whether news articles—as opposed to literary and artistic matter in newspapers—could be protected by copyright. In the 1918 Supreme Court case of *International News Service v. Associated Press*, the decision in *Clayton* was cited numerous times by the plaintiff, the defendant, and the justices in the majority and dissenting opinions.[11]

Given the various ways *Clayton* was treated as a precedent, it is important to closely examine the reasons that the court gave for denying copyright to the *Shipping and Commercial List*. The judgment provides a clear example of how attempts to protect news—in this case time-sensitive reports of commerce and finance—obliged judges to interpret the purpose and scope of copyright before deciding whether news publications deserved the protection of the law. Although the plaintiffs in *Clayton* failed to achieve what they wanted, their suit led the judge to articulate a principle that would be followed for decades to come: copyright was meant to promote works that made a lasting contribution to learning.

THE 1790 ACT AND ITS USES

As already mentioned, the Copyright Act of 1790 explicitly protected "maps, charts, and books." The bill had included the phrase "and other writings," but an amendment in the Senate removed this phrase from the title and throughout the law.[12] The concerns that motivated this change remain unknown, but it created uncertainty for works not easily identifiable as books. The explicit protection for maps and charts reflected the fact that lawmakers envisioned such works as indispensable for a newly independent and geographically expanding country. Moreover, the makers of maps and atlases, along with the authors of spelling books and histories, were among the first to lobby American lawmakers for copyright. These authors and their supporters in Congress argued that copyright would be an effective means of encouraging the production and diffusion of useful knowledge.[13]

Unlike today, copyright was not automatic. To obtain it, authors or their assignees had to perform a series of steps known as copyright formalities. Before publication, one had to deposit a printed copy of the title in the clerk's office of the local district court. Then one had to inform the public that the work had been registered for copyright by inserting a notice in at least one newspaper for four consecutive weeks. Finally, one had to deposit a copy of the work itself within six months of publication. Beginning in 1802, the statute also required a copyright notice on the work itself.[14] In the United States, unlike in Britain, strict compliance with these formalities was required to secure copyright. Registration, notice, and newspaper announcements were meant to ensure that other authors, printers, and the reading public had information about which works were protected and for how long. In Britain, failure to register a work did not affect the copyright, but in America it placed the work in the public domain.[15]

On the whole, a tiny minority of works published in the United States in the late eighteenth and early nineteenth centuries was registered for copyright. Although they remain estimates, the best figures that we have are for the first ten years after the 1790 act, a period for which most of the extant copyright records have been compiled in a printed edition and for which decades of research by bibliographers have produced a list of titles known to have been published. Out of roughly fifteen thousand imprints known to have been produced between 1790 and 1800, only about eight hundred of them (approximately 5 percent) were registered for copyright.[16] Although such figures may someday be revised, it is clear that the overwhelming majority of printed works remained in the public domain. The low incidence of copyright registration suggests that in many cases authors and publishers either did not see the need for copyright or did not think registration was worth the trouble and the cost. But some genres of publication were more likely to be registered than others. Practical and instructional works made up the majority of entries in the 1790s; these included maps, atlases, directories, grammar and spelling books, arithmetic primers, and lawbooks.[17] Informational and educational works were widely seen as being eligible for copyright, and producers of these works sought to protect their investments against rivals who might issue unauthorized reprints. Whether copyright could be used to stop others from copying portions of an existing work into a new work was less clear. The statute explicitly prohibited others from printing, reprinting, importing, publishing, or selling *copies* of a registered work, but it did not address the right to make abridgments or quotations. Whether partial copying constituted infringement had to be decided by judges on a case-by-case basis.[18]

Although most newspaper publishers did not express any interest in copyright in the early nineteenth century, the same cannot be said for those who specialized in business news. Price currents listing the prices at which goods were trading had existed since the sixteenth century in some European cities, and over time, related business newspapers developed, including stock exchange currents, bills of entry, and marine lists. Although these distinct genres continued to exist, by the nineteenth century there was a tendency toward more heterogeneous publications that contained a wider range of information but that still bore the title "Price Current," "Shipping List," or some combination of these.[19] (For the sake of brevity, I will also refer to them as price currents even though they contained more than just prices.) Price currents had been protected by patents in seventeenth-century England, and in the eighteenth century some of them were registered under the Statute of Anne. American publishers also sought copyright protection for price currents, probably because their subscriber base was more limited than most newspapers. Price currents also did not contain many paid advertisements, at least at first. The owners of price currents tended to be merchants and brokers who relied on their contacts in the business community to obtain the latest information. The time and labor required to gather this information led to a stronger desire for exclusivity.

PRICE CURRENTS AND COPYRIGHT

As early as 1791—only one year after the first federal copyright law was passed—the Philadelphia broker Vincent M. Pelosi registered *Pelosi's Marine List and Price Current* for copyright.[20] Within a year, Pelosi abandoned this publication to concentrate on other business, but over the next three decades, others followed his lead and registered their price currents for copyright. In 1812, when the Boston merchant Peter A. Grotjan started *Grotjan's Philadelphia Public Sale Reports*, he entered the title (as a book) with the clerk of the district court.[21] Although he registered the title only once (rather than entering each weekly issue), for six months his publication contained the notice "*Copy Right secured agreeably to Law.*"[22] But then Grotjan removed the copyright notice, and the following year he announced that he would enforce his copyright only against competitors in his home city of Philadelphia. Indeed, enforcing the copyright in other cities would have undermined Grotjan's goals. He believed that widespread access to reliable information would stimulate trade and that merchants would spend less time and money writing letters requesting information about prices and transactions. The only people that might oppose the circulation of such information, according to Grotjan, were speculators who put their own gains above the needs of the community. Still, Grotjan could not afford to allow local competitors to copy his information, since this would reduce the subscriber base on which he depended to keep the publication going. He therefore announced that he would waive the copyright in his "original matter" so long as it was published outside of Philadelphia.[23]

Other compilers of market news similarly envisioned copyright as a means of limiting what was copied and by whom. Peter Paul Francis Degrand, a French-born merchant based in Boston, started a weekly publication in 1819 in part to advertise his own services as a merchandise broker. *P. F. Degrand's Boston Weekly Report of Public Sales and Arrivals* (1819–1828) initially appeared without a copyright notice, and Degrand enjoyed seeing his work quoted by the leading newspapers.[24] But welcome publicity soon turned to unwelcome appropriation, and Degrand decided to register his *Report* for copyright and attach a notice to each issue.[25] Degrand's initial rationale for obtaining copyright was to dissuade others from reproducing a table of tariff duties that cost him significant effort to compile. Although the copyright notice appeared on each weekly issue of the *Report* for several more years, Degrand was mostly worried about protecting these tables, which had a longer shelf life than most of the information published in the *Report*. Degrand reissued some of these tables in separate pamphlets, sometimes including a warning, such as the following: "This tariff is extracted from the Boston weekly report and copy-right secured according to law. As it has cost me much labor, my brother-editors and other gentlemen of the type, will oblige me, by not giving it another edition."[26] Degrand was a merchant and broker rather than a printer or newspaper editor, but he knew that he had to appeal to the latter's sense of justice if he wanted to enjoy some degree of exclusivity over his information tables. Copyright remained a blunt tool in this context, and going to court was costly. So when a rival relied on his tariff guide to produce a competing work, Degrand tried the old tactic of publicly shaming the copyist. The competing guide cost less than Degrand's original, but it was also full of errors and was not updated to reflect rule changes issued by the Treasury since the publication of Degrand's edition. For Degrand, the only explanation was that his rival "aimed at making a servile copy of my Book, utterly regardless of my Copy-Right; and utterly regardless of his responsibility to the public" to provide current and reliable information.[27]

The legal validity of copyright in price currents was finally tested in court in 1828. The plaintiffs were Wakeman Burritt and Edwin B. Clayton, joint owners of the semiweekly *Shipping and Commercial List, and New York Price Current.* Clayton was a printer and bookseller in New York City. Burritt had a business background and was responsible for collecting the information from local merchants and preparing it for publication.[28] Shortly after their partnership began in 1824, the two men noticed that other publications were reproducing some of their material without acknowledgment. They published a note requesting credit for any material copied from them. The failure to give credit, according to Burritt and Clayton, was tantamount to passing off someone else's work as one's own, thereby deceiving the public about the source of the information.[29]

Burritt and Clayton initially claimed to be interested in receiving credit for their work rather than in stopping others from reusing it, but that soon changed. At the end of 1825, they registered the forthcoming year's volume of their price current for copyright (at that time, the titles of works had to be registered *before* publication).[30] The 1820s were a competitive time for New York publishers specializing in market news. Shortly after Burritt and Clayton registered their title, the *New York Mercantile Price Current* was also registered for copyright. About six months later, the *Comparative Price Current, and European and Commercial Reporter* followed suit.[31] But Burritt and Clayton were more worried about copying by daily newspapers than by other price currents. "For more than a year past," they explained, "two or more of the newspapers in this city, have regularly copied our Price Current, with our remarks on the state of the market, from beginning to end, immediately after its publication."[32]

The remarks, which appeared under the heading "Review of the New York Market," contained Burritt's comments on recent developments (the arrival of a shipment, a public sale, and so on) and how these affected the supply and demand for various goods. According to Burritt and Clayton, copying by newspapers enabled readers to obtain all the information they needed without subscribing to the *Shipping and Commercial List*, and this was particularly true for people outside of New York City. For those living in places served by the post two or three times per week, "the original and the copy both leave here in the same mail, and reach their destination at the same time." Burritt and Clayton asked newspapers to stop copying, and when that did not work, they decided to "adopt measures, to secure to ourselves and our families the benefit of our own labours."[33] Subsequent issues of the *Shipping and Commercial List* contained a notice that read "COPY RIGHT SECURED."[34]

Burritt and Clayton claimed that their publication was at a disadvantage compared to newspapers that bundled commercial information together with political news, editorials, letters to the printer, advertisements, and other features. In the 1820s, before the development of the so-called penny press, most of the New York dailies catered to the mercantile and political elite, so the list of subscribers to a price current would have been a subset of those who subscribed to business-minded newspapers such as the *Commercial Advertiser* or the *Courier and Enquirer.* Whereas those newspapers might have had up to two thousand subscribers, a price current would probably have been pleased to attract six hundred.[35] Given the more limited market for their publication, Burritt and Clayton were understandably worried about losing individual subscribers.

The copyright notice had its desired effect on one New York pa-

per, the *National Advocate*. Its editor admitted to having regularly relied on the *Shipping and Commercial List* to furnish readers with market news. He now felt obliged to obtain permission from Burritt and
Clayton, who agreed to allow him to copy the price list but not Burritt's
"Review of the New York Market."[36] It was the latter that Burritt and
Clayton treated as the unique product of their labor. But not all newspapers accepted the idea of treating market news as exclusive. In the
spring of 1828, the persistent use of their material by the *Commercial
Advertiser* motivated Burritt and Clayton to seek legal counsel in order
to comply more strictly with the copyright formalities and bring their rivals to court.

WHAT IS A BOOK?

By attempting to enforce a copyright in their publication, Burritt and
Clayton were breaking new ground. The copyright records reveal the
lengths they went to in order to comply with the statute. The first question they faced was how to register a price current. The 1790 act referred only to maps, charts, and books; an amendment in 1802 added
protection for prints (engravings). In May 1828, Burritt and Clayton
registered their title as a print, but they soon decided, probably on the
advice of counsel, to enter an individual number of their serial as a
book. After all, the *Shipping and Commercial List* was a work of letter-
press and not an engraving. To prepare for a lawsuit, they carefully entered the issue for June 21, being sure to specify the full title, date, and
issue number.[37] As required by the statute, they also deposited a copy of
the June 21 issue with the US Secretary of State's office. But the certificate of deposit they received referred to the work as a "paper" rather
than a "book." Worried that this discrepancy could create problems in
court, Burritt and Clayton insisted that it be corrected. "Our counsel
objects to the term 'Paper,' as not being in conformity with the certificate received from the District Court here at the time of depositing the
title—which specifies the publication as a Book." They asked for a new
receipt certifying that they had deposited "a certain Book consisting of
one Sheet."[38] Burritt and Clayton could thus come to court with proof
of having registered and deposited their price current as a book.

The case was heard in the fall of 1828 by Supreme Court justice Smith Thompson, acting in his capacity as a circuit court judge.[39] To reinforce the claim that their publication could be considered a book for the purposes of copyright, Burritt and Clayton introduced into evidence a volume of price currents bound in leather with marbled paper covers.[40] There was actually nothing disingenuous about referring to the annual volume of a serial as a book. Like many magazines, the *Shipping and Commercial List* had continuous pagination (that is, if one issue ended with page 80, the next one would begin with page 81). It also had an annual index, enabling readers to treat it as a reference work. At the end of each year, subscribers could send their semiweekly numbers to Burritt and Clayton to have them "neatly bound" with the index. They could also purchase back issues to complete their volumes.[41] The defendants were William L. Stone and Francis Hall, publishers of the *Commercial Advertiser.* They objected to the introduction of the bound volume as proof that Burritt and Clayton's publication was a book. Their counsel argued that "a newspaper could neither in common or legal parlance be denominated a book, and that both from its ephemeral nature, and from the objects to which it was devoted, it was utterly incapable of being the subject of a copy-right."[42] In an effort to disqualify the *Shipping and Commercial List* from copyright, counsel for the defendants assimilated price currents and newspapers, insisting that both were too "ephemeral" to be protected by copyright.

The term *ephemeral* was and is a value-laden term, and it is worth pausing here briefly to consider how it acquired traction in an argument that sought to exclude a whole class of publications from copyright. From the Greek *ephēmeros*, meaning something that lasted only one day, the English plural term *ephemera* was first applied to plants and insects with a short life span and then, beginning in the eighteenth century, to publications thought to be of only passing interest. Reacting to the proliferation of broadsides, pamphlets, newspapers, and journals in the early eighteenth century, writers such as Jonathan Swift and Alexander Pope used the term *ephemera* to denigrate these forms of publication, which they saw as stirring up religious controversy and corrupting literary culture. Swift and Pope distinguished between books that made a lasting contribution to literature and ephemera produced by "Grub Street" hacks. Their views did not go unopposed. Samuel Johnson, for example, argued that "small tracts and fugitive pieces" were a vital part of English literature. He also praised newspapers and journals. According to Johnson, the "papers of a day, the *Ephemerae* of learning, have uses more adequate to the purposes of common life than more pompous and durable volumes."[43] Although Johnson defended the ideas and information contained in ephemera, his use of the term nonetheless suggested a material object that was less substantial physically, and less obviously worth saving, than a book.

After hearing arguments on both sides, Justice Thompson stated that the question of whether a price current could be considered a book for the purposes of copyright deserved further consideration. He therefore let the plaintiffs proceed with their case, deferring his own opinion on the legal question until after the facts were presented. Since the copying was obvious, Thompson instructed the jury to enter a nominal verdict for the plaintiffs pending his own decision on whether a price current qualified for copyright as a book. After deliberating for an hour, the jury agreed that Hall and Stone were guilty of infringement and awarded nominal damages.[44]

As accounts of the trial traveled through the newspaper exchanges, some editors expressed interest in the legal question that Justice Thompson had put in suspense. A Boston newspaper offered a summary of the case under the headline "What Is a Book?"[45] In a report later copied by other newspapers, the Philadelphia *Aurora* asked, "Is a newspaper a book, and as such a subject of copy-right?"[46] Thompson finally gave his decision in early December, ruling that the *Shipping and Commercial List* did not qualify for copyright.[47] But in the end, his decision did not turn on the question of whether a price current or newspaper could be considered a book. Instead, Burritt and Clayton's attempt to claim exclusive rights in market news inspired Thompson to return to the Constitution and the federal statutes to interpret the fundamental purpose of copyright.

CLAYTON V. STONE: THE DECISION

At first glance, Justice Thompson's decision in *Clayton v. Stone* seems to follow a different logic than that of another copyright case he decided the same year. In *Blunt v. Patten*, Thompson held that a person could produce a nautical chart containing the same information as a copyrighted work only if he did his own field research; working directly from a copyrighted chart constituted infringement. The plaintiff in that case had sent a vessel with surveyors to two shoals off the northeastern coast of the United States. He used the resulting surveys to produce a chart of the coast that several mariners claimed to be more accurate than those previously in existence. The defendant, charged with copying these shoals "in form, position and bearings" into his own chart, argued that nobody could copyright the actual location of a shoal and that everyone was free to make charts of the coast that accurately represented its natural features. Thompson ruled that it was true that nobody could obtain a copyright in a shoal but that the plaintiff nonetheless "had a right to the results of his labors and surveys." Others were free to hire vessels and make their own surveys, but they did not have the right to rely on an existing copyrighted chart to compile their own charts.[48] Thompson's decision in *Blunt v. Patten* showed that he was willing to uphold copyright protection not only for the form of informational works—the particular arrangement of words and figures—but also for the facts they contained. As the legal scholar Robert Brauneis has explained, "Any factual representation that was the result of independent mental labor was copyrightable, and no one could copy wholesale that representation as a substitute for going out into the world and doing the hard work of gathering the factual details himself."[49] Why, then, did Thompson deny copyright to Burritt and Clayton's price current, which was also a fact-based work that required labor to produce?

Thompson mentioned the fact that newspapers and price currents were published at relatively short intervals and interpreted the registration and deposit requirements as evidence that the legislature had not envisioned copyright for them. In doing so, he echoed the *Commercial Advertiser*'s claim that such publications were "ephemeral." Thompson wrote, "The preliminary steps required by law, to secure the copyright, cannot reasonably be applied to a work of so ephemeral a character as that of a newspaper."[50] According to Thompson, the requirements of registration and deposit would have to be followed for every issue of a newspaper. He thought it was "improbable" that publishers would choose to do this and that the steps stipulated by the statute suggested that Congress had not intended to provide newspapers the same protection as books. In their case, however, Burritt and Clayton had entered and deposited the individual issue that was grounds for the suit. Consequently, Thompson's decision could not turn on the question of formalities.[51] He also was not troubled by the question of whether a price current could be considered a book. He held that the suitability of a work for copyright should not be determined by "the size, form, or shape in which it makes its appearance, but by the subject-matter of the work. Nor is this question to be determined by reference to Lexicographers, to ascertain the origin and meaning of the word book."[52] Relying on English legal precedents that had determined musical scores to be eligible for copyright even if printed on a single sheet, Thompson decided that "a book within the statute need not be a book in the common and ordinary acceptation of the word, viz, a volume made up of several sheets bound together; it may be printed only on one sheet, as the words of a song or the music accompanying it."[53] Thompson therefore found it irrelevant that each issue of the price current was printed on a single sheet and only later bound into a volume.

According to Thompson, the best guide for determining whether a work was eligible for copyright was the US Constitution, which empowered Congress "to promote the Progress of Science and useful Arts, by securing for limited Times to Authors and Inventors the exclusive Right to their respective Writings and Discoveries."[54] In this clause, the term *science* corresponds to the writings of authors who will be protected by copyright, whereas *useful arts* refers to the discoveries of inventors who will receive patents. The copyright statutes of 1790 and 1802 depended on the power granted to Congress by this clause in the Constitution, and since it referred to "science" (rather than say "literature" or "creativity"), determining the purpose of copyright required nineteenth-century judges to define that term. In his opinion, Justice Thompson referred to "the sciences" as though to recognize different branches of knowledge that should be encouraged by copyright. "It would certainly be a pretty extraordinary view of the sciences," he wrote, "to consider a daily or weekly publication of the state of the market as falling within any class of them. They are of a more fixed, permanent, and durable character. The term science cannot, with any propriety, be applied to a work of so fluctuating and fugitive a form as that of a newspaper or price-current, the subject-matter of which is daily changing, and is of mere temporary use."[55] Thompson thus focused on the subject of the articles being copied. As mentioned, Burritt and Clayton were not trying to protect price data so much as their "Review of the New York Market." For Burritt and Clayton, this was "original matter" written by one of the proprietors and therefore eligible for copyright.[56] Thompson held otherwise.

Although Thompson's decision did not consider whether other kinds of newspaper material—accounts of crimes or trials, editorials, political essays, biographical sketches, poems, and so on—might be protected by copyright, the language of his decision could be interpreted otherwise. By referring to the form of newspapers and price currents as "fluctuating and fugitive," the judgment might have led contemporary publishers to conclude that newspapers and other periodicals could not be protected because of their material form and expectations about their use, such as the notion that they were "ephemeral" publications to be read and discarded. In fact, apart from the extended debate between the *Shipping and Commercial List* and the *Commercial Advertiser* discussed later, few newspapers commented on this case, and those that did seem to have recognized that what mattered to the court was not the "size, form, or shape" of the price current but the fact that it did not make a lasting contribution to "science."[57] The problem for Thompson was that the information and observations made in the price current were "of mere temporary use" because prices and market conditions were always changing. Merchants who had their price currents bound with the index furnished by Burritt and Clayton may have valued the ability to consult back issues to identify historical trends, but Thompson did not see it this way. For him, the question was not whether a work was factual or creative but whether it contributed to the advancement of learning rather than just facilitating commercial transactions. "Although great praise may be due to the plaintiffs for their industry and enterprise in publishing this paper," Thompson wrote, "the law does not contemplate their being rewarded in this way: it must seek patronage and protection from its utility to the public, and not as a work of science."[58]

Most copyright decisions in the early nineteenth century depended on a similar understanding of science as what the legal scholar Lawrence B. Solum has characterized as "systematic knowledge or learning of enduring value."[59] Most judges of the period agreed with Thompson that the purpose of copyright was to encourage learning rather than industry and commerce (as the price current claimed to do) or entertainment and creativity (as the modern culture industries claim to do). In this context, the main obstacle to copyright protection for a price current or newspaper was the perception that the facts they contained would not remain relevant for very long. The owners of the *Commercial Advertiser* boasted that they had triumphed in "one of the most vexatious and unjustifiable pieces of litigation, that we recollect to have heard. No such case was ever tried, in this or any other country, before; and by contesting it, we have had the double satisfaction of establishing a principle heretofore unsettled, and of doing so at the expense of our opponents."[60] The principle that Stone and Hall claimed to have established was that price currents and newspapers could not be protected by copyright. The *Commercial Advertiser* sought to assimilate the two kinds of publications, and Thompson's decision also referred to the two almost interchangeably. Burritt and Clayton found this unfair. In their own published remarks on the case, they would insist on the differences between their own publication and a general newspaper such as the *Commercial Advertiser.*

THE COURT OF PUBLIC OPINION

Disappointed by Thompson's decision, Burritt and Clayton published a series of articles in their *Shipping and Commercial List* defending their rights and appealing to the public for support. These articles reveal aspects of the case that cannot be gleaned from the judge's published opinion. Relying on his business experience and contacts, Burritt had spent more than four years of hard work and "much expense" to improve his "Review of the New York Market." Although he and Clayton succeeded in increasing the circulation of their publication in New York and other cities, even attracting a few subscribers abroad, systematic copying by the *Commercial Advertiser* hindered their ability to obtain "a suitable remuneration for their exertions." Since February 1828, Stone and Hall's paper had been republishing the "Review" in full on the same day as it appeared in the *Shipping and Commercial List*. Burritt and Clayton complained that their work was being "reprinted and circulated through the city a few hours after it has made its appearance, and also sent to the other cities and towns in the United States, in the very same mails, *side by side* with the original." The proprietors of the *Commercial Advertiser* were also republishing the "Review" in their semiweekly newspaper, the *Spectator*, "thereby rendering the injury still more extensive and complete, by reaching through this *second channel* such persons and parts of the country as their daily paper might have escaped."[61]

Burritt and Clayton insisted that newspapers and price currents were not competing on a level playing field. The *Shipping and Commercial List* was intended for a specific audience, and its subject was more limited than most newspapers. The *Commercial Advertiser* had a broader appeal and a larger subscriber base because it contained foreign and domestic news, editorials, and advertisements as well as commercial information. According to Burritt and Clayton, it was the incorporation of their "Review" into such a newspaper that was especially damaging. They even claimed that this kind of copying was more harmful than republishing the whole *Shipping and Commercial List* "in the same shape and form, from beginning to end." A pirated edition of their work would do less harm, they claimed, "because the copy would have no preference over the original; while, in the case before us, the matter copied has the advantage of being incorporated into a general newspaper." Burritt and Clayton claimed that such copying had led to a loss of 220 subscribers in nine months. They quoted departing subscribers as saying, "We do not want your publication, as we have the same matter in the newspaper." Burritt and Clayton were so convinced of the dangers of newspaper republication that when another New York paper approached them about republishing their "Review," they refused to allow republication for less than two thousand dollars per year, a hefty sum in 1828. Eventually they reached an agreement whereby the newspaper could republish the "Review" once a week *two days after its publication by us,* and in such a way as not to be traced to the source, for a compensation at the rate of $500 per year."[62] They did not want their article "traced to the source" because they were convinced that newspapers and price currents were in direct competition: Burritt and Clayton reasoned that if readers recognized that they could get the same "Review" in the newspaper, they would abandon the *Shipping and Commercial List.* This reasoning led them to adopt a counterintuitive strategy. Instead of asking for credit, as most newspaper editors at the time did, they insisted that excerpts of their "Review" remain anonymous. The *Commercial Advertiser* had in fact been crediting the *Shipping and Commercial List* by name, but Burritt asked them to stop. Stone and Hall concluded from this that Burritt didn't care about credit; he merely sought to extract as much money as possible in republication fees.[63]

Responding to Burritt and Clayton's posttrial comments, Stone and Hall defended their right to copy the "Review of the New York Market" and any other information appearing in price currents or newspapers. They refused to believe that they had caused any harm, suggesting that the loss of subscribers to the *Shipping and Commercial List* could be attributed to the fact that similar market reviews were now appearing in several morning papers. Stone and Hall mocked Burritt and Clayton for "being tenacious about the labour of giving the prices of candles and pig tail tobacco." They wrote, "Newspapers always draw all the information they can from each other; and so little originality is there in the Price Current, that they cannot distinguish their own matter from that of other papers."[64] Burritt and Clayton replied that the information they collected necessarily bore the marks of their efforts because it came from their conversations and correspondence with merchants. Going out to collect such information was not the same as relying on exchange papers that arrived in the mail. According to Burritt and Clayton, well-informed merchants in New York knew better than "to be duped by so shallow an artifice, as that of an attempt to make them believe that two persons, of different education, habits, and pursuits, should go into the market, and both obtain precisely the same items of business, and communicate them to the public in the same language, with the exception of a word here and there transposed, or substituted for another of similar meaning, or the fractions of a sum lopped off."[65]

In the court ruling, Justice Thompson distinguished between works that contributed to "science" and those that promoted commerce; Burritt and Clayton argued that the law should protect everyone's labor, regardless of their field of endeavor. Although their publication catered to an elite clientele of merchants, Burritt and Clayton compared their own efforts to the daily struggle of the average worker. As they put it, "We have asked from the law no other reward, in the pursuit of a lawful calling, than that of being placed on an equal footing with the day labourer: that when we had earned our bread we might share it with our wives and children, without having it taken out of our mouths."[66] Burritt and Clayton did not object to competition. Others were free to compile their own reports but not to rob them of the fruits of their labor while deceiving the public as to the source of the information.

The idea of a property right resulting from one's labor, as formulated by John Locke, figured in many justifications for copyright, including Thompson's own opinion in *Blunt v. Patten*.[67] If counsel for Burritt and Clayton had known of this ruling, they might have asked why the same logic did not apply to the collection of commercial information. Later commentators would point to this discrepancy. George Ticknor Curtis, the author of one of the most influential legal treatises of the mid-nineteenth century, objected to Thompson's characterization of the price current as a work of industry rather than of learning, arguing that such a distinction was irrelevant. "Works of industry are as much the subjects of protection as works of genius," Curtis wrote. "Indeed, there can be no line drawn between a production, the fruit of learning, and one the fruit of mere industry. All learning is the accumulation of knowledge gathered by the exercise of industry."[68] Curtis had an expansive view of copyright and was writing two decades after *Clayton* was decided. Burritt and Clayton, for their part, insisted that the only distinction that mattered was between doing one's own work and copying. They thought that "the public [would] form its own opinion of the *merits* of the case."[69]

The *Commercial Advertiser* belittled Burritt and Clayton for "whining about the country, and laboring to excite the sympathies of the merchants about their fancied grievances." Its proprietors, Stone and Hall, accused Burritt and Clayton of hypocrisy for requesting payment to re-use their "Review" while copying other matter from newspapers without paying for it. The *Commercial Advertiser* boasted that it was part of a group of daily papers in New York that was currently spending ten thousand to twelve thousand dollars per year to collect shipping and commercial news. According to Stone and Hall, Burritt and Clayton did not contribute anything to this pool, but the news collected by the association made up at least one-third of every issue of the *Shipping and Commercial List*. (Burritt and Clayton denied ever copying from the *Commercial Advertiser*.)[70]

It is difficult to say how much of the merchant community, or the public more generally, endorsed Burritt and Clayton's arguments. The *Commercial Advertiser* claimed that the *Journal of Commerce* was the only paper to reprint Burritt and Clayton's editorials, but the *New York Evening Post* also did this, and the *National Advocate* (the paper that had made a deal with Burritt and Clayton) also featured a pseudonymous letter signed "Publicola" that argued on their behalf.[71] Publicola was astonished that the editors of the *Commercial Advertiser* would risk a lawsuit by "using the labors of industrious men without being willing to compensate them therefore." The same writer claimed that "the untiring industry, the practical knowledge, [and] the unbending integrity of Wakeman Burritt" were known to all the merchants in the city, and the writer asked:

Shall such a man be put down and crushed, because there is a defect in the law of copyright if such defect there be, and another trial will not prove the fact to be otherwise? Shall he have the products of his head and his hands go to enrich another, without any compensation? Shall *his* merchandize have the brand erased, and be sold as first quality, and because an action of trover cannot bring it back, shall he be told that it is worthless, when the whole community know better?[72]

Publicola hoped that respectable merchants and brokers would take a closer look at this case and not allow honest men such as Burritt and Clayton to be destroyed by an unscrupulous daily paper.

Whatever members of the business community might have thought, the *Shipping and Commercial List* was certainly not destroyed. Despite having their labor appropriated by other publishers, Burritt and Clayton found a winning formula, and their emphasis on accurate and fresh information enabled their publication to succeed. They expanded operations by hiring several clerks, who visited commission merchants to obtain price quotes and went to the waterfront to compile lists of vessels and their cargoes. One of these clerks, James W. Auten, joined the business in 1831 at age seventeen and stayed for forty-five years. He later recalled how busy the clerks were on the days immediately preceding publication, "for the information furnished was brought down to the latest possible moment." Around 1848, after both Clayton and Burritt had died, Auten took over the publication in partnership with two other clerks, and they ran the business for another thirty years. Auten claimed that the paper was widely recognized for its impartiality and correctness, making it indispensable to the business community.[73]

THE AFTERMATH OF *CLAYTON*

After Justice Thompson's decision in 1828, the *Shipping and Commercial List* no longer included a copyright line, but did the ruling affect other publishers? Discussion of the case in print was limited. Although a few newspapers supported Burritt and Clayton's position, most did not comment extensively on the case. At least two amused their readers with a parody in which the defendants were described as having taken "certain liberties with the Plaintiff's Logwood, Whiskey, Potash, and other 'Drysalteries.'" The plaintiffs were described as being disappointed by the decision that "a little folio containing the prices current of Short Staple and Ceyenne pepper, from its very nature much more variable than a Dutch weathercock, was hardly to be considered a 'book' protected by the United States law of Copy-Right."[74]

Yet the problem of copying market news did not go away, and publishers who specialized in this area had to find other strategies in the absence of copyright. Henry Billington and Joseph M. Sanderson, publishers of the *Philadelphia Price Current*, faced the same problem as Burritt and Clayton: it was difficult for them to compete with a local newspaper that included information from their price current plus everything else readers expected from a newspaper. Billington and Sanderson's operation was based at the Merchants' Coffee House in Philadelphia (Sanderson was superintendent), and this gave them privileged access to the latest news brought by merchants and ship captains who gathered there. Advertisements for the Merchants' Coffee House emphasized that the information available in the reading rooms was "the exclusive property of Subscribers" and would be "carefully protected from the intrusion of those who refuse to contribute toward their support." Ship captains enjoyed free entry because they were likely to contribute fresh news in lieu of money.[75]

The information published in Billington and Sanderson's price current was a subset of what was available in the reading rooms and could never be as fresh. Nevertheless, they were upset when they discovered in early 1829 that a local publisher named John Binns was "filching" information from them and inserting it into his newspaper, the *Democratic Press*. Binns would procure a copy of the price current when it appeared in the morning and copy its "Review of the Market" (by now a standard title for such articles) into his own paper in time for afternoon distribution. Binns credited the *Philadelphia Price Current* as the source of the "Review," but Billington and Sanderson remained frustrated. When he refused to heed their request to desist from copying, they denounced his "rapacity," "avarice," and "cupidity" in notices posted around the Coffee House. They had previously been exchanging their price current for Binns's *Democratic Press*, but they discontinued this exchange. They also refused to accept Binns as a paying subscriber in hopes that this would impede his access to their reports.[76]

Binns maintained that the amount of material being copied was reasonable and that he always gave credit to the *Philadelphia Price Current*. He felt a duty to provide his readers with the freshest and most accurate information available, and he admitted that Billington and Sanderson provided it in a handy, "condensed" form. To defend his right to reprint this material, Binns pointed to Justice Thompson's recent decision in *Clayton v. Stone*, which he republished in his newspaper. And in order to gain access to the price current, Binns relied on a friend who was a subscriber. Billington and Sanderson denounced this "clandestine" act in further printed notices, but Binns was unfazed.[77] Soon, however, Sanderson abandoned his share in the venture, and Billington settled on a new strategy for dealing with systematic copying. First, he expanded the scope of the publication to enable it to compete more effectively with newspapers. Second, he distributed his semiweekly paper in the evenings rather than the mornings, thereby making it impossible for Binns to copy from him the same day.[78] In October 1829, Billington issued the first number of a new series titled the *Philadelphia Price Current, and Commercial Advertiser*. In an address to his readers, Billington explained what had motivated the changes. By including political news alongside updates about trade useful to the business community, he hoped to "unite the objects of a Price Current with the usual variety of a newspaper" and thereby attract more subscribers and more advertisers.[79] Whereas Burritt and Clayton had emphasized the differences between price currents and newspapers, Billington sought profitability by combining elements from both.

Binns's *Democratic Press* stopped publication less than a month after Billington made the changes to his price current. Billington's tactic of delaying publication may have had an effect, but there were probably other factors at play in the demise of the *Democratic Press*. In any case, Billington took the opportunity to resume morning publication of his enlarged newspaper. The combination of commercial and political news seems to have been successful, and within a year, three out of four pages were filled with advertisements. In that respect, Billington had succeeded in his attempt to turn the price current into something more like a newspaper. The inclusion of advertisements in particular marked a major change from the price currents of earlier eras, which had contained few if any advertisements.[80]

The compilers of price currents sought exclusivity from an early date, especially when it came to copying by local newspapers. Compared to price currents, newspapers had higher circulations, more paid ads, and the ability to offer readers commercial information bundled together with political news, commentary, and other features. The effort required to compile the freshest possible information from local sources increased the sense of frustration when a local newspaper engaged in systematic copying. The 1828 dispute between the *Shipping and Commercial List* and the *Commercial Advertiser* revealed how the time-sensitive nature of news reporting challenged existing conceptions of copyright law. It should not be forgotten that Burritt and Clayton sued to protect their "Review of the New York Market," which was not a list of prices but a series of short written observations of market trends. The problem, according to Justice Thompson, was that their publication sought to promote commerce rather than "science" or learning, and the copyright clause in the Constitution was designed to promote the latter. Moreover, Thompson was troubled by the idea that the information and remarks contained in the price current would retain their usefulness for such a short period of time. According to him, only works that made a lasting contribution to learning should receive the privilege of copyright.

Significantly, it was a dispute over the right to republish news that led an influential judge to formulate this view of copyright's purpose. Although the Constitution referred to "the progress of science" and the Copyright Act of 1790 was titled "An Act for the Encouragement of Learning," neither text stated that a work's eligibility depended on how long it might remain useful. It was the circumstances of *Clayton v. Stone* that led Justice Thompson to think in terms of how long a publication's value was likely to last and to dismiss the price current as being "of mere temporary use." Thompson's vision of the purpose of copyright was cited in subsequent decisions, including by the Supreme Court in 1879.[81] Over time, however, the principle he espoused came under increasing pressure from those who argued that copyright should protect the market value of works independently of any judgment about their contribution to literature, science, or education.[82] But even after this more market-oriented approach gained ascendancy, the case of news would continue to test the boundaries of copyright law, as we shall see in subsequent chapters.

In Thompson's era, there were also political reasons for encouraging the copying of commercial and financial news. Uneven access to price information encouraged speculation, and beginning in the 1820s, the post office was expected to distribute market news as rapidly as possible to help curtail this problem.[83] Thompson's decision did not mention speculation, but his ruling did make it more difficult to monopolize commercial and financial information, even for a short period of time. After *Clayton*, publishers could reasonably claim that copying market news was not a violation of copyright. The implications of Thompson's decision for other kinds of newspaper material are less clear. Beginning around midcentury, copyright notices began to accompany some works of fiction, biography, and history published in newspapers, and later in the century, literary syndicates made more extensive use of copyright.[84] But even at the time of *Clayton* in the late 1820s, it could have been argued that at least some kinds of newspaper material did contribute to learning in terms that contemporary judges would have recognized. Indeed, some readers celebrated the value of preserving newspapers for future consultation. In an article titled, "Keep Your Newspapers," which was reprinted in various newspapers from the 1820s through the 1840s, the anonymous writer declared:

A volume of newspapers is a book unbound. Why then should it be wantonly destroyed? The man who receives a weekly journal during twenty years, receives twenty volumes at least as valuable, as those with which he furnishes his shelves from the bookstore. If, instead of procuring them to be bound, he suffers them to be destroyed, the loss is as real as the loss of any other property.[85]

But the real loss, our anonymous writer suggested, would be experienced by future generations. Since the seventeenth century, some publishers of news periodicals had incorporated features such as continuous pagination, indexes, and annual title pages that encouraged readers to bind successive issues into volumes. And some editors self-consciously described their newspapers and magazines as repositories of documents on which later historians could rely.[86] The anonymous contributor of "Keep Your Newspapers" recalled this tradition when he or she wrote: "What is news this week does indeed cease to be news the next; but then it becomes history, and the files of our periodical publications furnish many of the documents, from which the condensed histories of our country have been, and are to be compiled."[87]

If *Clayton v. Stone* had involved some other sort of newspaper matter besides market news, perhaps Justice Thompson would have agreed that newspapers could make a lasting contribution to learning and he would have upheld the copyright. But no such case was brought; newspaper republication at that time was governed not by copyright but by the exchange system and the customs that editors tried—with varying degrees of success—to impose on one another. Copyright was not invoked until much later in the century (see chapter 6). The irony of this today is that the consultation of nineteenth-century newspapers increasingly happens through proprietary databases, which rely on copyright and contract law to restrict access to paying subscribers. Fortunately, one can still sometimes consult the paper copies—perhaps even bound in marbled covers—at repositories like the American Antiquarian Society.

No American newspaper publisher claimed copyright in news reports during the first half of the nineteenth century. Doing so would have been unthinkable in a world in which copying was what enabled the news to spread. The fact that American newspapers were not taxed (as they were in Britain) but benefited from favorable postal policy also helps to explain why American news publishers did not seek copyright in the first half of the nineteenth century. The regulatory environment in Britain was very different, and this accounts for why London newspapers began to lobby for copyright in news reports as early as the 1830s. The policy changes that inspired these early efforts to protect news, and the reactions to these efforts, are the subject of the next chapter.

CHAPTER 5

Debating Copyright for News
in Industrial Britain

THE PERCEPTION THAT COPYING is a problem and that "piracy" will reduce the incentive to produce new works can depend on a number of factors. New technologies that facilitate the duplication or transmission of texts are sometimes a catalyst, but technology cannot be viewed in isolation from the policy decisions and business strategies that shape their use. In Britain, the idea that news publishers required special legislation to protect their investments arose at specific moments in response to changes in government regulations, new combinations of technology and business practice, and the personal vision of industry leaders. And in the nineteenth century, many discussions of news piracy were related to shifts in the relationship between London newspapers and "provincial newspapers," a term that was widely used to refer to publications based in towns other than London.[1]

The first attempt to enact a special copyright law for newspaper articles occurred in the 1830s, before the advent of the electric telegraph. Anticipating changes in taxation and postal policy that would affect their interests, a small group of London morning newspapers began to lobby for copyright. They argued that reducing the stamp duty on newspapers would lead to the creation of cheap "pirate" papers that would thrive on copying and thereby undermine investments in news gathering. This initial proposal did not get very far, but it was followed by further campaigns to secure copyright protection for news in the 1850s and again in the 1890s. By the early twentieth century, owing largely to the sustained efforts of *The Times*, a series of court rulings confirmed that newspaper articles could be protected by copyright. Significantly, however, the courts also restricted the scope of copyright by distinguishing between the language in which news was conveyed—protected by copyright—and the underlying factual details—free for all to use.

This outcome was not inevitable. Special laws protecting the substance of news contained in telegraphic dispatches were enacted in several British colonies during the late nineteenth century but never in Britain itself.[2] The fact that protection for news as such was repeatedly rejected in Britain is significant. The efforts described here sparked debates in Parliament and the press about how best to balance the interests of rival publishers and the public good. Returning to these debates reveals the kinds of rights that publishers sought, the arguments they developed, and the opposition they faced. In response to court cases and legislative proposals, editors, political leaders, and judges discussed what was special about news, which in turn led them to articulate what they saw as the acceptable boundaries of copyright. Disputes over news shaped the development of copyright law and vice versa.

THE STAMP DUTY AND COPYRIGHT

Access to printed newspapers in Great Britain remained limited throughout the eighteenth and early nineteenth centuries in large part because government duties substantially increased their prices. In addition to the stamp duty, first implemented in 1712 and raised several times over the next century, there were also taxes on newspaper advertisements and on the paper itself. From 1815 until the stamp duty was reduced in 1836, the average price of newspapers in England was seven pence, which was beyond the reach of most people. Although the duties were primarily intended to raise revenue (most of the increases happened when Britain was at war), they effectively hindered the publication of cheaper and more radical newspapers. Other measures sought to keep the press within bounds. All newspapers had to be registered with the government, and proprietors had to provide a hefty bond and two guarantors as security against seditious or blasphemous libel.[3] The combination of registration, security, and taxation meant that it cost a significant amount of money to operate legitimate newspapers, which tended to cater to an elite readership.

But there was also an unstamped press—illegal newspapers that were produced at low cost and sold for a penny or two to customers on the street. More than four hundred such papers were started during the 1830s.[4] Many writers and printers went to jail for selling unstamped papers, but it was impossible for the authorities to get rid of them, in part because of growing opposition to the stamp in and out of Parliament. In the early 1830s, radical editors and political leaders began referring to the duties as "taxes on knowledge," and this language was picked up by advocates of free trade and by radical MPs who saw wider access to newspapers as a necessary complement to the parliamentary reforms of the 1830s.[5] The stamp duty was also criticized for being unevenly applied, and part of the problem stemmed from the inherent difficulties in determining which publications were subject to it. Periodicals that did not contain news or commentary on recent events were exempt, but news was arguably a relative term: Did recent developments within a trade or profession count? What about literary news or reports of scientific discoveries? A Select Committee of Parliament in 1851 noted that an important factor fueling evasion of the stamp was "the difficulty of defining and determining the meaning of the word 'news.'"[6]

It was the campaign to end the stamp duty that led to the first attempt to create a special copyright for news reports. The owners of stamped newspapers worried that repealing or reducing the duty would lead to the creation of cheap papers that would copy news and sell it in competition with the newspapers that had actually collected it. Motions in favor of repeal, which highlighted the benefits of public access to knowledge of all kinds, came up against defenses of the business owner's right to protection of property.[7] The chancellor of the exchequer, Thomas Spring Rice, took fears of a piratical press seriously. In the summer of 1835, he announced in the House of Commons that "something in the shape of a principle of copyright is necessary to be established" before the stamp duty could be reduced.[8] He noted that newspapers spent considerable sums on foreign correspondence, parliamentary reporting, and the equipment and personnel necessary to distribute news early in the day. It would not be fair for others to profit from these investments. Some members of Parliament also endorsed the idea. George Grote, MP for the City of London, suggested that "a few lines in an Act of Parliament would be quite sufficient" to ensure protection against piracy. Henry Warburton, MP for Bridport, said that "an hour's conversation with the editors and proprietors of two or three newspapers" would lead to a workable copyright clause. Edward Baines, a reform-minded MP and printer-proprietor of the *Leeds Mercury*, also supported newspaper copyright, which he thought would be satisfactory to newspaper owners and beneficial to the public.[9]

The established morning papers saw copyright as a means of preventing unfair competition. Copying had long been central to the newspaper press, a fact that would have been hard for any editor to deny. But the stamp also created barriers to entry, because obtaining stamped paper in advance of printing required a certain amount of capital and business coordination. The stamp also artificially raised the price of newspapers, further restricting competition. The owners of stamped papers worried that a major change in the regulatory environment would lead to greater competition and a corresponding fall in profits. Their pleas for copyright stressed the right of business owners to profit from their labor and financial investments. The *Morning Chronicle*, for example, celebrated Spring Rice's promise to provide newspapers with "that protection for the fruits of their labour and their outlay of capital which individuals embarking in any branch of industry ought always to obtain."[10]

Speaking on behalf of the unstamped press, the *Poor Man's Guardian* denounced the proposed copyright as a ploy by the established newspapers to stifle competition. The *Poor Man's Guardian* was published by Henry Hetherington, a radical printer, founding member of the London Working Men's Association, and active leader in the campaign to repeal the stamp. He was imprisoned three separate times for publishing unstamped newspapers.[11] Instead of a stamp, each issue of the *Poor Man's Guardian* bore an image of a printing press surrounded by the phrase "Knowledge is Power." Although copyright was being envisioned as a way to stop cheap newspapers from copying more expensive ones, the *Poor Man's Guardian* insisted that it would be counterproductive because the stamped newspapers *all borrow and steal from each other on the very day of publication. To a great extent they are made up from each other, as every body may easily see.*"[12] Given how widespread copying was, it would have been impossible to determine who was the rightful owner of a given article. An editor could easily alter the phrasing of a news report, making allegations of infringement difficult to prove. In addition, the *Poor Man's Guardian* predicted that writers and printers who had gone to prison rather than pay the stamp duty were not likely to be intimidated by copyright suits.

In the spring of 1836, when Spring Rice announced that that he would introduce a bill to reduce the stamp duty to one penny, the owners of stamped newspapers organized to protect their interests. They were worried about two things: postal distribution and copying. By this time, payment of the stamp duty came with the privilege of free postage, including the right of customers to forward their newspapers to friends and family after they read them.[13] Celebrating the free postal transmission that came with the stamp became a politically defensible way of opposing repeal. A Manchester paper, for example, heard from one of its subscribers that he always sent his paper to a friend in Liverpool, who forwarded it on to friends in Glasgow, who then sent it to Dundee. "Think of the wonderful interchange that must take place in hundreds of thousands of such instances," wrote the Manchester editor. "Of the effects of this *secondary* circulation we have witnessed many proofs."[14] Representatives of London newspapers likewise argued that it was wrong to refer to the stamp as a "tax on knowledge" since it included the cost of postage. They feared that if the stamp were repealed, their distribution costs would go up.[15]

Stamped newspapers also worried about how copying by cheap newspapers would undermine their businesses. In a petition submitted to both Houses of Parliament in the spring of 1836, *The Times*, the *Morning Herald*, the *Morning Post* and the *Standard* complained that the proposed bill lacked "an equitable copyright as a protection to the capital and literary labour profusely expended by the daily journalists, in the constant acquisition and preparation of new matter to meet the wants of the community."[16] Referring to this petition, MP Henry Goulburn underscored the disparity between authors, who were protected by copyright, and newspaper owners, who received no protection "however great might be the expenditure of capital in the purchase of information" and "however extensive the literary labour employed."[17]

To bolster their argument in favor of copyright, newspapers gave examples of different sorts of piracy. The *Weekly Dispatch*, for example, complained that the unstamped *Twopenny Dispatch* had stolen its title as well as its news. The editor of the *Twopenny Dispatch* replied that his paper went to press several days before the *Weekly Dispatch* and was itself a victim of copying. As he put it, "Our articles have been ransacked and garbled extracts made from them into stamped newspapers."[18] The *True Sun* warned its readers that it had no connection to the unstamped *Weekly True Sun*. "This is the second piratical attempt, under the same false colours, to injure our property," the *True Sun* explained.[19] As had been the case after the creation of the stamp duty in 1712, the rivalry between stamped and unstamped publications involved accusations of attempting to "pass off" one publication for another. Meanwhile, resentment toward publications that did not pay the stamp led editors and publishers to pay more attention to copying than they might have otherwise.

An editorial in the *Morning Herald*, which was republished by other newspapers, explained why existing copyright law was inadequate for newspapers. The writer thought that newspaper articles could be considered "literary compositions" for the purposes of copyright but that existing procedures for obtaining an injunction were too slow. By the time a suit could be considered by a judge, the news would already be too old to be worth protecting. News had to be fresh to attract readers and advertisers. In cases of piracy, publishers needed to be able to ask for a summary judgment before a magistrate, who could quickly order the defendant to stop selling the news and pay damages to the copyright owner. It was hoped that the existence of such a swift remedy would dissuade newspapers from copying altogether.[20]

The advocates for legal protection against news piracy thus introduced several ideas that were foreign to the theory and practice of copyright. The first novelty was the claim that the speed of the news business justified a different set of legal procedures, namely the recourse to summary judgment, than those that applied to other works. The second novelty was that the term of protection for news would be much shorter— a few hours rather than twenty-eight years, let alone the lifetime of the author. But perhaps the most important novelty was the argument that accounts of current events were eligible for copyright at all. That idea was to attract considerable resistance on political and cultural grounds.

In the summer of 1836, a group of owners of stamped newspapers sent a draft copyright clause to Chancellor Spring Rice. Praising the speed and accuracy with which newspapers reported Parliament, the chancellor asserted that "it would be extremely unfair if, after being put to this expense the proprietors were, through the rapidity of print-ing, to be deprived of the advantages which they had obtained through their own labour and capital."[21] The example of parliamentary debates revealed how supporters of copyright for news saw no need to appeal to literary invention or originality to justify protection—labor and capital were sufficient. Yet Spring Rice and others also anticipated that copying would be harder to prove for news reports than for other literary works. A defendant could claim to have sent a reporter to cover the same event or to have an independent source for foreign news. It would take time to weigh the evidence, and this would defeat the purpose of summary judgment. Citing such difficulties, as well as the fact that it would be in-appropriate to tack copyright onto the stamp reduction bill, Spring Rice declined to move forward with the proposed clause.[22]

The stamp law that ultimately passed in 1836 was a compromise. The duty was reduced from fourpence to a penny, and the stamp came with the privilege of unlimited postal transmission. But newspapers were also subject to strict registration and security requirements, which made it difficult for smaller publications to get off the ground. Many thought the remaining stamp was an obstacle to the wider diffusion of news and knowledge. Although total circulation of newspapers rose by an esti-mated 70 percent between 1836 and 1856, most of the gains went to ex-isting publications. The single biggest beneficiary of the 1836 law was *The Times*, which reportedly doubled its readership over the next six years. The remaining stamp kept prices artificially high, reducing com-petition, and the postal privilege was a boon for *The Times*, which was heavier and contained more advertisements than other papers but paid the same effective rate of postage.[23]

MIDCENTURY DEBATES

After passage of the 1836 law, discussion of news piracy subsided. The copying of news no doubt continued, but it may not have been as much of a problem as some publishers had feared in 1835–1836.[24] The question of whether it was permissible to reproduce extracts from other newspapers and periodicals was addressed in the 1839 case of *Bell v. Whitehead*. The owners of the *Monthly Chronicle: A Journal of Politics, Literature, Science, and Art* sued the owners of a weekly paper called the *Railway Times* for reprinting parts of a railway engineer's report. The plaintiffs claimed that the report was prepared expressly for them and that by reproducing "the most material and valuable parts" of the article in a cheaper weekly publication, the defendants had infringed their copyright. The defendants responded that "considerable public interest" in controversies surrounding the Great Western Railway justified including excerpts of the engineer's report. The *Railway Times* sought to criticize specific aspects of the engineer's report, and it was necessary for the purpose of this criticism to provide the public with excerpts of it.[25] The Court of Chancery found that the copying was justified on these grounds and cited the tradition of the quarterly reviews, which often quoted from copyrighted books. In the course of his ruling, the lord chancellor suggested that awarding an injunction in this case could set a precedent that would adversely affect newspaper reporting. "If I were to entertain this application of the plaintiffs," he asked, "how could I decline to entertain a similar application in the case of those newspapers from the columns of which articles have been extracted and printed in other newspapers, for the purpose of questioning or criticizing the opinions expressed therein?"[26] Providing experts for the purposes of criticism or review was not the same as reproducing whole articles, but the decision in *Bell v. Whitehead* suggested that newspapers enjoyed an exception to copyright law allowing them to make limited use of material that was currently of interest to the public.

A major revision of British copyright law was passed in 1842. Although it provided explicit protection for contributions to magazines, reviews, and "periodical works," newspapers were not mentioned, and there is no evidence that newspaper publishers lobbied for any special provisions during the legislative process that led to the 1842 act.[27] Instead, it was the campaign to abolish the remaining "taxes on knowledge," reignited at midcentury, that brought the question of news copyright back to the fore. The National Stamp Abolition Committee, which was formed in 1849, and its successor, the Association for Promoting the Repeal of the Taxes on Knowledge, organized public meetings and press campaigns. Writers attacked the taxes as perpetuating a "monopolist" press, with *The Times* being the most frequent target. In Parliament, the fight was led by committed free traders, especially members of the Manchester School such as John Bright, Thomas Milner Gibson, and Richard Cobden. One of their motives was to bolster the provincial press at the expense of the big London dailies. Cobden, for example, hoped that repeal of the stamp would strengthen local journalism.[28]

Proponents of repeal had to deal with the objection—raised by *The Times* and others—that abolishing the stamp would lead to a proliferation of cheap papers that would engage in piracy and degrade the overall quality of the British press. The novelist Charles Dickens, who resented that the lack of an international copyright treaty allowed American publishers to freely publish British novels without permission, explained to Gibson why he would not support repeal of the stamp: "I am disposed to think that the tax increases [the newspapers'] respectability—that they have a fair return for it in the postage arrangements—and that if it were taken off, we might be deluged with a flood of piratical, ignorant and blackguard papers, something like that black deluge of Printer's Ink which blights America."[29] Collet Dobson Collet, the secretary of the National Stamp Abolition Committee (NSAC), employed similar metaphors when he recalled that in 1849 "there arose a fear that a flood of piracy would set in on the repeal of the stamp."[30] The NSAC had to deal with this fear. The editor of the London *Weekly News* suggested two potential ways of making news more accessible while preventing piracy. A law could be passed to secure copyright for news and leading articles for a few hours or, if necessary, a few days after publication. Alternatively, news gathering could be done at government expense, with the House of Commons hiring its own reporters, and foreign news appearing in cheap editions of the official *London Gazette*. Collet's committee rejected the second idea on the grounds that the government could not be trusted to criticize itself. One member of the NSAC felt strongly that copyright should be extended to news, but the others did not share this view.[31]

The subject of newspaper piracy received more sustained discussion after 1851, when Parliament appointed a Select Committee to look into the newspaper stamp and the potential effects of repeal. The committee, chaired by Gibson, was sympathetic to repeal, as were most of the witnesses. Among the questions considered by the committee was whether piracy would become more of a problem if the stamp were repealed. John Cassell, a respected publisher of several periodicals aimed at working-class families, was asked if the stamp were repealed and he were to start a cheap newspaper, would he feel free to "copy without restraint" from *The Times* or the *Morning Chronicle*? Cassell replied that if he started an evening paper he would conform to the established practice, which he claimed was to copy the previous day's news from the morning papers but to rely on one's own staff to gather news of the current day. He thought that news articles, unlike literary contributions, were free for the taking. "It is not like availing ourselves of a literary production," he said, "and it is not considered so."[32] Cassell thought that copying news was more acceptable because unlike fiction, news lost its value quickly, and the first to publish it had a major advantage. He assumed that piracy would not work as a business strategy; if newspapers outside of London wanted to compete with *The Times*, they would have to gather their own news.[33]

The Select Committee was interested in how the lack of taxation on newspapers in the United States affected readers and publishers. They interviewed Horace Greeley of the *New York Tribune*. Asked whether piracy was a problem, Greeley responded that it was "sometimes talked of for effect's sake" but that he saw copying as a form of flattery. "We have six or seven journals in the city, which form a combination, and spend, perhaps, 100,000 dollars a year in telegraphing." According to Greeley, "The evening journals all copy from us, and we rather like it."[34] Greeley and his partners were not concerned about the lack of legal protection for news; they knew that the public would seek out papers with the reputation for the earliest reports. Yet Greeley's testimony also revealed that the New York "combination" took steps to protect its investments. In order to keep rivals from copying, the partners sometimes agreed to delay publication of certain news items. Instead of copyright, they relied on exclusive partnerships and collusion.[35]

At the time of the 1851 Select Committee, the most vocal supporter of a property right in news was Frederick Knight Hunt, editor of the *Daily News*. This paper was founded in 1846 by Charles Dickens, who recruited Hunt and may have shaped the latter's views about the need for some kind of newspaper copyright. In any case, by 1851, Dickens was no longer at the *Daily News*, Hunt was the chief editor, and the paper was becoming profitable.[36] Testifying before the Select Committee, Hunt claimed that almost all of the news that appeared in British newspapers could be traced back to "four sets of proprietors" that controlled the "chief morning papers" in London. Citing the high cost of telegraphic dispatches and reporters covering the law courts and Parliament, Hunt argued that "all the special reports they pay for ought to be regarded as their property. If you give the newspaper proprietors some 12 hours' copyright in that which they pay for, I think they would then thrive by the removal of the penny stamp, and that all the papers might then be reduced in price."[37] He asserted that the amount of copying that currently took place was negligible compared to what would happen if the stamp were removed without new copyright measures in place. According to Hunt, the individuals who owned stamped papers were restrained by their "honesty and character." By contrast, the operators of unstamped papers "print anything they can take hold of." If the stamp were removed, then the number of cheap papers would increase, and copying would become widespread. As a result, the existing morning papers would reduce their investments and "cease to give you so complete a newspaper as they now offer."[38]

Hunt clothed his argument in the language of national honor. English newspapers were superior to American, French, and German ones, he claimed, but if their "property" was not secured, then English newspapers would decline in quality. Hunt said that removal of the stamp would lead to "little papers like the 'Cheltenham Looker-On,' to give local news," but if postage remained low and copyright was secured, then "papers emanating from large towns, such as London, Manchester, and Liverpool, would circulate over the country, and give more than ever a tone to national opinion."[39] According to Hunt, the major urban dailies had the potential to provide reliable information, untainted by local prejudices, to the whole country. His interest in copyright was not merely a reaction against the supposed piracy of the unstamped press; it reflected the ambitions of metropolitan newspapers to achieve a national circulation.

Committee member T. F. Lewis pressed Hunt to define the scope of the property right he envisioned. Would it be possible, Lewis asked, "to prevent persons from taking the substance of the news and, as it were, recompounding it, and putting it in somewhat different phraseology?" Hunt argued that the copyright should prohibit more than just verbatim copying. Acquiring news from India was very expensive, he said, and "no change in the verbiage of the telegraphic dispatch could so conceal the piracy as to protect the party guilty of it."[40] Today, copyright protects expressions but not facts or ideas. Although this point was not as clear in the mid-nineteenth century, the idea of owning the factual details of news was already controversial. Many newspaper editors were more concerned about getting credit for being first to publish news than with prohibiting copying per se. Hunt did not think credit was sufficient. Given the high cost of telegraph transmission, he thought the newspaper that paid this cost should have exclusive use of the news until it became available through the ordinary mail. He gave the example of a hypothetical event in Paris. If a newspaper paid for news to be sent by telegraph from Paris to London, then other newspapers should not be allowed to publish this news—even if they rewrote it—unless they made their own arrangements. Once the same news arrived by post, however, all exclusive rights over it would cease, and anybody could publish the news. Similarly, a report from India could be published by any newspaper editor "after he had, or might have, received it by way of post; when it had become public property in fact."[41] That Hunt considered the same news to be private or public depending on the channel of communication may have been related to the fact that the telegraph was at that time in private hands (after 1870 it would be managed by the post office). But the main point was the cost differential. According to Hunt, the expense of procuring a piece of news by telegraph justified a temporary monopoly on that news item. He did not imagine a copyright that would cover all the contents of a newspaper.

In its final report, the Select Committee recommended repeal of the stamp, citing the potential benefits for provincial readers in particular: a lower price would attract more readers to existing papers and encourage the creation of "small and cheap local papers" that would further expand access to "that most useful knowledge, the news of the day."[42] The argument that newspapers had the potential to educate the people was not new, but the emphasis on news was. The Society for the Diffusion of Useful Knowledge (1826–1848), for example, had stressed the importance of scientific and practical texts rather than news; its *Penny Magazine* was initially published as an alternative to the radical unstamped newspapers. By 1851, there were no more radical unstamped papers, and the Select Committee faced few objections to the idea of making news more accessible to workers.[43] But the committee also recognized the potential danger of piracy and recommended a copyright of short duration to protect the news-gathering efforts of the London press.[44]

TELEGRAPH COMPANIES AND NEWSROOMS

Despite the recommendations of the 1851 Select Committee, no action was taken for several years. Fiscal concerns worked against repeal of the stamp, as did political disagreements about how best to balance direct and indirect taxes.[45] When the government finally moved forward with a bill to repeal the stamp in 1855, there was no provision for copyright. The *Daily News* and *The Times* went on the offensive. London morning papers were relying increasingly on the railroads and news agents, especially W. H. Smith, to reach paying customers in other towns. They worried that if the stamp were removed, daily papers would be set up in the provinces, where newspapers were currently weekly or semiweekly. Using the telegraph, agents for provincial newspapers could take news from London papers and transmit it home in time to be printed and sold in competition with the same London papers arriving by railway. Such tactics had the potential to undermine the whole business. According to the *Daily News*, "If a piece of intelligence which costs us 100 [pounds] is to be published within an hour or less of the time of our publication, and sold for a penny, newspapers worthy of the name will cease to exist."[46]

The word *intelligence* had long been used to refer to both secret information (collected by a spy, for example) and published news, especially reports of foreign affairs and war. In the seventeenth century, the compilers of handwritten newsletters were referred to as *intelligencers*, a word that also appeared in the titles of printed newspapers such as the *Moderate Intelligencer*. In these contexts, the word *intelligence* had the connotation of news that was filtered, and sometimes interpreted, by a writer or editor.[47] The valences of *intelligence* in relation to *news* and *information* changed over time, but all three words were still being used in the nineteenth century. When the *Daily News* referred to the cost of a "piece of intelligence," it was likely referring to news of the Crimean War (1853–1856) that may have had its basis in official government sources but nonetheless required arrangements with third parties to procure and have transmitted across vast distances. In arguments about the need to protect investments in news gathering, the word *intelligence* also evoked the underlying information—names, dates, numbers of dead and wounded—that made up a published news report. When the *Daily News* and *The Times* referred to paying for intelligence, they sought to exclude others from copying these kinds of factual details from their columns.

In addition to concern about copying by provincial newspapers, *The Times* and the *Daily News* also complained about the activities of the telegraph companies. Beginning in 1848, the Electric Telegraph Company (ETC) created its own Intelligence Department to provide reports of Parliament, the law courts, the weather, horse racing results, market prices, and other news. Clerks working under Charles Vincent Boys in London would read the morning papers, select articles from them, and transmit summaries by telegraph to customers in the provinces. All of this could be done within an hour of London newspapers going on sale.

The customers of this news service included provincial newspapers as well as subscription newsrooms in stock exchanges, railway stations, hotels, clubs, and associations.[48] For locations not yet connected to the telegraph network, the railway remained crucial. In fact, even before the ETC set up its Intelligence Department, W. H. Smith pioneered the rapid, large-scale distribution of newsworthy texts—such as the queen's speech at the opening of Parliament—by carefully exploiting both the railway and the telegraph.[49]

Ventures like Boys's and Smith's, in combination with the newsrooms, encouraged the novel idea that news was something to be sought out throughout the day as intelligence arrived by telegraph. Time-sensitive information was now available in the newsrooms before it was printed in the local newspapers and before copies of London newspapers arrived by railway. Subscription newsrooms had existed in the eighteenth century, when Lloyd's Coffee House had such a service, but most of the early ones catered to merchants. By the 1850s, there were newsrooms for artisans and workers located in mechanics' institutes, clubs, and libraries. The Manchester Athenaeum for the Advancement and Diffusion of Knowledge, for example, had over 1,100 members in 1855, including many working men. During that year, the newsroom spent 273 pounds on a range of English newspapers and a few major titles from Ireland, Scotland, France, Germany, and the United States. They also spent fifty-seven pounds to provide members with almost hourly updates by telegraph. Interest in the Crimean War made 1855 a somewhat exceptional year in terms of demand for news, but the fact remains that the amount that the Athenaeum spent on books and magazines (82 pounds) was dwarfed by the amount it spent on newspapers and telegraphic dispatches (330 pounds).[50]

The cost of the service provided by the ETC and its competitors inspired some newsrooms to send agents to competing newsrooms and copy the news posted there. Newsrooms treated this as piracy, but they were able to stop it by denying entry to those suspected of copying. Some provincial newspapers may also have sent agents to the newsrooms to gather news, but over time a growing number of them paid to receive reports directly from the telegraph companies. By 1854, approximately 120 provincial newspapers were subscribing to such a service. Although they sometimes complained about the cost and quality of the news they received, provincial newspapers celebrated the potential of the telegraph to reduce the time lag between London and other cities.[51]

The Times denounced the activities of the telegraph companies and pointed to them as proof of the need for copyright in news.[52] In response, John Lewis Ricardo, MP for Stoke and chairman of the ETC, defended his company's service as being in the public interest. Ricardo was a committed free trader who believed in the potential of the telegraph to make news of "universal interest" available to every part of the country. He insisted that his company never violated the confidentiality of telegrams. Agents always waited until news appeared in print before transmitting it to newsrooms or provincial newspapers, and they always labeled the source of reports. If there were no telegraph, Ricardo said, then extracts of London papers would still be posted in the newsrooms and republished in other newspapers after a delay of several hours. His company merely sped up the process, enabling news to travel much faster than before.[53]

As in 1836, weekly papers, whether based in London or other towns, tended to oppose the idea of copyright for news. *Reynolds's Weekly Newspaper*, which was founded in 1850 by the novelist and radical journalist George William MacArthur Reynolds and was popular among working-class readers, even went so far as to argue that copying was central to journalism. "The Times affects to believe that the Chancellor of the Exchequer's measure [repeal of the stamp] will conjure up a host of piratical prints. If the transfer of news from one newspaper to another be piracy, then piracy is the basis on which the entire newspaper press is built up." According to this editorial, *The Times* had rarely complained about copying before because the stamp restricted competition. "Now that a measure is brought forward which promises to make newspapers plentiful and cheap, the Times suddenly finds out that the transfer of news from one print to another is nothing less than an infamous piracy!" The editorial in *Reynolds's Weekly Newspaper* also criticized the *Daily News* for supporting copyright, given that it had an evening edition that republished telegrams from the morning papers. *The*

Times and the *Daily News* should recognize that "all newspapers must be continuously laboring under a mutual indebtedness" and that copyright was inappropriate for news because of its importance to the public. The editorial continued by asserting, "The interests of the community plainly and pointedly demand that nothing which tends to the prompt diffusion of intelligence shall be branded as an illicit piracy at all."[54] The word *intelligence* will again be noted. The writer for *Reynolds's Weekly Newspaper* had used the word *news* several times, but when it came time to underscore the benefits of copying, the phrase "diffusion of intelligence" packed a stronger punch. The point was that many readers would not have access to this intelligence in any form if the law prohibited "the transfer of news from one newspaper to another."

A PROPOSED COPYRIGHT CLAUSE

The pressure that *The Times* and the *Daily News* put on the chancellor of the exchequer (now Sir George Cornewall Lewis) and members of Parliament initially worked. In the spring of 1855, Chancellor Lewis proposed a copyright clause to be inserted in the newspaper stamp bill. This clause offered newspaper proprietors a twenty-four-hour copyright for "any original article, letter, paragraph, communication, or composition" first published by them. This fairly exhaustive list was designed to bring as much of the newspaper as possible into the bounds of copyright law. Moreover, the clause aimed to protect much more than verbatim copying of an entire paragraph or article. Penalties applied to reproducing "any material part" or "any colourable abridgement or alteration of the same."[55] Even an editor who spent time reformulating an existing report might be guilty of infringement if he followed the original too closely. Finally, as requested in the past by Frederick Knight Hunt and others, the proposed clause offered a swifter legal remedy: instead of filing for an injunction, plaintiffs could recover financial penalties in summary proceedings before a local magistrate.[56]

The proposed copyright clause was widely criticized by provincial newspapers, which developed two main arguments against it. The first was that copyright would restrict the flow of intelligence. The *Leeds Mercury* denounced the proposal as "the first attempt of the kind to interpose an obstruction to the free circulation of intelligence in this country." According to the Leeds paper, it had always been assumed that when news was published it became public property. It would be absurd to require each newspaper to have an independent source for news that was already published.[57] At that time, the *Leeds Mercury* was run by Edward Baines Jr., who had started working for his father's paper as a reporter in 1815 and joined him in partnership in 1827. The elder Baines had supported copyright back in 1836, but his son saw copyright as inconsistent with his views as a free trader who opposed the dominance of London and championed local efforts to educate workers for the new industrial society. The younger Baines's opposition to newspaper copyright inspired him to join the owners of several other provincial newspapers in a petition to the House of Commons asserting that the proposed law would "obstruct the circulation of important intelligence, to the serious detriment of the public," while exposing newspaper proprietors to frivolous lawsuits.[58]

The other main argument advanced by provincial newspapers was that news was not eligible for copyright because it was different than other genres of writing. Some conceded that copyright might make sense for leading articles, biographies, criticisms, and reviews, but *The Times* and the *Daily News* were not asking for this. What they wanted was protection for breaking news, which they justified based on the expense of telegraph transmission. Their opponents claimed that such bulletins lacked the sort of originality associated with authorship. As a writer in the *Manchester Examiner and Times* put it, "The true originality in this case is found in the fact of occurrence, and this is the produce of the busy spirit of the world. . . . In news the element which confers proprietary rights upon the author or the translator, is altogether wanting. The work of origination is already done; it is furnished readymade, to everybody who can twist a tongue or handle a pen. The sender of news merely echoes what he has himself heard or seen."[59] The idea that news was collected rather than written by authors had been expressed as early as the 1730s when the *Grub-Street Journal* mocked the idea of literary property in news paragraphs.[60] The cost and complexity of the news business had changed significantly by 1855, but the fact that proponents of copyright focused on telegraphic dispatches rather than longer journalistic writings exposed them to this sort of criticism. The effort to extend copyright to telegraphic dispatches also led opponents to emphasize a view of copyright that stressed original authorship rather than labor or financial investment. According to the writer in the *Manchester Examiner and Times*, it was not a logical extension of copyright law to grant protection based solely on the cost of transmitting something. Copyright was a product of authorship. The just reward for incurring the cost of telegraphic tolls was not exclusive rights in the news, but the ability to publish it first, which was valuable in itself.[61]

Copyright was perhaps the wrong word for what *The Times* and the *Daily News* were requesting. They defined their efforts in terms of collection rather than authorship, and they justified protection based on the expense and coordination involved. As *The Times* put it, "We are collectors and importers of news" with "expensive agencies, offices, correspondences, credits, [and] lines of communication in all the principal cities and ports of the world." *The Times* described how it imported "articles," which then went through "processes of weeding, deciphering, interpreting, composing, and correcting" before expensive machinery was used to print them and make them available to the public. *The Times* acknowledged that "there are those who think that there ought to be no property in news, information, intelligence, ideas, or whatever can be comprehended by the mind," but its owners did not understand why standards should differ across genres. If novels were covered by copyright, why not foreign news? They called on the House of Commons to protect their investments against unfair competition.[62]

When the proposed copyright clause was debated in the Commons, Chancellor of the Exchequer Lewis defended it reluctantly. Lewis admitted that the republication of newspaper articles was a common practice even among the largest daily newspapers, "and it certainly would be a considerable detriment to the public at large if any attempt should now be made to abridge the rights thus conceded by practice."[63] But he did not think the leading newspapers would abuse the proposed copyright. They were subject to censure by the public and would lose customers if they acted in a way that restricted access to important news. In the debate that followed, a few MPs supported the general principle of a copyright for news, but most of the speakers objected to the proposed measure as unnecessary, impractical, or both. Gibson, who had chaired the 1851 committee and was prorepeal, did not see any "great army of pirates approaching" and said it would be unwise to create a remedy for a danger that may not exist.[64] Others pointed out that *The Times* was still thriving despite being copied, and they expressed faith that readers would continue to seek out the earliest source of news rather than buying cheap and derivative versions. Several speakers, including the government's own solicitor general, argued that the law would be unworkable. In many cases it would be difficult to establish the rightful owner of news, especially if the copyright encompassed the substance as well as the form. Echoing the fears expressed in newspaper editorials, some MPs worried that copyright would restrict the flow of intelligence. Benjamin Disraeli, then an MP for Buckinghamshire, stated that he felt a duty "to facilitate the communication of intelligence . . . so that the largest number of people in the country can become acquainted with it."[65] Finally, there was some objection to the idea that newspaper writings qualified for copyright at all. MP John Phillimore revealed a prejudice against "ephemeral" texts when he defined the newspaper as "an ephemeris—an insect of the day—which, having performed all its functions, in a few hours disappeared. It could not for a moment be put on the footing of great works—such as those of poets, orators, and historians."[66] Other speakers agreed, highlighting a distinction between newspapers and works of more "durable" interest. Lord Stanley said that copyright was appropriate for "original compositions" in newspapers but not for "the mere circumstances of making public a fact which had already taken place."[67]

The Times and the *Daily News* were fighting a losing battle. The *Era*, a Sunday paper based in London, explained that "the copyright clause met with so much opposition on both sides of the House that the Chancellor of the Exchequer withdrew it."[68] The *Examiner*, another London weekly, observed that the proposal had exposed fears of "oppression" and "monopoly" that could not be ignored, and that it would have been nearly impossible to prove piracy in cases in which the substance of the news was taken rather than the form. "A large portion of the contents of the principal daily papers, then, is found to be of the kind which it is impossible to fence round by enactments. Parliamentary debates, police reports, foreign intelligence, by a little skill in the re-setting, can all be presented in a form that would defy the rigid and jealous rules of legal evidence."[69] In other words, it might be possible to use copyright to stop the verbatim copying of news articles—an idea that had not yet been tested in the courts—but there was no way to prohibit others from presenting the same news in a different form.

THE NEWS INDUSTRY TRANSFORMED

In the summer of 1855, the hated stamp duty was abolished, and the stamp became an optional charge for postage. There was no provision for newspaper copyright, and yet concerns about piracy subsided quickly. Newspapers continued to copy from each other, and there were occasional complaints about the appropriation of news without acknowledgment, but the idea of a special copyright for news was largely forgotten.[70] Some of the cheap new publications launched after 1855 prided themselves on the fact that they did not copy. The *Birmingham Daily Post*, which began publication in 1857, defended the new penny papers against false assumptions when it declared, "Not only do [the penny papers] not pilfer their articles or their news from the columns of their more expensive rivals, but they meet them on their own ground, and not unfrequently beat them at their own weapons, and surpass them in the promptitude and accuracy of their information."[71] By 1859 the *Morning Post* in London was able to state that the "honourable and meritorious exertions" of the cheap press showed that the copyright proposed back in 1855 had proven "altogether unnecessary."[72]

Still, the news service operated by the Electric Telegraph Company remained a threat for *The Times*. In the absence of copyright, that paper's owners struck a deal with the ETC. *The Times* would provide the ETC with privileged access to its news, including use of telegraphic dispatches received by the editors between printed editions. The ETC was permitted to sell *The Times*'s news to subscription newsrooms and provincial newspapers, but it was not allowed to transmit the news to any

paper published within thirty miles of London. In addition, the ETC
had to stop serving any paper that did not credit *The Times* or otherwise deviated from using the news in "the usual way in their own columns."[73] The contract thus gave *The Times* some means of controlling
how others used its news. But the deal also provided something that no
copyright law could: *The Times* enjoyed free transmission of its messages over the ETC's wires in England, Scotland, and Ireland. The official history of *The Times* states that this agreement served the newspaper well, because it significantly reduced the cost of receiving news by
telegraph.[74] But it did not last long. When Ricardo died in 1862, the ETC
took a more hostile approach to newspapers, eliminating discounts for
press messages and rescinding the special agreement with *The Times*.[75]

Meanwhile, growing frustration with the private telegraph companies fueled a movement in support of nationalization, which set in
motion a series of arrangements that transformed the news industry in
Britain. Frustrated by the high cost and lack of choice in news provided
by the private telegraph companies, provincial newspapers supported
the campaign to place the telegraph under the control of the post office. The abolition of the stamp duty enabled the creation of daily newspapers outside London, a trend that was given a major boost by the removal of the duties on paper in 1861. All told, seventy-eight new dailies
were founded between 1856 and 1870.[76] Provincial newspapers were eager to take advantage of the telegraph to provide their readers with the
freshest possible news. They supported nationalization because the existing arrangement severely limited their ability to compete on par with
the London newspapers. The telegraph companies did not lease wires
to newspapers, which therefore had to be satisfied with whatever reports the companies provided. Provincial newspapers argued that placing the telegraph under post office control would reduce costs, increase
efficiencies, and enable more people to benefit from the new means of
communication.[77]

Although London newspapers sometimes claimed that their provincial counterparts relied overwhelmingly on them, this was not the case.
Provincial newspapers could turn to the London press for foreign news

and reports of Parliament, but most London papers contained little news from other parts of Britain. To provide regional and national coverage, provincial newspapers had to rely on each other.[78] If each newspaper gathered its own news by telegraph, then competition would increase and the costs of producing a newspaper would rise. The solution that the provincial publishers devised was to form the Press Association (PA), a nonprofit cooperative agency owned by its members. London newspapers were deliberately excluded, since one of the main goals was to protect the interests of provincial newspapers against those of the London press. The PA was created in 1868, as legislation authorizing the nationalization of the telegraph was making its way through Parliament.[79] The cooperative arrangement had several advantages. Provincial newspapers shared the cost of collecting telegraph news and gained greater control over the kinds of reports they received. By excluding London papers, the PA was also able to treat them as clients, selling them the local and regional news collected by PA members. Similarly, the PA sold selected reports to the newsrooms, reserving other stories for newspaper publication. Finally, cooperation gave the PA bargaining power to negotiate better rates with Reuters for access to foreign news.[80]

When the post office took over the telegraph in 1870, the PA, Reuters, and the major London newspapers effectively divided up the market for news in Britain. The PA and Reuters signed an agreement, variations of which continued until 1925, when the two entities merged completely. The PA had the exclusive right to publish Reuters' news outside of London in exchange for the PA agreeing not to gather its own foreign news or to support any other agency that did. The PA also provided Reuters with local news collected by its members for redistribution outside the United Kingdom. This arrangement ensured that most provincial newspapers would join the PA, since membership included cheap access to foreign news. London newspapers also contracted with Reuters, but they paid a much higher rate than provincial newspapers enjoyed as a result of the PA's agreement with Reuters. The PA's competitor Central News, a for-profit agency, offered both domestic and foreign news but had to rely on its own foreign correspondents because the

PA had exclusive use of Reuters' news outside London. Another agency called Exchange Telegraph Company (Extel) specialized in the rapid dissemination of financial and sporting news.[81]

The end of the so-called taxes on knowledge combined with the nationalization of the telegraph and the organization of the PA transformed the media landscape in Britain. In hindsight, it is possible to see these changes as responsible for a decline in *The Times*'s circulation outside the southeast. *The Times* invested heavily in news gathering, including hiring foreign correspondents, and was unable to reduce its cover price below threepence, making it difficult to compete with the new provincial dailies selling for a penny. Although *The Times* remained an important newspaper because of the quality of its reporting, its circulation declined significantly from about 65,000 in 1861 to 49,000 in 1883 and 32,000 in 1904. The highest circulation figures were achieved by the Sunday papers—*Lloyd's Weekly Newspaper*, the *News of the World*, and *Reynolds's Weekly Newspaper*—which were selling about 100,000 copies each at midcentury. Among the London dailies, the first major beneficiary of repeal of the "taxes on knowledge" was the *Daily Telegraph*, a penny paper founded in 1855 that was claiming sales of nearly 250,000 by 1876. By the 1880s the *Standard* was rivaling the circulation of the *Daily Telegraph*, and the *Daily News* and *Daily Chronicle* were selling about 100,000 copies each, more than double the circulation of *The Times*.[82] *The Times* was also somewhat atypical in its content, containing more commercial and foreign news and less coverage of arts, theater, and literature than could be found in many London and provincial weeklies. Moreover, *The Times*, like many London dailies, contained relatively little news from other areas of the country. For all of these reasons, *The Times* and other London dailies were not national newspapers so much as metropolitan ones; provincial newspapers were both more numerous and more widely read than any single London daily.[83]

The changes of the 1850s and 1860s thus marked a turning point in the importance of the provincial press relative to that of London, and this helps to explain why newspapers became less vocal about piracy. London newspapers could not with any justice claim that provincial newspapers survived on copying since they had their own news-gathering association and a contract with Reuters. Provincial newspapers that joined the PA had decided that it was better for everyone to have access to the same news and share the cost of collecting it rather than to engage in ruinous competition. In this context, copyright for news had little relevance. Disputes between agencies did arise, however. On one occasion in 1883, the rivalry between the PA and Central News led to an accusation that the latter had used a Reuters dispatch as the basis for its own report, a provocation that caused Central News to sue the PA and Reuters for libel, but this was settled out of court.[84] Publishers that chose to patronize another agency, such as Central News, or to procure their own news could not complain of being unfairly excluded from the PA, since all provincial newspapers were free to join. Such would not be the case with the Associated Press in the United States, as explained in chapter 6.

CAN NEWSPAPERS BE PROTECTED BY COPYRIGHT?

The failure to achieve a special copyright law for telegraphic dispatches did not necessarily mean that the contents of newspapers were ineligible for copyright, but since the 1842 Copyright Act did not mention newspapers, there was considerable doubt about this. Yet quite a few newspapers were registered at Stationers' Hall starting in the early 1860s, after the duties on paper were lifted. The registration of stock and commodity price lists and sporting newspapers also became more common in the 1860s and 1870s. And as early as 1870, Reuters made an entry at Stationers' Hall in an attempt to secure copyright for its dispatches.[85] It remained unclear whether articles in newspapers, let alone telegraphic dispatches, could be protected by copyright. But the fact that some publishers registered titles and paid the required fee of five shillings reveals that they sought to benefit from the protections of the 1842 act in case of piracy.[86]

Anyone could register a work at Stationers' Hall, but only the courts could decide whether a copyright claim was valid.[87] In 1869, the *Field*, a paper that specialized in hunting news, sued the *Land and Water Journal* for republishing a hunting list without permission. The plaintiff argued that although the information in question—the name of each hunt, the hunting days, the names of the masters, the number of hounds, and so on—could be obtained by anyone who made the effort, it was a violation of copyright to reproduce such information from an existing publication.[88] Courts had upheld copyright protection for fact-based works such as directories.[89] The question was whether such a compilation could be protected if it appeared in a newspaper. The defense contended that newspapers were not appropriate subject matter for copyright, citing the preamble of the 1842 act, which sought to encourage the production of "literary works of lasting benefit to the world." In addition, the proprietor of the *Field* had not entered the work at Stationers' Hall, and registration was required to initiate legal action under the 1842 act. The judge was Vice Chancellor Sir Richard Malins. He held that a newspaper could not be considered a "book" as defined by the statute, and since newspapers were not mentioned in the clause relating to "periodical works," the legislature must have meant to exclude them. Nevertheless, Malins asserted that the proprietors of newspapers had a property in the articles that they paid for and that to rule otherwise would be "a monstrous state of law, repugnant to common sense and common honesty."[90] According to Malins, the proprietors of the *Land and Water Journal* had made an "unfair use" of the plaintiff's newspaper. If they wanted to publish hunting lists they had to rely on their own labor and resources to collect the information. Malins thus recognized a property in newspaper articles that were paid for but remained vague on the source of such property.[91]

Malins's decision created confusion because it suggested that newspapers deserved protection even though they were not mentioned in the statute and that because they were not books they did not need to be registered at Stationers' Hall. Uncertainty about whether newspapers were eligible for copyright, and if so whether they needed to be registered, continued for more than a decade after Malins's ruling. In 1878, a royal commission appointed to examine the general state of copyright law concluded that "some sort of copyright has been recognized in newspapers, but it is impossible to say what it is." The commission recommended that future legislation clarify rules for newspaper registration and explicitly state "what parts of a newspaper may be considered copyright, by distinguishing between announcements of facts and communications of a literary character."[92] In line with this recommendation, a copyright reform bill proposed in 1879 envisioned copyright for "compositions of a literary character" published in newspapers but not for news reports.[93]

Legislative reform of copyright remained deadlocked for several decades to come, but in 1881 a case brought by *The Times* did lead the Court of Chancery to issue a clearer ruling on newspaper registration. The proprietors of *The Times* sued the publishers of a pamphlet that had reprinted a biography of Benjamin Disraeli that first appeared in *The Times*. The plaintiffs cited the *Land and Water Journal* decision to argue that newspapers were protected regardless of registration. The case was heard by Master of the Rolls Sir George Jessel. He rejected Malins's earlier ruling as incorrect, since according to the 1842 act all works had to be registered before an infringement suit could be brought. According to Jessel, in order to enjoy exclusive rights in the Disraeli biography, the proprietors of *The Times* needed to do two things: register their newspaper at Stationers' Hall and show that they had obtained the copyright from the author of the biography. Jessel thought that newspapers could be considered "books" or "periodical works" for the purposes of copyright but that in either case they needed to be registered.[94]

Later court decisions confirmed that newspapers were eligible for copyright, but the requirement that proprietors show proof that they had paid for each article and obtained an assignment of rights from the author created practical difficulties. Any newspaper that wanted to claim copyright in individual contributions would have to systematically require its contributors to sign over their rights.[95] Moreover, the question of whether news reports were eligible for copyright remained unsettled. Should news reports be treated the same way as works of fiction, biography, history, or science that were published in newspapers? As it turned out, the question of how to treat different genres of newspaper writing was addressed in the context of international copyright treaties before it was considered by British courts.

CAN NEWS BE PROTECTED BY COPYRIGHT?

The 1852 International Copyright Act, which integrated the recent Anglo-French copyright convention into British law, was not primarily concerned with newspapers—the goal was to establish reciprocal rights for British and French authors—but it did contain a provision for articles in newspapers and periodicals. According to this provision, "any article of political discussion" appearing in a foreign newspaper or periodical could be republished in the United Kingdom, either in the original language or in translation, so long as the original source was acknowledged. For articles on subjects other than politics, authors and publishers were allowed to reserve publication but only if they attached a copyright notice to the articles themselves. Any articles for which rights were not explicitly reserved could be reproduced without permission.[96]

This provision provided a model for the first multilateral copyright agreement, the Berne Convention for the Protection of Literary and Artistic Works (1886 and subsequent revisions). The initial agreement in 1886 was signed by Belgium, France, Germany, Great Britain, Haiti, Italy, Liberia, Switzerland, and Tunisia. Like the 1852 law in Britain just discussed, the text adopted at Berne in 1886 included specific rules for articles in newspapers and periodicals. The Haitian delegate, Louis-Joseph Javier, argued that a broad right to reproduce material from foreign newspapers and periodicals would allow knowledge to circulate internationally. Haiti's 1885 copyright law explicitly permitted the reproduction of articles from the foreign press. The British delegation also supported the idea of adopting a general rule rather than a complicated list of exceptions depending on the genre or subject of the articles in question.[97] Ultimately, it was decided that all articles published in foreign newspapers and periodicals could be reproduced, in the original language or in translation, unless accompanied by a notice explicitly prohibiting reuse. It was thus possible to reserve the right to republish material from newspapers and periodicals in other signatory countries, and a general notice at the head of the issue sufficed. Crucially, however, it was not possible to prohibit others from reproducing "articles of political discussion," "news of the day," or "current topics" (*fait di-*

vers in the original French).[98] News and political commentary were thus explicitly denied protection in the first major international copyright agreement.

Some newspaper editors and publishers expressed disappointment that the Berne Convention did not protect what they saw as their most valuable asset—breaking news. The International Congress of the Press (ICP), formed in 1894, discussed this issue at several of its early meetings. Some delegates urged for the need to recognize an exclusive right to news reports for a set number of hours after publication. Yet not everyone agreed with the premise that a newspaper's value to readers depended on the speed with which it reported events, and even those that did agree could not settle on a definition of what exactly should be protected. Many continued to insist that news should be open to copying so long as the source was cited. Ultimately, the ICP rejected the idea of international copyright for news because it might hinder the dissemination of important information. Instead, the group recommended treating unauthorized republication as unfair competition, leaving it to the national courts to decide on a case-by-case basis.[99]

When the Berne Convention was revised in Paris in 1896, the rules for articles in newspapers and periodicals became more genre specific. Haiti did not send a delegate, and this might have been a factor. Under the revised agreement, serial novels appearing in newspapers or periodicals could never be reproduced without permission, but other articles could be translated or republished in the original language unless they were accompanied by a notice reserving rights. In the absence of such a notice, reuse was allowed as long as the source was indicated. But once again, publishers were not allowed to prohibit republication of "articles of political discussion," "news of the day," or "current topics" [*fait divers*].[100] The Berne Convention was revised again in Berlin in 1908, when it was decided that publishers could reserve rights in newspaper articles on any subject except for "news of the day" and "miscellaneous news [*fait divers*] having the character merely of press information."[101] The removal of the exception for "articles of political discussion" and the restriction of the exception for *fait divers* to items of mere "press information" reduced the range of newspaper material that could be copied and translated without permission. But the point remains that in negotiations over international copyright, a distinction was being drawn between news and other kinds of literary and artistic material in newspapers and periodicals.[102] The current version of the Berne Convention continues to exclude "news of the day" and "miscellaneous facts having the character of mere items of press information" from protection internationally.[103] (Countries that adhere to Berne remain free to adopt national legislation covering these categories.)

Why was news excluded from the main international copyright agreement, and what did such an exclusion mean for those who sought to protect news articles internationally? Unfortunately, the records of the 1886 and 1896 conferences do not provide any clues. But the committee report from the 1908 conference suggests that "news of the day" was excluded not on the grounds of public policy—such as the desire for news to circulate freely—but because delegates saw it as being outside the scope of literary and artistic copyright. Indeed, the committee mentioned that news could conceivably be protected by other means—such as by laws relating to unfair competition—but that news was inappropriate subject matter for copyright.[104]

Some newspaper editors in Britain found the Berne Convention's original 1886 provisions for newspapers and periodicals to be wise. The *Birmingham Daily Post,* for example, celebrated that the agreement would "permit the reproduction of matter which is of immediate interest to the public at large, and allow the right to be reserved, by special announcement, in the case of articles which are in the nature of essays." The writer for the Birmingham paper did not think protection would be sought for most newspaper material because "the utility of the newspaper press depends in great degree on the freedom with which various publications extract matter from each other."[105] In 1888, when the widow of Emperor Frederick of Germany threatened to sue British and French newspapers that reproduced Frederick's diary—it had first appeared in a German newspaper without authorization—the *Pall Mall Gazette* reprinted it in full, citing the Berne Convention.[106]

PROTECTING THE FORM OF NEWS:
WALTER V. STEINKOPFF

When it came to republishing newspaper articles within Britain, the views of editors and publishers were more divided. At the end of the nineteenth century, the leading proponent of a copyright in news articles was Charles Frederick Moberly Bell, manager of *The Times*. In cooperation with the Walter family, the main proprietors of *The Times*, Bell spearheaded a series of lawsuits and lobbied for new legislation in an attempt to expand the scope of copyright protection for news. In *Walter v. Steinkopff* (1892), *The Times* sued an evening paper called the *St. James's Gazette* for reprinting part of a copyrighted story by Rudyard Kipling and several news paragraphs from *The Times* of the same morning. The Walters made sure to register this issue of the newspaper before commencing legal action.[107] The *St. James's Gazette* had copied two-fifths of the Kipling story as well as twenty-two news paragraphs taken largely verbatim from *The Times*. But the case centered on only three of these paragraphs, since these were the ones for which *The Times* could prove that the author had been paid and that the paragraphs had been composed with the understanding that the copyright would belong to *The Times*. On behalf of the other proprietors, Arthur Fraser Walter asserted that *The Times*'s foreign correspondents were "gentlemen of proved literary skill" who were carefully selected and well paid.[108] The plaintiffs recognized that it might seem trivial to mention the news paragraphs but claimed that the copying by the *St. James's Gazette* was "part of a system which is of serious injury" to *The Times*, justifying the intervention of the court.[109] The goal was to establish the principle that permission was required to republish news articles.

The proprietor of the *St. James's Gazette*, Edward Steinkopff, admitted fault with respect to the Kipling story and was willing to pay the costs of the suit if *The Times* dropped the charges relating to the news paragraphs. According to counsel for the *St. James's Gazette*, news was too "trivial" and "ephemeral" to be the subject of copyright.[110] Furthermore, they argued that there was a tacit convention whereby newspapers recognized the right to republish articles as long as credit was given.

Whereas Bell and the Walter family sought judicial confirmation of copyright for news articles, Steinkopff and his staff sought recognition of an established journalistic custom of copying. Sidney Low, the editor of the *St. James's Gazette*, described this custom as a "well-recognized rule in journalism, and one upon which *The Times* itself has frequently acted." According to Low, newspaper editors understood that copying was allowed as long as four conditions were met: (1) the source newspaper was acknowledged; (2) the publications were not direct competitors, by which he meant two papers published at roughly the same time (morning or evening) in the same city; (3) the source newspaper had copied in the past, "implying that it agrees to a free interchange of literary and other matter"; and (4) the editor of the source newspaper had not explicitly objected to material being taken from his paper.[111]

Low's claims about the tacit conventions of journalism were supported by affidavits from two of the subeditors of the *St. James's Gazette*. One of them had thirty years of experience working for various newspapers, and the other had twenty. They insisted that it had always been customary for newspapers to copy from each other and that they had never heard any objection to their paper's use of material from *The Times* until the present lawsuit.[112] To bolster their case, the *St. James's Gazette* arranged for additional affidavits to be submitted by the editors, managers, and proprietors of several evening and weekly newspapers. All of them swore that, for as long as they had been in the business, evening newspapers had taken material from morning newspapers and that this practice was considered acceptable as long as the source was acknowledged.[113] *The Times*'s proprietors replied that they had never acquiesced to such a custom and that it was no longer correct to assume that morning newspapers and evening newspapers were not competitors. Arthur Fraser Walter acknowledged that evening papers had often copied from morning papers in the past and that he had little reason to complain so long as these papers appeared relatively late in the day. Recently, however, several evening papers were issuing editions as early as 10:00 or 10:30 a.m., before the second edition of *The Times* went out to customers at about 1:00 p.m. Walter explained that *The Times* was taking legal action now because the evening papers were making "more copious extracts than formerly," and they were using this news to compete more directly with morning papers. He also pointed out that the *St. James's Gazette* had been registered at Stationers' Hall in 1888 (the year Steinkopff took it over), a claim of ownership that seemed to be at odds with the custom of copying now being defended by Steinkopff's own editors.[114]

The case was heard in the Court of Chancery by Sir Ford North, who found no compelling evidence that *The Times* had acquiesced to a "custom" of journalistic copying. Moreover, North ruled that even if such a custom existed, it could not override the copyright statute. Citing the source would show that there was no intention to pass off an existing work as one's own, but it did not eliminate the need to obtain permission from the copyright owner. North cited two earlier cases in which defendants had unsuccessfully referred to trade customs to justify copying from other periodicals. In both cases, the court ruled that such customs, however widespread, did not excuse violations of the copyright law enacted by the legislature.[115]

The most important aspect of North's decision was that it articulated, more clearly than had any previous judicial opinion, the distinction between copyrightable expressions and uncopyrightable information. During the hearing, North pushed the plaintiffs on what they thought copyright should protect. If *The Times* published a telegram announcing the death of a foreign leader, would other papers be prohibited from publishing the same news unless they obtained their own telegram? After some back and forth, counsel for *The Times* was willing to concede that other papers could not copy *The Times*'s report verbatim but that they could restate the facts.[116] North explained this principle fairly clearly: "It is said there is no copyright in news. But there is or may be copyright in the particular forms of language or modes of expression by which information is conveyed, and not the less so because the information may be with respect to the current events of the day."[117] The final court order recognized that the plaintiffs were "entitled to the copyright of and in the cablegrams, telegrams or communications" referred to in their complaint.[118] Although Bell and the Walters won in principle, North refused to grant an injunction for the three news paragraphs on the grounds that interest in them had passed and the *St. James's Gazette* was not likely to print them again. He also rebuked the plaintiffs for bringing a lawsuit without having previously asked the editor of the *St. James's Gazette* to stop copying.[119] In doing so, North essentially acknowledged that copying had been widespread for many years and that *The Times* was trying to use the law to impose a new custom in which copying was not allowed.

Despite North's criticisms, *The Times* celebrated the decision. An editorial, which was probably written by Bell, declared that "it has now been authoritatively laid down that the protection of literary products by copyright law extends fully over articles and news published in a newspaper."[120] North had distinguished between information and the form in which it was conveyed. By contrast, the editorial in *The Times* distinguished between events and news of events, insisting that news was already the product of labor and skill. As the editorial put it, "News is not a spontaneous product; it does not make itself; it is not found ready made. It is a creation of man's industry, and bears the same relation to facts and events that a manufactured article does to raw material. Facts by themselves are not news. They have to be converted into news by the process of speaking or writing." Bell and the Walters did not welcome the idea that others were free to reformulate their news. If *The Times* had incurred the expense of a foreign correspondent and that correspondent provided the only news from a given place, then "this news is its property, and its own creation."[121]

Commentators in the press could not agree on how the decision in *Walter v. Steinkopff* might affect newspapers. An editorial in the *Daily News* doubted that it would be possible to prohibit republication of news because it was in the very nature of news to be shared and excerpted. "In clubs, in exchanges, in various places of general resort," the *Daily News* declared, "summaries or detached sentences of articles are posted up for universal information."[122] The *Belfast News Letter* speculated that the decision would lead to "a great revolution in the matter of copying from the newspaper Press" because evening papers would now have to be more careful to reformulate news taken from morning papers.[123] An editorial in the *Pall Mall Gazette* found the decision inconclusive, revealing the need to settle the newspaper copyright question by statute. In the meantime, newspapers were advised to clearly mark any articles they wanted to remain exclusive. Setting an example, the *Pall Mall Gazette* announced "to all whom it may concern, in the provinces, the colonies, and elsewhere, that we have no objection to quotations from our columns, if the source of the quotation is given, except in cases where we may signify to the contrary, in the manner required by the Berne Convention."[124] (It should be remembered, however, that the Berne Convention excluded protection for "news of the day" internationally, whereas North's decision in *Walter v. Steinkopff* held that the form of news could be protected by copyright in Britain.)

Some British newspapers and agencies became more assertive about protecting their reports in the 1890s and early 1900s, attaching copyright notices to special items of foreign news. The desire for exclusivity increased in this period due to greater use of the telegraph to procure news from abroad, especially during imperial conflicts such as the First and Second Boer Wars (1880–1881 and 1899–1902) in South Africa. Moreover, the level playing field promoted by a post office–run telegraph with low rates for press messages was undermined by allowing newspapers to rent private wires. The leasing of private wires increased competition among newspapers, and it enabled those who were not paying for news from Reuters, for example, to copy reports from London papers and send them to the provinces to be printed.[125] In an attempt to secure copyright for its reports, Reuters printed selected telegrams in a daily publication called *Reuter's Journal*, which was entered at Stationers' Hall and made available for purchase. The hope was that this additional expense would bring its telegrams within the bounds of the copyright statute. Extel did something similar in an attempt to protect price quotations obtained through an exclusive contract with the London Stock Exchange. Extel sent the quotations by telegraph to subscribers, who accessed them through ticker machines installed in their offices. Because it was doubtful that the ticker tapes would qualify for copyright, Extel produced a typewritten publication called *Exchange Telegraph Company's Stock Exchange News*. This was also registered at Stationers' Hall.[126]

In 1895, a court recognized Extel's copyright. A broker named George Gregory subscribed to Extel's quotation service until 1894, when the Stock Exchange Committee required Extel to stop serving brokers who were not official members of the Stock Exchange. Since he was no longer able to subscribe, Gregory obtained the quotes surreptitiously from one of Extel's legitimate clients. (Subscribers were prohibited by contract from sharing the information with outsiders). Gregory argued that he had not violated copyright law because he obtained the price quotes from the ticker and not from the newspaper that was registered at Stationers' Hall. He also insisted that there could be no copyright in stock quotations. Counsel for Extel argued that on some occasions Gregory copied the information after Extel's typewritten newspaper was published, in which case he violated copyright, and that on other occasions he obtained the quotations before the newspaper was issued, thereby violating common-law property rights in the information. The court recognized that Extel was entitled to an injunction on both of these grounds. In the process, it affirmed that it was possible to copyright stock quotations. As one of the judges put it, "The written matter in the present case is, in my view, literature within the decided cases. It was the property of the plaintiffs before its publication in the newspaper, and after that publication they were entitled to copyright."[127] The fact that Gregory had taken the information surreptitiously, inducing a breach of confidence between Extel and one of its legitimate clients, clearly placed him in a bad light, making it hard to imagine any other outcome.[128]

BELL'S CRUSADE

The Times, which invested heavily in its own correspondents and relied less on Reuters than other newspapers did, was dissatisfied with copyright law for two reasons: the normal procedures for obtaining an injunction were too slow for news, and copyright was now understood to exclude protection for facts. For Bell, the manager of The Times, the decision in Walter v. Steinkopff confirmed both of these problems. Bell advocated summary proceedings leading to damages and penalties for infringement. He argued that such a process would dissuade newspapers from copying without permission. He also believed, like Frederick Knight Hunt had back in the 1850s, that the substance of news, not just the language in which it was expressed, should be protected. Bell made both of these arguments when he appeared as a witness before a Select Committee of the House of Lords in 1898. A comprehensive reform of copyright law was again on the agenda, and this time a bill being considered included a clause whereby "copyright in respect of a newspaper shall apply only to such parts of the newspaper as are compositions of an original literary character, to original illustrations therein, and to such news and information as have been specially and independently obtained."[129] By including protection for "news and information," this clause went beyond the recommendations of the Royal Copyright Commission of 1878, which had recommended copyright for literary contributions but not for "announcements of facts."[130] It also departed from the 1896 revision of the Berne Convention, which excluded "articles of political discussion," "news of the day," and "current topics."[131]

These disparities were noticed by members of the 1898 Select Committee. They pushed witnesses to explain exactly what it would mean to have copyright in news. Farrer Herschell, a lawyer who had previously served as solicitor general and lord chancellor, took the lead in these examinations. He stressed that copyright had always been limited to protecting the "form of expression" and that there was no copyright in ideas.[132] Witnesses who spoke in favor of the clause, such as the publisher John Murray; Frederic Richard Daldy, the secretary of the Copyright Association; and Bell of *The Times*, struggled to convince the committee that the substance of news should be treated as exclusive. They claimed that the goal was to protect newspapers' investments in foreign correspondents and that publishers would not monopolize facts. But when the committee pressed these witnesses to consider specific examples—such as a revolution in Mexico or the death of a world leader—their answers suggested that they envisioned copyright as a means to stop others from reporting any news that they had not obtained independently.[133]

The basic principle that Bell sought to establish was that each newspaper had to collect its own news. In support of his argument, he used the analogy of directories. The names of shops were facts that anybody was free to collect and publish, but courts had determined that others were not free to copy those facts from an existing directory. He wanted newspapers to be bound by the same principle. Any newspaper that made special arrangements—such as sending a correspondent abroad to cable news back to Britain—should have a limited copyright (he suggested twenty-four hours) that would dissuade others from copying. Other newspapers could obtain permission to reproduce this news for a fee. But Bell thought that such arrangements would be infrequent and that the main effect of the law would be to encourage more newspapers to gather their own news, leading to a greater diversity of coverage.[134]

In response to concerns that copyright could restrict the flow of news, Bell, Daldy, and others struggled to distinguish between the fact of an occurrence and the news of that fact. When pressed as to whether the "mere fact" of an event was protected, Daldy answered that the current law already protected "descriptions of anything more than the bare fact" and that the point of the proposed clause was to provide additional protection beyond that. When Bell was asked on what basis he would justify a copyright in news, he responded, "There is an enormous difference between the fact and news of the fact." When asked to define news for the purposes of copyright, he stated, "News would be the expression or the transmission of a fact."[135] Bell insisted that his goal was not to obtain exclusive use of a given set of facts, just the right to stop competitors from copying the facts collected by his newspaper. If they wanted to report the same facts, they should have to collect them independently.

The members of the Select Committee found this difficult to accept. Herschell raised the analogy of scientific discoveries. A chemist who was the first to ascertain a particular fact could have a copyright in his report of the discovery but not in the fact itself. Bell conceded that copyright could not be used to require other scientists to perform independent research before stating a fact. But he did not see Herschell's analogy as relevant, "because the newspaper does not claim any copyright in the fact, but in its publication of it."[136] The committee reminded him that verbatim copying was already prohibited by the current legislation, especially in light of *Walter v. Steinkopff*, but Bell insisted that this protection was practically useless. He cited the Tasmanian Newspaper Copyright Act of 1891 as a model, although he thought twenty-four hours would provide sufficient protection rather than forty-eight hours, as in Tasmania. By allowing for summary proceedings and specifying a remedy of damages and penalties rather than an injunction, Bell thought that such a law could be used to dissuade newspapers from copying and to encourage them to do more independent reporting. Although the bill being considered by the Select Committee in 1898 did not propose these remedies, Bell still thought it was a move in the right direction.[137] But the committee adjourned without coming to a conclusion about the 1898 bill.[138]

For a number of reasons, copyright reform in the years around 1900 was a convoluted process, but thanks to Bell, the question of news remained on the agenda as further bills were considered. A bill introduced in the House of Lords in 1899 provided for twelve hours of protection for newspaper articles. Herbert de Reuter, head of the news agency that bore his name, joined Bell in supporting the bill, in part because a special clause for news would relieve Reuters of the "considerable annual expenditure" of printing *Reuter's Journal* in an effort to secure copyright for its telegrams. Yet he suggested that twelve hours of protection would not be sufficient and that twenty-four would be better.[139] As they had back in the 1850s, provincial newspapers opposed the whole idea. Henry Whorlow, secretary of the Newspaper Society and of the Press Association (PA), told the Select Committee in the Lords that Bell's and Reuter's views were far from representative. Based on a survey sent to all 369 members of the Newspaper Society, Whorlow concluded that most newspaper proprietors found the existing copyright law to be adequate and feared that the special protection being proposed would "revolutionize the practice of journalism" in a way that would harm the public.[140]

Whorlow dismissed the argument that provincial newspapers copied their most valuable news from London newspapers. Several of the morning papers in Birmingham, Liverpool, Manchester, and Glasgow spent as much as any London newspaper—with the exception of *The*

Times—to procure foreign intelligence. The other provincial papers were almost all members of the PA, which meant that they paid to receive news from Reuters. The early editions of these newspapers consisted almost entirely of news procured through the PA or by the paper's own staff. Whorlow admitted that many papers had "town editions" that came out around 9:00 a.m. and that these contained extracts and summaries from London newspapers. He claimed that such news was generally credited and used with the "tacit approval" of the London newspapers. It was largely this custom that Whorlow and the provincial newspaper proprietors he represented sought to continue. An explicit copyright covering the substance of news would put an end to what he called the "system of interchange" that guaranteed "the free flow of information."[141]

The perspective of individual journalists was not considered by the Select Committee, a fact that was regretted by members of the Institute of Journalists when they gathered for their annual meeting in Liverpool in the summer of 1899. Delegates agreed with the justice of protecting investments in news gathering but suggested that piracy was not limited to the realm of telegraph news. Local and regional newspapers had staffs of reporters whose work was subject to "robbery" by other publications. Some members of the Institute of Journalists argued that individual reporters had the right to have their work protected, and they regretted that the current bill did not contain any provisions along these lines.[142]

Despite the objections of provincial proprietors and journalists, the Select Committee in the Lords endorsed the kind of copyright advocated by Bell and Reuter. The committee's report recommended a duration of eighteen hours, a compromise between the twelve hours initially proposed and the twenty-four hours desired by Bell and Reuter.[143] The copyright bill was modified and proposed again in 1900, and this one also envisioned protection for news. Newspapers and agencies that "obtained specially and independently news of any fact or event which has taken place beyond the limits of the United Kingdom" would have the exclusive right to publish it within the United Kingdom for eighteen hours. Protection extended to the factual details of the news. In cases in which two or more organizations had independently collected news of the same fact or event, they had equal rights against anyone who infringed, but all such rights were to cease eighteen hours after first publication of the news.[144] The 1900 bill was passed by the Lords but not the Commons. The news clause was hardly responsible for this failure, which was due to the persistent difficulty of reaching a consensus on copyright reform at the turn of the century.[145]

REPORTERS AS AUTHORS

Bell and *The Times* did obtain an important legal victory in *Walter v. Lane,* a case that went all the way to the House of Lords in 1900. The decision in *Walter v. Steinkopff* (1892) had shown that the form of news articles could be protected by copyright, but there was still a question about reports of public speeches. Was there any way to stop other newspapers or book publishers from reproducing accounts that *The Times* had paid a reporter to take down and prepare for the press? To answer this question, the Walter family sued the publisher John Lane for issuing a book containing five speeches by the liberal politician Lord Rosebery that had first appeared in *The Times*. These speeches had not been given in Parliament but in other public settings. Still, *The Times*'s proprietors sought a ruling that would enable them to control subsequent publication of work by their reporters covering Parliament and other public meetings, thereby placing newspaper syndication on a firmer footing.[146]

Walter v. Lane departed from the usual rivalries between London and provincial newspapers or between morning and evening papers by pitting a newspaper against a book publisher. In fact, another book publisher had previously issued an edition of Rosebery's speeches after asking permission from *The Times*. Lane had contacted Rosebery but not *The Times*, and Bell and the Walters wanted to establish that their permission was required. Rosebery in fact objected to the republication of his speeches on the grounds that they represented thoughts expressed spontaneously and should not be treated as anything other than "fleeting and transitory." But Rosebery also thought that he did not have any legal right to stop Lane or anyone else from publishing speeches that he delivered in public with reporters present. Most of all, Rosebery wanted to avoid being in the middle of a public lawsuit, and he pleaded in vain for Bell to drop the suit against Lane.[147]

The case came before Sir Ford North, the same judge who had decided *Walter v. Steinkopff*. North determined that Rosebery had abandoned his own rights over the speeches. A statute passed in 1835 theoretically gave lecturers the exclusive right to print or publish their speeches, but only if they gave prior notice to two magistrates near the place of the lecture. Rosebery had not done this, and in any case, lectures given in public institutions such as schools and universities were excluded from protection under the 1835 statute.[148] According to North, Rosebery had abandoned his rights, and the main question was whether *The Times* had a statutory copyright in its versions of the speeches. The court was presented with evidence that accounts of the same speech by different reporters showed variations in punctuation, diction, and phraseology. These variations supported *The Times*'s claim that skill and judgment were required to transform spoken utterances into printed accounts. North held that *The Times*'s copyright in Lord Rosebery's speeches was valid, and he issued an injunction prohibiting further sale of Lane's book.[149]

Lane appealed the decision. He was supported by the Publishers' Association and represented by two prominent authorities on copyright, T. E. Scrutton and Augustine Birrell. They argued that the skill employed by reporters was not "literary" but "mechanical" because reporters used shorthand to produce verbatim transcripts. If anyone was the author of the speeches, it was Rosebery, and *The Times* had not secured any rights from him. The Court of Appeal found these arguments compelling and reversed North's judgment. But Lane's victory was short-lived, for *The Times* appealed to the House of Lords, which was at that time the highest court of appeal. Birrell and Scrutton argued that the copyright statute applied only to "original compositions" and that the reporters of verbatim transcripts did not produce anything new. But several of the lords noted that the phrase "original composition" did not appear in the copyright statute and that there was no explicit requirement that a work must exhibit "literary merit" or "originality" of thought or language.[150] The lords concurred with the idea that skill and labor employed by reporters was sufficient to qualify them as authors for the purpose of copyright, even if their goal was to present speeches as accurately as possible. Indeed, some reporters were bound to be better at this than were others. Each reporter could therefore enjoy a copyright in his version of a speech, and this copyright could be transferred to a newspaper. The House of Lords reversed the decision of the Court of Appeal and awarded *The Times* a perpetual injunction against Lane's book.[151]

There was some comment in the press and among legal commentators that the House of Lords went too far in equating reporters with authors, but it was a clear victory for Bell and *The Times*. Any newspaper article that had been paid for and done with the understanding that the copyright belonged to the proprietor could now be protected by copyright. But *Walter v. Lane*, which stemmed from *The Times's* long-standing interest in being able to stop others from copying, had effects far beyond the realm of news. The low threshold for authorship advanced by the House of Lords—that copyright was justified by skill and labor rather than literary merit—became an important precedent in British law. The historical context of the case should not be forgotten: the low threshold for authorship was justified by the observation that reporters' versions of the same speech could be different. Their reporting involved skill and judgment, and if they had not performed this work, then the public of 1900, which did not have the benefit of recorded sound transmitted directly by radio or television, would not have had access to speeches in Parliament.[152]

Despite the rhetoric about reporters as authors, *Walter v. Lane* had nothing to say about the rights of newspaper contributors vis-à-vis proprietors. The reporters covering Rosebery's speeches had all signed their rights over to *The Times*. The situation was more complicated for freelance writers, as a court decision in 1903 revealed. The case involved a story about the near drowning of a prominent ophthalmologist. Having witnessed this event, a journalist named George Springfield composed a story titled "Doctor's Wonderful Escape" and sent it to several London papers, including the *Daily Mail* and the *Standard*. The *Daily Mail* published the story in exchange for payment but only after a subeditor condensed Springfield's account from eighty-three lines to eighteen lines and another "touched up" the text further. Later the same day, the *Daily Mail*'s version appeared in the *Evening Standard* with slight alterations. Springfield approached the *Evening Standard*, which initially refused to pay him. Eventually the *Evening Standard* offered Springfield payment, but by that time he had registered his article at Stationers' Hall and contacted the Institute of Journalists. The Institute saw Springfield's case as an opportunity to establish the principle that newspapers could not copy paragraphs from other papers without paying the writer who first composed them. Springfield therefore returned the payment offered by the *Evening Standard* and sued its publisher for copyright infringement.[153]

The strategy of the defense was to argue that Springfield should not be considered the author of the article that was published in the *Daily Mail* and then copied into the *Evening Standard*. As a result of the changes made by the first paper's subeditor, Springfield's contribution appeared "in a form so materially abridged and altered by the said editor as to constitute a new article."[154] In the hearing before the judge, counsel for the *Evening Standard*—the legal team again included Scrutton—cited North's ruling in *Walter v. Steinkopff* that only the form of news could be protected, not the underlying factual details. Springfield contributed the factual details, but it was the subeditors who shaped them into a new article, and so they should be considered the authors. Springfield's counsel responded that treating subeditors as the authors of the articles they revised would mean that "an outside contributor would never have any rights, since contributions are always adapted and rearranged."[155] Ultimately, the judge found that the published version was different enough from Springfield's original to disqualify him from being considered the author and hence the copyright owner. Springfield's suit was dismissed, and he was ordered to pay costs. His defeat showed how copyright law's emphasis on language and form could be turned against freelance writers whose work was heavily edited before publication.

NEWSPAPERS AND THE 1911 COPYRIGHT ACT

Comprehensive reform of copyright became more pressing following the Berlin revision of the Berne Convention in 1908, because British law was inconsistent with the amended agreement. The government moved forward with copyright reform in 1911, but explicit protection for news was no longer on the agenda. In fact, a bill introduced by Sydney Buxton, the president of the Board of Trade, contained a provision allowing newspaper articles to be reproduced as long as the source was credited, unless the original article appeared with a notice prohibiting republication. Not surprisingly, Bell was outraged. He began writing a letter to Buxton condemning this clause, but he died before he could finish it. Bell literally died defending newspaper copyright.[156]

In the end, however, the clause that infuriated Bell was dropped, and the 1911 act recognized copyright in newspapers and in contributions to them. But the new law did not protect the factual details of news as Bell and others before him had advocated. There was a work-for-hire clause by which works made by an employee automatically belonged to the employer unless otherwise stipulated by contract, but this did not apply to articles in newspapers, magazines, and other periodicals. In the absence of some other agreement, contributors retained the right to restrain further publication of their articles after their first appearance in a newspaper or periodical. This clause meant that publishers who wanted to be able to license articles to other newspapers or republish them separately had to first ask contributors to sign over their rights.[157] *The Times* developed a clever solution to this problem: it created special checks for contributors that contained a copyright assignment on them. When contributors endorsed their checks, they also signed the copyright over to *The Times*, thereby giving the proprietors written proof that they had obtained the rights from the author in exchange for payment. Taking advantage of copyright thus required newspapers to develop new business practices.[158]

The 1911 act contained several provisions that were welcomed by newspapers. First, a "fair dealing" clause made it possible to reproduce parts of works for the purposes of research, criticism, review, or "newspaper summary." In the case of public lectures, newspapers were allowed to publish full reports unless the lecturer had specifically reserved the right of publication, and even in those cases, newspapers were still allowed to provide summaries. There was also an exception for political speeches delivered at public meetings, which could always be reported in the newspapers.[159] But there was no provision to protect "news and information," even for a few hours.

The fact that efforts by Hunt, Bell, and others to enact a special copyright for news failed in the United Kingdom was not inevitable. Indeed, laws protecting news were passed in a number of British colonies in Australia, Asia, Africa, and the Middle East. These laws were adapted to the specific challenges of importing and retailing news in distant colonies. They tended to serve the interests of not only Reuters but also the local English-language publishers and agencies that partnered with Reuters.[160] The situation in Britain was very different because of the number and variety of newspapers and of long-held views about press freedom and the circulation of news. The decades-long struggle to remove the "taxes on knowledge" made it much harder to defend exclusive rights in news. After 1886 such rights would have also been against the spirit of the Berne Convention, although signatory countries remained free to protect news within their borders. The decision in *Walter v. Steinkopff* recognized copyright in news articles but also clarified that copyright did not extend to the substance of news, only its form.

The incentives-based argument in favor of copyright for news, which was articulated as early as the 1830s and elaborated in subsequent periods, repeatedly encountered the objection that such a right would restrict the flow of information of public concern. If not for this resistance, copyright might have expanded much further than it did by coming to protect factual details as well as expressions, at least in the case of news. These efforts also reveal how both proponents and opponents frequently insisted that news was different than other genres of writing, including other genres featured in newspapers. Cultural and political attitudes toward news thus helped to determine the acceptable boundaries of copyright. The kind of right sought by Hunt and Bell was ultimately recognized in the realm of unfair-competition law in the United States, but only after American news publishers engaged in their own struggle to incorporate news into copyright law. The shifts in the American news business that underpinned these efforts and led to the conception of a different kind of property right in news are the subject of the next chapter.

Press Associations and the Quest
for Exclusivity in the United States

EFFORTS TO CREATE a special copyright law for news in the United States did not begin until the 1880s, almost fifty years later than in Britain. The circumstances and rationale were very different. In Britain, the reduction and repeal of the stamp duty motivated the first efforts to secure copyright for news. American newspapers had never been taxed, and their distribution through the mail had long been subsidized, a policy that encouraged copying. Although editors expressed interest in receiving "credit" for copied news and sometimes retaliated against those who did not provide proper credit, they did not seek legal protection. Instead, they argued for shared protocols of citation and acknowledgment that would allow news to circulate while boosting the reputations of the most enterprising newspapers. The spread of the telegraph beginning in the mid-1840s made the exchange system more problematic. Due in part to the high cost of telegraph transmission, complaints about misattribution and failure to credit became more frequent, and copying was increasingly described as "stealing." But most editors continued to suggest that copying was acceptable as long as credit was given.

Interest in receiving credit and the expense of telegraph transmission were not by themselves enough to make newspapers seek copyright protection. Instead, the quest for exclusivity was motivated by a gradual but fundamental shift in relationships among newspapers. Beginning around 1850, the networks of editors and contributors that had characterized newspapers in the early nineteenth century gave way to more formal business arrangements. These included both cooperative associations, in which members spread the cost of collecting news among themselves, and for-profit agencies that treated newspapers as paying clients.[1] Even among equal members of a cooperative association, exchange functioned differently than it had in earlier periods. Instead of exchanging news after publication, in which case credit for having first published the news might be sufficient, press associations exchanged news *before* publication. Members of the association sent the local news collected by their staff to a central agent, who selected and aggregated reports into a consolidated dispatch that was sent back to members for publication. Over time, the dispatches came to include foreign news obtained through contracts with agencies abroad as well as reports prepared by the association's own staff. For these cooperative arrangements to work, press associations had to develop rules to ensure that members did not leak their local news to outside parties before it could be published by other members. They also had to stop rival agencies from taking news collected by their members and selling it to newspapers that competed for readers and advertisers in the same city. The growing emphasis on using breaking news to attract readers and advertisers and the particular cooperative arrangements that publishers created to collect and distribute this news generated a desire for exclusivity.[2]

The fact that the US Congress allowed the telegraph to develop through private enterprise rather than to be run as a branch of the post office (as was the case in Britain after 1870) was an important factor. The shift from a decentralized news environment in which postal policy encouraged the free exchange of news to a model in which newspapers formed partnerships with each other and with private telegraph companies fundamentally reconfigured the business of news. The decision not to nationalize or more closely regulate the telegraph companies was a political choice that had profound effects on the development of American media.[3] For our purposes, what matters is that the particular business model adopted by the press associations and the arrangements they made with the telegraph companies led them to treat news as a species of property, but one that did not fit into existing frameworks of copyright law. The press associations relied primarily on their own bylaws to maintain the exclusivity of their news, but when these mechanisms broke down or when the actions of rivals made certain kinds of copying problematic, they turned to copyright law in search of a solution. As in Britain, uncertainty about whether newspaper articles or telegraphic dispatches could be protected by copyright led to efforts to establish special laws for news as well as various attempts to assert rights under the existing statutes. These efforts were motivated by shifting alliances among newspapers, press associations, and for-profit agencies, and they revealed disagreements about the purpose of copyright and the best way to ensure public access to news.

COOPERATIVE NEWS GATHERING

Beginning in the 1820s, newspapers occasionally coordinated their efforts to send boats out to greet incoming ships carrying European news; they also shared the expense of horse expresses to obtain reports from other regions. Such cooperation tended to be ad hoc and short-lived until the late 1840s. The advent of a regular transatlantic steamer service and the spread of the telegraph motivated more formal cooperation.[4] The first telegraph line, which connected Washington, DC, to Baltimore in 1844, was initially operated by the post office, but subsequent development of the network was the result of private enterprise.[5] The cost of transmission was high, and initially only one message could be sent at a time. Newspapers began to see the virtues of cooperating rather than competing with each other to transmit redundant messages. Cooperation was also motivated by the fear of what would happen if the telegraph companies entered the news business, as some did briefly.[6]

In the spring of 1846, as the telegraph line was being extended from Albany to Buffalo, several publishers in upstate New York jointly hired a *reporter* (the term was beginning to be used) who compiled paragraphs from Boston and New York newspapers as well as the latest news from the local legislature and then sent this consolidated report out to the partners by telegraph. This consortium, which evolved into the New York State Associated Press, negotiated special rates with the telegraph company. As most future associations would do, this one sought to protect the value of its news by prohibiting members from sharing reports with other newspapers.[7] In New York City, meanwhile, several publishers joined efforts to procure news of the Mexican-American War (1846–1848) through a combination of telegraph and overland express mail. They also cooperated to obtain news from Europe, which arrived by steamer in Boston before being telegraphed to New York.[8]

These partnerships created a desire for exclusivity based on the idea that only those who contributed to the cost of collecting news should be able to profit from timely publication of it. Evidence of this can be seen in a written agreement from 1849, when six morning newspapers in New York formed a partnership called the Harbor News Association. The arrangement initially consisted of two small boats with agents to collect news from incoming ships. According to the contract, news obtained in this way was to be treated as the "common property" of the six partners and was not to be shared with outside parties. This rule applied to British or European newspapers carried by the ship, oral reports by the captain and crew, and any "loose papers or open letters which may be obtained on board." But any private correspondence addressed to one of the partners did not have to be shared, and the partners remained free to obtain exclusive information by interviewing passengers or crew once they were on shore.[9] Consequently, the "common property" referred to in the agreement consisted entirely of news that was already known by people on the ship and could be known by any newspaper that undertook the expense to meet the ship as it approached the harbor.

The idea of treating publicly available news as the property of a cooperative association might seem strange at first, but it made perfect sense given the primary goal of the partnership: to avoid ruinous competition in the race for foreign news. The members of the Harbor News Association had no legal claim to news that was printed in European newspapers or relayed by the captain. But by coordinating their efforts, they could ensure that they would be the first to publish this news in New York. Other publishers were at a disadvantage because they would have to pay significantly more to match the resources that the association enjoyed by spreading the cost among its members. The Harbor News Association's conception of a property in news was elaborated and refined by subsequent associations. Newspapers that shared in the expense of gathering news became frustrated at outsiders that copied. A year after its founding in 1851, the *New York Times* noted that "although property in *news* is not protected by law, it is just as dishonest to steal it as to steal the money which bought it."[10] Yet how could this property right be enforced? The perennially seductive idea of baiting copyists with false news was bound to backfire. The *New York Times* gave the example of a false report claiming that Louis-Napoleon Bonaparte, the current ruler of France, had been assassinated. It was circulated in an attempt to embarrass newspapers that were reprinting the latest telegraphic reports without sharing in the cost of their transmission. The *New York Times* acknowledged the injustice of such copying, but it also denounced the hoax for the way it misled readers.

The New York Associated Press (NYAP), which evolved out of these early cooperative ventures, created a fundamentally new way of distributing news. The NYAP was not a corporation but a partnership owned and managed by half a dozen newspapers that spread the cost of telegraphic transmission among themselves and, over time, an increasing number of members. In addition to paying weekly assessments (most of which were turned over to the telegraph companies that transmitted the news), members had to provide the NYAP with the news they collected locally. The NYAP digested this news and redistributed it to its members, who were bound by contract to keep it secret until their designated publication time. Morning and evening newspapers were not allowed to invade each other's time slots. In order to further limit competition, the bylaws also prohibited members from subscribing to rival news agencies.[11]

A NEWS MONOPOLY?

Over time, the NYAP improved its news report and convinced more and more newspapers to join the association. Many of these newspapers further protected their interests by forming local associations modeled on and affiliated with the NYAP. Indeed, until the 1890s, there was not one Associated Press but several regional and local associations that formed a loose and fragile confederation. As early as the 1850s, the name Associated Press was used casually to refer to this confederation, but it wasn't until 1892 that a single national organization called the Associated Press was incorporated in Chicago (it was reincorporated in New York in 1900).[12] Before 1892, affiliates of the NYAP included the New England Associated Press, the Southern Associated Press, the California Associated Press, and the Western Associated Press among others. The NYAP had considerable power over the other associations because it furnished news from Europe as well as from New York and Washington. Each of the affiliated associations created restrictive bylaws similar to those of the NYAP; members had to share their local news before publication, and they were forbidden from subscribing to other agencies. To enhance the value of membership, bylaws permitted existing members to block other newspapers in their circulation areas from joining the association. These so-called protest rights allowed members to enjoy exclusive access to the association's news in their territories. The fact that some newspapers were excluded from membership in this way fostered negative sentiment toward the NYAP and its affiliates as a news "monopoly."[13]

The early history of the California Associated Press (CAP) provides a good example of this dynamic. The core papers of the CAP were the San Francisco *Alta California*, the *Sacramento Union*, and the San Francisco *Evening Bulletin*. As the telegraph companies worked to link California and the East Coast in 1860–1861, the CAP negotiated exclusive deals with the telegraph companies and the NYAP. The latter deal was facilitated by the fact that James W. Simonton, an owner and editor of the *Evening Bulletin*, was also a shareholder of the *New York Times*, which was an NYAP paper. Simonton and his allies repeatedly blocked requests by other San Francisco papers to join the CAP or to obtain news directly from the NYAP. Unable to purchase the news, the excluded newspapers denounced the CAP as a monopoly. Some also resorted to copying. Taking advantage of the time difference between New York and California, they arranged for agents to take news from printed newspapers in New York and telegraph it west in time to be published at the same time or earlier than members of the CAP. But such tactics did not work for long, because the CAP was able to persuade the telegraph companies to charge prohibitively high rates to newspapers that were not part of the association.[14]

A more important problem was that the restrictive bylaws of the NYAP and its affiliates encouraged the formation of rival news agencies. During the 1870s, the main rival was the American Press Association (APA). The NYAP complained about the APA copying its news.

The threat of the APA, however, was severely limited by the fact that the NYAP had a highly advantageous contract with the telegraph company Western Union. As a result of consolidation, Western Union became the nation's dominant carrier. By 1880, it controlled 80 percent of the total miles of wire and sent 91 percent of total press messages in the United States. In exchange for steep discounts and privileged access to the wires, the NYAP and its affiliates were obliged to give all their business to Western Union, and they largely avoided criticism of the company. Western Union also agreed to stay out of the news business.[15]

James H. Goodsell, president of the APA and editor of the New York–based *Daily Graphic*, led a campaign in the press and before Congress against the "twin monopolies" of the NYAP and Western Union. Goodsell and others urged Congress to regulate the telegraph industry in a way that would enable a "free trade in news."[16] Allegations of collusion between the NYAP and Western Union were fueled by a general antimonopoly sentiment during the late nineteenth century, and there were several proposals to regulate or even nationalize the telegraph.[17] What matters for our story is that the particular business model of the NYAP and its affiliates led to the articulation of the idea that news was a form of property. Rather than sell its reports to all customers willing to pay, the NYAP and its affiliates were cooperative associations. Bylaws allowed members to block new entrants in their territories (in order to have exclusive use of NYAP news) but also forbid members from subscribing to other agencies (thereby stifling competition). These policies were attacked by critics such as Goodsell, whose own agency wanted to sell news to NYAP members. The NYAP's practices also received scrutiny from lawmakers concerned about how the agreement between Western Union and the NYAP limited the circulation of news.

It was during a Senate committee hearing on these issues in 1879 that James W. Simonton, now the general agent of the NYAP, stated, "I claim that there is a property in news, and that property is created by the fact of our collecting it and concentrating it."[18] Simonton had something specific in mind. He was not concerned about news being copied *after* publication. Rather, he was defending the right of the NYAP to decide who could join the association and thereby obtain timely access to its news. A senator had criticized the NYAP for excluding newspapers that wanted to join, effectively treating news as "private property of [their] own."[19] The question was whether the NYAP had a public duty to open up its membership, much in the same way that common carriers such as railroads were required to provide service to anyone willing to pay. Given the NYAP's relationship with Western Union and the dominant position of the latter, did Congress have the mandate or the duty to regulate telegraphy in a way that would promote increased access to news?[20]

Simonton asserted that it was wrong to consider the NYAP a monopoly because news could not be depleted; every newspaper and agency was free to collect as much as they wanted. Simonton used the analogy of fishing. When one fisherman pulled in his net, he necessarily reduced the amount of fish available to others. By contrast, when a press association used its resources to gather news, it did not reduce the amount of news that could be collected by others. Simonton was describing the fact that news is a nonrivalrous good, although he did not use this term. To drive home the point, he used the analogy of light. "When we have collected the news," Simonton said, "we have no more absorbed it and used it up or destroyed it than you and I have destroyed the light here."[21] Although news was nonrivalrous, Simonton thought it should be excludable. Everyone was free to gather news, but they should not be allowed to use news collected by others without permission. Simonton told the committee that it was regrettable that Congress denied news organizations the kind of copyright protection that it offered the authors of literary works.[22]

THE PUSH FOR COPYRIGHT

At the time of Simonton's testimony in 1879, it was not clear whether newspapers, let alone telegraphic dispatches, could be protected by copyright. The question became more urgent during the 1880s as the leadership of the NYAP and the Chicago-based Western Associated Press (WAP) attempted to create a more unified national press association. Such a goal had recently become more feasible thanks to changes in telegraphy. Until the 1870s, when duplex (1872) and quadruplex

(1874) were developed, only one message could be sent at a time. In the 1880s, as multiplex became more widely available, telegraph companies started to lease excess wire capacity to individual newspapers and press agencies, facilitating the development of national news organizations.[23] For the NYAP and its regional affiliates, the desire for stronger cooperation increased in 1882 when United Press (UP) emerged as a more formidable rival. UP was a for-profit agency rather than a member-owned association. It sold news to any customer willing to pay and grew rapidly from about 100 subscribers in 1882 to 166 in 1884. Concerned about the growth of UP and the need to maintain the exclusivity of their news, the joint executive committee of the NYAP and WAP decided to lobby Congress for a copyright bill that would prohibit the reuse of news stories for a certain number of hours after publication.[24]

This effort took place in 1884, the same year that Congress considered comprehensive reform of the telegraph. Antimonopoly sentiment was strong, as were fears about the ambitions of the financier Jay Gould, who had gained control of Western Union in 1881. Gould was also involved in newspapers, which he used to advance his own interests. He owned the *New York World* from 1879 until 1883, when it was acquired by Joseph Pulitzer, and he had a close relationship with the *New York Tribune*. In the run-up to the presidential election of 1884, some observers claimed that Gould was trying to take over the New York City press.[25] It was at this ill-chosen moment that the joint NYAP-WAP leadership pressed for a special copyright in news. They sent Henry Watterson, the editor of the *Louisville Courier-Journal*, to Washington to lobby on their behalf.[26]

Congress considered numerous copyright bills in the late nineteenth century, and it would not have been surprising to lawmakers that news publishers also had an interest in copyright.[27] Watterson's efforts led to the introduction of identical bills in the Senate and the House of Representatives in March 1884. The bills proposed an automatic copyright—without formalities of registration or deposit—for news reports published by any newspaper or "association of newspapers." For eight hours after going to press, the copyright owner would have "the sole right to print, issue, and sell . . . the contents of said daily or weekly newspaper, or the collected news of said newspaper association, exceeding one hundred words."[28] The references to newspaper *associations* may have been designed to exclude for-profit agencies such as UP. The time limit of eight hours was a compromise; the original draft had referred to forty-eight hours, which was reduced to twenty-four and then, finally, to eight. Watterson thought that much of the opposition to the bill might have been avoided if such a lengthy period had not been proposed initially.[29]

Watterson defended the proposed legislation in editorials and a published interview. A common objection was that the law would benefit only the NYAP, which critics liked to refer to as a monopoly. Watterson responded that "all honest newspapers and all honest news associations" supported the bill.[30] Newspapers in small towns and rural areas worried that the law would prohibit them from republishing news that originated in major cities. Watterson sought to reassure them that copying could continue so long as editors waited the specified number of hours, a delay he claimed would not affect weekly papers at all. He also suggested that other newspapers or associations could republish news before the copyright expired if they rewrote it. Watterson assumed that the delay caused by rewriting would effectively protect the investment of the organization that first broke the news.[31]

The distinction between the substance of news and its expression was in fact blurred by a number of supporters of the 1884 legislation, who referred to a "property in news." Their goal was clearly to protect the financial investments in the gathering and transmission of news rather than the intellectual effort made by reporters or editors who put the news into words. Watterson, for example, asserted that the physical assets of newspapers, "from the perfecting press to the newsman's pot of paste, is property, and he who steals it falls within the reach and compass of the law. But that which constitutes the real value of a newspaper property—its news franchises, costing vast sums of money and years of special enterprise, training, and labor—has no legal status whatever . . . anybody can steal it with impunity."[32] Other statements by supporters of the measure similarly stressed how the outlay of time, labor, and money justified a property in news. This led critics to denounce the proposed copyright as an attempt to create a monopoly on accounts of current events. As in Britain, supporters of copyright for news in America struggled to convince critics that it would be possible to protect a particular version of an event without monopolizing the underlying factual details.[33]

OPPOSING COPYRIGHT IN NEWS

Opponents of the 1884 proposal advanced political, economic, and cultural arguments against the idea of copyright in news. First, the owners and editors of newspapers serving small towns and rural areas claimed that copyright would strengthen the "monopoly" of the NYAP and large, urban newspapers. A petition signed by ten residents of Latrobe, Pennsylvania, protested against any law to copyright news "even for an hour," arguing that such a measure was "calculated to destroy the freedom of the press." Another petition, signed by twenty-eight residents of Missouri, described the bill as "a move in the interest of the large dailies to crush out their smaller competitors, thus giving them a monopoly of the business of furnishing news to the people. We believe in a Free Press and we are decidedly opposed to any such law."[34] Freedom of the press was clearly being envisioned as involving more than a lack of prior restraint; it was also about who had access to news and of what quality. In a letter to his congressman, the owner of a small Iowa newspaper complained that the publishers of big-city dailies sought to "choke off the rural brethren from publishing the news" and that "by and by these fellows will try to copyright the air we breathe."[35] The choking metaphor emphasized how the livelihood of rural printers depended on the right to copy, but it also signaled the extent to which they viewed news as a common resource—as vital as the air itself.[36]

Critics of the 1884 proposal highlighted the political dangers of copyright. In a letter to his senator, a newspaper publisher in New York State argued that the country press was "nearer the people than any metropolitan daily can ever be."[37] Copyright was seen as a threat because it would impede editors from reproducing news of interest to their local readers. The *Milwaukee Sentinel* worried that by limiting what others could copy, the law would necessarily hinder commentary. As an editorial put it, "To prevent other journals from commenting upon [news] is to stifle free discussion, and to permit them to comment is to permit them to re-publish the matter."[38] The fact that some news depended on government sources also raised concern. A trade journal called the *Printers' Circular* claimed that government officials often furnished important announce-ments to the NYAP with the understanding that "they are to be given to the public press for the use of the public." If a copyright in news existed, it could theoretically be used to enforce "a monopoly in the reports of Congressional proceedings, presidential proclamations, and important appointments by the President."[39] Many of the editorials and petitions to Congress in 1884 used this language of monopoly, which would have resonated with lawmakers. Indeed, the same week that the news copy-right bill was introduced, the Senate held hearings related to telegraph policy in which the NYAP and Western Union were once again accused of having a monopoly on the dissemination of news.[40]

Alongside these concerns about access to information, the argument arose that news was not a product of authorship and therefore not eli-gible for copyright at all. Copyright was supposed to encourage authors and artists to produce new works, and it was not clear how this logic applied to news. The owners and editors of newspapers that opposed the 1884 proposal sent Congress copies of a printed petition declaring that news was a business rather than a form of authorship. "Copyright and patent laws are not made to reward individuals or corporations for the expenditure of money," the petition argued, "but to stimulate cre-ative and inventive talent. If a copyright can be granted on news, it must be to him who creates or invents news, and not to the newspapers which are buyers of and dealers in news." Defining news as "the history of current events," the petition asked, "can anyone create or invent a fact or event? If he cannot create or invent a fact or event, how can he copy-right it? News is the history of the time. The law cannot make it any one's property."[41]

The notion that facts cannot be protected by copyright now seems familiar, but well into the twentieth century, a number of American courts held that the labor invested in compiling a fact-based work jus-tified copyright protection. In 1991, the Supreme Court firmly rejected the doctrines of the "sweat of the brow" and "industrious collection," insisting that the standard for copyright was original authorship. This decision meant that in the case of factual compilations, only the selection and arrangement could be protected, not the facts themselves.[42] But in the late nineteenth century, the idea that copyright required "creativity" or "originality" remained novel. Courts had long recognized copyright for informational works such as encyclopedias and directories, but the time-sensitive nature of newspapers made them seem less eligible for copyright, as the 1828 case of *Clayton v. Stone* showed.[43] By the 1880s, newspapers and press associations stressed not only the speed with which they delivered news but also the public value of the service they provided. They argued that the high cost of providing reliable information from around the world justified protection against "piracy." But as the petition quoted earlier suggests, attempts to justify copyright for news based on financial outlay could backfire. In response to the 1884 proposal, critics articulated, more clearly than before, the idea that copyright was intended to protect original authorship rather than financial investment.[44] Some of these critics might have accepted the idea that other forms of journalism, such as editorials or leading essays, could be protected by copyright. But the NYAP-WAP leadership was seeking protection for telegraphic dispatches rather than feature articles. They might have argued that telegraphic dispatches were the result of literary labor by reporters and editors. Instead, they focused on the capital and business organization required to collect and disseminate breaking news. That strategy provided opponents with an opportunity to articulate their vision of what copyright law was meant to do.

In the *Nation*, an article titled "Stealing News" elaborated the argument that news was not a form of authorship worthy of copyright protection.[45] The writer criticized Henry Watterson for fighting for a measure that "he very incorrectly calls a newspaper 'copyright' law." Citing Article I, section 8 of the US Constitution, which empowers Congress to secure to authors an exclusive right to their writings for a limited period of time, the writer for the *Nation* declared, "It is absurd to talk of a man who picks up a piece of news or an 'item' as an 'author' at all." According to this anonymous writer, the goal of copyright was "to secure the fruits of original, intellectual labor," whereas the collection of news was a passive activity that could be done by anyone:

Some people do it by listening at keyholes, most people in the ordinary course of conversation with the persons whom they meet in the way of business or pleasure. If a collector of news in London telegraphs to New York that Sir Stafford Northcote has just delivered a lecture on "Nothing," or that Lord Cairns has offered Miss Fortescue £10,000 to release his son from his marriage engagement, who is the person whose "property" in the news ought to be protected, or who is the "author" of it? Is it the collector of the "item"? If so, any one who has ears and eyes is an "author."[46]

The contention that news was collected rather than written was hardly new. As early as the 1730s, the *Grub-Street Journal* had dismissed the idea of literary property for news on the grounds that it was collected by paid hirelings who visited coffeehouses looking for the latest gossip.[47] By the 1880s, newspapers had large staffs, and press associations required a tremendous amount of coordination to function. Even so, the writer for the *Nation* viewed news as outside the bounds of authorship; he even went so far as to suggest that someone who fabricated news had a better claim to authorship than someone who reported factual occurrences. He conceded that other articles in the newspaper, such as anecdotes about remarkable people or places, could qualify for copyright because these were the result of "literary labor." But he thought most news reports lacked evidence of such labor and would be nearly impossible to protect anyway since a copyist could obscure the origins of the report by altering the phrasing. Even if it were possible to prove that one newspaper had unfairly copied from another, treating news as property would hinder legitimate reuse. As the writer for the *Nation* put it, "The same 'news' . . . which appears in one newspaper as a 'special cable' reappears immediately in another newspaper as a topic for a paragraph, editorial, or an 'item.' If this were made a criminal offense, most editors would be in jail all the time."[48] In other words, copying facilitated commentary and analysis. Editors depended on one another, and if copyright were applied to news, it is not clear how they could continue to do their jobs.

It was possible to agree that news did not rise to the level of literary authorship while also seeing copying as theft. Pulitzer's *New York World* admitted that it was "absurd" to put collecting news on the same footing as writing novels or plays. An editorial in that paper explained, "The one is enterprise and investment. The other is creation."[49] But the *World* nonetheless supported the idea that skill, enterprise, and money invested in news collection justified protection against "robbery" and "piracy." Interestingly, the comments of editors who weighed in on the question of copyright for news reveal that they envisioned the proposed legislation as a potential solution to a range of problems. The *World* claimed that copyright would stop individuals from obtaining news through surreptitious means and then publishing it at approximately the same time as the newspaper that had collected it. Such a claim conflated copyright infringement with bribery or theft of confidential information. The *Providence Journal* and the Portland *Oregonian* each expressed hope that the law being considered in 1884 would encourage unscrupulous editors to adopt "honester" methods, implying that copying might be allowed if certain norms were respected. A Chicago weekly called the *Current* speculated that the main objective was to put a halt to the tradition of afternoon newspapers taking news from morning papers.[50] Copyright clearly meant different things to different people.

Most small newspapers opposed copyright because they thought it would restrict their access to national and international news, but one editor in the Dakota Territory supported the 1884 proposal in hopes that it might save jobs for small-town printers. His idea was that copyright would hinder the growth of syndication companies offering services known as ready-print and boilerplate.[51] Ready-print services dated back to the 1860s. Small-town newspapers would contract with an outside company (usually located in a larger city) for sheets of paper containing news columns, feature stories, and advertisements preprinted on two pages. The other two pages would be left blank so that the local printer could add news and advertisements procured locally. These four-page weeklies became known as patent 'sides because advertisements for patent medicines were common on the preprinted "insides" (pages two and three) or "outsides" (pages one and four). The Wisconsin printer Ansel N. Kellogg set up the first major ready-print business in Chicago in 1865. By the following decade he and his competitors were also offering another product that came to be known as boiler-plate.[52] Whereas ready-print consisted of sending partly printed sheets in the mail, boilerplate involved producing lightweight stereotype molds that could be shipped out to local printers for use in their newspapers. By 1880, it was estimated that more than 3,000 of the country's approximately 8,600 weekly papers subscribed to either ready-print or boiler-plate services.[53]

Country printers who used such services were criticized by those who did not, and in 1884 a newspaper trade journal referred to ready-print as a "fraud on the reader" because the content appeared to be produced locally but was not.[54] The Dakota editor mentioned earlier supported the proposed copyright law because he thought it would stop the ready-print firms from taking news from major newspapers and press agencies. He thought that if the firms were cut off from their supply of free copy, their growth would be restricted, thereby preserving jobs for local printers.[55] In fact, the NYAP-WAP leadership did not cite ready-print and boilerplate services as a motivation for pursuing copyright in 1884, and it seems that some of the firms contracted with press associations to receive their news directly.[56] That the Dakota editor saw the proposed copyright law as a way to check the growth of ready-print underscores the extent to which copyright was optimistically looked to as a remedy for a variety of problems.

Some commentators in the press argued that the legislation proposed in 1884 was pointless because copyright could not protect the facts of news, and that was what the NYAP-WAP leadership actually wanted. As an editorial in *Harper's Weekly* put it, "The essential value in news lies in the fact and not in the form, and the moment that is published, in whatever form, the fact becomes the property of the public." The writer for *Harper's* offered the analogy of historical research. Three historians might use the same facts to prepare their histories, each of which would be eligible for copyright. The same went for news. As *Harper's* put it, "News as published is a description of certain events. Can anything but the description be copyrighted?"[57] The implication was that NYAP and

WAP board members were trying to use copyright to do something that it was not meant to do—protect facts.

The 1884 news copyright bills died before coming to a vote. A month after introducing the bill in the Senate, Senator John Sherman reported back that it should not go forward.[58] The NYAP-WAP leadership did not press the matter. They must have feared that a prolonged campaign would expose the organization to further accusations of attempting to monopolize news. In his autobiography, Watterson looked back on his time in Washington as a "fool's errand." He recalled that a number of his fellow editors criticized him for supporting copyright. Although he initially found allies among members of the Supreme Court, the attorney general, and the Joint Committee on the Library, he came to realize that the bills would never come to a vote because of fears that copyright could increase the power of the NYAP and its affiliates at the expense of small newspapers around the country.[59]

COPYRIGHT USE EXPLODES

The failure to pass a new law in 1884 did not end hopes for using copyright to protect news. In fact, in the late 1880s and early 1890s, newspapers and press agencies began to register individual articles for copyright and attach copyright notices to them. Copyright lines became more common in a variety of newspaper content, from poetry and illustrations to telegraphic dispatches, a change that was noticed by readers at the time. In the case of fiction, the word *copyright* was used in advertisements to signal that the material was exclusive and had been paid for. An 1885 advertisement for the Sunday *New York Tribune*, for example, promised readers "brilliant copyright articles by the brightest writers."[60] In 1890, the editor of the Chicago-based *Inter Ocean* complained that copyright restrictions prevented him from reproducing more than a few lines of poetry from another newspaper.[61] The remark revealed the extent to which the old exchange model had been replaced by one in which editors had to be much more careful about what they copied.

There was also a sudden increase in copyright notices attached to news reports, leading some observers to wonder how this was possible

given that the 1884 bills had failed.[62] In 1886, the Washington correspondent of a Wheeling, West Virginia, paper argued that by choosing
not to move forward with copyright for news, Congress had effectively
decided that "whatever was current and whatever was discussed by
tongue or pen in the daily press should be free, and that no one should
be hampered in using it."[63] Nevertheless, major East Coast newspapers
were attaching copyright notices to telegraphic dispatches. The correspondent looked into the process by which newspapers were registering
news articles for copyright and explained this to readers. Before each
edition was issued, employees would "clip the title, credit and date line
from the proof slips" and mail them to the Librarian of Congress.[64]

Copyright records confirm a sudden spike in registrations by newspapers and press associations in 1886. Admittedly, the use of copyright
by newspapers was not entirely new. Beginning in the 1850s, weekly papers that contained a high proportion of literary articles and illustrations, such as *Harper's Weekly*, the *New York Ledger*, and *Frank Leslie's Illustrated Newspaper*, registered each issue for copyright.[65] Robert
Bonner, the publisher of the *New York Ledger*, touted his exclusive contracts with authors and attached copyright notices, usually in his own
name, to contributions by Sylvanus Cobb Jr., Fanny Fern, and others.[66]
In 1870, responsibility for copyright registration was transferred from
local district courts to the Library of Congress. As the *New York Times*
explained, the policy of the new copyright office within the library was
to "give every applicant a copyright, and let him maintain its validity
before the Courts if he can." The office would not consider "questions
of priority, infringement, originality, usefulness, and the like."[67] This
statement made clear what had always been the case: the validity of
copyright claims could be decided only by the courts. Some major metropolitan newspapers registered the occasional article during the 1870s
and early 1880s, but these represented attempts to protect fiction and illustrations, not news reports. The New York *Sun,* for example, registered the titles of stories by Bret Harte and other authors for copyright
and then sold publishing rights to other newspapers, a model that was
also adopted by literary syndicates.[68]

The development of syndication publishing contributed to the sudden increase in copyright notices in American newspapers beginning in the late 1880s. The idea of syndication is often traced back to the English publisher William Frederic Tillotson. As the owner of a newspaper in Bolton, England, in the 1870s, Tillotson wanted to publish fresh literary material. He thought that exclusive rights to a serial novel by a popular author had the potential to boost his paper's circulation, but he couldn't afford to pay for exclusive rights. It occurred to him to contact publishers in other towns and arrange for joint publication. Partners would share the cost of a given story and then enjoy exclusive rights in their respective areas. Tillotson's business in England grew rapidly, and he opened an agency in New York in 1889.[69] In the mid-1880s, Irving Bacheller, Edward W. Bok, and S. S. McClure also began operating fiction syndicates in the United States. The syndicates would obtain copyright from the authors and then license concurrent publication to newspapers located in different places.[70] Syndication publishing took off quickly, and it represented a major change in how literature circulated. Previously, much fiction and poetry had been exchanged among editors or clipped from other publications. Syndicates persuaded newspapers to pay for original material by promising exclusivity in their area. Their business model contributed to a growing number of newspaper articles being marked off as proprietary.[71]

But the rise of syndicates was not the only factor responsible for the increase in newspaper copyright notices. In the late 1880s and early 1890s, some newspapers and press associations also began registering news reports for copyright. Before the mid-1880s, most publishers would have agreed with Frederic Hudson, who served as managing editor of the *New York Herald* before writing a history of American journalism in 1873. Hudson claimed that the speed with which major newspapers were printed and distributed provided adequate protection against piracy. The *Herald* had the capacity to print one hundred thousand copies in an hour. By the time a competitor could print and distribute the same news, it would be old. Hudson concluded that "our newspapers must continue to find their copyright in their superior enterprise, their superior machinery, their superior circulation, and in their superior means of delivering their papers to the public."[72] Legal protection was not needed because speed of distribution provided a sufficient advantage.

By the mid-1880s, only a decade after Hudson was writing, the situation had changed. In 1885–1886, several newspapers and press associations began registering telegraphic dispatches for copyright. The *Sun* may have been the first in December 1885, but it was quickly joined by the *New York Times*, the *Evening Post*, the *Herald*, the *World*, and the German-language *New Yorker Staats-Zeitung*, which was then one of the leading New York City papers.[73] Most of the dispatches came from Britain and were about the controversy over Irish Home Rule. This story was eagerly followed by American readers, and it appears that competition in the New York market as well as the desire to syndicate their "cable service" led these publishers to assert copyright in special reports that they paid for.[74] In 1886, several press agencies also began to claim copyright in their dispatches.[75]

But were such copyright claims valid? In 1886, the Colorado News and Press Association tried to find out. The association complained of being victim to acts of "journalistic piracy" by a "slick fellow named Colby."[76] Colby was copying dispatches from a newspaper that belonged to the association and transmitting them by telegraph to his own newspaper clients in Colorado and New Mexico. The Colorado News and Press Association began to attach a copyright notice to its reports and threatened to sue Colby for infringement, but Colby responded that it was not possible to copyright news. The association then wrote to the Librarian of Congress, Ainsworth Rand Spofford, for advice on how to secure copyright. Spofford's reply focused on the procedures for registration rather than on the question of validity, which his office was not in a position to address. Yet the Colorado association published Spofford's letter and celebrated it as proof that news could be copyrighted. Spofford explained that the association would have to make a separate entry for "each day's dispatches under its distinctive headline as they vary from day to day." He reported that such entries were being made by the *New York Evening Post*, the *Tribune*, the *Sun*, the *Omaha Bee*, and other papers. Spofford's office did not have any printed instructions for registering dispatches, so he enclosed a more general circular indicating that a new entry was required "for each change or variation, either of title or substance, in a publication secured by copyright."[77] The copyright office applied this same rule to periodicals and books published in parts: each issue or installment had to be entered separately. Although the copyright law did not explicitly mention newspapers, let alone telegraphic dispatches, Spofford's office had adapted to the times and was allowing publishers to enter individual news reports as "books."

The law required authors or publishers to deposit two copies of each registered work within ten days of publication.[78] Perusal of the record books of the copyright office reveals that not all newspapers and press associations that registered articles for copyright in the late 1880s complied with this requirement. The California Associated Press, for example, made more than four hundred copyright entries in 1887, presumably in an attempt to stop newspapers outside the association from printing its news. But the CAP did not consistently comply with the deposit requirement.[79] Of course, in the case of telegraphic news, it was not clear what should be deposited. The record books indicate that sometimes publishers deposited typewritten copies of the dispatches, but other times they did not deposit anything. The same was true for newspapers; some publishers were more compliant with the deposit requirements than others.[80] Failure to deposit a registered work would have invalidated the copyright. Whether a judge would accept the idea that news reports were eligible for copyright was another matter.

The first reported copyright decision related to telegraph news in the United States did not take place until after the turn of the century (discussed later), but in the meantime, an 1886 decision involving *Harper's Weekly* confirmed that at least some contributions to newspapers and magazines were eligible for copyright. The case centered on an engraved illustration that had appeared in *Harper's Weekly* back in 1873 and was reproduced by the *New York Illustrated Times* almost ten years later. Given this delay, it seems likely that Harper & Brothers envisioned this lawsuit as an opportunity to establish the legal principle that material published in periodicals, particularly illustrations, could be protected by copyright. The resulting judgment confirmed that periodicals could be registered as books for the purposes of copyright and that the copyright protected against infringement of any substantial part of the work.[81] The court cited the 1828 case of *Clayton v. Stone* on the point that even a work of a single page could be considered a book for the purposes of copyright. But the *Harper's Weekly* decision also signaled how much had changed since 1828. In *Clayton*, the judge had insisted that to be eligible for copyright a work had to make a lasting contribution to "learning" or "the sciences." The judge that decided the 1886 dispute saw no need to evaluate works in this way.[82]

Harper & Brothers relied on this court decision to stop others from reproducing their illustrations. Within months of the 1886 verdict, they reached a settlement with American Press Association, which had reproduced several cuts from *Harper's New Monthly Magazine* and distributed them to its own newspaper clients. As part of the settlement, American Press Association arranged for its clients to print notices apologizing for the infringement and praising Harper & Brothers for their role in advancing the art of engraving. These notices avowed that the New York firm deserved full credit and copyright protection for its illustrations.[83]

For newspaper publishers, the 1886 decision involving *Harper's Weekly* suggested that at least some articles and illustrations in newspapers could be protected by copyright, but the question remained whether news reports were eligible. Commentators weighed in on this question. At this time, one of the most knowledgeable observers of how publishers made use of copyright was Richard Rogers Bowker. In addition to being owner of *Publishers Weekly* and head of the Publishers' Copyright League, Bowker had experience as a newspaper and magazine editor. In an 1886 book about copyright law, Bowker suggested that newspapers could be protected as long as each issue was registered separately. According to him, "All copyrightable matter contained in the issue would then be copyrighted." That begged the question of what parts of a newspaper qualified for copyright. Bowker thought that the primary motivation for registering each issue of a daily or weekly newspaper would be "to protect all its original material of substantial literary value."[84] Other publishers did not necessarily agree. Bowker had learned from the copyright office that a daily publication listing prices on the New York Cotton Exchange had been entered for a while and that the New York *Sun* was also entering its "cable letter" for copyright, but such claims had not yet been tested in court.[85] The *Harper's Weekly* decision occurred the same year that some major newspapers and press agencies began registering telegraphic dispatches. The ruling may have strengthened their resolve, but it did not prompt their turn toward copyright, which began much earlier in the year. The use of copyright for newspaper material, however, was in the air with the rise of the syndicates, and specific rivalries among news brokers—such as the Colorado association's dispute with Colby, the resolution of which remains unknown—motivated registration in an attempt to secure exclusivity.

Copyright was not the only means, or even the most effective one, for dealing with copying. The NYAP, which had lobbied for new legislation in 1884, did not register its dispatches in the late 1880s, even though other agencies were doing so. The reason for this was that the NYAP and its main rival, United Press (UP), found another means of restricting competition: collusion. The NYAP wanted to prevent its members from defecting to UP; meanwhile, UP wanted access to NYAP news. The NYAP executive committee and the main shareholders of UP therefore enacted a series of "gentlemen's agreements" and covert stock pools beginning around 1885. The NYAP agreed to supply news to UP, which sold this news to its clients and then disbursed the profits to the shareholders involved in the secret deal. UP promised to stop raiding NYAP papers, and NYAP benefited from maintenance of the UP brand, which helped to ward off the creation of other news agencies. By 1892, the collusion was exposed, and the resulting shake-up led to the creation of a new Associated Press based in Chicago, built on the foundations of the old Western Associated Press. The members of the NYAP were initially excluded from the Chicago AP, leading them to dissolve their association and join UP.[86]

Over the next several years, the new Chicago-based AP battled the New York–based United Press in an effort to become the dominant nationwide news organization. Crucially, a contract with Reuters gave the AP exclusive access to the reports of the main European agencies (Havas, Wolff, and Reuters, which formed a cartel). This was a decisive advantage in its battle with UP. The AP quickly gained the upper hand, growing from 207 members in 1893 to 396 members in 1895 and 637 in 1897. UP went bankrupt in 1897, and most of its clients became AP members. The absorption of former UP clients was possible in part because the AP's board of directors worked hard to convince AP members to forgo their protest rights for the sake of building a stronger national network. At the AP's 1897 annual meeting, the board of directors celebrated the end of a costly four-year war with UP and explained that most of UP's former members had been accepted into the AP fold.[87]

The shifting alliances among newspapers in the 1890s motivated a number of publishers to register news articles for copyright. The major New York papers, several of which were temporarily aligned with UP during its battle with the AP, entered individual stories and whole issues for copyright. The *Sun,* whose editor Charles A. Dana was also president of UP, began to register each daily issue in 1892; starting in 1894, the *Sun* registered all 365 daily issues in a batch at the beginning of each calendar year.[88] The *New York Times,* which had been registering dispatches since 1886, began to register each issue of its newspaper in 1893.[89] The *Herald* began daily registration in 1895.[90] During its war with UP, the Chicago-based AP also registered dispatches for copyright. But competition over coverage of the Spanish-American War (1898) was also a factor. The number of copyright entries by the AP peaked in 1898, when it entered and deposited 509 articles for copyright.[91] Also in 1898, the board of directors ordered all members to regularly print a copyright line over any material copyrighted by AP, and this order was renewed in subsequent years.[92]

TESTING COPYRIGHT IN COURT: *TRIBUNE V. AP*

The validity of copyright for news articles remained uncertain in the 1890s because most accusations of "stealing" news did not lead to lawsuits. Some editors used the tactic of publicly shaming copyists by baiting them with false news. During the Spanish-American War, for example, accusations of news theft were one component of a larger rivalry between William Randolph Hearst's *New York Journal* and Joseph Pulitzer's *New York World.* On one occasion the *Journal* sought to em-

barrass the *World* by printing an article that referred to an Austrian ar-
tillerist named Reflipe W. Thenuz. The whole point was to catch the
World in the act of copying a name that could be rearranged to read
"We pilfer the nuz."[93] The use of bogus news to humiliate rivals had a
long history, and the technique of spelling insults backward went back
to at least 1876, when Melville E. Stone of the Chicago *Daily News* set
a similar trap for the McMullen brothers, owners of the *Post and Mail.*
In retaliation for what he claimed to be the brothers' daily acts of "piracy," Stone arranged for a story about starvation in Serbia to include
a quotation from the local mayor. The quote meant nothing in Serbian
but when read backward in English stated, "The McMullens will steal
this sure." According to Stone's autobiography, the resulting mockery
in the press helped to erode the value of the *Post and Mail*, which Stone
purchased at a discount two years later.[94]

In the 1890s, some copyright suits were initiated by syndicates and
newspaper publishers. Newspapers and magazines that reproduced articles or illustrations without permission might now receive letters from
lawyers explaining that providing credit for copied material was no substitute for obtaining permission. Such letters would urge publishers to
settle by mentioning the much larger sums that might be recovered at
trial.[95] Fiction and feature articles seem to have been more closely policed than news paragraphs, but in the right circumstances, such as the
intense rivalry among newspapers and agencies in the 1890s, annoyance
over the "theft" of news could lead to copyright suits being filed, although these did not necessarily make it to court.[96]

One dispute that did lead to a court ruling at the turn of the century involved rights to news first published abroad. The *Chicago Tribune* sued the AP in an effort to protect news of the Second Boer War
(1899–1902) that the Chicago paper obtained through a contract with
The Times of London. The contract specified that *The Times* would
provide the *Chicago Tribune*'s London correspondent with advanced
access to its news and would release its copyright in any articles that
the correspondent chose to wire to Chicago. The *Chicago Tribune* registered each issue of its daily paper for copyright, and when it found
that the AP was distributing some of the same stories to its members,

it sued for copyright infringement, requesting damages of $100,000.[97] Although the bill of complaint alleged that the AP had copied from the *Chicago Tribune*, the AP's correspondent in London had actually taken the articles from printed editions of *The Times* and cabled them back to America. The AP questioned whether either *The Times* or the *Chicago Tribune* had actually taken the proper steps to secure copyright. In addition, the AP argued that neither paper could claim exclusive rights to any information or documents provided by the British government. The AP contended that much of the news and "statements of facts" appearing in *The Times* were "public property."[98] *The Times*'s manager, Charles Frederick Moberly Bell, did not accept this idea. As discussed in chapter 5, Bell expended considerable energy trying to protect the news collected by *The Times*.

Judge William Henry Seaman, who wrote the opinion in *Tribune v. AP*, sought to balance the Tribune Company's rights to "the fruits of its enterprise and expenditure" against the rights of the public to news published in a leading foreign newspaper. He closely examined the procedures that had been followed by the Tribune Company in order to determine whether the articles were protected by American copyright. Every evening the company would mail a printed copy of the title "Chicago Daily Tribune" along with the issue number and date of the next morning's paper to the copyright office. They perfected this registration by depositing copies of each day's issue at the Library of Congress. The fact that the London articles had not been registered separately troubled Judge Seaman, who was of the opinion that "there can be no general copyright of a newspaper composed in large part of matter not entitled to protection."[99] To support this assertion, Seaman cited Justice Thompson's 1828 opinion in *Clayton v. Stone* that copyright "cannot with any propriety be applied to a work of so fluctuating and fugitive a form as that of a newspaper or price current, the subject-matter of which is daily changing and is of mere temporary use."[100] Judge Seaman did not know all the details about *Clayton* that were revealed in chapter 4. That case had actually centered on reports of market trends rather than on accounts of war or political events, but Seaman found the language of the opinion compelling.[101]

Ultimately, however, Judge Seaman's ruling did not turn on an analysis of whether news reports were eligible for copyright. Instead, he determined that the Tribune Company did not have a valid copyright at the moment that the AP's London correspondent found the news in *The Times*. The London paper had agreed to release its American rights over any material that the Tribune Company wanted, but in the meantime the AP had no way of knowing which articles the Tribune Company would choose and no notice that American rights had been reserved. The International Copyright Act of 1891 (also known as the Chace Act) made it possible to obtain American copyright for works by British authors, but only if identical editions were published simultaneously in both countries. The news articles in question were not published simultaneously, and they were components of larger works—*The Times* and the *Chicago Tribune*—that were anything but identical.[102] The requirements of the Chace Act thus made it very difficult to secure American copyright for news first published abroad. The *New York Times* faced the same problem a few years later. It was unable to stop other American newspapers from copying reports that it had obtained through an exclusive contract with *The Times*.[103]

LOBBYING FOR NEWS COPYRIGHT, AGAIN

Frustration with the ineffectiveness of the current law in protecting news led to renewed efforts to pass new legislation around the turn of the century. In 1899, the AP's board of directors resolved to appoint a committee to begin the process of drafting and proposing "a news copyright law."[104] Nothing seems to have come of this, and Judge Seaman's opinion in *Tribune v. AP* suggested that most newspaper matter would fall outside the bounds of copyright even if publishers complied fully with the requirements of the statute. But was Seaman correct? In 1903, a contributor to a law journal asked the US Register of Copyrights, Thorvald Solberg, whether newspapers were covered by the current statute. Solberg responded that newspapers and periodicals had long been registered as books and that such registration, if perfected by deposit, "is supposed to secure protection upon so much of the contents of the periodical as is subject to copyright protection."[105] It was up to the courts, when confronted with specific disputes, to decide whether a newspaper item qualified for copyright. As Register, Solberg merely recorded the claims, but he assumed that a fair amount of newspaper material would not be eligible for copyright. The writer for the law journal who quoted Solberg was of a different opinion. He wrote, "Why has not a newspaper proprietor who employs the best thought, appliances and resources to collect, write up and arrange the news of the day, the same right to protection as a historian who delves deep in dusty volumes of the past and collects, writes up, and arranges in original form the history of former ages?"[106] This author was expressing a view of copyright that was becoming more common in the years around 1900. The idea that copyright provided a crucial incentive for business owners, not just authors, and that copyright should protect the market value of works regardless of their literary or artistic merits was also gaining traction in the courts.[107]

In the first decade of the twentieth century, Solberg was at the center of efforts to produce a general revision of American copyright law. Some lawyers and newspaper publishers saw this process of copyright reform as an opportunity to clarify protection for news. In an address to the Maine Bar Association in 1903, a Boston lawyer argued that newspapers should enjoy a copyright that was automatic—because registration and deposit were too cumbersome for daily publications—but also of shorter duration than that enjoyed by literary works. A short copyright term was justified by what he called the "transitory character" of much newspaper material. But the lawyer also argued that the high cost of collecting news justified that this temporary copyright should extend beyond the language in which the news was expressed. As he put it, "The news itself, the facts stated, should be protected, and not merely the literary vehicle in which it is conveyed."[108] The same idea had recently been advocated in Britain by Bell of *The Times*, and it would be broached during the legislative process leading to the passage of the Copyright Act of 1909.

The first step in this process was a series of conferences convened by the Librarian of Congress, Herbert Putnam, in 1905–1906. Putnam sent invitations to associations representing authors, publishers, artists, composers, dramatists, photographers, typographers, and other interested parties. The idea was to work toward a draft bill that could be sent to Congress.[109] Newspaper publishers were represented by the American Newspaper Publishers Association (ANPA), which had been formed in 1887 mainly to provide a common front against advertising agencies and paper manufacturers.[110] The AP was not initially invited to participate because of Putnam's mistaken assumption that news publishers were adequately represented by the ANPA.[111] Although the AP did receive a last-minute invitation to attend the second conference, its general manager, Melville E. Stone, declined. Stone explained that he had already given up on copyright. "Our interest in the protection of our news service from piracy must be obvious," Stone wrote to Putnam, "but I have no great hope that it can be accomplished through a modification of the copyright law."[112] Stone regretted that it would probably be impossible to pass a special law protecting telegraphic dispatches for a certain number of hours, as had been done in several British colonies. He thought that the proposal would "arouse such hostility as to not only insure failure of the effort, but probably would do damage to the whole cause" of copyright reform.[113] Stone thought that the only useful protection for news would come from common-law property rights. (As explained in chapter 7, Stone and the AP would finally test this idea in the courts during World War I.)

The ANPA's representative at the conferences was Don C. Seitz, business manager of Pulitzer's New York *World*. He had not yet reached the same conclusions as Stone. Seitz spent most of his time at the first conference arguing for a copyright in telegraphic dispatches. He acknowledged that the *World* and other papers currently registered dispatches by sending proof slips to the Library of Congress each day. But this registration did not provide effective protection for timely news. Seitz cited the example of George Dewey's victory at Manila Bay at the beginning of the Spanish-American War in 1898. The *World* received the news at 4:00 a.m., after the bulk of its morning edition had been printed. The *World* put out a few thousand "extras" with the news, but their rivals across the street copied the news into their early-evening editions, beating the *World*'s own evening edition to market. "News comes from var ious points," Seitz said, "and only occasionally we suffer, but when we do we suffer greatly. Our enterprise and our forethought or luck, or whatever it is termed, are lost to us."[114] By stumbling over how to refer to the genesis of news—enterprise, forethought, or luck—Seitz revealed the rhetorical difficulties faced by those who sought to treat it as property. They saw the problem in practical business terms rather than as a matter of authors' rights. Given that newspapers were being published earlier and earlier in the day, Seitz said that the old tactic of holding important news until competitors went to press no longer worked. What was needed was a special clause in the copyright law similar to those that he knew existed in Tasmania and South Africa. Such precedents suggested that it should be feasible to draft a workable law that would protect newspapers for a certain number of hours after they first printed a dispatch. Seitz thought that twenty-four hours of protection would suffice; at the very least, he said, "we ought to have more than ten or fifteen minutes, between editions."[115] Seitz favored an automatic copyright; rather than requiring publishers to register each dispatch, they could keep records of when they received each item of news by telegraph, and these records could be used to prove infringement.

Seitz's contention that current copyright law was ineffective for newspapers echoed the remarks of other members of the ANPA when the subject arose at their 1905 annual meeting. H. F. Gunnison of the *Brooklyn Eagle* explained that his paper had abandoned efforts to copyright news, although sometimes they registered "special articles." Representing the *Boston Globe*, Charles H. Taylor Jr. admitted that although his paper registered each issue, "it is a bluff. It is absolutely invalid. The copyright office will tell you so. You go through the form, but the copyright covers nothing."[116] As Taylor understood it, each individual article or illustration had to be registered and published with a copyright notice attached to it. In his view, the notice that appeared at the head of a newspaper was "about as good as a trespass sign." He added, "The copyright people in Washington tell you it does not do any good, but they cheerfully take your money."[117] Other publishers registered their titles daily but were similarly unconvinced of the value of doing so. Adolph S. Ochs, publisher of the *New York Times*, asked legal counsel in 1904 if it was a good idea to copyright "important items of news." The lawyer responded that "in view of the condition of the copyright law it is a useless expense and with no hope whatsoever of successfully prosecuting a claim for damages. All that you can get out of it, is the prestige of the advertisement, if that is worth anything, which I hardly think it is."[118]

At the second copyright conference in November 1905, Seitz pushed for "a twenty-four or thirty-six hour embargo on special cable despatches [sic]."[119] He promised that local news would not be covered by such a clause, only foreign news. The AP would have disagreed with this, since it sought exclusive use of the local news gathered by its members. This difference showed that the ANPA and the AP did not have identical interests. Seitz argued that protection for the form of reports would be insufficient. What the ANPA wanted was exclusive use of the news in telegraphic dispatches for a certain number of hours. "We are not trying to protect our intellects," he told participants of the copyright conference, "but are trying to protect our energies, and if that can be done I can not see why there should be any objection."[120] But it was objected that newspapers in rural areas might want to republish foreign news that they could not obtain on their own. Seitz did not think that these papers would be harmed by a short embargo, but Putnam, the Librarian of Congress, feared that including a clause along the lines proposed by Seitz "might imperil the whole bill."[121] Putnam asked Seitz to provide a draft of his proposed clause, but the ANPA gave up in the face of skepticism by Putnam and others.[122] The lack of support from the AP did not help their cause.

PHOTOGRAPHY AND THE NEWSPAPER

Abandoning the idea of copyright for news, the ANPA focused its lobbying efforts on concerns about newspaper photographs. In the 1890s, newspapers suddenly found themselves vulnerable to infringement suits brought by photographers. The reproduction of photographs in the form of engravings and then halftone images was becoming more common, but initially many publishers were not careful about obtaining permission to reproduce photographs. Copyright law stipulated penalties of one dollar per copy of an infringed photograph, and in the case of mass-circulation newspapers, damages could potentially reach hundreds of thousands of dollars. In 1895, the ANPA's copyright committee persuaded its members of the need to lobby Congress to change the law, and their efforts led to an 1895 amendment limiting penalties for newspaper reproductions of copyrighted photographs to a maximum of five thousand dollars per suit.[123]

Although the penalties were now capped, newspaper publishers still claimed to be victims of blackmail by photographers. In 1897, John Norris of the *New York World* warned his peers that "there exists in New York a Photographers' League with an attorney that is thriving on the settlements and compromises made with American publishers of newspapers."[124] The *World* had been sued for publishing a portrait of the actress Marie Jansen given to the reporter by Jansen herself. To avoid court, it settled for five thousand dollars.[125] The ANPA lobbied for an amendment that would make newspaper reproductions of photographs noninfringing. It argued that halftones were necessarily "inferior" to the original photographs and could not possibly hurt the sale of the originals.[126]

The ANPA's efforts were vigorously opposed by photographers. Some petitioned Congress, arguing that the proposed amendment would "deprive photographers of their property rights so far as newspapers are concerned; and would destroy privacy rights in photographic portraits."[127] The threat to privacy became a refrain among opponents of the ANPA's proposed amendment. The idea was that if newspapers did not have to request permission to reproduce photographs, then they would be violating not only the copyrights of photographers but also the privacy rights of the individuals pictured.[128] Writing to the chairman of the Senate Judiciary Committee, the head of the Photographers Association of America protested that the ANPA sought "to take all privacy from the Photograph, thereby using it wherever they see fit, and destroying the value of a Portrait which you or I may deem too sacred to be hawked about the country in an ordinary newspaper."[129] The Photographers' Copyright League of America combined moral and economic arguments against the ANPA's efforts. Testifying before the Joint Committee on Patents (which had responsibility for copyright reform), the League's representative appealed to the sensibilities of congressmen, suggesting that the time may come when they needed to protect themselves or their families from unauthorized reproductions of photographs in newspapers. But the League, which claimed to represent thirty thousand photography studios with two hundred thousand total employees, also highlighted the potential economic harm for photographers. Newspaper publishers knew that photographs constituted a record of passing events and sought to use these photographs without paying the photographers.[130] A major photography studio provided evidence that newspaper reproduction rights had become an important source of income for photographers. The studio rejected the argument that newspaper reproductions acted as an advertisement for the photographers, insisting that most newspapers did not print credit lines.[131]

While photographers emphasized their economic rights and concerns about privacy, the ANPA stressed the need to protect newspapers in cases in which they had no way of knowing that a particular photograph had been registered for copyright. If it was not possible to classify all newspaper reproductions as noninfringing, then the ANPA wanted the law modified to require clear copyright notices on photographs and a strict limitation of penalties for infringement. If such changes were not made, they argued, newspapers would remain vulnerable to "unscrupulous photographic copyright proprietors in semi-blackmailing operations" that sought to extract enormous sums from publishers who unwittingly reproduced copyrighted photographs.[132]

THE 1909 ACT AND NEWSPAPERS

The ANPA partly achieved its objectives. Although the 1909 Copyright Act did not allow newspapers to reproduce photographs without permission, it did further limit damages in cases of unauthorized newspaper reproductions of photographs.[133] But what about copyright for newspaper articles? With the AP declining to participate in discussions leading up to the 1909 act and the ANPA shifting its attention to photographs, news publishers were largely absent from the legislative process. The publishers of magazines and other periodicals were keen to modify the registration requirements, with some suggesting that periodicals should have to register their titles only at the beginning of each volume or calendar year.[134] Authors also sought to protect their rights over contributions to newspapers and periodicals. The American Copyright League, for example, suggested that absent some other agreement between the author and the publisher, all rights to a contribution should revert to the author after three years.[135]

Two of the most important people involved in drafting the bills that became the 1909 Copyright Act were Solberg, the Register of Copyrights, and Bowker, the editor, publisher, and copyright expert. Neither man doubted that newspapers and periodicals should be included as copyrightable subject matter, and the 1909 act was the first American statute to do so.[136] The new law also changed formalities in important ways. After 1909, it was no longer necessary to register titles before publication. To secure copyright, one simply had to publish the work with a copyright notice affixed to it. Registration and deposit of the work "promptly" after publication was still required before any action for infringement could be initiated.[137] Solberg had long advocated the removal of the advanced registration requirement in order to reduce administrative burdens and avoid legal misunderstandings. In his experience, many titles were registered that were never actually published or were published under a different title than what had been registered. Some people also had the mistaken belief that registering a title gave them exclusive use of it.[138] Although the removal of the advanced registration requirement applied to all kinds of works, it was particularly useful for the publishers of newspapers and periodicals, since they no longer had to scramble to send in titles before a daily newspaper or weekly magazine went to press.

Magazine publishers wanted the new law to clarify what was covered by the copyright in a periodical. After reading a draft bill that Solberg sent him in 1906, Charles Scribner II, whose firm published *Scribner's Magazine*, urged Solberg to add a clause "stating clearly that the copyright of a number of a periodical protected all its contents, both text and illustrations, in so far as the same is proper subject of copyright." Scribner also wanted to make sure that one copyright notice would suffice for the entire issue of a periodical; it was cumbersome to attach notices to individual articles.[139] *Life* magazine supported similar changes, complaining of the additional labor and expense required to register individual articles for copyright.[140] In line with these requests, the 1909 act explicitly stated that the copyright in a periodical provided the same rights as if each part were individually copyrighted and that a single copyright notice at the head of each issue sufficed. One could also secure copyright in contributions by registering them separately and depositing one copy of the periodical in which they appeared.[141] Solberg wanted to ensure that it was possible to protect selected articles in cases in which the periodical itself was not registered, but some publishers ended up filing redundant applications, making separate entries for individual articles in addition to the general entry for each issue of their periodical.[142]

Despite these changes, it was still unclear what kinds of newspaper material qualified for copyright. In Bowker's well-informed view, the 1909 act protected "all the copyrightable component parts of the work copyrighted," but it was left to the courts to decide what was "copyrightable" by determining which parts of the work were original.[143] Newspapers had long been interested in being the first to publish a particular story in their own circulation area, but whether the text of the news originated with them was another matter. Although the procedures for registration and deposit had been simplified, the question of whether reports of recent events were copyrightable remained unresolved. Part of the reason for this may be that the AP declined to participate in the copyright conferences, and once the ANPA encountered resistance on the question of telegraphic dispatches, it shifted its focus to photographs. That left Bowker, Solberg, and magazine publishers, especially Scribner, as the ones involved in drafting the clauses affecting newspapers. Solberg knew that news dispatches had long been registered as books, but like Putnam back in 1906, he may have thought the idea of copyright for news articles was too controversial to insert in the bill. The comments of Scribner and Bowker suggest that they assumed that the main point of copyright for newspapers, as for other periodicals, was to protect their "literary and artistic contributions."[144]

In his 1912 copyright treatise, updated to reflect the 1909 act, Bowker suggested that if a daily newspaper decided to deposit each issue with the copyright office and spend $365 per year ($1 per entry), the reason would be to protect its "original matter of substantial literary value." Although he did not have any clear American precedent to cite, Bowker speculated that copyright could protect "the form of a dispatch, letter, or article containing news" but could not stop another newspaper from reporting the same news in a different form.[145] He probably could not have predicted what would happen next. Six years later, the AP would appear before the Supreme Court and argue forcefully that news was not appropriate subject matter for copyright. Instead, the AP would claim that the factual details of news reports should be treated as property that deserved to be protected against unfair use by competitors. In a decision that continues to elicit debate one hundred years later, the Supreme Court agreed with the AP. The next chapter considers the origins and consequences of that decision.

CHAPTER 7

International News Service v. Associated Press and Its Legacy

THE US COPYRIGHT ACT OF 1909 made it possible to protect newspaper articles against verbatim copying and to license their republication, providing a legal basis for syndication. To secure copyright, one had to affix a notice to the publication and complete the formalities of registration and deposit. Some publishers found these requirements confusing and ill-suited to the speed of the news business.[1] Still, in 1921, a federal court provided a clear precedent that the form of news articles could be protected by copyright and that copying substantial parts of an article without permission constituted infringement, even if credit was given.[2] That continues to be the law today, with the important difference that copyright now subsists from the moment a work is "fixed in any tangible medium of expression." Registration and notice on the work are no longer necessary to secure copyright, although one still has to register before filing a lawsuit.[3]

In 1918, however, a completely different remedy against "piracy" was established by the Supreme Court in *International News Service v. Associated Press* (hereafter *INS*).[4] In *INS*, the court recognized what the majority opinion called a *"quasi* property" in news that was entirely independent of copyright. The property was quasi in the sense that it could be enforced only against business competitors, not against members of the public. Although readers were free to discuss and share news, press agencies were not allowed to reproduce news gathered by a competitor until its "commercial value" had passed. *INS* established the tort of misappropriation (later known as the "hot news" doctrine), which protects organizations that collect time-sensitive information from "free riding" by direct competitors. The most revolutionary aspect of *INS*, and one of the reasons that it remains controversial, is that the court recognized certain exclusive rights over the factual details of news *after* publication.[5]

INS had no parallel in the United Kingdom. Although British courts issued injunctions to stop unauthorized reuse of information (such as stock quotations and cricket scores), these cases always involved some element of theft, bribery, or breach of confidence.[6] Once facts were published, any property in them ended. In *INS*, the Supreme Court ruled that the AP's competitors could not copy *or rewrite* AP news for as long as it had commercial value. Obtaining this legal victory required convincing the justices to accept a new definition of publication and to stretch existing conceptions of property and unfair competition law. The case has long been a staple of law school curricula and law reviews, in part because the majority and dissenting opinions touch on fundamental questions of intellectual property. The case exposed competing rationales for temporary monopoly rights—the utilitarian idea that incentives for creators will benefit society versus the theory that individuals have a natural right to the rewards of their labor. It also addressed the question of who should have the authority to make rules about intellectual property—the legislature or the courts—and proposed the novel idea of "quasi property," which was controversial even in 1918. Justice Louis Brandeis issued a powerful dissent, and two other justices argued in favor of a different remedy than the one decided by the majority. Ever since, people have questioned the legal basis of the ruling and its consequences for news organizations and the public.

For the history of journalism, *INS* matters because of the ways its principles have been interpreted and adapted to changes in the media landscape. In the age of radio, the precedent was invoked in efforts to prohibit broadcasters from reading news on the air. More recently, it has been revived in attempts to stop the unauthorized reuse of news and financial information online. For these reasons, it is important to take a closer look at the genesis of the case, the AP's motivations in bringing it, the principles that were at stake, and the ongoing tension between property rights and public access to news that *INS* embodies. It is also important not to assume that *INS* was the dramatic turning point that it appeared to be in 1918. A closer look at the decision's legacy reveals a legal principle that has often been controversial and difficult to enforce.

QUALIFIED PUBLICATION

The AP's victory in establishing a "property in news" is generally credited to its general manager at the time, Melville E. Stone. In his autobiography, Stone claimed that he always knew that copyright was inappropriate for news. He worried less about the burdens of registration and deposit than about the fact that copyright did not protect facts, making it ineffective against rivals that reproduced the same news in different form. Stone claimed that what was needed was "a successful revolution in all of the accepted theories of the law so far as literary property was concerned. It meant new and wider definitions of the words 'property' and 'publication,' and it meant forward-looking men of no mean order both upon the bench and at the bar."[7] Stone's retrospective account provided a neat narrative, as though he had a plan to enact a revolution in legal thinking and then carried it out. In fact, this process depended on a series of court cases involving property rights in stock quotations beginning in the 1870s.

The struggle to protect financial information entered a new phase in the 1870s due to the development of multiplex telegraphy and ticker machines. Multiplex allowed for the simultaneous transmission of four messages on a single wire. Telegraph companies could now lease excess wire capacity to newspapers, press agencies, and brokerage firms. Tickers were printing telegraph machines installed in financial firms, hotels, saloons, and other establishments that paid to receive updates of market prices or sports scores. These changes in communications infrastructure encouraged the continuous trading of stocks and commodities and led to fierce competition among those providing the latest price quotations.[8] This competition in turn led some firms to enter price quotations for copyright in the early 1870s.[9] But they soon turned away from copyright in favor of a common-law property right in unpublished information.

In 1876, a New York court recognized this type of property. The case was brought by J. J. Kiernan, who had a business distributing news of foreign financial markets to clients via tickers installed in their offices. Kiernan purchased the information from the Gold and Stock Tele-

graph Company, which had obtained it from the New York Associated Press (NYAP).[10] Although the information was publicly available
in London, the NYAP paid for it to be transmitted by telegraph to New
York. Kiernan's clients paid a premium for access to these ticker reports before they were distributed to Gold and Stock's own clients or
the newspapers of the NYAP. But a competitor of Kiernan's called the
Manhattan Quotation Telegraph Company gained access to the reports
from some of Kiernan's subscribers and then transmitted the information to its own clients. When Kiernan sued to stop this practice, the defendant argued that there could be no property in financial news that
was already publicly known in Europe. The court disagreed. Although
everyone was free to make arrangements for an agent in London to collect news and transmit it to New York, it was not lawful to profit from
the "superior diligence" of one's rivals. The court ruled that the NYAP
had "a right of property in all news transmitted to it by its agents, until
it abandons that right by publication."[11]

The Kiernan case hinged on the question of what constituted publication. The Manhattan Quotation Telegraph Company insisted that
the appearance of the quotations on ticker tapes in multiple offices
made them public. But Kiernan successfully argued that his clients were
bound by contract; they knew that they were not supposed to share the
information with outside parties. When the Manhattan Quotation Telegraph Company asked Kiernan's clients for access, it induced a breach
of trust. To explain why the ticker tapes did not constitute publication
in the sense of abandonment to the public, the court referred to the
rights of authors or artists in their unpublished works. The performance
of a play did not deprive the dramatist of the exclusive right to print and
sell her work. The public display of a painting did not entitle viewers to
make copies for sale to the public. Similarly, receiving a letter did not
entitle the recipient to publish the letter without the author's consent.
The court did not see any reason why the private transmission of news
by telegraph was any different than sending a letter. Kiernan's transmission of the quotations to clients was therefore a "qualified publication,
which did not forfeit his right of property therein."[12]

THE VALUE OF TIMELINESS

Kiernan's information was considered unpublished because access was restricted to subscribers. The case of tickers installed in public places such as hotels and saloons was more complicated. By the late nineteenth century, such venues were providing their customers with up-to-the-minute news through arrangements with telegraph companies.[13] Did casual public access to news on the tickers mean that it had been published? This question was central to a case at the turn of the twentieth century involving Western Union and one of its competitors, National Telegraph News Company. Western Union was primarily a telegraph company, but it had a subsidiary that furnished clients with market news and sports scores via tickers. National Telegraph, which had a similar business, copied some of its reports from Western Union's tickers and transmitted them to its own paying clients. Western Union obtained a preliminary injunction prohibiting National Telegraph from copying for sixty minutes after news appeared on the tickers. National Telegraph appealed, arguing that the ticker tapes were not protected by copyright because they had not been registered or deposited with the copyright office. Because Western Union failed to secure copyright, any common-law property in unpublished information necessarily ended once it appeared on tickers that could be viewed by members of the public visiting a hotel or saloon that subscribed to the service.[14]

To get around this problem, Western Union's lawyers made a surprising argument. Although news organizations in Britain and America had long claimed that the labor and financial resources required to collect news justified copyright protection, Western Union asserted that it would be absurd to treat news as literary property. In court filings, the company's lawyers wrote, "We respectfully protest at the outset, and in the holy name of art and letters, that the reports of passing events sent over [Western Union's] tickers to saloons, hotels and brokers' offices, is not, properly speaking, literature."[15] In *Clayton v. Stone* (1828), a federal court had denied copyright to a weekly publication of market news on the grounds that it did not contribute to "learning." Citing this precedent, counsel for Western Union argued that sports scores and stock prices should also be excluded from copyright. But they also claimed that the information on the tickers "may appropriately be called quasi— or pseudo—literary property."[16] The goal was to have the court recognize a common-law property in information akin to that enjoyed by authors before publication but one that would continue after the news became available to the public via tickers.

Western Union received a sympathetic hearing from Judge Peter S. Grosscup, who wrote the opinion of the Court of Appeals for the Seventh Circuit. Grosscup's thinking had been shaped by conversations with Melville E. Stone of the AP.[17] Grosscup clearly understood that Western Union's strategy was to exclude news from copyright in order to seek a common-law property right, and he found their arguments compelling. Over time, the courts had recognized copyright protection for a wider range of works, but Grosscup maintained that "there is a point at which this process of expansion must cease." He did not think that the copyright clause of the Constitution justified giving "a monopoly of narrative" to those who were the first to print "the bare recital of events." A true work of authorship, Grosscup wrote, "would not have found existence in the form presented, but for the distinctive individuality of mind from which it sprang."[18] Similar rhetoric was used back in 1884 to oppose the idea of a special copyright law for news.[19] Now it was being used by a business that sought to establish a property right in news and by a judge who endorsed this idea. In both contexts, the push for legal protection for news led individuals to articulate, more clearly than before, the idea that copyright was meant to protect "creative" and "original" works of authorship.[20] Although this rhetoric was part of a legal strategy by Western Union, once it was affirmed by the Court of Appeals for the Seventh Circuit it could be used to exclude certain kinds of fact-based works from copyright. Once again, a dispute over news had led a judge to articulate what he saw as the appropriate boundaries of copyright law.

Grosscup accepted that informational works could qualify for copyright if they showed evidence of an author's mind at work, but sports scores and stock quotations did not rise to this level. Still, he thought some form of legal protection was needed to protect organizations that gathered and distributed news. The solution was to see Western Union not as an author eligible for copyright but as a "carrier" of news. Customers were willing to pay for this news because of the speed with which Western Union delivered it. And it was the commercial value of this *timeliness* that deserved to be protected as intangible property. Although the court's main justification for enjoining National Telegraph was the harm done to Western Union's property in the commercial value of its news, Grosscup also raised the issue of the public interest. The business of gathering and transmitting news involved considerable expense and coordination. If such news was freely appropriated by a competitor, he reasoned, then Western Union might withdraw from the business. As Grosscup put it, "The parasite that killed, would itself be killed, and the public would be left without any service at any price."[21]

SETTING UP A TEST CASE

Within the newspaper industry, Western Union's victory was hailed as establishing "a right of property in the news" that was "broader even than copyright."[22] It was broader than copyright because it protected facts, but the right was also of much shorter duration. After a sixty-minute embargo imposed by the court, National Telegraph and others were free to republish information from Western Union's tickers. Could the same principle be applied to news distributed by press associations? Because tickers were printing machines attached to telegraph wires, customers were able to read stock quotations and sports scores as soon as they were transmitted. News collected and distributed by press associations was not released to the public in this way. Customers accessed it by reading newspapers. In major cities, breaking news also appeared on bulletin boards outside of newspaper offices. Publishers used these bulletins to attract customers on the street. A vivid example is shown in figure 10, which portrays crowds gathering in front of the *New York Herald*'s bulletin board to learn the latest updates on the health of President James A. Garfield after he was shot in 1881.[23] Such bulletins had existed in New York since at least the 1830s, when letters were painted on paper or wood attached to the building; by the early twentieth century, New York publishers were experimenting with electric light displays.[24]

FIGURE 10. An example of an outdoor news bulletin from an earlier period. Crowds gather to learn the latest updates about President James A. Garfield's health after he was shot in 1881. *Frank Leslie's Illustrated Newspaper,* September 3, 1881.

What was to stop other newspapers or press agencies from republishing news announced in this way? Relying on the ticker cases to protect news that was already available to the public required challenging existing legal definitions of *publication*. And this is precisely what the AP would do.

Stone, the general manager of the AP, had long been interested in the idea of a property right in news, and the unscrupulous activities of International News Service (INS) during World War I provided a perfect opportunity to test this idea in court. INS was owned by William Randolph Hearst, who also operated several newspapers with AP franchises. Hearst wanted AP news for all of his papers, but in some cities his applications were blocked because existing members wanted to enjoy exclusivity in their areas. Hearst's inability to obtain AP membership for all of his papers provided the initial motivation for setting up the agency that became INS, although it soon began selling news and other syndicated material to other newspapers.[25]

The context of censorship and propaganda during World War I was crucial for setting up the AP's test case. Before the United States entered the war in 1917, Hearst papers were seen as sympathetic to Germany, against American intervention, and pro-Irish. In Britain, newspapers and press agencies were closely monitored during the war, and on October 10, 1916, the British government barred INS from using the transatlantic cable on the grounds that Hearst papers were propagating rumors and misinformation.[26] With INS's access to European news restricted, AP leadership suspected that they might now catch Hearst's agency in the act of "stealing" news. Someone immediately made the decision to register selected AP stories for copyright. In the previous 15 years, the AP had not claimed copyright in any stories; in the two months after October 10, it registered and deposited 16 articles.[27] This fact has not been noticed in previous studies of *INS*, no doubt because in court, the AP insisted that news reports were not eligible for copyright. But the registrations show that in the fall of 1916, the AP sought to catch INS by any means available. The AP soon gathered evidence that INS had obtained news surreptitiously, enabling it to forget about copyright and use the precedent of the ticker cases to enjoin INS. Evidence of surreptitious taking enabled the AP to build a case against INS and put it in a bad light. But Stone's real goal was to exploit the situation to establish the principle of a property right that would protect news even after it appeared on public bulletin boards or in early editions of newspapers. The fact that Hearst was already a controversial figure did not hurt Stone's cause. Hearst was an outspoken critic of war censorship, and under the Sedition Act of 1918, his papers would be closely watched by the War Department.[28]

The AP accused INS of appropriating news in three ways. The first two involved surreptitious taking before publication and were easily dealt with by the district court. First, INS paid a telegraph editor at the *Cleveland News*, an AP paper, for access to local news gathered by that paper and foreign news transmitted to Cleveland by the AP. Second, employees of INS visited the offices of the *New York American*, a Hearst paper with an AP franchise located in the same building as INS. Employees of INS were allowed to linger in the *American*'s offices and glean details of AP news as soon as it arrived.[29] As Hearst knew, AP bylaws forbid members from furnishing news to nonmembers or rival agencies. The problem of leaks was widespread enough in 1915–1916 that the AP's board of directors ordered an inspection of "the physical conditions of every office in which the report is received" to ensure that members did not allow representatives of other news organizations to enter their offices.[30] Hearst was far from alone in being accused of this practice, but the fact that he was the head of a rival agency presented a clear conflict of interest. Some AP members cited this conflict as a reason for the association to relax its policies and make AP news available to any newspaper willing to pay.[31] But according to the bylaws in force at that time, Hearst the AP member was not allowed to share news with Hearst the head of INS. Given the evidence of surreptitious taking in Cleveland and New York, the district court showed no hesitation in issuing injunctions to stop INS from obtaining news by these two methods.[32]

The third accusation involved the reuse of news after it had appeared on public bulletin boards and in early editions of AP member newspapers. As soon as news was released in one of these ways in New York, INS could transmit it by telegraph to its newspaper clients on the West Coast. Because of the time difference between the two coasts, INS's clients in California could print the news at the same time or earlier than could local members of the AP who paid for it. The problem was not new. In the 1860s, California newspapers that were excluded from the

California Associated Press (CAP) engaged in this practice, but the CAP was able to persuade the telegraph company not to transmit the "stolen" news. Thanks to increased line capacity (which allowed newspapers to lease wires) and the intervention of Congress and the courts, it became increasingly difficult to monopolize the wires in this way. A 1910 law explicitly classified telegraph companies as "common carriers," meaning that they were required to serve all customers willing to pay reasonable rates.[33] But the problem of multiple time zones remained. Theoretically, the AP could have avoided the problem by requiring its members to publish the news simultaneously regardless of their location. But that would have been highly impractical because early morning in New York was the middle of the night in San Francisco. The AP wanted its consolidated report and the local news gathered by AP newspapers to remain exclusive until all members had had a chance to publish it in their respective regions at their usual time of publication. Such exclusivity was seen as crucial to maximizing sales and advertising revenue in each local market.

An important study of *INS* referred to the case as a "concocted controversy," suggesting that INS did not mount a very strong defense because as a leading AP member Hearst had an interest in protecting the exclusivity of AP news.[34] Meanwhile, a detailed study of the AP during this period concluded that the association was less worried about INS than about the growing strength of United Press (UP), which was founded in 1907 when E. W. Scripps consolidated several existing agencies. By 1914, UP had over five hundred clients (INS had about four hundred clients, and the AP close to nine hundred members).[35] With the AP facing growing competition in the nationwide distribution of news, INS's actions during World War I provided Stone with an opportunity that he was eager to exploit. Hearst's relationship to the AP complicated the case and revealed how the interests of newspapers did not always match those of the association. That does not mean that INS colluded with AP during the litigation, however. INS appealed the case all the way to the Supreme Court, and it was represented by Samuel Untermyer, one of the country's most prominent antitrust lawyers.

REDEFINING PUBLICATION
AND UNFAIR COMPETITION

At the district court, Judge Augustus Hand stopped short of issuing an injunction against the reuse of news from public bulletin boards and early editions. The question was novel, and he preferred to have it decided by the Court of Appeals for the Second Circuit. On appeal, the AP requested that the court enjoin INS from "copying, transmitting, selling, using, or causing to be copied" any AP material from bulletins or printed newspapers belonging to its members, which now numbered about one thousand.[36] INS admitted that its agents purchased early editions, scanned them for fresh news, and rewrote selected stories. This practice was perfectly legal, according to INS, because there could be no property in facts after they were published. INS also claimed that taking news from early editions was a long-standing custom among newspapers and press agencies. According to INS, the AP came to the case with "unclean hands" because it had engaged in the same practice. Finally, INS argued that there was no justification for awarding the AP the kind of monopoly it sought. Being the first to publish news was sufficient reward. If the court prohibited INS and other agencies from reusing AP news, then the association would have a monopoly on facts.[37]

The AP denied that it copied or rewrote news from INS or other agencies. If there was an industry custom, according to the AP, it involved using competitors' reports as "tips." Employees would examine early editions of newspapers looking for interesting news that the AP may have missed. Instead of copying the story or rewriting it, they would conduct an independent investigation and prepare their own report. Because the AP expended labor and resources to gather news based on tips, it was not guilty of taking anyone's property or engaging in unfair competition. The AP maintained that everyone was free to report news of a particular event, but they had to rely on their own efforts to obtain the information. As the AP put it in its brief, "The raw material is the event and the final product is the message by which the event is brought to the purchaser; and whoever creates this product is entitled to it as his property."[38]

INS insisted that any such property ended with publication. The AP responded that INS was giving undue weight to a legal definition of publication that had no relevance outside of copyright law. Since news reports were not eligible for copyright, according to the AP, their appearance in newspapers or on bulletin boards did not constitute publication in the sense of abandonment to the public. The AP contended that the central principle of the ticker cases was that organizations that invested in collecting information were entitled to exclusive use of that information until they obtained a fair return. In a 1905 ruling on the ownership of commodity price quotations, the Supreme Court had held that "information will not become public property until the plaintiff has gained his reward."[39] Given that AP members paid assessments and contributed their local news to the association, they should each be given time to profit from AP news before competitors were allowed to reuse it. "Owing to the nature of the news distributing business," the AP argued, "the publication involved is necessarily a nation-wide publication. In other words, the publication throughout the country is a *single* publication."[40] If others were free to print AP news without permission, then the newspapers that contributed their local news to the AP would withdraw from the association. Piracy, if left unchecked, would undermine the cooperative model of news gathering.[41]

To argue its case before the Court of Appeals for the Second Circuit, Stone recruited Peter Grosscup, who was no longer a judge but whose decision in *National Telegraph v. Western Union* was one of the most important precedents cited in the case. In his oral argument, Grosscup elaborated on the idea that property in news depended on the "commercial value" of the AP's service. Admitting that there was no property in "facts" or "events," Grosscup explained that "what we do is to bring to the reader the *intelligence* of these events." The commercial value of this intelligence depended on the AP delivering it before any other agency, a quality that Grosscup referred to as "firstness."[42] The AP was not claiming to own the news, Grosscup insisted, only the exclusive right to profit from the *service* created by its members' investments in news gathering. Judge Charles Merrill Hough, who wrote the opinion for the court of appeals, accepted this distinction between the *facts* of the news and the

AP's *service*. In doing so, he acceded to the AP's demands to stretch the definition of publication to fit the circumstances of a press association operating in a country with multiple time zones. Hough agreed that INS and other agencies should not be allowed to reuse AP news until the association's westernmost member had a chance to publish it free from local competition. The court of appeals ruled that INS had invaded AP's property rights in news and engaged in unfair competition.[43]

Both rulings broke new ground. The ticker cases had upheld property rights in unpublished information, but the AP's news was available on outdoor bulletin boards and in early editions sold to the public. Findings of unfair competition had previously been limited to cases in which a defendant appropriated the reputation of another firm. INS had not labeled the news as coming from the AP. Arguably, it had deceived the public by failing to indicate the source of the news. Although there was no act of imitation or passing off, Hough nonetheless found INS's actions "immoral." But the court's decision was not unanimous. Judge Henry Galbraith Ward issued a dissent arguing that the court was wrong to stretch the definition of publication to fit the AP's circumstances. The fact that a rival was able to use the telegraph to transmit the news to its own clients did not justify creating a new property right or extending unfair competition law to cases in which there was no surreptitious taking or passing off. As Ward put it, "That the rotation of the earth is slower than the electric current is a physical fact the complainant must reckon with in doing its business."[44]

Despite this dissent, the court of appeals instructed the district court to issue an injunction against "any bodily taking of the words or substance of the plaintiff's news" until its commercial value had passed.[45] The AP's board of directors immediately began requiring members to print the following notice in their newspapers: "The Associated Press is exclusively entitled to the use for republication of all news dispatches credited to it or not otherwise credited in this paper and also the local news published herein."[46] In other words, any news that was not explicitly labeled as belonging to someone else belonged to the AP. Nothing was said about using the news after a certain number of hours.

NEWS IS DIFFERENT

INS contested the ruling of the court of appeals, and since the decision was not unanimous, the AP also preferred to have the case settled by the Supreme Court. The two sides returned to many of the same arguments used in the lower courts, but they now placed greater emphasis on the public interest.[47] In oral arguments for INS, Samuel Untermyer stressed that a property in news would impede the flow of information. He reminded the court that the current AP had been reorganized in New York in 1900 after the Illinois Supreme Court made a highly unfavorable ruling against its predecessor, the Chicago-based AP. The Illinois court found that the AP's rules prohibiting members from receiving news from other agencies was in restraint of trade. The court also cited a clause in the AP's articles of incorporation that allowed it to erect, purchase, lease, and operate telegraph wires. According to the court, the existence of this clause meant that the AP could be regulated as a public utility. In other words, like railroads and telegraph companies, the AP had to provide its news to all newspapers willing to pay for it.[48] Following the order of the Illinois Supreme Court would have made it impossible to maintain the exclusivity of news reports on which the value of AP franchises was based. The AP therefore left Chicago and reorganized as a membership corporation under New York law, where it continued to allow members to block applications by other newspapers in their territories. Untermyer explained that the AP's current rules made it impossible for many newspapers to obtain AP news, even though such news was essential to the success of any newspaper. Now the AP was asking for exclusive use of its news after it was released to the public. Untermyer warned that if the Supreme Court recognized such a right, then the AP would have "the most intolerable and despotic monopoly on the face of the earth."[49]

Untermyer was seconded by Hiram Johnson, the former governor of California and current senator. Like Hearst, Johnson was an outspoken critic of wartime censorship. He fought against passage of the Sedition Act of 1918, declaring it a threat to First Amendment rights.[50] But the INS case was not technically about censorship, so Johnson focused on the dangers of treating news as exclusive. He claimed that from "time immemorial" newspapers and agencies had relied on each other for news. Recalling the long tradition of exchange editors clipping news from other papers, Johnson told the court that if given more time he could deliver "an apostrophe to the Paste Pot and the Shears."[51] To deny the right to republish news—even if it was reformulated—would destroy the traditions of the country press and would hinder the activity of large urban dailies as well. Johnson also objected to the idea of basing an injunction on the time differential between the coasts. If the AP wanted to, it could require members to publish news simultaneously in all regions. Instead, it was trying to create a new property right that would help its own business while restricting access to news.[52]

In response to the charge that it sought a monopoly on news, the AP recalled that every agency was free to gather its own information. News reports were not like other kinds of writing because "their source is not locked in the brain of the producer, but is the *event* to which all persons have equal access."[53] But it was unfair to appropriate news collected by other agencies or associations and sell it in competition with them. Moreover, the AP claimed that exclusivity in news was in the public interest. If each agency collected its own news, then the public would have access to a greater variety of coverage. In cases in which two or more agencies conducted independent investigations of the same event, readers could have greater confidence in the facts. The rights of one agency over its reports would not prevent other agencies from gathering information for their own reports. As counsel for the AP put it, "In this field the law can find a middle ground between a complete monopoly in the creator and no rights at all."[54]

There were numerous precedents to show that common-law property in writings ended as soon as they were printed and sold to the public. Published works could be protected by copyright, but the AP knew that the court was extremely unlikely to uphold copyright protection for facts independently of their expression. For these reasons, the AP expended considerable energy trying to entirely exclude news from the realm of literary property. This strategy led counsel to accentuate the differences between news and other forms of writing. The AP's brief claimed:

News has no resemblance of any kind to literary property except the accidents that, like trade-marks, it is expressed in words, and in print and on paper. There is no imaginative or intellectual quality in its production, except the imagination and intellect which go into the organization for its collection and distribution. Indeed its character as news disappears when invention or imagination is introduced into its substance, and it then becomes what is known as a "fake."[55]

The idea that fake news might qualify for copyright because it was the product of imagination had actually been tested in court in 1913. The case was heard by none other than Judge Hough, who would later write the opinion of the Court of Appeals for the Second Circuit in *INS*. In the 1913 case, a writer for the New York *Sun* had penned a fictional account of a courtroom scene but framed it as though it were a journalistic report of a real occurrence. Believing the story to be true, another author used the report in the *Sun* as the basis for a stage play. The first author sued, claiming that the play represented an infringement of his right to dramatize the work. Judge Hough denied the injunction on the grounds that it was immoral to present fiction as news. Since the story was framed as news, the public had reason to believe it was true, and nobody had the exclusive right to dramatize factual occurrences.[56] In its dispute with the AP, INS cited this earlier case because of Hough's statement that "there can be no piracy of the facts, because facts are public property."[57] Hough's decision in the fictional-news case emphasized the importance of morality and expressed doubts about whether a real news story would qualify for copyright at all. In that sense, it was consistent with the AP's own strategy. According to the AP, news was out there waiting to be collected, and anybody who expended labor and financial resources could perform this work of collection.[58]

This representation of telegraphic news obscured the various forms of mental labor that went into the articles appearing in newspapers. The AP's correspondents and telegraph agents condensed reports into an economical form for transmission by wire to the AP's headquarters. Then employees unpacked the "cablese" and composed the consolidated report to be sent out to members. Finally, local newspaper editors modified and embellished these reports, more or less treating the dispatch as the basis for a story (although some printed the dispatch word for word).[59] In most cases, agencies did not furnish headlines with their dispatches. Those were the choice of the local editors who selected and prepared reports for the press.[60] But the idea that news was collected rather than created and the claim that invention or creativity would compromise the value of the news were consistent with the AP's ideals and ambitions. The AP catered to all of its members, regardless of region or political affiliation, and these members in turn sought to have the widest customer and advertiser base possible. The AP thus sought to strip news reports of signs of religious or political affiliation, regional dialect, or personal voice that might make the report less acceptable to newspaper readers in various parts of the country. The argument that news was a "business commodity" rather than a form of authorship thus dovetailed with the ideal of impersonal factual reporting.[61]

According to counsel for the AP, copyright should be reserved for literary works of enduring value, and news was of passing interest only. This view of copyright was in fact largely out-of-date. By the early twentieth century, a more minimalist approach to originality in copyright law prevailed as a result of pressure from industries that sought to protect works that had significant market value but might not quality for copyright if courts set strict standards for original authorship.[62] The case of *Bleistein v. Donaldson Lithographing Co.* (1903), in which the Supreme Court upheld copyright protection for circus posters, was a watershed. The plaintiff insisted that advertisements and show bills represented a significant share of the trade in lithographic prints. If firms could not copyright them then there would be no incentive to invest in new designs, and the industry would collapse. The defendant cited numerous precedents in which courts denied protection to works that did not make a lasting contribution to literature or science. But the tide had turned against this view of copyright in favor of one that was oriented toward the market value of works. The Supreme Court in 1903 held that the circus posters exhibited enough evidence of independent intellectual effort to qualify for copyright and firmly rejected the idea that courts should judge the artistic or literary merits of works.[63]

The AP might have easily satisfied the threshold for originality by showing that its agents and the reporters for its member papers expended intellectual effort to shape the news into a distinct product that had a recognizable market value. But the AP's desire to protect factual details made copyright counterproductive, and this led its counsel to reject the kind of approach embodied by the *Bleistein* decision. The AP insisted that news was different than other genres of writing. In the case of a scientific treatise or historical study, future generations would seek out the work for its form, not just the facts it conveyed. Their brief put it this way: "The value of the book is the original way in which the thought is presented. The commercial value of news, on the contrary, is not in the way the events are presented, but in its being the *first* to bring to the person's notice the happening of such event."[64]

Counsel for the AP repeatedly stressed the idea that "firstness" constituted the primary value of news for customers. There was no sense that readers might enjoy how events were described, the particular words or phrases employed, or the viewpoint of the journalist. As had been the case in previous attempts to protect telegraph news in Britain and America, there was little discussion of how one reporter's coverage of an event might differ from that of another. The goal was to stop competitors from reporting the same event unless they had investigated it independently. As the AP's counsel Frederick W. Lehmann said in oral arguments, "The essential element, the thing of value in the news, is not the literary form in which it is expressed, but the report of the event or the occurrence."[65] In the case of most writings, it might be acceptable to reformulate ideas or facts in order to create a new and different work. But in the case of news, no amount of rewriting could possibly avoid damaging the property of the organization that first collected the news. Since the property adhered not to the expression but to the "firstness" of the news, there was no difference between announcing, "The Austrian Emperor died today," and "The death of the Austrian Emperor occurred today."[66]

INS objected to the idea of excluding news from the realm of literary property in order to obtain stronger property rights than those available to authors. How could it be correct that the ideas and conceptions of great writers belonged to the public as soon as their books were published but that a news agency could claim the exclusive right to report facts as long as they had commercial value? To justify special treatment for news on the grounds that it was "worthless as literature" seemed perverse. As INS's brief stated, "That is tantamount to saying, that legal protection is dependent on the lack of literary merit. Gibbon, Grote, Macauley, Prescott, and Parkman would have lost the property right inhering in their classical historical compositions, by publication without securing a copyright, whilst the ephemeral news of the day would continue to retain its character of private property though published a millionfold."[67]

CONFLICTING OPINIONS

The AP was trying to exclude news from the realm of copyright for strategic reasons, but ultimately they did not need to do this, because the majority of the Supreme Court sympathized with the AP's idea that news needed to be protected from unfair use by a competitor. In the majority opinion, Justice Mahlon Pitney distinguished between the "substance of the information" being conveyed and "the particular form or collocation of words" used to communicate it. Acknowledging that news articles "often possess a literary quality," Pitney stated that they could be protected by copyright. Counsel for the AP had referred to *Clayton v. Stone* (1828), but Pitney determined that precedent to be outdated since the Copyright Act of 1909 offered protection for "all the writings of an author" and specifically mentioned newspapers. Pitney even cited the regulations of the copyright office to show that it was possible to register individual articles or entire issues of a newspaper for copyright and that specific application cards were available for these purposes. According to Pitney, a glance at the newspapers of the day made clear that some publishers were taking advantage of the law.[68] Pitney did not comment on the fact that prominent members of the AP regularly entered their newspapers for copyright, a practice that stretched back to the 1890s.[69] Either he was unaware of these registrations or he considered them irrelevant because the AP was not suing for copyright infringement. INS might have used these registrations to try to undermine the AP's repeated claim that news reports could not be copyrighted. The AP could have replied, however, that the registrations were intended to protect not news reports but other literary and artistic matter in the newspapers, thereby holding on to the argument that news was not eligible for copyright.

In any case, Pitney affirmed that news reports could be copyrighted but that the underlying factual details could not be. If he had stopped there, his reasoning would have been consistent with the English decision of *Walter v. Steinkopff* (1892) discussed in chapter 5.[70] Yet Pitney dismissed the distinction between facts and expressions as irrelevant to the case, saying, "We need spend no time, however, upon the general question of property in news matter at common law, or the application of the copyright act, since it seems to us the case must turn upon the question of unfair competition in business."[71] Pitney's turn away from copyright here has been criticized by legal scholars who have claimed that *INS* gave rise to a tradition in which punishing those who "reap where they have not sown" often takes priority over issues of free speech and public access to information.[72] But once Pitney determined that INS's actions were "contrary to good conscience," he could ignore most of the legal arguments that had been levied against exclusive rights in news. By framing the case in terms of unfair competition rather than the rights of authors and the public, he was able to sidestep the whole question of whether publication constituted abandonment. He acknowledged that once news was printed or announced on bulletin boards, members of the public were free to use it as they wished. Different rules applied to INS and its clients because they used the telegraph and printing presses to sell news in competition with the AP. The neologism used by Pitney—he referred to news as "quasi property"—reflected the fact that he was trying to find a middle ground between those who saw news as private property and those who defined it as a public good.

The Supreme Court upheld the decision of the Court of Appeals for the Second Circuit, recognizing that the AP had the exclusive right to use its news until all of its members had a chance to publish it free from local competition. But the decision was not unanimous; the vote was 5–3. Justice John Clarke recused himself because he had a financial interest in newspapers. Justices Louis Brandeis and Oliver Wendell Holmes Jr. each authored a dissenting opinion, and Justice Joseph McKenna concurred in the latter. Holmes, who had authored the opinion in the circus poster case, did not see any reason why news reports could not be copyrighted. Because the AP chose not to claim copyright, neither the combination of words nor the factual details could be protected. For Holmes, the court could not recognize a property based on the "exchangeable value" of the news. Property rights had to be created by law; they did not automatically result from the commercial value of something. Holmes also disagreed with the majority's finding of unfair competition since INS had not "palmed off" its product as that of the AP. By republishing AP news without acknowledging the source, INS had actually done the opposite. Holmes thought that the solution for this kind of misrepresentation was simply to require news agencies to cite their sources. He therefore favored a different kind of injunction than the one granted by the majority. He suggested that the court should prohibit INS from republishing AP news for a certain number of hours after publication "unless it gives express credit to the Associated Press."[73]

It is tempting to connect Holmes's opinion in *INS* to his more famous dissent in the case of *Abrams v. United States* the following year. In *Abrams*, Holmes argued that allowing critical or unpopular views to be aired was crucial to democracy because a "free trade in ideas" would eventually allow truth to prevail.[74] In *INS*, the Supreme Court did not consider the First Amendment, but issues of censorship and patriotism formed the background of the case given Hearst's reputation and the fact that the British government had denied him access to the transatlantic cable. In this context, it may be instructive to see Holmes's dissent in *INS* as part of his turn toward a greater emphasis on press freedom after the war ended. If in *Abrams* Holmes was concerned with the circulation of critical or unpopular views, in *INS* he seems to have been concerned about allowing newspapers to report published information as long as they cited the source.

Justice Brandeis issued a longer and more critical dissent. Like Holmes, he rejected the idea of property arising from market value. Just because something could be sold for a profit did not make it property, nor did the fact that it required labor or money to produce. Here Brandeis offered one of the most widely quoted statements about the limits of intellectual property: "The general rule of law is, that the noblest of human productions—knowledge, truths ascertained, conceptions, and ideas—become, after voluntary communication to others, free as the air to common use. Upon these incorporeal productions the attribute of property is continued after such communication only in certain classes of cases where public policy has seemed to demand it."[75] Brandeis knew perfectly well that arguments based on labor and financial outlay had often been employed to justify copyrights and patents, but he insisted that these statutory monopolies were the exception rather than the rule. Brandeis thought his colleagues in the majority were wrong in claiming that the ticker cases had established a property right in news. Although the judges in the ticker cases sometimes employed the language of property, their rulings were always based on breach of confidence, and this element was lacking in *INS*. British courts, according to Brandeis, had been more consistent in offering relief only in cases of surreptitious taking. If what INS did was unfair, then existing law offered no remedy.

Brandeis insisted that if a new law were needed to protect news gatherers, then it should be created by Congress, not by a court dealing with a dispute between two businesses. He wrote that "the rule for which the plaintiff contends would effect an important extension of property rights and a corresponding curtailment of the free use of knowledge and of ideas; and the facts of this case admonish us of the danger involved in recognizing such a property right in news, without imposing upon news-gatherers corresponding obligations."[76] The reference to obligations here hinted at the restrictive nature of the AP's bylaws, which made it difficult for many newspapers to obtain AP news even if they were willing to pay for it. Brandeis recalled that the attempt in 1884 to legislate a special copyright for news had failed. He also pointed out that international agreements such as the Berne Convention (which the United States had not yet signed) and the Pan-American Copyright Convention (which the United States had ratified in 1911) explicitly denied protection to "news." Consequently, the courts should be wary of recognizing a new property right. Congress should determine whether such a right was needed, define its limits, and provide for the "administrative machinery" necessary to enforce it.[77]

UNCERTAIN EFFECTS

Notwithstanding the dissents of Holmes and Brandeis, the AP had obtained a major legal victory. The organization celebrated the fact that other agencies would no longer be able to take the substance of AP news from bulletin boards or early editions.[78] *Editor & Publisher* described *INS* as "one of the most important decisions in the history of news gathering, deciding that there is a property right in news."[79] The *New York Times*, an AP member, applauded the court's recognition of a property in the "freshness" of news. They wrote, "The moment of distribution to the public through early editions of newspapers or by posting of bulletins is the one seized upon by the news pirate for converting it to its own use. That is where protection is needed, that is where it is extended by the decision of the Supreme Court."[80] The Portland *Oregonian*, also an AP member, praised the court's ruling but saw it primarily as a condemnation of Hearst's deviant actions rather than as a new departure in journalism. "There is a certain comity of fair dealing between newspapers and news associations," the *Oregonian* claimed, "but Hearst has been a most persistent and unscrupulous violator of its reasonable rules. He takes what he can get, wherever and however he can get it."[81]

The extent to which *INS* marked a change in industry customs with respect to copying is difficult to answer. The ongoing digitization of newspapers and the use of computational analysis to locate substantially similar texts may one day help to answer this question.[82] But archival evidence suggests that the AP's competitors saw the Supreme Court's decision as introducing new norms rather than confirming existing ones and that the decision may have had a greater effect on United Press (UP) than on INS. Hearst already had access to AP news for some of his newspapers, and INS traded in syndicated feature stories as well as breaking news. Whether INS stopped using factual details from AP papers remains difficult to know, but UP's general manager Roy Howard explicitly acknowledged that his agency would have to change its practices since it was no longer permissible to rewrite news from AP papers. Stone described this admission as even more gratifying than the decision of the Supreme Court.[83] UP's response to the case confirms that INS was not the only agency to take news from the AP and that the problem was not caused by Hearst losing access to the transatlantic cable. In that sense, INS established a right that had not previously been recognized, either in custom or at law.[84]

As the AP quickly learned, its victory in INS represented a double-edged sword in America and abroad. Stone—the longtime champion of a property in news—worried that the decision could effectively destroy the AP's competition, once again exposing the association to charges of monopoly. Meanwhile, the INS decision constrained what the AP was able to do internationally. Although the Supreme Court ruling had no validity abroad, the AP felt obliged to abide by its principles in order to avoid charges of hypocrisy. The organization could not champion exclusive rights in news while copying from other newspapers, even foreign ones. As Stone put it to the board of directors in 1919, the INS decision "necessarily put an end to our pirating news from the London papers."[85] Based on a sample of news collected by the AP in England, Stone concluded that an overwhelming majority of stories came not from Reuters (with which the AP had an exclusive contract) but from London newspapers. The AP asked a number of London publishers for permission to reuse their material; all but one denied the request. Meanwhile, UP saw no obligation to ask permission and continued to lift stories from London papers.[86]

Under the leadership of Kent Cooper in the late 1920s, the AP hoped for an international agreement that would recognize the kinds of rights established by INS. In 1927, the Conference of Press Experts of the League of Nations considered a resolution on this subject, and although the United States was not a member of the League of Nations, the AP was invited to participate. Cooper jumped at the chance to speak. The draft resolution suggested that official news issued by governments should flow freely but that news gathered by a newspaper or agency should be protected as property for a certain number of hours after publication. Cooper and the AP fully supported this idea, as did the British and French news agencies, Reuters and Havas. Unsurprisingly, International News Service was against the proposal on the grounds that it would restrict the flow of information. The British delegation was also divided. Representing newspaper publishers, Baron George Riddell of the *News of the World* saw the measure as an attempt by the agencies to advance their own interests. He also mocked the participation of the AP given that the United States was not a member of the League of Nations or the Berne Convention. The German delegation, which played an important role in the negotiations, favored recognition of a property right in unpublished news but argued that each country should be left to make its own laws regarding protection after publication.[87] In line with a compromise proposed by the Germans, the final resolution of the Conference of Press Experts declared that news organizations were "entitled to the fruits of their labour, enterprise and financial expenditure on the production of news reports" but that "this principle shall not be so interpreted as to result in the creation or encouragement of any monopoly in news."[88] Although the conference endorsed the idea that reproducing published news without permission should be considered an act of "unfair trade," it could not agree on anything more specific and thus decided to leave such questions to the national governments.[89]

The head of Reuters, Sir Roderick Jones, also sought international recognition for a property right in news. His goal was to protect Reuters news throughout the British empire. Since the Berne Convention excluded news from copyright protection internationally, Jones tried to rally European news agencies around the idea that news could be classified as a form of industrial property. In 1932, he sent a proposal to Agences Alliées, a federation of European agencies, suggesting that "all news obtained by a newspaper or news agency, whatever its form or content and whatever the method by which it has been transmitted, shall be regarded as the property of such newspaper or agency for as long as it retains its commercial value."[90] Jones thus adopted the language of *INS*, which he celebrated as having "imposed upon U.S. journalists, for their eternal salvation, the doctrine that news after publication as well as before is as much an article of property as coal, or cabbages, or diamonds."[91] Of course, news was intangible. The almost absurd list of goods mentioned by Jones, coupled with his over-the-top religious language, betrayed the rhetorical difficulties of arguing for a property right in news. In 1934, during a conference to revise the International Convention for the Protection of Industrial Property, a proposal to protect news for twenty-four hours after publication actually came to a vote. Thirteen countries voted in favor, five voted against (including the United States), and twelve abstained (including Britain). The idea came up again at the 1938 conference, but delegates could not agree on exactly what should constitute illicit use of news or what the terms of protection should be. The outbreak of World War II precluded further efforts to establish an international agreement.[92] Protection for news would be decided on a national basis, not only because of disagreements among the parties at each international conference but also because news did not seem to fit into prevailing conceptions of either literary or industrial property.[93]

Even within the United States, it proved difficult to translate the legal victory in *INS* into a lasting change in industry norms. Roy Howard of UP had assured Stone in writing that his agency accepted the principles of the Supreme Court's decision, but in the 1920s Cooper found that UP sometimes took AP news or solicited AP members to provide reports before publication. Cooper exchanged several letters with his counterpart at UP, Karl Bickel, on the mutual benefits of respecting the *INS* decision. Bickel maintained that UP did not publish any news for which it did not have its own sources, but Cooper became aware of several violations, and he sought legal advice in 1927–1928. The lawyers determined that Cooper did not have enough evidence to show that UP had a deliberate policy of taking AP news but that if he found such evidence an injunction could be obtained. The AP's counsel also reported that UP staff thought they had the right to republish AP news as long as they gave proper credit. Such an assumption was based on Holmes's dissenting opinion, which suggested that copying news should be allowed if the source was named, rather than on the majority decision, which prohibited any use of the news as long as it still had commercial value.[94] But Cooper sought to avoid litigation. He wanted Bickel to explicitly acknowledge the principle of a property in news and ensure that UP employees respected that principle. The exchange of letters on this subject reveals that this was easier said than done.[95] For Cooper, the desire to have UP respect the AP's exclusive rights over news it collected was part of a broader effort to establish agreements with rival agencies—such as the agreement not to publicly disparage each other—that he thought would be of mutual benefit.[96]

INS did not mark the end of the relevance of copyright for AP or for newspapers in general. The changing uses of copyright by news organizations over the course of the twentieth century merits a detailed study of its own. But a preliminary examination of the records indicates that many newspapers registered their daily issues for copyright, both before and after 1918.[97] As for the AP, management sought the advice of the copyright office in the 1920s, and there were internal discussions about whether copyright was worth the trouble and expense of registration and deposit. Members of the AP also wondered whether all the copyright notices they saw on newspaper stories were legitimate. Thorvald Solberg, the Register of Copyrights, confirmed that many large newspapers entered each day's issue and made separate entries for selected stories. But Solberg also suspected that many newspapers displayed a copyright line without complying with the other formalities.[98] In 1926, when the AP sought to protect a series of high-profile interviews, they learned that registration alone would not suffice if the full copyright notice did not appear in member papers.[99] The AP instructed members to give proper credit to AP and reproduce copyright notices where applicable, but some members remained confused about the requirements. In 1931, the Washington bureau chief suggested that with the exception of very special material, the AP could save time and money by forgoing registration entirely. Printing the copyright notice at the head of an article served as a warning, and if copying took place, then the AP could proceed with registration. Cooper agreed with this strategy, which was in line with the requirements of the Copyright Act of 1909.[100]

Occasional disputes revealed that copyright was a blunt instrument for controlling rights over news stories in an organization as complex as the AP. The AP sought to protect its dispatches as well as the local news stories furnished by its members. But AP members often modified the stories they received over the wires. Whenever a newspaper added interpretation, explanation, or other editorial comments to an AP report, it was required to label these changes clearly so that readers would not hold the AP responsible for the views expressed. And if a newspaper wanted to mix AP reports with material from other agencies, then they had to remove the AP credit line entirely.[101] News stories were almost always the product of collective authorship, and reliance on freelancers complicated matters, especially if the writer refused to transfer rights to the member newspaper or the AP. A lawsuit threatened by one such freelancer in 1932 led the AP to create new guidelines advising newspaper editors to systematically obtain written permission for any story that originated outside their staff.[102]

LEGAL RECEPTION OF *INS*

From a legal perspective, the legacy of *INS* has been mixed. Immediately after the decision, articles in law reviews celebrated the Supreme Court's decision for holding businesses to higher ethical standards and affirming the principle that it was wrong to appropriate the fruits of someone else's labor.[103] The decision initially provided some hope for legal protection in industries or situations in which copyright law did not apply. In the 1920s, for example, copyright law did not explicitly protect fabric designs. When a silk manufacturer found that another company had copied one of its most popular designs, it sought rights similar to those the AP had obtained. The silk manufacturer admitted that fashion was "ephemeral" and demanded protection only for the current season. But the Court of Appeals for the Second Circuit refused to see Pitney's decision in *INS* as a general rule that could be applied to other industries. Writing for the court, Judge Learned Hand echoed Brandeis's view that only Congress could create laws protecting writings or inventions. According to Hand, it was wrong to see *INS* as creating "a sort of common-law patent or copyright for reasons of justice." Courts that did so would be usurping the constitutional mandate of Congress to establish copyright and patent laws.[104] If this logic had been followed by the majority of the Supreme Court in *INS*, as Brandeis said it should have been, then the AP would have lost.

Still, Hand's decision in the silk designs case was not the end of the story. In the news business, the precedent of *INS* offered hope at a time when radio challenged the business models of newspapers and press agencies. The 1918 decision underpinned efforts to stop the unauthorized broadcasting of news stories and sporting events.[105] Yet such cases need to be put in context. We should not assume that each new combination of technology and business practice inevitably led news organizations to seek legal redress. The first radio broadcasts took place in the early 1920s. It was more than a decade later that the AP and a few newspapers relied on *INS* to sue radio stations. As we shall see, the outcome of these cases reveals that even when restricted to the news business, relying on *INS* to obtain an injunction was not straightforward. The repeated difficulty sustaining a misappropriation claim shows that *INS* has always been controversial and cautions us against assuming that the decision created a lasting remedy that transformed the business of news. It was invoked in quite specific contexts and with mixed results.

THE AGE OF RADIO

Although some newspaper publishers initially feared that broadcast news would cut into the circulation and advertising revenue of newspapers, others seized the opportunity to operate radio stations in conjunction with their newspapers, creating the first multimedia news businesses. Newspapers that owned or were affiliated with radio stations wanted to be able to broadcast their own news as well as that of the AP and other agencies. But newspapers that were not affiliated with a station saw radio stations as competing with them for readers and especially advertisers.[106]

Unlike in the United Kingdom, where the BBC was given a monopoly on broadcasting, the American spectrum was opened to private companies that were free to develop their own programming.[107] Newspapers and press agencies in the United Kingdom initially put pressure on the government and negotiated with the BBC to limit competition between newspapers and radio. At first the BBC promised to limit its news coverage to reports furnished by press agencies and to broadcast them at designated times. The compromise was meant to preserve newspaper readership. Over time, the BBC significantly expanded its news-gathering operations, but the BBC's monopoly on broadcasting meant that newspapers in various parts of the country did not face additional competition from local stations that collected their own news or took it from newspapers. Newspapers and press agencies generally supported the monopoly of the BBC because it restricted competition in the business of using news to attract advertising revenue.[108]

In the United States, by contrast, broadcasting remained in private hands. Newspapers were among those who obtained licenses to operate stations, and the law did not in any way restrict the broadcasting of news. Within the AP, there arose tensions between members who operated stations and those who did not. The cooperative model of the AP was predicated on the advantages of sharing one's local news in exchange for the consolidated AP report containing news gathered by members in other parts of the country, AP correspondents, and foreign news agencies that partnered with the AP. The value of membership depended in part on having the exclusive use of AP news in one's vicinity at a designated time of publication (morning or evening). Radio broadcasts did not respect such boundaries. It was possible for a station operated by one member to reach the circulation area of another, thereby making AP news available for free before the local paper could be delivered to all of its subscribers. The use of broadcasting by some AP members and not others thus had the potential to undermine the cooperative model of news gathering.[109]

For publishers who did not own stations, the Great Depression heightened the sense that radio was a threat. Between 1929 and 1932, advertising revenue for newspapers fell from $800 million to $490 million; over the same period, revenue for radio doubled from $40 million to $80 million.[110] From the perspective of newspaper publishers, broadcasters were doing well despite the Depression, and the fact that they used news (among other forms of programming) to attract advertisers was upsetting. Although advertising revenues would largely recover by the end of the 1930s, the situation looked dire in 1932 and 1933. The question of how to deal with radio therefore took center stage at the annual meetings of the AP and the American Newspaper Publishers Association (ANPA) in the spring of 1933. The AP announced that it would no longer supply news to radio stations and that members of the AP who owned stations had to limit news broadcasts to occasional thirty-word bulletins without commercial sponsors. INS and UP took a similar approach. Although these agencies had previously been supplying broadcasters with news, they realized that unlimited broadcasts harmed their core clients—newspapers. The ANPA recommended that newspapers stop printing schedules of radio programs unless these were paid for as advertisements. It also encouraged newspapers to take legal action against broadcasters that violated their "property" in news.[111]

In the fall of 1933, the two main radio networks, CBS and NBC, negotiated a deal with the AP, INS, and UP known as the Biltmore Agreement. CBS and NBC agreed to stop gathering their own news. In exchange, the AP, INS, and UP promised to provide news to a new Press-Radio Bureau, which would prepare two five-minute broadcasts for the networks each day. The networks would air these broadcasts without commercials and at designated times in the late morning and late evening. The goal was to allow newspapers to reach customers before the same news was announced on the radio. Stations that were not affiliated with one of the two networks did not accede to the Biltmore Agreement, a fact that hindered its success from the start. Some of the independent stations gathered their own news; others purchased it from Transradio Press, an agency started in 1933 to serve independent broadcasters that were not part of the Biltmore Agreement. There was also opposition from a number of newspapers, including AP members that owned stations and found that the agreement restricted their own businesses. From their perspective, battling radio was misguided.[112]

It was in this context of economic depression and differences of opinion about radio that the *INS* decision was looked to as a means of controlling broadcasters' use of printed news.[113] In 1933, the AP sued KSOO, an independent station in Sioux Falls, South Dakota. KSOO defended itself on the grounds that radio stations affiliated with AP newspapers were airing the same stories and that it would be discriminatory if the AP stopped KSOO from doing so. The station thus revived the old charge that the AP was attempting to create a "monopoly" in news. The AP countered that its activities were in no way violating the Sherman Anti-Trust Act and that its own members were allowed to engage only in limited broadcasts of extraordinary events. After hearing the arguments on both sides, the judge granted a preliminary injunction restraining KSOO from broadcasting AP news—whether it was rewritten or not— for twenty-four hours after publication. The judge justified this duration on the grounds that the news had commercial value for the AP and its members for at least this long.[114] KSOO initially announced that it would appeal but then decided to accept the ruling.[115]

A subsequent attempt by the AP was less successful, and it revealed how judges examining the same case could advance different interpretations of the Supreme Court's ruling in *INS*. In 1934, the AP sued KVOS, another independent station in Bellingham, Washington, on behalf of three AP members in the region. KVOS had taken stories from the three local AP newspapers and read them on the air. At the district court, KVOS obtained a clear victory. Judge John C. Bowen stressed that the news was used by KVOS after it was printed in the regular editions of the newspapers; there were no bulletin boards or early editions as in *INS*. Once news appeared in newspapers, according to Bowen, it unquestionably belonged to the public. Bowen held that *INS* did not establish any absolute property right in news and that the "quasi property" right applied only to direct competitors. KVOS and AP were not direct competitors, according to Bowen, because KVOS did not supply news to other broadcasters, as AP did to newspapers. Moreover, KVOS could not be said to be competing with newspapers, because it offered the news for free. Finally, echoing Brandeis's dissent in *INS*, Bowen insisted that only Congress had the power to create new property rights that might restrict the public benefits of a new means of communication such as radio. According to Bowen, protecting AP's contracts and its investment in news "cannot justify withholding from the public the more speedy and more extensive dissemination of news through the improved instrumentalities."[116]

The *Washington Post* reported that Bowen's decision was "a shock to newspaper publishers" because it contradicted the recent ruling in South Dakota. The *Post* also denounced Bowen for using the bench to promote a particular policy agenda with respect to radio. According to the *Post*, Bowen was a "protégé" of Senator Clarence Dill, who was actively seeking to expand the role of radio in the dissemination of news. Dill was the most vocal critic of the AP's current policy toward radio and proposed to set up a nationwide agency to supply broadcasters with news. In the meantime, the *Post* suggested, Bowen was making it possible for the stations to simply take news from printed newspapers.[117]

The AP appealed, arguing that radio stations and newspapers were direct competitors when it came to using news to attract advertisers. Against Bowen's narrow reading of *INS*, the AP claimed that the Supreme Court had recognized that an organization such as the AP could not function without some protection against unfair competition and that it was in the public interest to promote an efficient news-gathering association. KVOS, meanwhile, claimed to be serving the public by offering news to everyone for free, including the illiterate and visually impaired. The Court of Appeals for the Ninth Circuit sided with the AP, holding that radio stations and newspapers were in direct competition for advertising revenue and that they both used breaking news to attract these advertisers. Because KVOS provided the news for free and while it was still "hot," it reduced the value of that news for readers, some of whom might choose to abandon their newspaper subscriptions. Advertisers would necessarily follow, and the ability of the AP and its members to gather news of public concern would be impaired. The court of appeals ordered the district court to enjoin KVOS from broadcasting any news gathered by the AP "for the period . . . during which the broadcasting of the pirated news to KVOS's most remote auditors may damage the complainant's papers' business of procuring or maintaining their subscriptions and advertising."[118] The court of appeals thus extended *INS* to a very different economic situation. In 1918, newspapers still had a monopoly on using breaking news to attract advertising revenue. By 1934 this was no longer the case, and the Depression made things seem worse.

But the AP's victory was short-lived. KVOS appealed, and the Supreme Court overturned the decision of the court of appeals on technical grounds. In order to enjoy the protection of the federal courts, the AP had argued that its damages were in excess of the statutory minimum of three thousand dollars. The AP cited the potential loss of eight thousand dollars in assessments if the three Washington newspapers located in KVOS's broadcast area abandoned their AP memberships. The Supreme Court ruled that this did not represent actual damages suffered as the result of KVOS's broadcasts and that the case should have been immediately dismissed by the district court.[119] Reporting on this decision, the *Chicago Tribune*, an AP member, predicted that the practical effect would be the "removal of all limitations on the 'pirating' and broadcasting of news by radio stations."[120] But the *Tribune* had its own station, WGN, whose call letters stood for "World's Greatest Newspaper."[121] The *Tribune* was not against radio, only stations that appropriated news from local newspapers.

KVOS took place at the height of what contemporaries and historians have referred to as the "Press-Radio War" of the early 1930s (see figure 11). The litigation was part of a moment that passed. Although the Press-Radio Bureau remained in operation until 1938, by that time UP and INS had backed out of the Biltmore Agreement and about 30 percent of radio stations were owned by newspapers, making the agreement totally unworkable. The Biltmore Agreement was also criticized on Capitol Hill, especially by Senator Dill, who claimed that newspapers were hampering the potential benefits of radio. Dill sought to encourage the formation of an AP-like entity for radio. Although this never happened, the proposal represented a threat for the AP, and everybody could see that the Biltmore Agreement was not working. In the spring of 1939, the AP finally lifted its restrictions on member broadcasts and its ban on selling AP news to broadcasters, including those that ran commercials during the news.[122] By the end of the 1930s, it

FIGURE 11. A cartoon from the period of the "Press-Radio War" depicting a broadcaster "chiseling" news from the newspapers. *Editor & Publisher*, April 21, 1934. Reproduced courtesy of *Editor & Publisher*.

had become clear that owning radio stations was a winning strategy for newspapers. The label "Press-Radio War" is misleading, because many newspapers sought to exploit the potential of radio from an early date. As Michael Stamm has shown, the real competition was not between two rival media—newspapers and radio—but among companies that developed ways to use both media to inform the public and attract advertising revenue in the process.[123]

RESTRICTING *INS*

Over time, the usefulness of *INS* was also limited by changes in the law that had nothing to do with communications technologies or the news business. In 1938, the Supreme Court put an end to federal common law, which meant that the principles of *INS*, like other common-law doctrines, were no longer binding.[124] States remained free to recognize common-law doctrines within their jurisdictions, and some courts upheld claims of "hot news" misappropriation, citing *INS*. In 1963, for example, the Pennsylvania Supreme Court held that a radio station that used news collected by a local newspaper without permission had engaged in unfair competition and violated the newspaper's property right in news.[125] But the ability to use *INS* to protect news was limited by the Copyright Act of 1976, which codified the notion of preemption.[126] Preemption means that if a particular right is available through the federal copyright statute, then it is not possible to turn to the statutes or common law of any state to obtain an equivalent right. Courts now had to consider whether claims of misappropriation were preempted by copyright. If equivalent relief could be had through the copyright statute, then *INS* could not apply. Since copyright could be used to protect only the form of news reports and not the underlying factual details, news organizations could argue that the misappropriation doctrine was not preempted by copyright. But they would face resistance on precisely those grounds: since copyright explicitly placed facts in the public domain, how could the courts justify protecting them by other means?

In the 1990s, a case involving the transmission of sports scores via pagers and America Online's (AOL) dial-up service provided an opportunity for the courts to clarify the circumstances in which a misappropriation claim could survive preemption. The National Basketball Association (NBA) sued Motorola and another company known as STATS for providing their customers with real-time updates of NBA games through Motorola's pagers and STATS's AOL site. Citing *INS*, the district court ruled against the defendants, finding that they had "reaped where they have not sown" and taken the NBA's most valuable property, "the excitement of an NBA game in progress."[127] The defendants appealed, arguing that *INS*-type claims were preempted by copyright. Ultimately, the Court of Appeals for the Second Circuit held that a misappropriation claim could survive preemption in cases in which timesensitive information gathered by one firm was appropriated by a direct competitor and in which this "free riding" undermined the first firm's incentive to gather information.[128] In the case at hand, however, the court determined that the plaintiffs and the defendants were not direct competitors because the NBA's primary business was to organize basketball games whereas Motorola's was to manufacture and sell pagers. Moreover, Motorola collected the information about the games independently (from within the arena or by following radio and television broadcasts) rather than copying the information directly from a competing pager service run by the NBA. Therefore, Motorola could not be said to be free riding on the information-gathering efforts of the NBA.[129]

The decision in *NBA v. Motorola* left some important questions unanswered, such as what constituted direct competition, what kind of evidence of harm was needed, and how long protection against the reuse of factual information might last.[130] In *INS*, the duration of the exclusive right remained vague, since it was supposed to continue for as long as the news had commercial value. But the emphasis on the time difference between the East and West Coasts suggested that the protection would last several hours. As was pointed out by counsel for INS in 1918, the AP might have solved the problem of copying from early editions if it had chosen to impose simultaneous publication on all its members. But forcing newspapers in California to go on sale in the middle of the night rather than early in the morning would have undermined their businesses, and this in turn would have harmed the association as a whole. That's why the AP asked the court to stretch the definition of publication to fit its needs as a nationwide cooperative association. Radio changed the dynamic, since now the problem was appropriation by a broadcaster that had the ability to reach readers faster than the physical newspapers could be distributed. The South Dakota court ordered an embargo of twenty-four hours, whereas the Court of Appeals for the Ninth Circuit suggested that KVOS should desist from broadcasting AP news until doing so would no longer harm the local newspapers' ability to attract subscribers and advertisers. Because the Supreme Court reversed the decision, the injunction was never issued, but presumably the idea was for KVOS to wait at least as long as it took for the newspapers' most far-flung subscribers to receive their papers and read them.

The internet transformed the time-space nexus of news. It became possible for readers in California, or any place connected to the network, to read an article in a New York paper as soon as it was published online. In addition, stories could be updated online as they unfolded. The time advantage enjoyed by the first newspaper to announce news—which had long been used as an argument against the need for a property right—was reduced to seconds. Networked computers also made it easier to copy and retransmit text (and later images and videos), thus creating new opportunities for free riding. But what about the kind of appropriation at issue in the *INS* case, in which the details but not the language of news reports are reproduced? Now that the kinds of time differentials at the heart of the *INS* dispute no longer exist, should the misappropriation doctrine still apply?

A test case was brought in 2008, when the AP sued a website called All Headline News for both copyright infringement and hot news misappropriation. The context was very different than it had been in 1918 or the 1930s. For one thing, in 2008 the AP no longer had the restrictive bylaws that had blocked Hearst from obtaining access to AP news for all of his papers. In 1945, the Supreme Court ruled that the protest rights allowing AP members to block new entrants in their territories were in restraint of trade.[131] The rationale of the Supreme Court's decision was that AP membership had become indispensable to the success of major newspapers. Without access to AP news, there was little chance that a publisher would start a new title in a city dominated by one or two AP papers. By denying applications for membership, the AP was restricting competition and potentially reducing the diversity of reporting and commentary available to readers. As a result of the 1945 Supreme Court decision, the AP changed its bylaws, opening its news to any newspaper willing to pay. But this did not necessarily increase diversity of coverage in the long run. A growing proportion of

American newspapers came to rely on the AP for nonlocal news, and in 1958, UP and INS merged, further reducing choice when it came to wire services.[132]

The other major difference between 1918 and 2008 was that the financial health of newspapers had declined dramatically. At the time of *INS*, newspapers were highly profitable, in large part because they still had a monopoly on using breaking news to sell advertising. By 2008, newspaper sales had been declining for decades, and the web was claiming a growing share of advertising revenue, upsetting the business model on which newspapers had relied for centuries. In 2008 and 2009, news organizations became more assertive about protecting their intellectual property. They turned to the law as one tool among others they used to adapt to the new media landscape.[133]

In its suit against All Headline News (AHN), the AP claimed that the defendant did not engage in original reporting; it merely paid employees who located news stories online and then either copied them verbatim or rewrote them and changed the headline. Verbatim copying was clearly an infringement of copyright, but what about the stories that AHN reformulated? The AP argued that this constituted free riding. AHN was profiting from the labor and financial resources that the AP used to produce the stories, and it was selling this news in competition with the AP. AHN filed a motion to dismiss the misappropriation charge on the grounds that it was preempted by copyright, but the district court denied this request, confirming that the doctrine was recognized under New York law.[134] The AP was able to use this ruling to force a settlement with AHN, suggesting that the *INS* decision was alive and well in the digital age.[135]

But a subsequent case involving the republication of stock recommendations revealed serious disagreements about the legal viability and social consequences of using the hot news doctrine to control the flow of information online. Several investment banks sued a specialized website called theflyonthewall.com (Fly) for republishing their stock recommendations online. In 2010, the district court ordered Fly to delay reporting those recommendations for two hours after they were released, on the grounds that immediate republication was a form of free riding that constituted hot news misappropriation.[136] Fly appealed, and there were amicus briefs entered on both sides. The AP joined several other prominent news organizations, including Agence France Presse, Gannett Company, the McClatchy Company, E. W. Scripps Company, the New York Times Company, and the Newspaper Association of America, in a brief arguing for the relevance of the hot news doctrine. "Unless generalized free-riding on news originators' efforts is restrained," the brief explained, "originators will be unable to recover their costs of newsgathering and publication, the incentive to engage in the news business will be threatened, and the public will ultimately have fewer sources of original news."[137]

Champions of the public domain responded that the hot news doctrine could interfere with free speech and restrict the democratic potential of the internet.[138] Technology firms and internet advocacy groups submitted amicus briefs against the idea of adapting the logic of INS to the current situation. In one brief, Google and Twitter argued that banning a website from immediately disseminating news of stock recommendations would set a dangerous precedent that could "seriously impair the distribution of factual information on the Internet." The brief explained, "In a world of modern communications technology, where anyone with a cell phone may disseminate news throughout the world even as it is occurring, the notion that a single media outlet should have a monopoly on time-sensitive facts is not only contrary to law, it is, as a practical matter, futile."[139] In a separate brief, Citizen Media Law Project, the Electronic Frontier Foundation, and Public Citizen argued that the hot news doctrine could threaten free speech by restraining internet users' ability to gather, share, and comment on news.[140]

When the case came before the Court of Appeals for the Second Circuit, the court chose not to engage with the First Amendment issue but nonetheless held that the investment firms' misappropriation claims were preempted by copyright. The banks' reports were protected by copyright, but since copyright does not protect facts, Fly and others were free to report the recommendations as facts. In the words of the court, "In this case, a firm's ability to make news—by issuing a recommendation that is likely to affect the market price of a security—

does not give rise to a right for it to control who breaks that news and how."[141] Some lawyers who commented on the decision claimed it was now unlikely that the misappropriation doctrine could be used to stop the republication of factual information online. But representatives of news organizations suggested that in other circumstances, such as in cases of free riding on the news-gathering efforts of a direct competitor, the tort remained viable.[142] Indeed, it should be remembered that neither the banks that brought the suit nor Fly were news organizations and that the stock recommendations were not news so much as professional opinions aimed at encouraging stock trades. The court referred to the banks as "making news" and Fly as "breaking" it, but the published opinion failed to adequately define news.[143] As has been the case for centuries, the definition of news continues to elude those who seek to control its flow.

BUSINESS REALITIES AND NOTIONS OF PROPERTY

In 1918, the Supreme Court's ruling in *INS* seemed to some like the beginning of a new era. The AP's legal victory was celebrated not just by Stone and the AP's board of directors but also by Reuters, which sought similar protection for its own news throughout the British empire. It proved impossible to create an international agreement that offered the kind of protection promised by *INS*, and even in the United States, the AP found that it was hard to translate a legal victory into a lasting change in industry practices. As Stone recognized, *INS* turned out to be a mixed blessing, since the AP felt obliged to respect the principle of a property in news even where other agencies did not. And the attempt to use *INS* to limit broadcasting was not a viable long-term solution. The *INS* decision has been controversial since the beginning, as the dissents by Brandeis and Holmes showed, and by the 1930s the attempt to use *INS* to restrict what broadcasters could do was already seen as hindering the benefits of a new communications medium. The same criticism has been raised in response to recent attempts to resuscitate the misappropriation doctrine in the digital age.

In the wake of these attempts, legal scholars analyzed the continued viability and potential usefulness of the misappropriation doctrine.

While some argued for codifying a similar principle in the statute, others insisted that the flexibility of the common-law tort was one of its strengths. Among those who criticized the doctrine, some argued that it should be abandoned because it posed a danger to freedom of expression. Others stressed the idea that, regardless of the legal principles involved, the tort was not likely to help solve the fundamental problem of revenue loss faced by news organizations.[144] Discussions of *INS* and its legacy were thus part of a larger and ongoing discussion about how to fund quality journalism. Those who emphasized the problem of free riding echoed some of the arguments that had been used by proponents of legal protection for news going back to the nineteenth century in Britain and America. The idea that news is political and socially vital but expensive to produce remains central to these discussions. The related idea that news needs to be treated differently from other kinds of human creativity also has deep roots: the cultural argument that news does not seem like the product of authorship and the political argument that exclusive rights would restrict public access to information have been aired repeatedly in different contexts.

But from the perspective of publishers and news agencies, the economic model of using news to attract advertising revenue helps to explain why the copyright laws designed to protect other literary, artistic, and scientific works never seemed like a good fit for news. Unlike a book or film, which might be read or watched for decades to come, interest in news is time sensitive. More importantly, its value for businesses comes from being able to capture attention that can be sold to advertisers. Seen in its historical context, the *INS* case was really about protecting the cooperative arrangements of the AP at a time when its membership was restricted and newspapers did not yet face competition in using breaking news to sell advertising. In that sense, the 1918 decision offers little real hope for news organizations today that might look to the case as a source for a "property in news."[145]

The View from the Digital Age

IN THE FAST-PACED WORLD of social media, news seems more protean and intractable than ever. The tension between access and control that characterized many of the episodes in this book—a tension that has been at the heart of so many discussions of intellectual property—is back with a vengeance. The history recounted here has been one of recurring challenges and debates, some of which remain unresolved or have taken on new dimensions in the digital age. But major changes have occurred during the long sweep of this book, and a few of these should be recalled before considering ongoing issues.

In the seventeenth century, a combination of censorship and state-sanctioned monopoly meant that it was possible to claim exclusive rights in news publications of various sorts. Licensing enabled governments to favor certain writers and publishers and to watch them closely; in some cases, patents gave an individual or group a monopoly on the publication of certain kinds of information. The Stationers' Company recognized exclusive and perpetual rights in all sorts of printed works, including news publications. The copyright statutes passed in Britain and the United States in the eighteenth century represented an entirely different approach. Literary property was divorced from censorship. Authors were free to write and printers free to publish; their investments were protected by a copyright that was limited in duration and scope. Statutes and judicial decisions emphasized that the goal of copyright was to "encourage learning" and "promote the progress of science" by incentivizing the creation of "useful books" and informational works such as maps and charts.

Meanwhile, the business and culture of news publishing as it developed in the eighteenth and early nineteenth centuries led to a situation in which copyright was seen as largely unnecessary. Those who seek to make money selling news and time-sensitive information have always faced what the late economist Kenneth J. Arrow called a "fundamental paradox in the determination of demand for information." According to Arrow, the value of information for a purchaser "is not known until he has the information, but then he has in effect acquired it without cost."[1] But publishers did find ways to make readers and advertisers pay for news and time-sensitive information. The development of the periodical newspaper sold by subscription was fundamental in this respect. Issuing a publication with a stable title at regular intervals created an appetite for news and attracted a community of readers who looked forward to the next installment, whatever it might include. Selling by subscription locked readers in and made it easier to determine how many copies to print and where to deliver them. Crucially, it also attracted advertisers who wanted to reach these subscribers, and advertising revenue was essential to making news profitable. News as such did not need to be treated as proprietary, especially when it was bundled with the other features—letters, essays, poems, stories, and practical information—that filled the pages of British and American newspapers. In the eighteenth and early nineteenth centuries, editors and publishers actively exchanged their newspapers, treating news as a shared resource.

There was no eureka moment when copyright for news suddenly made sense. Attitudes and practices evolved unevenly, and copying became more problematic as a result of shifts in the media landscape. Sometimes these shifts were related to changes in government policy, such as the repeal of the "taxes on knowledge." Sometimes new business arrangements—such as the development of press associations—or new communications technologies—the telegraph and radio—motivated attempts to create a special copyright or property right in news. In Britain and America these efforts were actively resisted, an important reminder that political and cultural arguments have blocked copyright expansion in the past. Disputes over news also generated debates on the purpose and acceptable boundaries of copyright law. In the early twentieth century, newspapers were integrated into the copyright statutes in both countries, but protection did not extend to the factual details of news as some publishers and press agencies had hoped it would.

Of course, the duration, subject matter, and scope of copyright have expanded dramatically over time. In the eighteenth century, copyright lasted for a maximum of twenty-eight years after publication; now it generally lasts for the lifetime of the author plus seventy years.[2] Initially only books were explicitly protected; now copyright automatically applies to many kinds of works that satisfy a minimum threshold of originality. Moreover, the bundle of rights enjoyed by copyright owners has expanded from the sole right to print and sell copies of the work to the right to authorize performances, translations, adaptations, and all sorts of derivative works. But despite the undeniable expansion of copyright during the nineteenth and twentieth centuries, no new statutory provisions were created for news in Britain or the United States. This was not for lack of trying, as the efforts of publishers and press agencies going back to the 1830s reveal. Their failures were victories for those who argued that news belonged to the public.

Concerns about the need for news to circulate underpinned opposition to special legislation protecting news on both sides of the Atlantic, and the legacy of this can be found in the Berne Convention, which continues to exclude "news of the day" from copyright protection internationally. The Berne Convention is generally understood as allowing copyright for the expression of news reports, thereby excluding only the factual details from protection.[3] But the current version of the agreement also includes a mandatory requirement to permit quotations from copyrighted works, including "quotations from newspaper articles and periodicals in the form of press summaries."[4] Press summaries (*revues de presse* in the original French) compare and juxtapose accounts by several news outlets, facilitating public access to a plurality of coverage. They are the twentieth- and twenty-first-century equivalents of experiments by magazines and weekly journals in the early eighteenth century. Some of those early digests were accused of piracy, but their editors and publishers began to articulate arguments about the public utility of excerpts that eventually carried the day.

FACT VERSUS EXPRESSION AND FAIR USE

Today the expressive content of news reports is clearly protected by copyright regardless of the medium of transmission. This protection makes it possible for news organizations to syndicate their material.[5] But the laws in Britain and the United States also have important exceptions that have developed over time to ensure that copyright does not stifle creativity or overly restrict access to knowledge. The most important of these limitations is the recognition that copyright does not protect facts or ideas independently of the manner in which they are expressed. This means that authors may use facts or ideas contained in a protected work to create a new work that is the result of their own labor and intellectual creativity.[6] The fear that copyright might be used to restrict access to news or political commentary—such as a critical account of a political leader—was aired as early as the eighteenth century. But it was in response to nineteenth-century efforts to create a special copyright for news that this fear was articulated most clearly and consistently. Similarly, attempts by newspapers and agencies to protect the substance as well as the form of news eventually led judges on both sides of the Atlantic to clearly distinguish between copyrightable expressions and uncopyrightable facts.

Having helped to expose this boundary, some news organizations turned away from copyright in search of a property right that would extend beyond the words to protect the underlying details of news reports. In *International News Service v. Associated Press* (1918), the US Supreme Court referred to a "quasi property" in news and extended unfair-competition law to protect against the reuse of time-sensitive information by a competitor. In hindsight, *INS* could be seen as the high-water mark of legal protection for news, but in fact the decision has always been controversial and difficult to translate into industry-wide norms. The exclusion of facts as such from copyright protection is crucial for journalism, just as it is for all kinds of research and scholarship. News organizations often rely on each other's published reports. Although it is certainly beneficial for the public to have journalists check facts and corroborate sources, it would be highly inefficient to require permission to reproduce factual information that has been published by another news organization, even if the value of that information is time sensitive and it cost money to collect.

Additional flexibilities are provided by statutory exceptions for fair use in the United States and fair dealing in the United Kingdom.[7] In both countries, news organizations are allowed to reproduce parts of a protected literary, artistic, or scientific work in the course of their reporting. To qualify for this exception in the United Kingdom the reporting must be of a current event, the material used has to be relevant and justified for the purposes of the reporting, and the original work must be acknowledged. Significantly, photographs are not part of the statutory exception in the United Kingdom, which means that permission is required to reproduce them. Courts have parsed all of these terms—*reporting*, *current*, and *event*—in order to distinguish between fair and unfair dealing for news reporting.[8] The American doctrine of fair use is somewhat broader than its British counterpart, but that does not mean that journalists always take full advantage of it. A 2012 survey of American journalists revealed that the extent to which they understand and rely on fair use to do their jobs varies widely. This survey led to the creation of a code of copyright best practices for journalists.[9] Fair use and fair dealing also apply to the content produced by news organizations. In the United States, for example, individuals may reproduce excerpts of a news story for the purposes of teaching, research, criticism, comment, or news reporting (as when one news outlet reports what another is saying).[10] In the United Kingdom, the law allows individuals to reproduce excerpts for the purposes of criticism or review and to make quotations regardless of the purpose, as long as use of the work is "fair" and accompanied by sufficient acknowledgment.[11]

To the extent that they are recognized by courts and taken advantage of by individuals, the exclusion of facts from copyright protection and the fair-use exceptions act as safeguards that enable news to be shared and commented on. But in some situations, these safeguards might be insufficient to guarantee public access to newsworthy material protected by copyright. Indeed, the boundary between fact and expression is often blurred. In some cases, the fact that someone wrote X or Y is newsworthy in itself, and it is only by reproducing some of the author's original words that a journalist can persuade the public of the authenticity of what's being reported. Photographs add another dimension to this problem, since it is difficult if not impossible to separate the facts from the expression. One could try to use words to describe a photograph or attempt to convey a similar message by creating a new visual representation, but sometimes there would be no adequate substitute for allowing the public to see the actual image.[12] In such cases, copyright might be seen to be in conflict with freedom of expression. For most of the history recounted in this book, the potential conflict between free speech and copyright law received little attention, but in recent decades there has been more interest in this area.[13] It is possible that in certain situations courts could decide that issues of freedom of expression and the public interest in access to newsworthy material might trump the rights of the copyright owner. But to date, most courts have deemed that the statutory exceptions for fair use and fair dealing are sufficient to avoid conflict between freedom of expression and copyright law.[14]

WHAT IS FAIR?

Just what constitutes fair use or fair dealing is particularly contentious in the digital environment. In the first decade of the twenty-first century, when technology firms such as Google and Yahoo developed aggregators that reproduced headlines and short snippets of news accompanied by hyperlinks, many publishers and press agencies claimed that these activities were not fair. In 2005, Agence France Presse (AFP) sued Google News in France and the United States, insisting that Google was reproducing the most valuable parts of its stories. Headlines and ledes, according to AFP, are "qualitatively the most important aspects of a story and are painstakingly created. They capture the readers' attention and describe what the rest of the article is about."[15] The attention of readers is what makes it possible to sell advertisements, and although Google and Yahoo were not in the news business, they were using news along with other content to capture attention and sell ads. Ultimately, the case was settled out of court, leading to a licensing agreement for the use of AFP content. Reuters and the AP have also made licensing deals with Internet aggregators.[16]

The limits of fair use were also tested by media-monitoring companies, which provide the electronic equivalent of press "clippings" to clients interested in tracking news of a particular industry or topic. In 2012, the AP sued a company called Meltwater, claiming that the excerpts of AP stories that Meltwater sent to clients were in violation of copyright law. Meltwater argued that its use of AP content was "transformative" and therefore fair because it helped users locate the most relevant articles based on their interests. But the extracts included the headline and part of the lede, which the AP referred to as "the heart of the story." Meltwater wanted to be compared to search engines, but the court did not accept this analogy because Meltwater's service was restricted to paying clients. In addition, it was shown that Meltwater's subscribers clicked through to the original source far less often than users of Google did. Because the AP licensed its content to other websites, Meltwater's product could also be seen as providing a substitute for the sites authorized by the AP. For these and other reasons, the district court rejected the defense of fair use.[17] Meltwater initially planned to appeal, but then the two sides announced that they were developing a partnership. Because the appeal was dropped, the fair use question did not receive as much scrutiny as it might have, leading to worries about a potential problem of circularity in the licensing market: uncertainty about whether judges will accept a fair-use defense can lead parties to obtain a license in order to be safe; the existence of this licensing "market" can then be used in court as evidence of the potential harm created by unauthorized uses of a work.[18]

Meltwater was also sued by news organizations in the United Kingdom, but the legal questions were different. The plaintiff was the Newspaper Licensing Agency, which managed rights on behalf of newspapers. By the time the suit came to trial in 2010, a decision of the Court of Justice of the European Union (CJEU) involving another firm called Infopaq had ruled that extracts as small as eleven words could be protected by copyright as long as they were the expression of the intellectual creativity of an author. (Infopaq's extracts for its clients included a key word and five words on each side of the key word.) The CJEU also determined that the automated processes of scanning, storing, and reproducing these extracts were acts of copying that required the permission of the copyright owner.[19] So when Meltwater was sued in the United Kingdom, it did not dispute the need to obtain a license to reproduce snippets from newspapers. The question was whether Meltwater's subscribers also needed an end-user license on the grounds that by viewing excerpts on Meltwater's website they necessarily created copies of protected works. This case went all the way to the UK Supreme Court and then to the CJEU, which ruled that copies created in the course of browsing by internet users do not constitute copyright infringement.[20]

The UK Meltwater case offers another example of how a dispute involving the reuse of news obliged courts to interpret broader principles of copyright, such as what constitutes a protected "part" of a work. Notably, the trial judge ruled that some headlines could be protected by copyright because they involve "considerable skill in devising and they are specifically designed to entice by informing the reader of the content of the article in an entertaining manner."[21] The court of appeal agreed, departing from a long-standing tradition in which British courts (like American ones) have refused to recognize copyright for titles and short phrases. Although it seems likely that most titles will still fall outside the bounds of copyright, the suggestion that some news headlines qualify for protection could lead individuals or firms to hesitate before reproducing them, thus restricting free expression and innovation online.[22]

In the late 2000s and early 2010s, most of the complaints of unfair use or free riding were aimed at aggregators and media-monitoring services. At the time of this writing, the attention of news organizations has shifted to social media sites, especially Facebook, in an effort to exert control over how their content is used, to capture a share of ad revenue, and to gain access to reader analytics. It would be folly to try to predict the next chapter in this ongoing struggle. Setting aside tensions between news organizations and technology firms such as Google and Facebook, it seems that even among journalists and publishers, the question of copyright for news remains a live one. Two disputes from 2017 are revealing in this respect.

In the first dispute, Glyn Bellis, a freelancer based in Wales, covered a case in a local court and then sold the story to *Wales Online*. The *Independent* in London relied entirely on this story to create its own account. The *Independent* credited *Wales Online* and linked to the original story but refused to pay Bellis a licensing fee on the grounds that "there is no copyright in news."[23] According to the *Independent*, their version did not copy Bellis's language, and the factual information contained in his story could not be protected. But Bellis had been the only reporter present in court that day. The *Independent* relied on his account of the evidence presented at trial and included a police quote obtained by him. *Press Gazette*, a trade journal for journalists, drew attention to the dispute, and the National Association of Press Agencies supported Bellis. Ultimately, the *Independent* agreed to pay him forty pounds for the story while still insisting that no copyright infringement had taken place. According to a spokesperson for the *Independent*, "What began as a dispute about copyright had seemingly become a debate about the importance of local journalism and court reporting." The *Independent* agreed with Bellis that it was important to support work like his even if they were not required by law to obtain his permission.[24] Even in its resolution, this case reveals the extent to which copyright continues to mean different things to different people.

Another dispute over a local news story in 2017 ended up in small-claims court. *Rochdale Online*, which covers news in Greater Manchester, England, complained that the *Manchester Evening News* relied entirely on one of its stories about a local MP, failing to credit or link to the original source. The *Manchester Evening News* argued that since it had not copied the language of the original story there was no infringement; *Rochdale Online* could not claim exclusive rights over information contained in public documents just because it had made the effort to obtain those documents. But the county court found in favor of *Rochdale Online* and ordered the *Manchester Evening News* to pay two hundred pounds plus court fees. The fact that the *Manchester Evening News* had not credited the website was probably a factor in the decision to sue, although *Rochdale Online*'s chairman, Malcolm Journeaux, also made it clear that the case was about securing the ability to syndicate news stories. According to Journeaux, the existence of local journalism depended on copyright protecting the "'sweat of the brow' involved in researching and writing articles."[25]

What these two relatively minor disputes reveal is that ideas about what is protected by copyright and standards for crediting or paying for the use of other journalists' reports continue to be the subject of debate.

Copyright claims are not only about money; they are also about control and acknowledgment. The statements of the protagonists in the 2017 cases provide another reminder of how the rationale for legal protection depends on the context. Bellis and Journeaux sought to rally publishers and the reading public around the idea that a strong view of copyright could help prop up local journalism.

NEW LEGISLATION

Litigation is not the only weapon in the ongoing battle over who owns the news. Publishers in several countries have recently sought new legislation in order to have greater control over how their content is used online. New laws were ultimately passed in Germany and Spain. In Germany, a 2013 law gave news publishers the exclusive right to make their articles—in whole or in part—available to the public for commercial purposes for one year after publication. The goal was to force internet aggregators to pay for displaying snippets of news. Although the law excluded "very short text excerpts," it did not define "very short." Google sought to avoid the law altogether and obliged German publishers to waive their rights to compensation if they wanted to be indexed on Google News. The publishers had no choice but to go along with this, effectively eliminating any benefit from a law they had worked several years to obtain.[26] In 2014, Spain also passed a law to protect news publishers against aggregators. But whereas in Germany the publishers agreed to waive their rights, the Spanish law did not allow for this possibility, which meant that aggregators had to either pay a license fee to include excerpts from Spanish news sites or face heavy fines. As a result, Google removed Spanish publications from Google News and closed its news site in Spain. Spanish publishers reported a serious loss in traffic.[27]

At time of writing, these examples are being cited as warnings for policy makers in the European Union, where a neighboring right for press publishers is currently under consideration as part of a proposal for a directive on copyright in the digital single market.[28] Although news articles are already protected by the author's copyright, a group of publishers in several EU countries have argued that a separate right for publishers would facilitate licensing deals with online platforms. But there is disagreement about what exactly such a right would entail, how it would affect access to news online, and whether it could help resolve the underlying revenue problems faced by news organizations. Even before a draft clause was circulated in 2016, a two-year UK Arts and Humanities Research Council (AHRC)–funded project, though sympathetic to the idea of supporting quality journalism, concluded that changing copyright law was not an appropriate solution to the economic problems faced by publishers. The project's final report, based on a review of recent legislation and litigation, interviews with industry actors in eight countries, and a series of academic workshops, argued that both policy concerns and journalistic practices weighed heavily against any new right for press publishers.[29]

What will happen is difficult to predict—the answer will probably be known by the time you read these pages—but in any case, the EU proposal for a new press publishers' right represents another chapter in the centuries-old history presented here. A central thread in this history has been the oft-repeated contention that news is different than other forms of authorship protected by copyright law. As we have seen, the argument that news is different, or should be treated differently, was used by both proponents and opponents of legislation protecting news. Whereas some claimed that news should be ineligible for copyright because information needed to circulate freely, others urged that providing an incentive to collect and distribute timely news was in the public interest. The latter conviction has underpinned various efforts to create special copyright provisions for news, including the recent proposal in the European Union. Copyright law is a form of public policy, and the fact that phrases such as "in the public interest" can be easily co-opted by corporate interests should not lessen our will to shape policy decisions through informed debate and to use the built-in flexibilities of copyright law to ensure that information and ideas circulate freely, stimulating discussion and creativity of all kinds.[30]

NEWS VERSUS COPYRIGHT LAW

Another leitmotif in this history has been the sense that news does not fit comfortably into Anglo-American copyright law. There are several reasons for this, but a major factor has always been the temporal dimensions of news. To count as news, something needs to be new to the person encountering it. Of course, even after we know of an occurrence we might consider it news so long as people are talking about it and we want to be part of the conversation. News means little outside of the human interactions that produce it and are generated by it. But when it comes to copyright law, the time-sensitive nature of news has generated practical and conceptual problems. The practical problem was that the procedures for copyright registration and deposit were designed for books, whose commercial and social value were not as time sensitive as news publications. The registration problem was resolved, at first through ingenuity—such as registering newspapers or telegraphic dispatches as books—and then by changes in the law, especially the shift toward a system in which registration is not required to secure copyright.[31]

The conceptual problem is more profound. Copyright in Britain and the United States has its origins in statutes that explicitly sought to promote the "encouragement of learning." Copyright was meant not only to reward authors but also to benefit society by providing an incentive for the creation of new works. Legislators decided to grant authors a temporary monopoly on the printing and sale of their works in exchange for publishing them (thereby making these works available to readers), depositing copies for libraries (preserving the work and facilitating public access), and—not least—allowing the work to fall into the public domain after the expiration of the copyright. Legal scholars have used the term "copyright bargain" to describe the quid pro quo of authors accepting these obligations in exchange for certain exclusive rights.[32]

In the case of news and time-sensitive information, a temporary monopoly could restrict public access, potentially contradicting the goal of encouraging learning. Moreover, if the news will be of interest only for a short period of time, then the copyright bargain no longer seems like such a good deal. The bargain could be seen to pay off in the case of some books: once they fall into the public domain, cheap editions can be published, not to mention translations and adaptations of all kinds. A lengthy copyright on news publications is not without consequence since it allows publishers to license back issues to database companies, which make them available by paid subscription. Indeed, the questions of who has a de facto monopoly on historical newspapers today and how partnerships between public libraries and for-profit digital publishers affect access to news of the past are of considerable importance for teachers, students, and anyone interested in historical or genealogical research.[33] But even in the hours and days after news is published, the copyright bargain seems like a bad deal. The primary social value of news comes from being able to share and comment on it immediately. In that sense, news publications have always been different than other fact-based works. Recognizing this problem, publishers and press agencies that supported copyright for news in the nineteenth and early twentieth centuries proposed a much shorter duration; they said twenty-four hours or even eight hours would suffice. But they encountered resistance on the grounds that even a copyright of very short duration would disproportionately benefit larger publishers and restrict public access to news. The ideal of the press as a fourth estate that developed in the nineteenth century did not help the cause of those who sought a property right in news. Consider this famous statement by *The Times* in 1852:

The first duty of the press is to obtain the earliest and most correct intelligence of the events of the time, and instantly, by disclosing them, to make them the common property of the nation. The statesman collects his information secretly and by secret means; he keeps back even the current intelligence of the day with ludicrous precautions, until diplomacy is beaten in the race with publicity. The press lives by disclosures; whatever passes into its keeping becomes a part of the knowledge and the history of our times.[34]

The rhetoric of disinterest and public service was increasingly common, but it was often at odds with the business of news.[35] It was therefore entirely possible for an editorial to refer to "intelligence" of recent events as "the common property of the nation" while the same newspaper's management lobbied for a law to prohibit competitors from republishing news that had just been disclosed to the public. The same tension can be seen today.

The fundamentally collaborative nature of news is another important factor differentiating it from some—though not all—forms of authorship protected by copyright. Most news articles are shaped by several writers and editors. Journalists also depend on common sources and are in constant dialogue with each other. Today, bloggers and users of social media are involved in this collective process, raising questions about how fair dealing for news reporting might apply to "citizen journalists" who use mobile devices to capture and share copyrighted material related to a current event.[36] In response to legislative proposals to protect news in the past, some editors and publishers pointed out that newspapers were interdependent and that if copying without permission were made illegal, then it would be much harder for editors and reporters to do their jobs. In 1855, *Reynolds's Weekly Newspaper* stated, "If the transfer of news from one newspaper to another be piracy, then piracy is the basis on which the entire newspaper press is built up."[37] The same objection was raised in response to the American attempt to create a special copyright for news in 1884. An editorial in the *Nation* noted that if the reuse of news became illegal, "most editors would be in jail all the time."[38]

Even after copyright was recognized for newspaper articles, the way journalists drew on each other remained a powerful argument for limiting the scope of copyright for news reports. Settling a dispute between two newspapers in 1990, a British judge observed that if copyright in a news story protected against anything more than verbatim copying it would "strike at the root of what I think is the practice of the national press, namely to search the columns of other papers to find stories which they have missed and then using the story so found in their own newspaper by re-writing it in their own words."[39] Moreover, in the case of a story based on confidential sources, a copyright that extended beyond the expressive form would create a monopoly on that piece of news. In the 1990 decision, the British judge highlighted how the factual basis of news and the public interest in access to it meant that news stories did not enjoy the same degree of protection as certain kinds of literary works. He wrote, "There is no copyright in a current news story corresponding to the copyright which a novelist, for example, enjoys in the plot of his novel in addition to the actual words used to express the plot."[40] Here was another example of a dispute between news publishers that led a judge to articulate how news stories were different than other kinds of writings. Over time, the scope of copyright for literary works has expanded to protect against much more than verbatim copying, but there remain good reasons for limiting the scope of protection for news.

WHEN CREDIT IS NOT ENOUGH

Many professional journalists insist on the importance of giving credit to those who first break a story or bring new information to light.[41] But as the 2017 disputes over local news reporting discussed earlier reveal, not everyone agrees on what can be copied and whether giving credit constitutes sufficient reward. The digital environment may appear to be particularly porous, but it has always been difficult to wall off news. For news publishers, the problem with the internet is not the fact that it is easier to copy and transmit texts and images online; the problem is that it is so much harder to generate advertising revenue now that news organizations compete with all sorts of websites jockeying for the attention of consumers and the internet giants Google and Facebook dominate the market for digital advertising.[42]

As early as the eighteenth century, newspaper publishers recognized advertising as the primary source of profits. Bundling news with other features and selling newspapers by subscription helped publishers to generate revenue, but it was the ability to use this subscriber base to attract advertisers that made newspapers as a whole so profitable for much of their history. The subscription model is still available, and some have argued that it is now the only viable way for newspapers in their digital incarnations to survive.[43] Bundling no longer works well online given how many specialized websites and smartphone applications exist. Although the subscription model may be sufficient for some news organizations, in many cases it will not be, making it necessary to look for other sources of funding, both private and public.[44] The idea of public funding for print journalism has long been treated as anathema in Britain and the United States, despite the fact that postal subsidies were a boon for the American press in the nineteenth century and the nationalization of the telegraph in Britain was crucial to the growth of the provincial press, to say nothing of the public nature of the BBC.[45]

History provides reminders that public policies, from press licensing and the stamp tax to postal and telegraph regulations, have shaped the production and circulation of news in important ways. But with copyright as with other policies, it is difficult to measure the effects, both positive and negative. Copyright is supposed to stimulate the production of new works, but it can also restrict access and provide a chilling effect for those who need to use existing works to produce new ones. In the case of news, policy makers have long been hesitant to pass laws that might restrict the flow of information of public concern, and for good reason. The risks simply outweigh the potential benefits.

News publishers have turned to copyright at specific moments and imagined it as a solution to particular problems. Most discussions of copyright for news were prompted by changes in the media landscape brought on by new combinations of regulation, technology, and business practice. That has also been the case for recent litigation and legislative proposals for controlling news online. At such moments it is important to recall the history and first principles of copyright, to think about what differentiates news from other domains of knowledge and creativity, and to engage in informed debate about what policies will best serve the public interest.

Abbreviations Used in the Notes and
a Note on Newspaper Sources

ABBREVIATIONS USED IN THE NOTES

AAS: American Antiquarian Society.

AP Archives: Associated Press Corporate Archives, New York.

CCE: *Catalog of Copyright Entries* (Washington, DC: GPO, 1906–1978). For a convenient portal to digital scans, see http://onlinebooks.library.upenn.edu/cce/index .html.

CP: *Censorship and the Press, 1580–1720.* Edited by Geoff Kemp and Jason McElligott. 4 vols. (London: Pickering and Chatto, 2009).

CTE: *Catalogue of Title Entries of Books and Other Articles* (Washington, DC: GPO, 1891–1906). Available through http://onlinebooks.library.upenn.edu/cce/index.html.

HC Deb: Followed by the date, volume, and column number, this refers to the electronic version of the *Hansard Parliamentary Debates,* consulted through http://hansard .millbanksystems.com/index.html. In early 2018, the Parliamentary Digital Service announced that it was in the process of migrating this content to https://hansard .parliament.uk.

LMA: London Metropolitan Archives, City of London.

LOC: Library of Congress.

MN: *Making News: The Political Economy of Journalism in Britain and America from the Glorious Revolution to the Internet.* Edited by Richard R. John and Jonathan Silberstein-Loeb (Oxford: Oxford University Press, 2015).

NARA: National Archives and Records Administration (Washington, DC, site unless otherwise indicated).

NYPL: New York Public Library.

PP: Followed by the session year and serial number of the document, this refers to sessional papers of the UK Parliament, accessed through ProQuest House of Commons Parliamentary Papers Online.

PSC: *Primary Sources on Copyright (1450–1900).* Edited by Lionel Bently and Martin Kretschmer, http://www.copyrighthistory.org/.

SC Myers: *Records of the Worshipful Company of Stationers 1554–1920.* Edited by Robin Myers. 115 reels of microfilm (Cambridge, UK: Chadwyck-Healey, 1985). For a concordance between the microfilm reels and the original documents (some of which are now being made available digitally), see Robin Myers, *The Stationers' Company Archive: An Account of the Records, 1554–1984* (Winchester, UK: St. Paul's Bibliographies, 1990).

TNA: The National Archives, Kew, United Kingdom.

USCO: US Copyright Office, Library of Congress.

A NOTE ON NEWSPAPER SOURCES

Unless otherwise indicated in the notes, newspapers were consulted using one of the digital databases listed here. In cases in which paper copies were consulted, the repository is indicated after the reference in the notes. Note also that before 1752 the civil year in Britain began on March 25 (sometimes referred to as Old Style dating). For the sake of consistency, in citing newspapers published between January 1 and March 25 I have used New Style dates, in which the year begins on January 1.

Proprietary Databases

Seventeenth- and Eighteenth-Century Burney Newspapers Collection (Gale Cengage)
British Library Newspapers, 1800–1900 (Gale)
The Times Digital Archive (Gale)
America's Historical Newspapers, 1690–1922 (Readex)
ProQuest Historical Newspapers
Nineteenth-Century US Newspapers (Gale)

Free Databases

Chronicling America: Historic American Newspapers, https://chroniclingamerica.loc.gov
California Digital Newspaper Collection, https://cdnc.ucr.edu/cgi-bin/cdnc
Colorado Historic Newspapers Collection, https://www.coloradohistoricnewspapers.org
Georgia Historic Newspapers, https://gahistoricnewspapers.galileo.usg.edu

Notes

INTRODUCTION

1. *Grub-Street Journal* (London), 5 Apr. 1733. See chapter 2.

2. See Richard Pérez-Peña, "AP Seeks to Rein in Sites Using Its Content," *New York Times*, 6 Apr. 2009, http://www.nytimes.com/; Mercedes Bunz, "Rupert Murdoch: 'There's No Such Thing as a Free News Story,'" *The Guardian*, 1 Dec. 2009, https://www.theguardian.com/; Arianna Huffington, "Journalism 2009: Desperate Metaphors, Desperate Revenue Models, and the Desperate Need for Better Journalism," *Huffington Post*, 18 Mar. 2010, updated 25 May 2011, http://www.huffingtonpost.com/.

3. See Robert Denicola, "News on the Internet," *Fordham Intellectual Property Media & Entertainment Law Journal* 23 (2013): 68–131; and Pam Spaulding and Michelangelo Signorile, "Copyright Shakedown: The Rise and Fall of Righthaven," in *Media Authorship*, ed. Cynthia Chris and David A. Gerstner (New York: Routledge, 2013), 37–55. A study of legal interventions in several countries was undertaken by Lionel Bently, Richard Danbury, and Ian Hargreaves for the AHRC-funded project titled "Appraising Potential Legal Responses to Threats to the Production of News in a Digital Environment" (2014–2016), https://www.cipil.law.cam.ac.uk/projects/copyright-and-news-project-2014-16.

4. See Robert W. McChesney and John Nichols, *The Death and Life of American Journalism: The Media Revolution that Will Begin the World Again* (New York: Nation Books, 2011); Ian Hargreaves, *Journalism: A Very Short Introduction*, 2nd ed. (Oxford, UK: Oxford University Press, 2014).

5. *Grub-Street Journal*, 3 Jan. 1734.

6. International News Service v. Associated Press, 248 U.S. 215 (1918). See chapter 7.

7. For the recent court cases, see chapter 7. A proposal to codify the misappropriation doctrine was included in "Federal Trade Commission Staff Discussion Draft: Potential Policy Recommendations to Support the Reinvention of Journalism" (2009), https://www.ftc.gov/sites/default/files/documents/public_events/how-will-journalism-survive-internet-age/new-staff-discussion.pdf.

8. Referring to Britain instead of England has the advantage of brevity but remains problematic given that most of the developments discussed here took place in England. It also glosses over important political changes. In 1707, the Act of Union combined England and Scotland into Great Britain. In 1801, Great Britain and Ireland were combined to form the United Kingdom of Great Britain and Ireland. After the creation of the Irish Free State in 1922, the name became the United Kingdom of Great Britain and Northern Ireland.

9. For a comparative history of policy, see Paul Starr, *The Creation of the Media: Political Origins of Modern Communications* (New York: Basic Books, 2004). The international dimensions of copyright for news merit more study, but some good work

has been done on Reuters and the AP in an international context. See Michael D. Birn-hack, *Colonial Copyright: Intellectual Property in Mandate Palestine* (Oxford: Oxford University Press, 2012), 212–38; Jonathan Silberstein-Loeb, *The International Distribution of News: The Associated Press, Press Association, and Reuters, 1848–1947* (New York: Cambridge University Press, 2014); Heidi J. S. Tworek, "Protecting News before the Internet," in *MN*, 196–222; Sara Bannerman, *International Copyright and Access to Knowledge* (Cambridge: Cambridge University Press, 2016), 80–98; and Gene Allen, "Catching Up with the Competition: The International Expansion of Associated Press, 1920–1945," *Journalism Studies* 17, no. 6 (2016): 747–62.

10. See Peter Baldwin, *The Copyright Wars: Three Centuries of Trans-Atlantic Battle* (Princeton, NJ: Princeton University Press, 2014). Such differences should not be exaggerated, however.

11. For a recent analysis, with references to studies that posit a distinct Anglo-American tradition, see John Maxwell Hamilton and Heidi J. S. Tworek, "The Natural History of the News: An Epigenetic Study," *Journalism* 18, no. 4 (April 2017): 391–407. For a summary of research on cross-influences, see Bob Nicholson, "Transatlantic Connections," in *The Routledge Handbook to Nineteenth-Century British Periodicals and Newspapers*, ed. Andrew King, Alexis Easley, and John Morton (London: Routledge, 2016), 221–33.

12. See *MN*.

13. Several books with variations on the title *Who Owns the Media?* have explored the problem of media concentration. On the history of press commercialization, see Gerald J. Baldasty, *The Commercialization of News in the Nineteenth Century* (Madison: University of Wisconsin Press, 1992); James Curran and Jean Seaton, *Power without Responsibility: The Press and Broadcasting in Britain*, 7th ed. (London: Routledge, 2009); and John Nerone, *The Media and Public Life: A History* (Cambridge, UK: Polity, 2015).

14. The economic concepts are clearly presented in James T. Hamilton, *All the News That's Fit to Sell: How the Market Transforms Information into News* (Princeton, NJ: Princeton University Press, 2004), 7–10; and Gerben Bakker, "How They Made News Pay: News Traders' Quest for Crisis-Resistant Business Models" (Economic History Working Papers 206/2014, London School of Economics and Political Science, 2014), http://eprints.lse.ac.uk/59304.

15. For an overview of the law-and-economics approach, see Anne Barron, "Copyright Infringement, 'Free-Riding' and the Lifeworld," in *Copyright and Piracy: An Interdisciplinary Critique*, ed. Lionel Bently, Jennifer Davis, and Jane C. Ginsburg (Cambridge: Cambridge University Press, 2010), 93–127.

16. William St. Clair, "Metaphors of Intellectual Property," in *Privilege and Property: Essays on the History of Copyright*, ed. Ronan Deazley, Martin Kretschmer, and Lionel Bently (Cambridge, UK: Open Book Publishers, 2010), 369–95.

17. See the essays in Helena R. Howe and Jonathan Griffiths, eds., *Concepts of Property in Intellectual Property Law* (Cambridge: Cambridge University Press, 2013).

18. The discussion of property is in chapter 5 of Locke's *Second Treatise*, first published in 1690. See Mark Rose, *Authors and Owners: The Invention of Copyright* (Cambridge, MA: Harvard University Press, 1993).

19. St. Clair, "Metaphors," 391–93.

20. Adrian Johns, *Piracy: The Intellectual Property Wars from Gutenberg to Gates* (Chicago: University of Chicago Press, 2009), 23–24, 35–48.

21. See Meredith L. McGill, *American Literature and the Culture of Reprinting, 1834–1853* (Philadelphia: University of Pennsylvania Press, 2003); and Catherine Seville, "Nineteenth-Century Anglo-US Copyright Relations: The Language of Piracy versus the Moral High Ground," in Bently, Davis, and Ginsburg, *Copyright and Piracy*, 19–43.

22. Robert Spoo, *Without Copyrights: Piracy, Publishing, and the Public Domain* (New York: Oxford University Press, 2013).

23. On the importance of geography, see Johns, *Piracy*, 13–14, 41–56.

24. Michael Birnhack, "Copyright Pioneers," *WIPO Journal* 5, no. 1 (2013): 118–26. See also Melissa J. Homestead, *American Women Authors and Literary Property, 1822–1869* (Cambridge: Cambridge University Press, 2005); and Mark Rose, *Authors in Court: Scenes from the Theater of Copyright* (Cambridge, MA: Harvard University Press, 2016).

25. The literature is vast and will be cited throughout. For a survey, see Meredith L. McGill, "Copyright and Intellectual Property: The State of the Discipline," *Book History* 16 (2013): 387–427.

26. This point also emerged from a study of German publishers' efforts to protect news in the age of radio and, more recently, online. Heidi J. S. Tworek and Christopher Buschow, "Changing the Rules of the Game: Strategic Institutionalization and Legacy Companies' Resistance to New Media," *International Journal of Communication* 10 (2016): 2119–39.

27. These definitions are quoted in James W. Brown to A. H. Sulzberger, 11 Mar. 1932, box 96, folder 28, New York Times Company Records, Adolph S. Ochs Papers, NYPL. The same folder contains further correspondence related to the definition of news.

28. See Robert Darnton, "Writing News and Telling Stories," *Daedalus* 104, no. 2 (Spring 1975): 175–94; Michael Schudson, *The Power of News* (Cambridge, MA: Harvard University Press, 1995); and Howard Tumber, ed., *News: A Reader* (Oxford: Oxford University Press, 1999).

29. See Joad Raymond and Noah Moxham, eds., *News Networks in Early Modern Europe* (Leiden: Brill, 2016). Computational studies of news circulation are also becoming more transnational. An example of an ongoing project is "Oceanic Exchanges: Tracing Global Information Networks in Historical Newspaper Repositories, 1840–1914," http://oceanicexchanges.org.

30. Terhi Rantanen, *When News Was New* (Chichester, UK: Wiley-Blackwell, 2009), 2–3, 75.

31. "The News Copyright Bill," file S48A-H14, RG 46, Sen. Cmte. Library, NARA.

32. Clayton v. Stone, 5 F. Cas. 999 (C.C.S.D.N.Y 1829). See chapter 4.

33. Walter v. Steinkopff [1892] 3 Ch. 489; Walter v. Lane [1900] AC 539. See chapter 5.

CHAPTER ONE

1. Joad Raymond, ed., *News, Newspapers, and Society in Early Modern Britain* (London: Frank Cass, 1999); Paul Arblaster, "Posts, Newsletters, Newspapers: England in a European System of Communications," *Media History* 11, nos. 1–2 (2005): 21–36; Andrew Pettegree, *The Invention of News: How the World Came to Know about Itself* (New Haven, CT: Yale University Press, 2014).

2. I refer to the Stationers' Company as a guild because most studies do, but during

its early history it was referred to as a "mistery" or "craft." Note also that the history of the company goes back further than the 1557 charter. Peter W. M. Blayney, *The Stationers' Company and the Printers of London, 1501–1557* (Cambridge: Cambridge University Press, 2013), 1:14–19.

3. Adrian Johns, *The Nature of the Book: Print and Knowledge in the Making* (Chicago: University of Chicago Press, 1998), 187–90, 213–30; John Feather, "From Rights in Copies to Copyright: The Recognition of Authors' Rights in English Law and Practice in the Sixteenth and Seventeenth Centuries," in *The Construction of Authorship: Textual Appropriation in Law and Literature*, ed. Martha Woodmansee and Peter Jaszi (Durham, NC: Duke University Press, 1994), 191–209.

4. Adrian Johns, *Piracy: The Intellectual Property Wars from Gutenberg to Gates* (Chicago: University of Chicago Press, 2009), 13–14, 23–24, 41–47.

5. See Brendan Dooley, ed., *The Dissemination of News and the Emergence of Contemporaneity in Early Modern Europe* (Farnham, UK: Ashgate, 2010); and Joad Raymond and Noah Moxham, eds., *News Networks in Early Modern Europe* (Leiden, NL: Brill, 2016).

6. A classic study of this transition is Lyman Ray Patterson, *Copyright in Historical Perspective* (Nashville: Vanderbilt University Press, 1968).

7. Paul Arblaster et al., "The Lexicons of Early Modern News," in Raymond and Moxham, *News Networks*, 64–101; Pettegree, *Invention of News*, 8–11; Will Slauter, "The Rise of the Newspaper," in *MN*, 19–46.

8. Richard Cust, "News and Politics in Early Seventeenth-Century England," *Past and Present* 112 (Aug. 1986): 60–90; David Zaret, *Origins of Democratic Culture: Printing, Petitions, and the Public Sphere in Early-Modern England* (Princeton, NJ: Princeton University Press, 2000), 44–67.

9. Carolyn Nelson and Matthew Seccombe, "The Creation of the Periodical Press, 1620–1695," in *The Cambridge History of the Book in Britain*, ed. John Barnard and D. F. McKenzie, vol. 4, *1557–1695* (Cambridge: Cambridge University Press, 2002), 535.

10. David Cressy, *Dangerous Talk: Scandalous, Seditious, and Treasonable Speech in Pre-Modern England* (Oxford: Oxford University Press, 2010), 12–16; Jason Peacey, *Print and Public Politics in the English Revolution* (Cambridge: Cambridge University Press, 2013), 16–17, 214–24.

11. Joad Raymond, "Censorship in Law and Practice in Seventeenth-Century England: Milton's Areopagitica," in *The Oxford Handbook of English Law and Literature, 1500–1700*, ed. Lorna Hutson (Oxford: Oxford University Press, 2017), 507–28.

12. Geoff Kemp and Jason McElligot, "General Introduction: The Constitution of Early Modern Censorship," in *CP*, 1:xiii–xxxiii.

13. Raymond, "Censorship"; Cyndia Susan Clegg, *Press Censorship in Elizabethan England* (Cambridge: Cambridge University Press, 1997), 37–44; Johns, *Nature of the Book*, 230–35.

14. Ian Gadd, "The Stationers' Company in England before 1710," in *Research Handbook on the History of Copyright Law*, ed. Isabella Alexander and H. Tomás Gómez-Arostegui (Cheltenham, UK: Edward Elgar, 2016), 81–95; Johns, *Nature of the Book*, 248–62; Clegg, *Elizabethan England*, 7–13; Cyndia Susan Clegg, *Press Censorship in Jacobean England* (Cambridge: Cambridge University Press, 2001), 23–24; Arnold Hunt, "Book Trade Patents, 1603–1640," in *The Book Trade and Its Customers,*

1450–1900: Historical Essays for Robin Myers, ed. Arnold Hunt, Giles Mandelbrote, and Alison Shell (Winchester, UK: St. Paul's Bibliographies, 1997), 27–54.

15. Gadd, "Stationers' Company," 85–88; Cyprian Blagden, *The Stationers' Company: A History, 1403–1959* (London: George Allen and Unwin, 1960), 19–21, 101–4.

16. The distinction between seditious and blasphemous libel was often blurred, and the definition of both terms remained vague. Cressy, *Dangerous Talk*, 33–34, 41, 55; Philip Hamburger, "The Development of the Law of Seditious Libel and the Control of the Press," *Stanford Law Review* 37, no. 3 (Feb. 1985): 661–765.

17. Blagden, *Stationers' Company*, 20–21, 65–66, 70–74; Clegg, *Elizabethan England*, 20–21; Joseph Lowenstein, *The Author's Due: Printing and the Prehistory of Copyright* (Chicago: University of Chicago Press, 2002), 42–43.

18. Gadd, "Stationers' Company," 88–91; Feather, "Rights in Copies," 196–99; John Feather, "The British Book Market, 1600–1800," in *A Companion to the History of the Book*, ed. Simon Eliot and Jonathan Rose (Oxford, UK: Wiley-Blackwell, 2007), 232–46.

19. Clegg, *Elizabethan England*, 14–19; Gadd, "Stationers' Company," 88–89.

20. Johns, *Nature of the Book*, 213–30; W. W. Greg, "Introduction," in *Records of the Court of the Stationers' Company: 1576–1602 from Register B*, ed. W. W. Greg and E. Boswell (London: Bibliographical Society, 1930), v–lxxvii; H. Tomás Gómez-Arostegui, "What History Teaches Us about Copyright Injunctions and the Inadequate-Remedy-at-Law Requirement," *Southern California Law Review* 81 (2008): 1256–62.

21. Johns, *Nature of the Book*, 221–28. But see Lowenstein, *Author's Due*, 132–51; and Rebecca Schoff Curtin, "The Transactional Origins of Authors' Copyright," *Columbia Journal of Law and the Arts* 40, no. 2 (2016): 175–235.

22. The main legislative orders recognizing the stationers' printing rights were the Star Chamber decrees of 1566, 1586, and 1637; the parliamentary ordinances of 1643, 1647, and 1649; and the Printing Act of 1662. See Michael Treadwell, "The Stationers and the Printing Acts at the End of the Seventeenth Century," in Barnard and McKenzie, *Cambridge History of the Book*, 4:755–78.

23. I will refer to newspapers as periodicals, but note that librarians employ more precise definitions in order to catalog and classify their collections, leading to a distinction between newspapers and periodicals. See Joan M. Reitz, *Online Dictionary for Library and Information Science*, ABC-CLIO, last updated 10 Jan. 2013, https://www.abc-clio.com/ODLIS/odlis_p.aspx#periodical. Newspapers can also be defined by the type of material they contain.

24. C. John Sommerville, *The News Revolution in England: Cultural Dynamics of Daily Information* (New York: Oxford University Press, 1996); Joad Raymond, "News," in *The Oxford History of Popular Print Culture*, ed. Joad Raymond, vol. 1, *Cheap Print in Britain and Ireland to 1660* (Oxford: Oxford University Press, 2011), 377–97; Pettegree, *Invention of News*.

25. Angela McShane, "Ballads and Broadsides," in Raymond, *Oxford History of Popular Print*, 1:339–62.

26. Hyder Rollins, "The Black-Letter Broadside Ballad," *PMLA* 34, no. 2 (1919): 258–339. Rollins described ballads as furnishing news, an idea questioned by Angela McShane, who stressed their political functions. Angela McShane Jones, "'Rime and Reason': The Political World of the Broadside Ballad, 1640–1689" (PhD diss., Warwick

University, 2004), wrap.warwick.ac.uk/2708. Numbers from Angela McShane, "Typography Matters: Branding Ballads and Gelding Curates in Stuart England," in *Book Trade Connections from the Seventeenth to the Twentieth Centuries*, ed. John Hinks and Catherine Armstrong (New Castle, DE: Oak Knoll Press, 2008), 19.

27. Una McIlvenna, "When the News Was Sung: Ballads as News Media in Early Modern Europe," *Media History* 22, nos. 3–4 (2016): 317–33.

28. McShane Jones, "Rime and Reason," 67–70.

29. Hyder Rollins, *An Analytical Index to the Ballad-Entries (1557–1709) in the Registers of the Company of Stationers of London* (Chapel Hill: University of North Carolina Press, 1924), 1; Rollins, "Black-Letter," 281.

30. But in some cases the desire not to waste materials led to more complex agreements. See Gómez-Arostegui, "What History Teaches," 1260–62; Greg and Boswell, *Records*, lxxv, 109–10 (index entries for "Copyright, Customs and orders respecting"); and Alison Shell and Alison Emblow, *Index to the Court Books of the Stationers' Company, 1679–1717* (London: Bibliographical Society, 2007), 11–26.

31. Tessa Watt, *Cheap Print and Popular Piety, 1550–1640* (Cambridge: Cambridge University Press, 1991), 74–78; Cyprian Blagden, "Notes on the Ballad Market in the Second Half of the Seventeenth Century," *Studies in Bibliography* 6 (1954): 161–80; McShane Jones, "Rime and Reason," 72–74. The initial partnership may have been formed as an effort to counteract the claims of Thomas Symcock, who obtained a patent in 1618 for all works printed on one side of a single sheet. The patent was immediately contested by the Stationers' Company, and in 1631 it was declared invalid by the Court of Chancery. *Records of the Court of the Stationers' Company*, ed. William A. Jackson, vol. 2, *1602–1640* (London: Bibliographical Society, 1957), xvi–xxii.

32. Joad Raymond, *Pamphlets and Pamphleteering in Early Modern Britain* (Cambridge: Cambridge University Press, 2003), 5, 16–17, 98–160.

33. Pamphlets were registered as "books" and paid the same fee of sixpence. Edward Arber, *A Transcript of the Registers of the Company of Stationers of London; 1554–1640 AD*, vols. 2–3 (London: privately printed, 1875–1894). I am not making any claim about the proportion of news pamphlets that were registered. My point is that the stationers' customary rights also applied to news publications.

34. *A True Relation of a Most Desperate Murder, Committed upon the Body of Sir John Tindall* (London: Printed by Edw. All-de for L. L. [Lawrence Lisle], 1617). The pamphlet may have been commissioned or supervised by Sir Francis Bacon. See Ken MacMillan, ed., *Stories of True Crime in Tudor and Stuart England* (London: Routledge, 2015), chap. 11, which includes a transcription of the pamphlet.

35. Arber, *Transcript*, 3:598.

36. Watt, *Cheap Print*, 148–49; Alastair Bellany, *The Politics of Court Scandal in Early Modern England: News Culture and the Overbury Affair, 1603–1660* (Cambridge: Cambridge University Press, 2002), 127. The history of property claims in visual representations of news merits further study.

37. Rollins, "Black-Letter," 294.

38. Johns, *Nature of the Book*, 218; Arber, *Transcript*, 2:25; Fredrick Seaton Siebert, *Freedom of the Press in England 1476–1776: The Rise and Decline of Government Control* (Urbana: University of Illinois Press, 1965), 152.

39. Arber, *Transcript*, 3:200; Greg and Boswell, *Records*, 85.

40. Only the work deemed to be infringing appears to have survived, so it is impos-

sible to know whether it was a verbatim reprinting of the first work or a retelling of the news in a new form. The offending work was *A Letter from a Souldier of Good Place in Ireland* (London: Imprinted for Symon Waterson, 1602), STC 7434. No similar work by the complainant stationers, Thomas Pavier and John Hardie, has been located.

41. John McCusker, "British Commercial and Financial Journalism Before 1800," in *The Cambridge History of the Book in Britain*, ed. Michael F. Suarez and Michael L. Turner, vol. 5, *1695–1830* (Cambridge: Cambridge University Press, 2009), 448–65; John J. McCusker and Cora Gravesteijn, *The Beginnings of Commercial and Financial Journalism: The Commodity Price Currents, Exchange Rate Currents, and Money Currents of Early Modern Europe* (Amsterdam: NEHA, 1991), 291–99.

42. Quoted in McCusker and Gravesteijn, *Beginnings*, 293.

43. Ibid., 293–94.

44. John J. McCusker, *European Bills of Entry and Marine Lists: Early Commercial Publications and the Origins of the Business Press* (Cambridge, MA: Harvard University Library, 1985), 18–33.

45. This section on the bills of mortality draws on Will Slauter, "Write Up Your Dead: The Bills of Mortality and the London Plague of 1665," *Media History* 17, no. 1 (2011): 1–15. See also J. C. Robertson, "Reckoning with London: Interpreting the Bills of Mortality before John Graunt," *Urban History* 23, no. 3 (Dec. 1996): 325–50.

46. Stephen Greenberg, "Plague, the Printing Press, and Public Health in Seventeenth-Century London," *Huntington Library Quarterly* 67, no. 4 (2004): 508–27.

47. Jackson, *Records of the Court*, 8. Although Windet had entered the bills in the register (Arber, *Transcript*, 3:243), he did not make a separate entry for each week's edition. There is no evidence that the Court of Assistants was concerned about this. The Stationers' Company recognized the rights of patent holders, and Windet was the official city printer.

48. Jackson, *Records of the Court*, 441.

49. James Christie, *Some Account of Parish Clerks* (London: privately printed, 1893), 132–35, 187–88; Papers relating to grant of new charter, 1635, Collection of the Worshipful Company of Parish Clerks, CLC/L/PB/A/003/MS04893, LMA.

50. Hunt, "Book Trade Patents," 53.

51. A. W. Pollard and G. R. Redgrave, eds., *A Short-Title Catalogue of Books Printed in England, Scotland, and Ireland and of English Books Printed Abroad, 1475–1640*, 2nd ed. (London: Bibliographical Society, 1976), 2:112–13.

52. Christie, *Some Account*, 136–39; Copy Extracts from the Minutes of the Parish Clerks' Company, 1610–1926, pp. 10, 14–15, 33–34, 36, 39, 41–44, 50, CLC/478/MS03706, LMA; Orders and Rules dated 14 Oct. 1695, in Scrapbook of Collectanea for the History of the Company, 1187–1697, CLC/L/PB/F/001/MS04894/001, LMA.

53. Order dated 8 Jan. 1666, in Copy Extracts from the Minutes of the Parish Clerks' Company, 1610–1926, p. 10, CLC/478/MS03706, LMA; Orders and Rules dated 14 Oct. 1695, in Scrapbook of Collectanea for the History of the Company, 1187–1697, CLC/L/PB/F/001/MS04894/001, LMA.

54. Petition, [1621?], SP 14/124, fol. 230, TNA, accessed via *State Papers Online, 1509–1714*, http://gale.cengage.co.uk/state-papers-online-15091714.aspx. The petition is not signed, but it refers to "Mr. Porey" (presumably John Pory, a compiler of newsletters) as coapplicant. The letter has been attributed to Sir Thomas Wilson. See Mary Anne Everett Green, ed., *Calendar of State Papers, Domestic Series, of the Reign of*

James I. 1619–1623 (London: Longman, Brown, Green, Longmans, and Roberts, 1858), 330; and Fritz Levy, "The Decorum of News," in Raymond, *News, Newspapers, and Society*, 28. The document is partly reproduced in William S. Powell, *John Pory, 1572– 1636: The Life and Letters of a Man of Many Parts* (Chapel Hill: University of North Carolina Press, 1977), 52–53, where it is confusingly attributed to Thomas Locke.

55. "A Proclamation against Excess of Lavish and Licentious Speech in Matters of State (London, 1620)," in *CP*, 1:201–2. See also *CP*, 1:197–98.

56. The first English-language corantos available in London in 1620–1621 were printed in Amsterdam, the work of Dutch publishers who arranged for their own publications to be translated for an English audience. Soon London stationers were issuing their own corantos, translated from sources on the continent. Folke Dahl, *A Bibliography of English Corantos and Periodical Newsbooks, 1620–1642* (Stockholm: Almqvist and Wiskell, 1953), 31–54; Pollard and Redgrave, *Short-Title Catalogue*, 2: 178.

57. Raymond, *Pamphlets*, 130; Nelson and Seccombe, "Creation," 536.

58. Arber, *Transcript*, 4:60–61, 68–70, 77–78.

59. Raymond, *Pamphlets*, 101–34; Nicholas Brownlees, *The Language of Periodical News in Seventeenth-Century England* (Newcastle upon Tyne: Cambridge Scholars, 2011), 55–56.

60. Dahl, *Bibliography*, 19, 86; Nelson and Seccombe, "Creation," 535–37. Other scholars tend to refer to this as a *syndicate*, but I have employed the word *consortium* to avoid confusion with the kinds of literary syndicates discussed in chapter 6.

61. Jackson, *Records of the Court*, 154.

62. Dahl, *Bibliography*, 124.

63. Sommerville, *News Revolution*, 23–26; Raymond, *Pamphlets*, 131–36; Brownlees, *Language*, 55–69; Pettegree, *Invention of News*, 196–97.

64. Anthony B. Thompson, "Licensing the Press: The Career of G. R. Weckherlin during the Personal Rule of Charles I," *Historical Journal* 41, no. 3 (1998): 653–78; Kevin Sharpe, *The Personal Rule of Charles I* (New Haven, CT: Yale University Press, 1992), 646–47; Raymond, *Pamphlets*, 149; Pettegree, *Invention of News*, 198–200; "Privy Council Order to Cease News Publication (17 October 1632)," in *CP*, 1:290.

65. Petition of N. Butter and N. Bourne, 30 Sept. 1633, SP 16/246, fol. 177, TNA, via *State Papers Online*.

66. W. W. Greg, ed., *A Companion to Arber: Being a Calendar of Documents in Edward Arber's Transcript of the Registers of the Company of Stationers of London, 1554–1640* (Oxford, UK: Clarendon Press, 1967), 292; Siebert, *Freedom of the Press*, 157–58.

67. Raymond, "Censorship," 516; Raymond, *Pamphlets*, 150–51; *Calendar of State Papers, Domestic Series*, ed. John Bruce and William Douglas Hamilton, vol. 13, *Sept 1638–Mar 1639* (London: Longman, 1871), 182.

68. Siebert, *Freedom of the Press*, 159–60; Thompson, "Licensing," 675.

69. Jason McElligott, "1641," in *CP*, 2:15–17.

70. Joad Raymond, *The Invention of the Newspaper: English Newsbooks, 1641–1649* (Oxford, UK: Clarendon Press, 1996), 101–11; Peacey, *Print and Public*, 57.

71. Raymond, *Invention*, 20–24, 32–33.

72. Carolyn Nelson and Matthew Seccombe, *Periodical Publications, 1641–1700: A Survey with Illustrations* (London: The Bibliographical Society, 1986), 78–81.

73. Philip Gaskell, *A New Introduction to Bibliography* (New Castle, DE: Oak Knoll Press, 2006), 139–41. See also Raymond, *Invention*, 234–36.

74. The year on the title page is 1641 because it follows the Old Style calendar, in which the civil year began on March 25. Nelson and Seccombe note that the variations in spelling and wording also suggest that there were two copies of the manuscript, one given to each printer. Nelson and Seccombe, *Periodical Publications*, 42–45.

75. Ibid., 62–63. In 1643, Parliament passed an ordinance requiring all books, pamphlets, and papers (including newsbooks) to be authorized by a licenser and registered with the Stationers' Company, but not all publishers of newsbooks complied with these requirements. See Raymond, *Invention*, 28–29, 60–61, 77–78; and [G. E. B. Eyre], *A Transcript of the Registers of the Worshipful Company of Stationers; from 1640–1708 AD*, 3 vols. (London: privately printed, 1913), 1:58–326.

76. Jason Peacey, "'The Counterfeit Silly Curr': Money, Politics, and the Forging of Royalist Newspapers during the English Civil War," *Huntingdon Library Quarterly* 67, no. 1 (2004): 27–58.

77. Petition of John Dillingham, 23 June 1648, and remonstrance and petition of Gilbert Mabbott, abstracted in *Seventh Report of the Royal Commission on Historical Manuscripts* (London: H. M. Stationery Office, 1879), 33; Order of 23 June 1648, *Journal of the House of Lords*, 10:345–46, http://www.british-history.ac.uk/lords-jrnl/vol10/pp345-346.

78. Petition of Robert White, in *Seventh Report*, 33.

79. William Clyde, *The Struggle for Freedom of the Press from Caxton to Cromwell* (Oxford: Oxford University Press, 1934), 145–47; Raymond, *Invention*, 65–67.

80. Laurent Curelly, *An Anatomy of an English Radical Newspaper: The Moderate (1648–9)* (Newcastle upon Tyne, UK: Cambridge Scholars, 2017), 17–31.

81. Raymond, *Invention*, 54–79; Nelson and Seccombe, "Creation," 537–43.

82. Joad Raymond, "'A Mercury with a Winged Conscience': Marchamont Nedham, Monopoly and Censorship," *Media History* 4, no. 1 (1998): 7–18.

83. James Sutherland, *The Restoration Newspaper and Its Development* (New York: Cambridge University Press, 1986), 5–7; Harold Love, *Scribal Publication in Seventeenth-Century England* (Oxford, UK: Clarendon Press, 1993), 10–13. This and subsequent paragraphs in this section draw closely on Slauter, "Rise of the Newspaper."

84. "L'Estrange to bee Surveyor of the Printing Presse &c (15 August 1663)," in *CP*, 3:50–51.

85. Sutherland, *Restoration Newspaper*, 8–11. On the *Gazette* during a later period, see Natasha Glaisyer, "'The Most Universal Intelligencers': The Circulation of the *London Gazette* in the 1690s," *Media History* 23, no. 2 (2017): 256–80.

86. Susan E. Whyman, *The Pen and the People: English Letter Writers, 1660–1800* (Oxford: Oxford University Press, 2009), 49–52.

87. An Act for Preventing Abuses in Printing Seditious, Treasonable, and Unlicensed Books and Pamphlets, and for Regulating of Printing and Printing Presses [referred to in text as Printing Act], 1662, 13 & 14 Car. II c. 33, available in *PSC*.

88. The earliest recorded use in the *Oxford English Dictionary* is from 1667. *OED Online*, 3rd ed. (Sept. 2003), s.v. "newspaper, n.," http://www.oed.com.

89. Hamburger, "Seditious Libel," 682–83; Louis G. Schwoerer, "Liberty of the Press and Public Opinion: 1660–1695," in *Liberty Secured? Britain before and after 1688*, ed. J. R. Jones (Stanford, CA: Stanford University Press, 1992), 199–230.

90. "A Proclamation for Suppressing the Printing and Publishing Unlicensed News-Books, and Pamphlets of News (12 May 1680)," in *CP*, 3:175–76.

91. "The Trial of Henry Carr" (1680), in *A Complete Collection of State Trials*, ed. T. B. Howell (London: T. C. Hansard, 1816), 7:1114. See also Hamburger, "Seditious Libel," 688.

92. Geoff Kemp, "Restoration Crisis, 1679–81," in *CP*, 3:169–72; Geoff Kemp, "The Tory Reaction I," in *CP*, 3:233–36; Sutherland, *Restoration Newspaper*, 10–18.

93. Michael Harris, "Trials and Criminal Biographies: A Case Study in Distribution," in *Sale and Distribution of Books from 1700*, ed. Robin Myers and Michael Harris (Oxford: Oxford Polytechnic Press, 1982), 1–36; Andrea McKenzie, "From True Confessions to True Reporting? The Decline and Fall of the Ordinary's *Account*," *London Journal* 30, no. 1 (May 2005): 55–70.

94. Mark Goldie, "Introduction," in *CP*, 4:ix–x; Schwoerer, "Liberty," 227–29.

95. James Raven, *Publishing Business in Eighteenth-Century England* (Woodbridge, UK: Boydell Press, 2014), 10–11, 85.

96. McCusker and Gravesteijn, *Beginnings*, 291–352.

97. See Natasha Glaisyer, *The Culture of Commerce in England, 1660–1720* (Woodbridge, UK: Boydell Press, 2006), 145–71.

98. Treadwell, "Stationers," 770–71; Mark Goldie, "The Printing Act in Question, 1692–3," in *CP*, 3:347–50; Mark Goldie, "The Rejection of Licensing," in *CP*, 3:413–21.

99. Johns, *Piracy*, 41–43. On Stationers' Company leadership, see Michael Treadwell, "1695–1995: Some Tercentenary Thoughts on the Freedoms of the Press," *Harvard Library Bulletin* new series 7, no. 1 (Spring 1996): 3–19.

100. Mark Goldie, "Introduction," in *CP*, 4:ix–xxv.

101. Treadwell, "Stationers," 776.

102. Hamburger, "Seditious Libel"; C. G. Gibbs, "Press and Public Opinion: Prospective," in Jones, *Liberty Secured*, 231–64.

103. Alex Barber, "'It Is Not Easy What to Say of Our Condition, Much Less to Write It': The Continued Importance of Scribal News in the Early 18th Century," *Parliamentary History* 32, no. 2 (2013): 293–316.

104. Carolyn Nelson and Matthew Seccombe, *British Newspapers and Periodicals, 1641–1700. A Short-Title Catalogue of Serials Printed in England, Scotland, Ireland, and British America* (New York: Modern Language Association, 1987); Michael Harris, "London Newspapers," in Suarez and Turner, *Cambridge History of the Book in Britain*, 5:417–18.

105. Hannah Barker, *Newspapers, Politics and English Society, 1695–1855* (Harlow, UK: Longman, 2000), 29–30.

106. McShane, "Typography Matters," 28.

107. Printing Bill (Nov. 1695), quoted in Ronan Deazley, *On the Origin of the Right to Copy: Charting the Movement of Copyright Law in Eighteenth-Century Britain (1695–1775)* (Oxford, UK: Hart, 2004), 15.

108. Deazley, *On the Origin*, 18.

109. "A Proclamation, for Restraining the Spreading of False News, and Printing and Publishing of Irreligious and Seditious Papers and Libels (26 March 1702)," in *CP* 4:107–8. See also J. A. Downie, "The Development of the Political Press," in *Britain in the First Age of Party, 1680–1750*, ed. Clyve Jones (London: Hambledon, 1987), 117.

110. Order of the Court of Assistants, 4 Aug. 1707, Court Book G, fol. 144v, *SC Myers*, reel 57.

111. John How, *Some Thoughts on the Present State of Printing and Bookselling* (London, 1709), 11.

112. Ibid., 8–16.

113. An Act for the Encouragement of Learning, 1710, 8 Ann. c. 19, § 1, available in *PSC*.

CHAPTER TWO

1. See Hannah Barker and Simon Burrows, eds., *Press, Politics and the Public Sphere in Europe and North America, 1760–1820* (Cambridge: Cambridge University Press, 2002).

2. Mark Goldie, introduction to *CP*, 4:ix–xx; John Feather, "The British Book Market: 1600–1800," in *A Companion to the History of the Book*, ed. Simon Eliot and Jonathan Rose (Chichester, UK: Wiley-Blackwell, 2009), 239–43.

3. Mark Rose, "The Public Sphere and the Emergence of Copyright: Areopagitica, the Stationers' Company, and the Statute of Anne," in *Privilege and Property: Essays on the History of Copyright*, ed. Ronan Deazley, Martin Kretschmer, and Lionel Bently (Cambridge, UK: Open Book Publishers, 2010), 67–88.

4. An Act for the Encouragement of Learning, 1710, 8 Ann. c. 19 [hereafter Statute of Anne], §§ 1–3, 5, 11, available in *PSC*.

5. William St. Clair, *The Reading Nation in the Romantic Period* (Cambridge: Cambridge University Press, 2004); James Raven, *The Business of Books: Booksellers and the English Book Trade, 1450–1850* (New Haven, CT: Yale University Press, 2007); Isabella Alexander, *Copyright Law and the Public Interest in the Nineteenth Century* (Oxford: Hart, 2010), 20–28, 47–49.

6. Mark Rose, *Authors and Owners: The Invention of Copyright* (Cambridge, MA: Harvard University Press, 1993); Ronan Deazley, *On the Origin of the Right to Copy: Charting the Movement of Copyright Law in Eighteenth-Century Britain (1695–1775)* (Oxford, UK: Hart, 2004); and H. Tomás Gómez-Arostegui, "Copyright at Common Law in 1774," *Connecticut Law Review* 47, no. 1 (Nov. 2014): 1–57.

7. Statute of Anne, § 1.

8. The Commons and Lords did make amendments to the original bill that revealed a desire to limit the duration of the monopoly and increase public access to books. Ronan Deazley, "Commentary on the Statute of Anne (1710)," in *PSC*.

9. See, for example, James Sutherland, *The Restoration Newspaper and Its Development* (New York: Cambridge University Press, 1986), 42; and Iona Italia, *The Rise of Literary Journalism in the Eighteenth Century: Anxious Employment* (London: Routledge, 2005), 114.

10. For more on the scope of protection, see Simon Stern, "Creating a Public Domain in Eighteenth-Century England," in *Oxford Handbooks Online*, published online Aug. 2015, http://www.oxfordhandbooks.com/view/10.1093/oxfordhb/9780199935338 .001.0001/oxfordhb-9780199935338-e-39; and Isabella Alexander, "Determining Infringement in the Eighteenth and Nineteenth Centuries in Britain: 'A Ticklish Job,'" in *Research Handbook on the History of Copyright Law*, ed. Isabella Alexander and H. Tomás Gómez-Arostegui (Cheltenham, UK: Edward Elgar, 2016), 174–94.

11. Statute of Anne, §§ 1–2.

12. H. Tomás Gómez-Arostegui, "What History Teaches Us about Copyright Injunctions and the Inadequate-Remedy-at-Law Requirement," *Southern California Law Review* 81 (2008): 1218–50. *Stationers v. White* (1716) and subsequent rulings are summarized in H. Tomás Gómez-Arostegui, "The Untold Story of the First Copyright Suit under the Statute of Anne in 1710," *Berkeley Technology Law Journal* 25 (2010): 1322–23, n. 407.

13. Questions about the registration requirement were bound up with the issue of library deposit. A 1775 statute provided that the financial penalties for infringement specified in the Statute of Anne could not be recovered if the registration and deposit requirements had not been fulfilled, but courts still allowed proprietors of unregistered works to obtain an injunction or to sue for damages at common law. Alexander, *Copyright Law*, 47–56, 93. The 1814 Copyright Act, which sought to resolve the long-standing controversy about library deposit, made explicit that failure to register a work did not forfeit the copyright. An Act to Amend the Several Acts for the Encouragement of Learning, 1814, 54 Geo. III c. 156, § 5.

14. Entries of Copies 1710–1746, *SC Myers*, reel 6. For some examples, see fols. 11, 14, 17, 21–22, 24–25, 36, 56, 64, 78.

15. Brian Cowan, *The State Trial of Doctor Henry Sacheverell* (Chichester, UK: Wiley-Blackwell, 2012), 1.

16. Gómez-Arostegui, "Untold Story," 1260–65; Cowan, *State Trial*, 273; Entries of Copies 1710–1746, fols. 24, 32.

17. Entries of Copies 1710–1746, fol. 40 (Roper's entry); Cowan, *State Trial*, 17–18 (Tonson quotes).

18. Gómez-Arostegui, "Untold Story," 1266–74; Cowan, *State Trial*, 18–21.

19. Adrian Johns, *The Nature of the Book: Print and Knowledge in the Making* (Chicago: University of Chicago Press, 1998), 218.

20. Gómez-Arostegui, "Untold Story," 1292–1311; Statute of Anne, § 3. A Stationers' Company committee met in the spring of 1710 to determine "the most proper method of keeping the Register Book," but there is no record of what they decided. Entry dated 18 Apr. 1710, Court Book G, fol. 178v, *SC Myers*, reel 57.

21. Gómez-Arostegui, "Untold Story," 1311–20.

22. In the case of another trial in the House of Lords in 1716, Tonson's nephew Jacob Tonson Jr. was able to successfully use the Lords' order to suppress a rival edition and punish those responsible for it. Gómez-Arostegui, "Untold Story," 1324.

23. Graham Pollard, "The English Market for Printed Books: The Sandars Lectures, 1959," *Publishing History* 4 (1978): 27–29. See also Isabella Alexander, "All Change for the Digital Economy: Copyright and Business Models in the Early Eighteenth Century," *Berkeley Technology Law Journal* 25 (2010): 1358–61.

24. Entries of Copies 1710–1746. From 1710–1719, the serials entered include, in chronological order, *Tatler*; *Athenian News, or Dunton's Oracle*; *Examiner*; *Post Man*; *Medley*; *Monthly Weather Paper*; *Spectator*; *British Mercury*; *Rhapsody*; *Guardian*; *Englishman*; John Freke's *Prices of Stocks &c*; *Flying Post*; *Weekly Packet*; John Applebee's *Weekly Journal*; *Grumbler*; Robert Mawson's *Weekly Journal*; *Examiner*; *Post Man*; *Robin's Last Shift*; *Shift Shifted*; *Shift's Last Shift*; *Freeholder*; and *Great-Britain's Weekly Pacquet*.

25. Entries of Copies 1710–1746, fol. 12. The first entry covered numbers 1–200. A

later entry asserted similar rights over numbers 201–400 (fol. 76). In both cases, a single fee of sixpence was paid.

26. On this whole affair, see Richmond P. Bond, "The Pirate and the *Tatler*," *The Library*, 5th ser., 18, no. 4 (Dec. 1963): 257–74; and Calhoun Winton, "*The Tatler*: From Half-Sheet to Book," *Prose Studies* 16, no. 1 (Apr. 1993): 23–33.

27. Entries of Copies 1710–1746, fols. 113, 118, 129, 134, 136, 149, 165, 173, 219, 227. The case of *Tonson v. Collins* (1761, retried 1762) centered on the *Spectator*, but neither side mentioned the serial form of the initial publication. By the 1760s, the value of the copyright resided in the exclusive right to reprint the collected essays in book form. Also, by that time the protection specified by the statute had already lapsed, and so the case turned on the question of whether authors had common-law rights that could outlast the terms specified by the statute. Ronan Deazley, "Commentary on *Tonson v. Collins* (1762)," in *PSC*.

28. An Act for Laying Several Duties, 1711, 10 Ann. c. 19, § 101. Note that § 112 revoked all "property" rights in pamphlets of more than two sheets that did not comply with the terms of the statute, but newspapers were not mentioned in this clause.

29. Michael Harris, *London Newspapers in the Age of Walpole: A Study of the Origins of the Modern English Press* (Cranbury, NJ: Associated University Presses, 1987), 19–22.

30. *Weekly Journal* (London), 19 Feb. 1715, quoted in Sutherland, *Restoration Newspaper*, 34.

31. Entries of Copies 1710–1746, fols. 214, 227, 229.

32. *News Letter* (London), 7 Jan. 1716.

33. *Oxford Post*, 6 Jan. 1718, quoted in Harris, *London Newspapers*, 142.

34. Ephraim Chambers, *Cyclopaedia: Or, An Universal Dictionary of Arts and Sciences* (London, 1728), 1:xxix, quoted in Jeff Loveland and Joseph Reagle, "Wikipedia and Encyclopedic Production," *New Media and Society* 15, no. 8 (2013): 1300.

35. Richard Yeo, *Encyclopaedic Visions: Scientific Dictionaries and Enlightenment Culture* (Cambridge: Cambridge University Press, 2001), 208–9, 215–16.

36. Loveland and Reagle, "Wikipedia," 1298.

37. Entries of Copies 1710–1746, fols. 88–91, *SC Myers*, reel 6.

38. In addition to the example of Mawson cited earlier, James Roberts entered two numbers of the *Post Man* in 1716. Entries of Copies 1710–1746, fol. 233.

39. *Evening Post* (London), 26–28 Jan. 1710.

40. John Toland, "Proposal for Regulating ye Newspapers [1717?]," in *CP*, 4: 204.

41. Ibid., 204–5.

42. John Locke, *Two Treatises of Government*, ed. Peter Laslett, student ed. (Cambridge: Cambridge University Press, 1992), 287–89.

43. See Rose, *Authors and Owners*.

44. Toland, "Proposal," 204–6.

45. Harris, *London Newspapers*, 21–22, 29–30.

46. R. M. Wiles, *Freshest Advices: Early Provincial Newspapers in England* (Columbus: Ohio State University Press, 1965), 14–16, 23–24; G. A. Cranfield, *The Development of the Provincial Newspaper 1700–1760* (Oxford, UK: Clarendon Press, 1962), 10–12, 28–29.

47. Victoria E. M. Gardner, *The Business of News in England, 1760–1820* (Basingstoke, UK: Palgrave Macmillan, 2016), 2–4, 24–28, 138–61.

48. Gardner, *Business of News*, 27, 38; Michael Warner, *Letters of the Republic: Publication and the Public Sphere in Eighteenth-Century America* (Cambridge, MA: Harvard University Press, 1990).

49. Harris, *London Newspapers*, chap. 4; and Michael Harris, "London Newspapers," in *The Cambridge History of the Book in Britain*, ed. Michael F. Suarez and Michael Turner, vol. 5, *1695–1830* (Cambridge: Cambridge University Press, 2009), 413–33.

50. R. B. Walker, "Advertising in London Newspapers, 1650–1750," *Business History* 15, no. 2 (July 1973): 122.

51. Entries of Copies 1710–1746. The 1720s entries were *The Church-Man's Last Shift; or, Loyalists Weekly Journal* (fol. 278); *St. James's Post* (fol. 293); and *Heathcote's Intelligence, Being a Collection of the Freshest Advices Foreign and Domestick* (fol. 310).

52. See notes 12 and 13.

53. Although original essays and poems made up little more than 10 percent of each issue in 1735, by Cave's death in 1754 they accounted for more than 90 percent of the magazine. James Tierney, "Periodicals and the Trade, 1695–1780," in Suarez and Turner, *Cambridge History of the Book in Britain*, 5: 488–89.

54. Ad for *Gentleman's Magazine, Grub-Street Journal* [hereafter *GSJ*], 4 May 1732.

55. "To Mr. Edward Cave," *GSJ*, 18 May 1732.

56. John Wilford was the main shareholder of *Fog's Weekly Journal*; John Clarke and the printer Charles Ackers had a stake in the *Weekly Register*. D. F. McKenzie and J. C. Ross, eds., *A Ledger of Charles Ackers: Printer of "The London Magazine"* (Oxford: Oxford Bibliographical Society, 1968), 4–5.

57. *Weekly Register* (London), 3 June 1732, quoted in McKenzie and Ross, *Ledger*, 6.

58. *GSJ*, 25 May 1732.

59. Italia, *Rise of Literary Journalism*, 114–16.

60. *GSJ*, 18 May 1732.

61. The shareholders were John Clarke and John Wilford. See "The Minute Book of the Partners in the *Grub Street Journal*," *Publishing History* 4 (1978): 58–59; and note 56.

62. Contribution signed "Bavius," *GSJ*, 15 Mar. 1733. It seems likely that Bavius was one of Richard Russel's pseudonyms. For the sake of simplicity, I will refer to Russel even though the attribution is not certain. See Bertrand A. Goldgar, introduction to *The Grub-Street Journal, 1730–33*, 4 vols. (London: Pickering and Chatto, 2002), 1:vii–xv.

63. *GSJ*, 5 Apr. 1733.

64. These ideas are further developed in Will Slauter, "A Satirical News Aggregator in Eighteenth-Century London," *Media History* 22, nos. 3–4 (2016): 371–85.

65. *Daily Courant* (London), 12 Mar. 1702.

66. Cranfield mentions the examples of the *North Country Journal* (Newcastle) and the *Reading Journal*. Cranfield, *Development*, 30–31.

67. *GSJ*, 3 Jan. 1734.

68. *GSJ*, 8 Apr. 1736.

69. See Nick Groom, "Unoriginal Genius: Plagiarism and the Construction of 'Romantic' Authorship," in *Copyright and Piracy: An Interdisciplinary Critique*, ed. Lionel Bently, Jennifer Davis, and Jane C. Ginsburg (Cambridge: Cambridge University Press, 2010), 271–99.

70. Quoted in Harris, *London Newspapers*, 162. Spelling silently corrected here.

71. *GSJ*, 3 Mar. 1737.

72. *GSJ*, 10 Mar. 1737.

73. *Memoirs of the Society of Grub-Street*. 2 vols. (London: J. Wilford, 1737), 1:xiii.

74. Ibid.; and Robert Hume, "The Economics of Culture in London, 1660–1740," *Huntington Library Quarterly* 69, no. 4 (Dec. 2006): 514.

75. Michael Harris, "Journalism as a Profession or Trade in the Eighteenth Century," in *Author/Publisher Relations During the Eighteenth and Nineteenth Centuries*, ed. Robin Myers and Michael Harris (Oxford, UK: Oxford Polytechnic Press, 1983); Jeremy Black, *The English Press in the Eighteenth Century* (London: Croom Helm, 1987), 87–104; J. A. Downie, "Periodicals, the Book Trade and the 'Bourgeois Public Sphere,'" *Media History* 14, no. 3 (2008): 261–74.

76. *Memoirs of the Society*, 1:xiii–xvii.

77. Ibid., 1:xiv–xix, quote at xix.

78. Ibid., 1:xviii, xxii.

79. "Booksellers Bill, London (1737)," available in *PSC*. See also Alexander, "All Change," 1367.

80. Court filings in *Austen v. Cave* (1739), quoted in Alexander, *Public Interest*, 166.

81. Gyles v. Wilcox (1741) 2 Atk. 141, 142–43. See Ronan Deazley, "The Statute of Anne and the Great Abridgment Swindle," *Houston Law Review* 47, no. 4 (2010): 793–818; and Alexander, "All Change," 1364–67.

82. *The Monitor; or The British Freeholder* (London), 17 Sept. 1757, and subsequent issues through Aug. 1758. The *Herald* also registered individual issues in 1757–1758. Entries of Copies 1746–1773, fols. 172–85, SC *Myers*, reel 6.

83. Entries of Copies 1746–1773, fols. 147, 198, 199.

84. Printed copy of royal license granted to Richard Baldwin, 23 Oct. 1759, bound with *London Magazine* for Jan. 1782, in AAS Historical Periodicals Collection, digitized by EBSCO in partnership with AAS. Baldwin and his partners had previously been sued by Thomas Jefferys for reproducing an engraving claimed by Jefferys in the *London Magazine*. The court found that Jefferys was not entitled to relief because he had not designed the engraving but only procured it. Jefferys v. Baldwin, [1753] Amb. 164 (Ch.). The outcome of this case may have been a motivation for Baldwin and his partners seeking a royal license to protect works that they commissioned. It is unclear, however, whether it could have been enforced. For more on royal licenses, see Shef Rogers, "The Use of Royal Licences for Printing in England, 1695–1760: A Bibliography," *The Library* 1, no. 2 (June 2000): 133–92.

85. Entries of Copies 1746–1773, fols. 321–23.

86. Entries of Copies 1774–1792, SC *Myers*, reel 7. The only exception found among newspapers was the *News-Examiner, or Considerations on the State of Public Affairs to Be Published Every Tuesday, Thursday, and Saturday*, entered by Jean-Louis De Lolme in 1780 (fol. 178), but this probably focused on political commentary rather than news reporting, and only the prospectus has survived.

87. Harris, "London Newspapers"; Gardner, *Business of News*, 117–61; Slauter, "Rise of the Newspaper," 34–35.

88. These ideas are further developed in Will Slauter, "The Paragraph as Information Technology: How News Traveled in the Eighteenth-Century Atlantic World," *Annales: Histoire, sciences sociales* [English edition] 67, no. 2 (2012): 253–78.

89. Gardner, *Business of News*, 117–61.

90. Quoted in John Brewer, *Party Ideology and Popular Politics at the Accession of George III* (Cambridge: Cambridge University Press, 1976), 224.

91. "From the Lying Intelligencer," *Lloyd's Evening Post and British Chronicle*, 11 Feb. 1763.

92. Entries of Copies 1746–1773, fols. 228, 269; *Gazetteer*, 7 Aug. 1762 (ad for *North Briton* no. 10).

93. Advertisements in *Lloyd's Evening Post*, 23–25 Nov. 1763; *Public Advertiser*, 4 Mar. 1767; and *Gazetteer*, 11 Mar. 1767.

94. Advertisements for accounts of crimes by Elizabeth Brownrigg in *Public Advertiser*, 18 Sept. 1767; and *Saint James's Chronicle*, 12–15 Sept. 1767.

95. Entries of Copies 1746–1773, fol. 360.

96. Ledger containing the accounts of the *Public Advertiser* from Jan. 1765 to Dec. 1771, Add. Ms. 38,169, BL.

97. Peter D. G. Thomas, "The Beginning of Parliamentary Reporting in Newspapers, 1768–1774," *English Historical Review* 74, no. 293 (Oct. 1959): 623–36.

98. Quoted in Thomas, "Beginning," 636.

99. See Dror Wahrman, "Virtual Representation: Parliamentary Reporting and Languages of Class in the 1790s," *Past and Present* 136 (Aug. 1992): 83–113; and Will Slauter, "A Trojan Horse in Parliament: International Publicity in the Age of the American Revolution," in *Into Print: Limits and Legacies of Enlightenment. Essays in Honor of Robert Darnton*, ed. Charles Walton (University Park: Pennsylvania State University Press, 2011), 15–31.

100. John J. McCusker, *European Bills of Entry and Marine Lists: Early Commercial Publications and the Origins of the Business Press* (Cambridge, MA: Harvard University Library, 1985), 28–29, 42–51.

101. John J. McCusker and Cora Gravesteijn, *The Beginnings of Commercial and Financial Journalism: The Commodity Price Currents, Exchange Rate Currents, and Money Currents of Early Modern Europe* (Amsterdam: NEHA, 1991), 315–16.

102. Entries of Copies 1710–1746, fol. 206.

103. McCusker and Gravesteijn, *Beginnings*, 315–16.

104. Ibid., 316–22. See also James Raven, *Publishing Business in Eighteenth-Century England* (Woodbridge, UK: Boydell Press, 2014), 161–72.

105. McCusker and Gravesteijn, *Beginnings*, 311–13.

106. Ibid., 323–26; John J. McCusker, *Essays in the Economic History of the Atlantic World* (London: Routledge, 1997), 162–67.

107. Quoted in Cranfield, *Development*, 97–98.

108. McCusker and Gravesteijn, *Beginnings*, 325. *Lloyd's List* does not seem to have been entered under the Statute of Anne, but other business papers were. Between 1789 and 1796, Jane Elizabeth Prince, who managed the *London Price Current* after the death of her husband, registered each weekly issue. Entries of Copies 1786–1792, fol. 217, *SC Myers*, reel 7, with subsequent issues entered through 22 July 1796; En-

tries of Copies 1795–1797, *SC Myers*, reel 8. In 1797, J. B. Davallon entered "Prix Courant, de John Hiriart, & Cie. À Londres" once. Entries of Copies 1795–1797, fol. 265. In 1802, J. Abraham entered one number of his price current. Entries of Copies 1799–1806, fol. 232, *SC Myers*, reel 9.

109. George Man Burrows, "Strictures on the Uses and Defects of Parish Registers and Bills of Mortality," in *The Development of Population Statistics: A Collective Reprint of Materials Concerning the History of Census Taking and Vital Registration in England and Wales*, ed. D. V. Glas (Westmead, UK: Gregg International, 1973), 40.

110. James Christie, *Some Account of Parish Clerks* (London: privately printed, 1893), 143–45. Christie reports that the bills continued, albeit somewhat irregularly, until 1858.

111. "Introduction to Mortality Statistics in England and Wales: 17th–20th Century," Subject Guide, Wellcome Library, accessed 29 Jan. 2018, https://wellcomelibrary.org/collections/subject-guides/introduction-to-mortality-statistics-in-england-and-wales/.

112. Andrea McKenzie, "From True Confessions to True Reporting? The Decline and Fall of the Ordinary's *Account*," *The London Journal* 30, no. 1 (May 2005): 55–70.

113. Simon Devereaux, "The City and the Sessions Paper: 'Public Justice' in London, 1770–1800," *Journal of British Studies* 35, no. 4 (1996): 466–503.

114. See Leonard W. Levy, *The Emergence of a Free Press* (New York: Oxford University Press, 1985), chaps. 4–5; J. A. Downie, "The Development of the Political Press," in *Britain in the First Age of Party, 1680–1750*, ed. Clyve Jones (London: Hambledon, 1987), 111–27; Richard D. Brown, *The Strength of a People: The Idea of an Informed Citizenry in America, 1650–1870* (Chapel Hill: University of North Carolina Press, 1996), chaps. 1–2.

115. See Trevor Ross, "Copyright and the Invention of Tradition," *Eighteenth-Century Studies* 26, no. 1 (Autumn 1992): 1–27.

116. Major interpretations include Rose, *Authors and Owners*, 92–112; Deazley, *On the Origin*, 191–210; and Gómez-Arostegui, "Copyright at Common Law."

117. *The Cases of the Appellants and Respondents in the Cause of Literary Property, before the House of Lords* (London, 1774), 6.

118. *The Pleadings of the Counsel before the House of Lords, in the Great Cause Concerning Literary Property* (London, 1774), 39.

119. Edward L. Carter, "Choking the Channel of Public Information: Re-Examination of an Eighteenth-Century Warning about Copyright and Free Speech," *N.Y.U. Journal of Intellectual Property and Entertainment Law* 1 (2011): 79–127.

120. On manipulation, see Will Slauter, "Forward-Looking Statements: News and Speculation in the Age of the American Revolution," *Journal of Modern History* 81 (Dec. 2009): 759–92. On the depersonalized voice, see Warner, *Letters of the Republic*.

CHAPTER THREE

1. At that time Bache was just beginning his career, and he sought to produce a newspaper with broad appeal. He would later become an outspoken Republican. See Marcus Daniel, *Scandal & Civility: Journalism and the Birth of American Democracy* (New York: Oxford University Press, 2009), 109–47.

2. *General Advertiser* (Philadelphia), 25 Oct. 1790.

3. For Britain, see Catherine Feely, "Scissors and Paste Journalism," in *Dictionary of Nineteenth-Century Journalism in Great Britain and Ireland*, ed. Laurel Brake and

Marysa Demoor (Gent, BE: Academia Press, 2009), 561; and ongoing work by scholars cited in note 7.

4. See also Meredith L. McGill, *American Literature and the Culture of Reprinting, 1834–1853* (Philadelphia: University of Pennsylvania Press, 2003); Leon Jackson, *The Business of Letters: Authorial Economies in Antebellum America* (Stanford, CA: Stanford University Press, 2008), 89–141; and Laura J. Murray, "Exchange Practices among Nineteenth-Century US Newspaper Editors: Cooperation in Competition," in *Putting Intellectual Property in Its Place: Rights Discourses, Creative Labor, and the Everyday*, ed. Laura J. Murray, S. Tina Piper, and Kirsty Robertson (New York: Oxford University Press, 2014), 86–109.

5. Richard B. Kielbowicz, *News in the Mail: The Press, Post Office, and Public Information, 1700–1860s* (Westport, CT: Greenwood Press, 1989); Richard R. John, *Spreading the News: The American Postal System from Franklin to Morse* (Cambridge, MA: Harvard University Press, 1995); Richard D. Brown, *The Strength of a People: The Idea of an Informed Citizenry in America, 1650–1870* (Chapel Hill: University of North Carolina Press, 1996).

6. An Act for the Encouragement of Learning, ch. 15, 1 Stat. 124 (1790), available in *PSC*. The 1790 act is further discussed in chapter 4.

7. See David A. Smith, Ryan Cordell, and Elizabeth Maddock Dillon, "Infectious Texts: Modeling Text Reuse in Nineteenth-Century Newspapers," *Proceedings of the Workshop on Big Humanities* (IEEE Computer Society Press, 2013), http://www.ccs.neu.edu/home/dasmith/infect-bighum-2013.pdf; Ryan Cordell, "Reprinting, Circulation, and the Network Author in Antebellum Newspapers," *American Literary History* 27, no. 3 (Aug. 2015): 417–45; and M. H. Beals, "Scissors and Paste: The Georgian Reprints, 1800–1837," *Journal of Open Humanities Data* 3 (2017), http://doi.org/10.5334/johd.8. For transatlantic dimensions, see Bob Nicholson, "'You Kick the Bucket; We Do the Rest!': Jokes and the Culture of Reprinting in the Transatlantic Press," *Journal of Victorian Culture* 17, no. 3 (2012): 273–86; and Stephan Pigeon, "Steal It, Change It, Print It: Transatlantic Scissors-and-Paste Journalism in the Ladies' Treasury, 1857–1895," *Journal of Victorian Culture* 22, no. 1 (2017): 24–39.

8. As discussed in chapter 6, it was only in the 1880s that the publishers of American newspapers sought legal solutions to the problem of copying. Much earlier, however, some editors assumed that copyright could be secured if the statutory formalities were fulfilled; see, for example, "Wanting Credit," *Baltimore Gazette and Daily Advertiser*, 13 Nov. 1826.

9. Ann Blair, *Too Much to Know: Managing Scholarly Information before the Modern Age* (New Haven, CT: Yale University Press, 2010), 213–29; Ann Blair and Peter Stallybrass, "Mediating Information, 1450–1800," in *This is Enlightenment*, ed. Clifford Siskin and William Warner (Chicago: University of Chicago Press, 2010), 139–63.

10. See Philip Gaskell, *A New Introduction to Bibliography* (New Castle, DE: Oak Knoll Press, 2006), 40–51.

11. Quoted in Blair, *Too Much to Know*, 228.

12. There is less evidence of using paste, although commentary on the editorial process often referred to "scissors and paste" together. Paste might have been useful if an editor sought to arrange clipped material onto sheets of paper to create a mock-up, but I have found no evidence of this.

13. Thanks to Vincent Golden and Thomas G. Knowles of AAS for help in locat-

ing these exchange copies. In addition to AAS, see the exchange copies that make up much of the Ebeling Collection at Houghton Library (Harvard), and the newspaper volumes owned by Mathew Carey held by the Library Company of Philadelphia. Thanks to James N. Green for assistance with the latter.

14. *Massachusetts Spy* (Worcester), 29 Aug. 1782; Isaiah Thomas's copy of *New Jersey Journal*, 24 July 1782, AAS; *Freeman's Journal: or, The North-American Intelligencer* (Philadelphia), 17 July 1782.

15. Thomas's copy of *New Jersey Journal*, 30 July 1783, AAS.

16. Thomas's copy of *New Jersey Journal*, 11 July 1781, AAS; *Massachusetts Spy*, 26 July 1781. Thanks to Joseph Adelman for this example. See Joseph M. Adelman, "'Meer Mechanics' No More: How Printers Shaped Information in the Revolutionary Age," *Age of Revolutions* (blog), 11 Sept. 2017, https://ageofrevolutions.com/2017/09/11/.

17. Richard B. Kielbowicz, "The Press, Post Office, and Flow of News in the Early Republic," *Journal of the Early Republic* 3 (Fall 1983): 259–60. In the 1840s, postage rates were lowered, enabling letter writing to become a mass phenomenon. David Henkin, *The Postal Age: The Emergence of Modern Communications in Nineteenth-Century America* (Chicago: University of Chicago Press, 2006).

18. John, *Spreading the News*, 36–39; and Richard R. John, "Recasting the Information Infrastructure for the Industrial Age," in *A Nation Transformed by Information*, ed. Alfred Chandler and James Cortada (New York: Oxford University Press, 2000), 60–62.

19. Kielbowicz, "Press," 258–60; John Nerone, "Representing Public Opinion: US Newspapers and the News System in the Long Nineteenth Century," *History Compass* 9, no. 9 (2011): 746.

20. Joseph Adelman, "'A Constitutional Conveyance of Intelligence, Public and Private': The Post Office, the Business of Printing, and the American Revolution," *Enterprise and Society* 11, no. 4 (2010): 1–44.

21. Kielbowicz, *News in the Mail*, 17–18, 142–45; John, *Spreading the News*, 32–33; John Nerone, *The Media and Public Life: A History* (Cambridge, UK: Polity, 2015), 56–57.

22. Nerone, *Media and Public Life*, 57, which gives the estimate of 10 percent.

23. *Sentinel* (Burlington, VT), 14 July 1837, AAS, quoted in Jackson, *Business of Letters*, 126.

24. *Niles' Weekly Register* (Baltimore), 31 Aug. 1816.

25. *Niles' Weekly Register*, 15 Sept. 1832, quoted in Nerone, *Media and Public Life*, 68.

26. See Nerone, "Representing Public Opinion," 748–54; and Nerone, *Media and Public Life*, 66–73.

27. *Morning Courier and New-York Enquirer*, 31 May 1831, AAS.

28. See Jackson, *Business of Letters*, 95–97, 120–26.

29. "Georgia and the Indians," *Georgia Journal*, 13 Nov. 1830. The AAS copy, which was digitized by Readex for "America's Historical Newspapers," is missing the relevant article for reasons explained in the text, but a complete copy of this issue of the *Georgia Journal* can be viewed online at Georgia Historic Newspapers, https://gahistoricnewspapers.galileo.usg.edu.

30. Reprintings include *The Georgian* (Savannah), 18 Nov. 1830; *Daily National Intelligencer* (Washington, DC), 24 Nov. 1830; *United States' Telegraph* (Washington,

NOTES TO CHAPTER 3

DC), 23 Nov. 1830; *Weekly Eastern Argus* (Portland, ME), 30 Nov. 1830; *Pawtucket (RI) Chronicle and Manufacturers' and Artizans' Advocate*, 3 Dec. 1830; *Boston Recorder*, 8 Dec. 1830; *Christian Watchman* (Boston), 10 Dec. 1830.

31. *Daily National Journal* (Washington, DC), 23 Nov. 1830.

32. *Columbian Phenix* (Providence, RI), 11 May 1822; *Daily National Intelligencer*, 29 Jan. 1825, 1 March 1825.

33. The Library of Congress's US Newspaper Directory contains information for 161 newspapers in print in 1792, and 1,863 newspapers in 1838. Note that some of these titles are redundant and that the list is incomplete. Estimates by year available at http://web.stanford.edu/group/ruralwest/cgi-bin/drupal/visualizations/us_newspapers.

34. Kielbowicz, *News in the Mail*, 146–47; Richard R. John, *Network Nation: Inventing American Telecommunications* (Cambridge, MA: Harvard University Press, 2010), 69–81.

35. An Act Making Appropriations for the Service of the Post-Office Department, ch. 231, § 3, 17 Stat. 556, 559 (1873). For reactions, see *Daily State Gazette* (Trenton, NJ), 11 June 1873; *Daily National Republican* (Washington, DC), 11 Dec. 1873; *Auburn (NY) Daily Bulletin*, 16 Dec. 1873; *Providence (RI) Evening Press*, 19 Feb. 1874; and *Albany (NY) Evening Journal*, 15 May 1874.

36. See Nick Groom, "Unoriginal Genius: Plagiarism and the Construction of 'Romantic' Authorship," in *Copyright and Piracy: An Interdisciplinary Critique*, ed. Lionel Bently, Jennifer Davis, and Jane C. Ginsburg (Cambridge: Cambridge University Press, 2010), 271–99; and Margreta De Grazia, "Sanctioning Voice: Quotation Marks, the Abolition of Torture, and the Fifth Amendment," in *The Construction of Authorship: Textual Appropriation in Law and Literature*, ed. Martha Woodmansee and Peter Jaszi (Durham, NC: Duke University Press, 1994), 281–302.

37. *Providence (RI) Journal, and Town and Country Advertiser*, 16 Oct. 1799.

38. *National Gazette* (Philadelphia), 13 Mar. 1793; reprinted in *Argus* (Boston), 26 Mar. 1793.

39. "A Mistake Corrected," *New York Evening Post*, 16 Jan. 1805. Spelling silently corrected here.

40. Ibid.

41. "Scissors Editors," *Aurora General Advertiser* (Philadelphia), 19 Jan. 1805.

42. Jeffrey Pasley, *'The Tyranny of Printers': Newspaper Politics in the Early American Republic* (Charlottesville: University of Virginia Press, 2001), chaps. 6 and 9.

43. "Scissors Editors."

44. Pasley, *Tyranny*, 130, 237–38; Jackson, *Business of Letters*, 144.

45. "Scissors Editors."

46. *State Gazette of South Carolina* (Charleston), 18 Jan. 1787.

47. "Scissors Editors."

48. William St. Clair, "Metaphors of Intellectual Property," in *Privilege and Property: Essays on the History of Copyright*, ed. Ronan Deazley, Martin Kretschmer, and Lionel Bently (Cambridge, UK: Open Book Publishers, 2010), 369–95; and Catherine Seville, "Nineteenth-Century Anglo-US Copyright Relations: The Language of Piracy versus the Moral High Ground," in Bently, Davis, and Ginsburg, *Copyright and Piracy*, 19–43. As Meredith McGill shows, American printers and publishers often defended reprinting on political grounds (McGill, *American Literature*, 76–108). The Chace Act of 1891 allowed for copyright in works by nonresidents of the United States but contained

a number of requirements (not least that the book be manufactured in the United States) that kept many foreign works outside the bounds of US copyright. See Robert Spoo, *Without Copyrights: Piracy, Publishing, and the Public Domain* (New York: Oxford University Press, 2013).

49. Benjamin Russell to Charles Prentiss, 20 Dec. 1806, quoted in Pasley, *Tyranny*, 173.

50. Andie Tucher, "Newspapers and Periodicals," in *A History of the Book in America*, vol. 2, *An Extensive Republic: Print, Culture, and Society in the New Nation, 1790–1840*, ed. Robert Gross and Mary Kelley (Chapel Hill: University of North Carolina Press, 2010), 396.

51. *American Citizen* (New York), 19 Sept. 1807; *Republican Watch-Tower* (New York), 22 Sept. 1807.

52. "An Editor at Home," in Joseph T. Buckingham, *Personal Memoirs and Recollections of Editorial Life*, 2 vols. (Boston: Ticknor, Reed, and Fields, 1852), 1:237. Buckingham claimed that he wrote and published this piece in 1824.

53. *American Beacon* (Norfolk, VA), 9 May 1817.

54. "Miseries of Editors," *New-England Galaxy* (Boston), 21 Aug. 1818, AAS.

55. Ibid.

56. *New England Galaxy*, 20 Nov. 1818, AAS.

57. *Pittsfield (MA) Sun*, 11 Apr. 1833.

58. See the excellent account in Ellen Gruber Garvey, *Writing with Scissors: American Scrapbooks from the Civil War to the Harlem Renaissance* (Oxford: Oxford University Press, 2013), 29–37.

59. "Regrets," *Alexandria (VA) Gazette*, 9 Dec. 1845, credited to the *Chillicothe (OH) Gazette*.

60. "Scissors," *Fremont (OH) Journal*, 29 Dec. 1854, quoted in Cordell, "Reprinting," 435.

61. "Anabaptists," *Christian Watchman* (Boston), 24 Oct. 1850.

62. "How to Make Old Things New," *Commercial Advertiser* (New York), 25 Aug. 1826.

63. Ibid.

64. Cordell, "Reprinting," 424.

65. "Food for Thought," *Boston Daily Bee*, 30 Oct. 1844.

66. Garvey, *Writing with Scissors*, 7–10, 29–37.

67. J. Parton, *The Life of Horace Greeley, Editor of the New York Tribune* (New York: Mason Brothers, 1855), 394–95, 407–8.

68. A. F. Hill, *Secrets of the Sanctum: An Inside View of an Editor's Life* (Philadelphia: Claxton, Remsen and Haffelfinger, 1875), chap. 9.

69. *Baltimore Patriot*, 7 Dec. 1821.

70. *Connecticut Herald* (New Haven), 25 June 1822.

71. *Washington Whig* (Bridgeton, NJ), 16 Sept. 1822.

72. For examples, see *Baltimore Patriot*, 23 Sept. 1828; *Boston Evening Transcript*, 29 Apr. 1842.

73. *Vermont Chronicle* (Bellows Falls, VT), 9 Aug. 1833.

74. *Baltimore Patriot*, 24 Apr. 1822.

75. *New Bedford (MA) Mercury*, 17 Sept. 1824.

76. *Public Ledger* (Philadelphia), 14 Feb. 1838.

77. *National Gazette*, quoted in *North American* (Philadelphia), 17 June 1841.

78. *Journal of Commerce*, quoted in *North American* (Philadelphia), 17 June 1841.

79. Kevin G. Barnhurst and John Nerone, *The Form of News: A History* (New York: Guilford, 2001), 196–202; W. Joseph Campbell, *The Year That Defined American Journalism: 1897 and the Clash of Paradigms* (New York: Routledge, 2006), 124–26; Zvi Reich, "Constrained Authors: Bylines and Authorship in News Reporting," *Journalism* 11, no. 6 (2010): 707–25.

80. *The Journalist*, launched in 1884, was one of the first trade journals devoted to newspaper writing (trade journals for printers and typographers appeared earlier). Early journalism schools include the University of Missouri (1908) and Columbia University (1912).

81. Slips became more widespread in the late 1830s, when the post office briefly experimented with a horse-express service. John, *Network Nation*, 69–81.

82. *Morning Courier and New-York Enquirer, for the Country*, semiweekly edition [hereafter *Morning Courier*], 11 Oct. 1831, AAS.

83. See Victor Rosewater, *History of Cooperative News-Gathering in the United States* (New York: Appleton, 1930); and Richard A. Schwarzlose, *The Nation's Newsbrokers*, 2 vols. (Evanston, IL: Northwestern University Press, 1989–1990), 1:1–32.

84. "Ourselves," *Morning Courier*, 8 Nov. 1831, AAS.

85. *Morning Courier*, 19 Aug. 1831, AAS.

86. [Isaac Clarke Pray], *Memoirs of James Gordon Bennett and His Times* (New York: Stringer and Townsend, 1855), 135; Rosewater, *History*, 19.

87. *Morning Courier*, 31 Oct. 1831, AAS.

88. The content of the bogus report can be viewed in the *Journal of Commerce* (New York), 2 Nov. 1831, evening edition, 2:00 p.m., AAS, where it is labeled as a fabrication.

89. David Henkin, *City Reading: Written Words and Public Spaces in Antebellum New York* (New York: Columbia University Press, 1998), 1–2, 87–88, 169.

90. "Piratical," *Morning Courier*, 4 Nov. 1831, dateline 1 Nov.; *Morning Courier*, 8 Nov. 1831, dateline 5 Nov., AAS.

91. It is now very difficult to determine how many newspapers unwittingly copied the false news. By this time the major New York papers were issuing more than one edition per day, and many of these editions have been lost or are not easily accessible. But the online databases and surviving copies at AAS reveal that some newspapers were initially fooled. See, for example, "Fall of Warsaw," *New-Hampshire Statesman and State Journal*, 5 Nov. 1831, which reprints a paragraph from the *New York Gazette*; and *Morning Courier*, 8 Nov. 1831, which quotes from the *New York Gazette*.

92. *Morning Courier*, 8 Nov. 1831, dateline 5 Nov., AAS.

93. "Small Talk in Small Type," *New York Mercury*, 23 Nov. 1831; "The Courier's Hoax," *Journal of Commerce*, 3 Nov. 1831, evening edition, 2:00 p.m., AAS.

94. *New York Mercury*, 2 Nov. 1831; *Mercantile Advertiser* (New York), quoted in *Providence (RI) Patriot*, 5 Nov. 1831; "Forged News," *New York Spectator*, 8 Nov. 1831.

95. See the example described in the *New York Times*, 10 Mar. 1852.

96. See, for example, *New York Herald*, 14 May 1844; *New Orleans Times Picayune*, 28 June 1844, quoted in Fayette Copeland, *Kendall of the Picayune* (Norman: University of Oklahoma Press, 1943), 111–12; *Hudson River Chronicle* (Sing Sing, NY), 29 June 1841; *Baltimore Sun*, 12 Aug. 1841; *North American* (Philadelphia), 17 June

1841; *New Hampshire Patriot,* 24 Feb. 1842; *Boston Evening Transcript,* 29 Apr. 1842; *Ohio Statesman,* 24 Mar. 1848; *Barre (MA) Gazette,* 30 June 1843; and *Daily Scioto Gazette* (Chillicothe, OH), 3 Jan. 1851.

97. Bennett, quoted in Murray, "Exchange Practices" (full reference in note 4), 99. Note that Bennett singled out Hall and Stone of the *Commercial Advertiser,* who were also the defendants in *Clayton v. Stone,* discussed in chapter 4.

98. Andie Tucher, *Froth and Scum: Truth, Beauty, Goodness, and the Ax Murder in America's First Mass Medium* (Chapel Hill: University of North Carolina Press, 1994), 51–60.

99. "Credit Where Due," *Baltimore Sun,* 24 Apr. 1841.

100. "Autobiography of Matthew Carey. Letter 2," *New England Magazine* 5 (1833): 492. Carey was referring to newspapers here, but he did his fair share of reprinting books. See Adrian Johns, *Piracy: The Intellectual Property Wars from Gutenberg to Gates* (Chicago: University of Chicago Press, 2009), 185–95.

101. For an excellent discussion of this dynamic with respect to literary texts, see Melissa Homestead, *American Women Authors and Literary Property, 1822–1869* (Cambridge: Cambridge University Press, 2005), 154–63.

102. "Scissors," *Fremont (OH) Journal,* 29 Dec. 1854.

CHAPTER FOUR

1. Tanya Aplin and Jennifer Davis, *Intellectual Property Law: Text, Cases, and Materials,* 2nd ed. (Oxford: Oxford University Press, 2013), 63–64.

2. An Act for the Encouragement of Learning, ch. 15, 1 Stat. 124 (1790) [hereafter 1790 Act], available in *PSC.* See Oren Bracha, "The Adventures of the Statute of Anne in the Land of Unlimited Possibilities: The Life of a Legal Transplant," *Berkeley Technology Law Journal* 25, no. 3 (Summer 2010): 1427–73.

3. An Act to Amend and Consolidate the Acts Respecting Copyright, ch. 320, § 4, 35 Stat. 1075, 1076 (1909) [hereafter 1909 Act].

4. Brad Sherman and Lionel Bently, *The Making of Modern Intellectual Property Law: The British Experience, 1760–1911* (Cambridge: Cambridge University Press, 1999); Oren Bracha, *Owning Ideas: The Intellectual Origins of American Intellectual Property, 1790–1909* (Cambridge: Cambridge University Press, 2016).

5. On lithographs, see Erika Piola, "Drawn on the Spot: Philadelphia Sensational News-Event Lithographs," in *Philadelphia on Stone: Commercial Lithography in Philadelphia, 1828–1878,* ed. Erika Piola (University Park: Pennsylvania State University Press, 2012), 177–200; and Elizabeth Hodermarsky, "The Kellogg Brothers' Images of the Mexican War and the Birth of Modern-Day News," in *Picturing Victorian America: Prints by the Kellogg Brothers of Hartford, Connecticut, 1830–1880,* ed. Nancy Finlay (Hartford: Connecticut Historical Society, 2009), 73–83. It is not difficult to find examples of accounts of crimes, trials, and executions that were registered for copyright, although the extent to which other publishers respected these claims is not clear.

6. Clayton v. Stone, 5 F. Cas. 999 (C.C.S.D.N.Y. 1829). The case is usually cited as 1829, but newspaper reports confirm that it was decided in 1828. *Commercial Advertiser* (New York), 11 Dec. 1828.

7. Elijah Paine Jr., *Reports of Cases Argued and Determined in the Circuit Court of the United States for the Second Circuit,* ed. Thomas W. Waterman, vol. 2 (New York: Banks, Gould and Co., 1856), 382; *Clayton,* 5 F. Cas. 999. The 1856 compilation was

issued after Paine's death. The editor explained that Paine had obtained written opinions from the judges themselves and was particularly indebted to those of Smith Thompson, who decided *Clayton*. It seems likely that Thompson furnished a written decision
that was the basis for the published reports. The headnotes were prepared by Waterman.
Paine, *Reports*, iv–vi.

8. Baker v. Selden, 101 U.S. 99, 105 (1879). Note that *Baker* had nothing to do with
newspapers. The Supreme Court cited *Clayton* for the more general point that the purpose of copyright was to promote learning rather than commerce.

9. Tribune Co. of Chicago v. Associated Press, 116 F. 126, 127–28 (C.C.N.D. Ill.
1900). See chapter 6.

10. 1909 Act, §§ 3, 5 (b).

11. International News Service v. Associated Press, 248 U.S. 215 (1918). See chapter 7.

12. Oren Bracha, "Commentary on the U.S. Copyright Act 1790," in *PSC*.

13. Bracha, "Commentary"; Jane C. Ginsburg, "A Tale of Two Copyrights: Literary
Property in Revolutionary France and America," *Tulane Law Review* 64, no. 5 (1990):
1000–1005.

14. 1790 Act, §§ 3–4; An Act Supplementary to an Act Intitled "An Act for the Encouragement of Learning," ch. 36, § 1, 2 Stat. 171 (1802) [hereafter 1802 Act]. Beginning in 1831, newspaper announcements were required only for renewals. An Act to
Amend Several Acts Respecting Copy Rights, ch. 16, §§ 3–4, 4 Stat. 436, 437 (1831)
[hereafter 1831 Act].

15. In Wheaton v. Peters, 33 U.S. (8 Pet.) 591 (1834), the Supreme Court held that
compliance with all formalities was required to obtain copyright. In Britain, the 1814
Copyright Act codified the existing principle that failure to register or deposit the work
did not forfeit the copyright, although it did affect the ability to sue for statutory remedies. An Act to Amend the Several Acts for the Encouragement of Learning, 1814, 54
Geo. III c. 156, § 5. In the United States, the number of copies required and the deposi-
tory changed several times. See G. Thomas Tanselle, "Copyright Records and the Bibli-
ographer," *Studies in Bibliography* 22 (1969): 77–124.

16. Imprints include new editions of the same work, separate impressions of the
same edition, and separate issues of the same impression. Figures from James Gilreath,
"American Literature, Public Policy, and the Copyright Laws before 1800," in *Federal
Copyright Records, 1790–1800*, ed. James Gilreath (Washington, DC: Library of Congress, 1987), xxii. Compare Christopher Sprigman, "Reform(aliz)ing Copyright," *Stanford Law Review* 57 (Nov. 2004): 503. The North American Imprints Project (NAIP) at
AAS continues and expands the work originally undertaken by Charles Evans to catalogue all works known to have been printed in early America.

17. Ginsburg, "Tale of Two Copyrights," 1000–1005; Gilreath, "American Literature," xxii. Molly O'Hagan Hardy is currently preparing a study of the works that were
registered for copyright in the 1790s.

18. 1790 Act, § 2. On what constituted infringement, see R. Anthony Reese, "Inno-
cent Infringement in U.S. Copyright Law: A History," *Columbia Journal of Law and the
Arts* 30, no. 2 (2007): 133–84.

19. John J. McCusker, "The Demise of Distance: The Business Press and the Origins
of the Information Revolution in the Early Modern Atlantic World," *American Historical Review* 110, no. 2 (April 2005): 295–321.

20. Gilreath, *Federal Copyright*, 6.

21. Entry dated 17 Mar. 1812, Copyright Records, District of Pennsylvania, 1811–1817, fol. 487, vol. 264, reel 62. Original record books for before 1870 are in the Rare Books Division of the LOC, and a microfilm copy is available in the USCO. But not all pre-1870 records made it to the LOC. See Zvi Rosen, "Announcing the Release of Over 2,000 Pages of Lost Pre-1870 Copyright Records," *Mostly IP History* (blog), 6 Apr. 2017, http://zvirosen.com/2017/04/06/.

22. *Grotjan's Philadelphia Public Sales Report* [hereafter *Grotjan's*], 25 May 1812–19 Oct. 1812. Grotjan's notice was not in full compliance with the statute. Between 1802 and 1831 (when a shorter form of copyright notice was introduced), one had to insert the full text of the copyright registration at the district court. A full notice would be about a hundred words or more in length. 1802 Act, § 1; 1831 Act, § 5.

23. *Grotjan's*, 21 June 1813.

24. *P. P. F. Degrand's Boston Weekly Report of Public Sales and Arrivals* [hereafter *Degrand's*], 17 July 1819. Degrand immigrated to Boston from Marseilles by 1804. He was a merchant and broker all his life but seems to have been active in publishing only from 1819 to 1826. Printers File, AAS.

25. Entry dated 2 Sept. 1819, Copyright Records, District of Massachusetts, 1814–1825, fol. 295, vol. 46, reel 8, USCO; *Degrand's*, 4 Sept. 1819. Like Grotjan, he registered the title only once, and he does not seem to have deposited a copy of his work as required by the statute. A search of the incoming letter books of the secretary of state's office related to copyright deposit did not turn up anything from Degrand in 1819 or 1820. MS Copyright Letters 1818–1856, Archives of the Library of Congress Copyright Series, Manuscript Division, LOC.

26. *Tariff of Duties, on Importations into the United States, Compiled for P. P. F. Degrand's Boston Weekly Report of Public Sales and of Arrivals* (Boston: Elisha Bellamy, [1820]), 3. The first and second editions of this work contained a copyright date of 2 Sept.1819, corresponding to Degrand's registration of the *Report*; the third edition (1824) and fourth edition (1828) were registered separately.

27. *Degrand's*, 11 Dec. 1824.

28. David P. Forsyth, *The Business Press in America: 1750–1865* (Philadelphia: Chilton Books, 1964), 49–53. Burritt's name first appears on the masthead in the *Shipping and Commercial List, and New York Price Current* [hereafter *Shipping*], 7 Feb. 1824, AAS.

29. *Shipping*, 1 Sept. 1824, 4 Sept. 1824, AAS.

30. Entry dated 16 Nov. 1825, Copyright Records, Southern District of New York, 1824–1828, fol. 167, vol. 136, reel 30, USCO.

31. Entries dated 7 Jan. 1826 and 10 Aug. 1827 in Ibid., fols. 185, 364.

32. *Shipping*, 4 Jan. 1826, AAS.

33. Ibid.

34. These notices appeared for more than two years. They temporarily disappeared with the issue for 27 Feb. 1828 while Burritt and Clayton developed their lawsuit against the *Commercial Advertiser*.

35. Circulation estimates are unreliable. For price currents, see Forsyth, *Business Press*, 49–50. On the penny press, see Michael Schudson, *Discovering the News: A Social History of American Newspapers* (New York: Basic Books, 1979), 12–60.

36. "Price Current," *National Advocate* (New York), 5 Jan. 1826.

37. Entries dated 21 May 1828 and 19 June 1828, Copyright Records, Southern District of New York, 1824–1828, fols. 494, 509, vol. 136, reel 30, USCO.

38. W. Burritt and E. B. Clayton to Henry Clay, 2 Sept. 1828, MS Copyright Letters 1818–1856, Archives of the Library of Congress Copyright Series, Manuscript Division, LOC.

39. At that time, circuit courts were staffed by the local district court judges and one Supreme Court justice assigned to that circuit. In 1819, the circuit courts were empowered to hear copyright cases and issue injunctions. Such cases were heard by a single judge from the circuit. An Act to Extend the Jurisdiction of the Circuit Courts of the United States to Cases Arising under the Law Relating to Patents, ch. 19, 3 Stat. 481 (1819).

40. "United States Circuit Court," *Commercial Advertiser*, 1 Nov. 1828.

41. *Shipping*, 29 Dec. 1824, 1 Jan. 1825, 30 Dec. 1826, 29 Dec. 1827, AAS.

42. "United States Circuit Court," *Commercial Advertiser*, 1 Nov. 1828.

43. Johnson, quoted in Paula McDowell, "Of Grubs and Other Insects: Constructing the Categories of 'Ephemera' and 'Literature' in Eighteenth-Century British Writing," *Book History* 15 (2012): 53. My discussion in this paragraph relies on McDowell's excellent analysis.

44. "United States Circuit Court," *Commercial Advertiser*, 1 Nov. 1828; *Shipping*, 5 Nov. 1828.

45. *American Traveler* (Boston), 11 Nov. 1828.

46. *Southern Patriot* (Charleston, SC), 11 Nov. 1828, credited to the Philadelphia *Aurora*. See also *Georgian* (Savannah), 12 Nov. 1828.

47. *Commercial Advertiser*, 11 Dec.1828.

48. Blunt v. Patten, 3 F. Cas. 763 (C.C.S.D.N.Y. 1828).

49. Robert Brauneis, "The Transformation of Originality in the Progressive-Era Debate over Copyright in News," *Cardozo Arts & Entertainment Law Journal* 27, no. 2 (2009): 344–45.

50. *Clayton*, 5 F. Cas. at 1003.

51. Entry dated 19 June 1828, Copyright Records, Southern District of New York, 1824–1828. fol. 509, vol. 136, reel 30, USCO. Note that in *Wheaton v. Peters* (1834), Thompson entered a dissent in which he recommended that Wheaton be granted a perpetual injunction. By contrast, the majority held that Wheaton was not entitled to relief if he had not complied with all the statutory formalities. 33 U.S. (8 Pet.) 591, 668–98 (1834).

52. *Clayton*, 5 F. Cas. at 1000.

53. *Id.* at 1000.

54. U.S. Const. art. 1, § 8, cl. 8.

55. *Clayton*, 5 F. Cas. at 1003.

56. *Shipping*, 17 Dec. 1828, AAS.

57. "Law of Copy-Right," *Pawtucket (RI) Chronicle and Manufacturers' and Artizans' Advocate*, 20 Dec. 1828, credited to *Journal of Commerce*.

58. *Clayton*, 5 F. Cas. at 1003.

59. Lawrence B. Solum, "Congress's Power to Promote the Progress of Science: Eldred v. Ashcroft," *Loyola of Los Angeles Law Review* 36, no. 1 (2002): 3.

60. "Law of Copyright," *Commercial Advertiser*, 11 Dec. 1828.

61. *Shipping*, 20 Dec. 1828, AAS.

62. Ibid.

63. "Our Own Affairs," *Commercial Advertiser*, 30 Dec. 1828.

64. Ibid.

65. *Shipping*, 27 Dec. 1828, AAS.

66. *Shipping*, 17 Dec. 1828, AAS.

67. *Blunt*, 3 F. Cas. 763.

68. George Ticknor Curtis, *A Treatise on the Law of Copyright* (Boston: Charles C. Little and James Brown, 1847), 108.

69. *Shipping*, 27 Dec. 1828, AAS.

70. *Commercial Advertiser*, 30 Dec. 1828; *Shipping*, 31 Dec. 1828, AAS.

71. *Commercial Advertiser*, 30 Dec. 1828; *New York Evening Post*, 30 Dec. 1828; *National Advocate* (New York), 27 Dec. 1828.

72. *National Advocate* (New York), 27 Dec. 1828, excerpts of which appeared in *Shipping*, 31 Dec. 1828, AAS.

73. James W. Auten, *Personal Reminiscences: What Fifty Years Have Done!* (New York: Angell, 1882), 1–4 (quote at 3–4).

74. "Copy Right," *Southern Patriot* (Charleston, SC), 3 Jan. 1829, credited to *Camden Journal*.

75. *Poulson's American Daily Advertiser* (Philadelphia), 2 Jan. 1824.

76. *Democratic Press* (Philadelphia), 26 Jan. 1829, AAS. I have not been able to consult the *Philadelphia Price Current* of 24 Jan. 1829, and have based this account on Binns's response. See also Forsyth, *Business Press*, 61–62.

77. *Democratic Press* (Philadelphia), 24 Jan., 26 Jan., and 31 Jan. 1829, AAS.

78. Forsyth, *Business Press*, 61–62.

79. "To Our Patrons," *Philadelphia Price Current and Commercial Advertiser*, 24 Oct. 1829, AAS.

80. Forsyth, *Business Press*, 62.

81. See note 8.

82. See Bracha, *Owning Ideas*, chap. 2.

83. Richard R. John, *Network Nation: Inventing American Telecommunications* (Cambridge, MA: Harvard University Press, 2010), 20–22, 69–70.

84. See chapter 6.

85. "Keep Your Newspapers," *Boston Traveler*, 10 Feb. 1826, credited to *Montpelier Watchman*; *Christian Watchman* (Boston), 17 Feb. 1826; and *Washington Review and Examiner*, 17 June 1826; *National Banner and Nashville Whig*, 16 Sept. 1835; *Newburyport (MA) Herald*, 5 Aug. 1842.

86. Noah Millstone, "Designed for Collection: Early Modern News and the Production of History," *Media History* 23, no. 2 (2017): 177–98. In 1778, for example, the *Gentleman's Magazine and Historical Chronicle* (vol. 48, unpaginated preface) promised to be impartial so that "our labours may justly be considered as something more than a brief chronicle of the times—they are authentic materials for future historians."

87. "Keep Your Newspapers."

CHAPTER FIVE

1. On the London-provincial relationship, see Andrew Hobbs, "Provincial Periodicals," in *The Routledge Handbook to Nineteenth-Century British Periodicals and Newspapers*, ed. Andrew King, Alexis Easley, and John Morton (London: Routledge, 2016), 221–33.

2. See Lionel Bently, "Copyright and the Victorian Internet: Telegraphic Property Laws in Colonial Australia," *Loyola of Los Angeles Law Review* 38 (2004): 71–176; Kathy Bowrey and Catherine Bond, "Copyright and the Fourth Estate: Does Copyright Support a Sustainable and Reliable Public Domain of News?" *Intellectual Property Quarterly* 4 (2009): 399–427; and Lionel Bently, "The Electric Telegraph and the Struggle over Copyright in News in Australia, Great Britain and India," in *Copyright and the Challenge of the New*, ed. Brad Sherman and Leanne Wiseman (Alphen aan den Rijn, NL: Wolters Kluwer, 2012), 43–76.

3. Hannah Barker, *Newspapers, Politics and English Society, 1695–1855* (Harlow, UK: Longman, 2000), 38–39, 66–67; and Graham Law, "Distribution," in King, Easley, and Morton, *Routledge Handbook*, 42–45.

4. Kevin Williams, *Read All About It! A History of the British Newspaper* (London: Routledge, 2010), 87; Law, "Distribution," 57.

5. Joel Wiener, *The War of the Unstamped: The Movement to Repeal the British Newspaper Tax, 1830–1836* (Ithaca, NY: Cornell University Press, 1969); and Patricia Hollis, *The Pauper Press: A Study in Working-Class Radicalism of the 1830s* (London: Oxford University Press, 1970).

6. *Report from the Select Committee on Newspaper Stamps; With the Proceedings of the Committee*, PP 1851, no. 558, xii [hereafter *SCNS*]. See also Laurel Brake, "Markets, Genres, Iterations," in King, Easley, and Morton, *Routledge Handbook*, 237–48.

7. See, for example, HC Deb, 14 June 1832, vol. 13, cols. 619–42.

8. HC Deb, 21 Aug. 1835, vol. 30, col. 848.

9. Ibid., cols. 852, 854, 857–58.

10. *Morning Chronicle*, 22 Aug. 1835.

11. *Dictionary of Nineteenth-Century Journalism in Great Britain and Ireland*, ed. Laurel Brake and Marysa Demoor (Gent, BE: Academia Press, 2009), s.v. "Hetherington, Henry (1792–1849)."

12. *Poor Man's Guardian*, 29 Aug. 1835.

13. See Joseph M. Adelman and Victoria E. M. Gardner, "Making News in the Age of Revolution," in *MN*, 63–64.

14. "Effects of Free Postage of Newspapers," *Manchester Times and Gazette*, 21 May 1836.

15. "Repeal of the Newspaper Stamp Duty," *Times* (London), 5 Mar. 1836.

16. HC Deb, 25 Apr. 1836, vol. 33, col. 203.

17. HC Deb, 3 May 1836, vol. 33, col. 517.

18. *Twopenny Dispatch*, n.d., ca. May 1836?, quoted in Hollis, *Pauper Press*, 150.

19. *True Sun*, 13 July 1836, quoted in Hollis, *Pauper Press*, 150.

20. "Newspaper Duties," *Caledonian Mercury* (Edinburgh), 23 May 1836 (attributed to *Morning Herald*).

21. HC Deb, 18 July 1836, vol. 35, col. 297–98.

22. Ibid.; *Hull Packet*, 15 July 1836; see also HC Deb, 11 July 1836, vol. 35, cols. 122–23.

23. Wiener, *War of the Unstamped*, 266–77; and Williams, *Read All About It*, 5, 92–96, 106–9.

24. M. H. Beals is currently using computational methods to study the extent of duplicated texts across digital corpora of British newspapers.

25. Bill and answer, Bell v. Whitehead [W1839 B1], C13/400/13, TNA.

26. Bell v. Whitehead (1839) 8 LJ Ch. 141, 142.

27. An Act to Amend the Law of Copyright, 1842, 5 & 6 Vict. c. 45, § 18 [hereafter 1842 Act]. See Elena Cooper, "Copyright in Periodicals in the Nineteenth Century: Genre and Balancing the Rights of Contributors and Publishers," *Victorian Periodicals Review* 51, no. 4 (forthcoming).

28. Martin Hewitt, *The Dawn of the Cheap Press in Victorian Britain: The End of the 'Taxes on Knowledge,' 1849–1869* (London: Bloomsbury, 2014), 16–19.

29. Charles Dickens to Thomas Milner Gibson, 12 Feb. 1850, quoted in Hewitt, *Dawn*, 28.

30. Collet Dobson Collet, *History of the Taxes on Knowledge: Their Origin and Repeal* (London: T. Fisher Unwin, 1899), 1:96.

31. Ibid., 1:96–97.

32. *SCNS*, 1449.

33. Ibid., 1441–49.

34. Ibid., 2644.

35. Ibid., 2644–51.

36. *Oxford Dictionary of National Biography*, s.v. "Hunt, Frederick Knight (1814–1854)," by Richard Garnett, revised by C. A. Creffield, 2004, https://doi.org/10.1093/ref:odnb/14191.

37. *SCNS*, 2319.

38. Ibid., 2320–22.

39. Ibid., 2358–60, quote at 2360.

40. Ibid., 2321.

41. Ibid., 2321–47, quote at 2336.

42. Ibid., xi.

43. On changes in readership and political attitudes, see Alan J. Lee, *The Origins of the Popular Press in England: 1855–1914* (London: Croom Helm, 1976); and Mark Hampton, *Visions of the Press in Britain, 1850–1950* (Urbana: University of Illinois Press, 2004).

44. *SCNS*, xi.

45. See Hewitt, *Dawn*, 61–66.

46. *Times*, 20 Mar. 1855; *Daily News*, 26 Mar. 1855. See also *Daily News*, 14 Apr. 1855. On distribution, see W. H. Smith's testimony in *SCNS* (starting at 2810); and Charles Wilson, *First with the News: The History of W. H. Smith, 1792–1972* (London: Jonathan Cape, 1985).

47. See Paul Arblaster et al., "The Lexicons of Early Modern News," in *News Networks in Early Modern Europe*, ed. Joad Raymond and Noah Moxham (Leiden: Brill, 2016), 94.

48. Bently, "Electric Telegraph," 62–66; Roger Neil Barton, "New Media: The Birth of Telegraphic News in Britain, 1847–68," *Media History* 16, no. 4 (2010): 379–406; and Steven Roberts, *Distant Writing: A History of the Telegraph Companies in Britain between 1838 and 1868*, published online 2006–2012, http://distantwriting.co.uk/index.htm (pages 210–11 of 2012 PDF version).

49. Thomas Smits, "Making the News National: Using Digitized Newspapers to Study the Distribution of the Queen's Speech by W. H. Smith & Son, 1846–1858," *Victorian Periodicals Review* 49, no. 4 (Winter 2016): 598–625.

50. Roberts, *Distant Writing*, 210–11.

51. Barton, "New Media," 385–87.

52. *Times*, 30 Apr. 1855.

53. HC Deb, 30 Apr. 1855, vol. 137, col. 2003–4; Barton, "New Media."

54. *Reynolds's Weekly Newspaper* (London), 25 Mar. 1855.

55. "Proposition of the Chancellor of the Exchequer for Newspaper Copyright," *Daily News*, 19 Apr. 1855.

56. As Lewis remarked, the "model for this cheap remedy already exists in the Act with respect to the copyright of designs." HC Deb, 30 Apr. 1855, vol. 137, col. 1984.

57. *Leeds Mercury*, 21 Apr. 1855.

58. *Oxford Dictionary of National Biography*, s.v. "Baines, Sir Edward (1800–1890)," by J. R. Lowerson, 2004, http://dx.doi.org/10.1093/ref:odnb/1090; "House of Commons," *Manchester Examiner and Times*, 25 Apr. 1855.

59. "Copyright in News," *Manchester Examiner and Times*, 28 Apr. 1855.

60. See chapter 2.

61. "Copyright in News."

62. *Times*, 30 Apr. 1855.

63. HC Deb, 30 Apr. 1855, vol. 137, cols. 1984–85. This paragraph draws on the research in Bently, "Electric Telegraph," 66–69.

64. HC Deb, 30 Apr. 1855, vol. 137, col. 1994.

65. Ibid., col. 2011.

66. Ibid., col. 1991.

67. Ibid., cols. 1999–2000.

68. *The Era* (London), 6 May 1855.

69. "The Press Question," *The Examiner* (London), 5 May 1855.

70. See, for example, *Preston Chronicle*, 1 Dec. 1855.

71. *Birmingham Daily Post*, 3 Jan. 1860.

72. *Morning Post* (London), 28 Apr. 1859.

73. Contract quoted in *The History of the Times* (London: Office of the Times, 1935–1939): 2:90–91.

74. Ibid. See also Barton, "New Media," 390.

75. Barton, "New Media," 391–94; Roberts, *Distant Writing*, 213.

76. Williams, *Read All About It*, 116.

77. Jonathan Silberstein-Loeb, "The Structure of the News Market in Britain, 1870–1914," *Business History Review* 83, no. 4 (Winter 2009): 763–64.

78. Andrew Hobbs, "When the Provincial Press Was the National Press (c. 1836–1900)," *International Journal of Regional and Local Studies* 5, no. 1 (2009): 21–29.

79. Silberstein-Loeb, "Structure," 766–72; and George Scott, *Reporter Anonymous: The Story of the Press Association* (London: Hutchinson, 1968), 19–30.

80. Silberstein-Loeb, "Structure," 766–72.

81. Ibid., 769–78; Scott, *Reporter Anonymous*, 114–19.

82. Williams, *Read All About It*, 5, 101–2, 109, 119.

83. Andrew Hobbs, "The Deleterious Dominance of *The Times* in Nineteenth-Century Scholarship," *Journal of Victorian Culture* 18, no. 4 (2013): 472–97.

84. Scott, *Reporter Anonymous*, 119.

85. Copyright Registry Books, Entries and Assignments, series COPY 3, TNA. The 1846 entry for the *Daily News* is in COPY 3/3, fol. 163. The 1870 entry for Reuters is in

COPY 3/18, fol. 163. Further entries for newspapers and price lists for 1861–1880 are in COPY 3/10 through COPY 3/26, TNA. The post-1842 registers have not yet been made available digitally, making a detailed study of registration patterns difficult. When the title is known, entries can be located using the *Index to Entries (Literary) in the Book of Registry of the Stationers' Company*, 4 vols. (London: Harrison and Sons, 1896–1907).

86. In Britain, copyright began with publication, and registration was not required until one wanted to sue for infringement. As early as 1814, the statute said that failure to register did not affect the copyright. An Act to Amend Several Acts for the Encouragement of Learning, 1814, 54 Geo. III c. 156, § 5, available in *PSC*; 1842 Act, § 24.

87. See Bently, "Victorian Internet," 90–91.

88. Cox v. Land and Water Journal Company [1869] LR 9 Eq 324, 324–26. See also Platt v. Walter [1867] 17 L.T.R. 157, in which the court suggested that newspapers may be eligible for copyright under the 1842 Act.

89. Kelly v. Morris [1866] LR 1 Eq 697.

90. *Cox*, LR 9 Eq at 327.

91. *Id*. at 332–33; Alexander, *Public Interest*, 206.

92. *Copyright Commission. The Royal Commissions and the Report of the Commissioners*, PP 1878, no. 2036, viii, xvii.

93. Catherine Seville, *The Internationalisation of Copyright Law: Books, Buccaneers and the Black Flag in the Nineteenth Century* (Cambridge: Cambridge University Press, 2006), 276.

94. Walter v. Howe [1881] 17 Ch.D. 708.

95. *The Times* later began to do this. See Jose Bellido and Kathy Bowrey, "From the Author to the Proprietor: Newspaper Copyright and *The Times* (1842–1956)," *Journal of Media Law* 6, no. 2 (2014): 206–33.

96. International Copyright Act, 1852, 15 & 16 Vict. c. 12, § 7.

97. Sara Bannerman, *International Copyright and Access to Knowledge* (Cambridge: Cambridge University Press, 2016), 85.

98. Convention de Berne, 1886, art. 7, http://www.wipo.int/wipolex/en/treaties/text .jsp?file_id=278701. English text available in *International Copyright Union: Berne Convention, 1886. Paris Convention, 1896. Berlin Convention, 1908* (Washington: GPO, 1908), 35.

99. Jonas Bjork, "The First International Journalism Organization Debates News Copyright, 1894–1898," *Journalism History* 22 (Summer 1996): 56–63.

100. Acte additionnel de Paris, 1896, art. 7, http://www.wipo.int/wipolex/en /treaties/text.jsp?file_id=278700; English version in *International Copyright Union*, 35.

101. Acte de Berlin, 1908, art. 9, http://www.wipo.int/wipolex/en/treaties/text.jsp ?file_id=278699; English version in *International Copyright Union*, 20.

102. For more on the international dimensions, see Heidi J. S. Tworek, "Protecting News before the Internet," in *MN*, 196–222.

103. Berne Convention, amended 28 Sept. 1979, art. 2 (8), http://www.wipo.int /treaties/en/text.jsp?file_id=283698.

104. Sam Ricketson and Jane Ginsburg, "Intellectual Property in News? Why Not?" in *Research Handbook on Intellectual Property in Media and Entertainment*, ed. Megan Richardson and Sam Ricketson (Cheltenham, UK: Edward Elgar, 2017), 10–46.

105. *Birmingham Daily Post*, 24 Oct. 1887.

106. "Copyright, Not Censorship," *Pall Mall Gazette*, 11 Oct. 1888.

107. Walter v. Steinkopff [1892] 3 Ch. 489; Entry dated 13 Apr. 1892, Copyright Entries and Assignments, COPY 3/37, fols. 233, 304, TNA.

108. Affidavit of Arthur Fraser Walter, Walter v. Steinkopff [1892 W. 1281], 29 Apr. 1892, J4/4477/1890, TNA.

109. *Walter*, 3 Ch. at 492.

110. *Id.* at 493.

111. Affidavit of Sidney James Low, 3 May 1892, J4/4477/1937, TNA.

112. Affidavits of James Watson and David Brenner, 4 May 1892, J4/4477, fols. 1959–62, TNA.

113. Affidavits of James Watson, William Thomas Madge, Thomas Power O'Connor, David Brenner, James Stuart, Frederick William Wilson, and Walter Herries Pollock, 4–5 May 1892, J4/4477, fols. 1960–79, TNA. See also *Birmingham Daily Post*, 14 May 1892; and *Leeds Mercury*, 14 May 1892.

114. Affidavit of Arthur Fraser Walter, 6 May 1892, J4/4478/2012, TNA.

115. *Walter*, 3 Ch. at 497–99. In 1814, a defendant argued that it was "the usual Practice among Publishers of Magazines and monthly Publications" to take articles from each other but the court ruled that "the Custom among Booksellers could not control the Law." Wyatt v. Barnard (1814) 35 Eng. Rep. 408. In 1874, the proprietor of the *Bristol Mercury* was sued by the publisher of the *Belgravia Magazine* for republishing stories without permission. The defendant claimed that the magazine was sent to him with the expectation that articles would be republished in his newspaper and that he had been doing this for years without complaint. But the plaintiff had sent the copies in hopes that his magazine would be reviewed, not copied, and the judge granted an injunction. Maxwell v. Somerton [1874] 22 W.R. 313.

116. *Leeds Mercury*, 18 May 1892.

117. *Walter*, 3 Ch. at 495.

118. Final order dated 2 June 1892, J15/2037/1072, TNA.

119. *Walter*, 3 Ch. at 500–501. The defendants also complained about this. Note that Walter's first affidavit referred only to the Kipling story. Another affidavit two weeks later added the complaint about the news paragraphs. Affidavits of Arthur Fraser Walter, 13 Apr. 1892 and 25 Apr. 1892, J4/4476, fols. 1705, 1791, TNA.

120. *Times*, 3 June 1892.

121. Ibid.

122. *Daily News*, 3 June 1892.

123. *Belfast News Letter*, 3 June 1892.

124. "The Copyright Tangle, and How to Untie It," *Pall Mall Gazette*, 3 June 1892.

125. Jonathan Silberstein-Loeb, "The Political Economy of Media," in *The Routledge Companion to British Media History*, ed. Martin Conboy and John Steel (London: Routledge, 2015), 80–81.

126. Tworek, "Protecting News," 203–4; 1890 entry for Reuters in COPY 3/35, fol. 242, TNA; 1894 entries for Exchange Telegraph in COPY 3/40, fols. 158, 190, TNA.

127. Exchange Tel. Co., Ltd. v. Gregory & Co. [1896] 1 Q.B. 147, 157.

128. See Tanya Aplin et al., *Gurry on Breach of Confidence: The Protection of Confidential Information*, 2nd ed. (Oxford: Oxford University Press, 2012), 53–65 (section written by Lionel Bently); and Megan Richardson, Michael Bryan, Martin Vranken,

and Katy Barnett, *Breach of Confidence: Social Origins and Modern Developments* (Cheltenham, UK: Edward Elgar, 2012), 66–67.

129. Copyright Bill [H.L.] 1898, quoted in Alexander, *Public Interest*, 250.

130. *Copyright Commission*, viii (see note 92).

131. See note 100.

132. *Report from the Select Committee of the House of Lords on the Copyright Bill [H.L.] and the Copyright (Amendment) Bill [H.L.]*, PP 1898, no. 393, 17.

133. Ibid., 18, 39, 54, 63.

134. Ibid., 53–64.

135. Ibid., 39, 53, 63.

136. Ibid., 54.

137. Ibid., 53–64.

138. Alexander, *Public Interest*, 238–39.

139. Herbert de Reuter to C. F. Moberly Bell, 7 July 1899, in *Report from the Select Committee of the House of Lords on the Copyright Bill [H.L.] and the Copyright (Artistic) Bill [H.L.]*, PP 1899, no. 362, 235.

140. Ibid., 110–14, quote at 110.

141. Ibid., 181–82.

142. "The Journalists' Conference," *Aberdeen Weekly Journal*, 31 Aug. 1899.

143. *Report . . . on the Copyright (Artistic) Bill [H.L.]*, 247.

144. Copyright Bill [H.L.], PP 1900, no. 295, § 12. It was not clear whether protection for the form of news also expired after eighteen hours, an ambiguity that Daldy pointed out before the 1899 committee. *Report . . . on the Copyright (Artistic) Bill [H.L.]*, questions 313–15, p. 22.

145. Alexander, *Public Interest*, 238–39.

146. Megan Richardson and Julian Thomas, *Fashioning Intellectual Property: Exhibition, Advertising and the Press, 1789–1918* (Cambridge: Cambridge University Press, 2012), 117–21; and Bellido and Bowrey, "From the Author," 212–15.

147. Barbara Lauriat, "Walter v. Lane (1900)," in *Landmark Cases in Intellectual Property Law*, ed. Jose Bellido (Oxford, UK: Hart, 2017), 149–80 (Rosebery quote at 152).

148. Publication of Lectures Act, 1835, 5 & 6 Will. IV c. 65, available in *PSC*; and Lauriat, "Walter v. Lane," 157–61.

149. Walter v. Lane [1899] 2 Ch. 749.

150. Walter v. Lane [1900] AC 539 at 546, 548.

151. Id. at 545–62; Alexander, *Public Interest*, 209–11; and Lauriat, "Walter v. Lane," 168–69.

152. Lauriat, "Walter v. Lane"; and Richardson and Thomas, *Fashioning*, 119–22.

153. Statement of Claim, 27 Mar. 1903, Springfield v. Thame [1902 S. 3280], J54/1202, TNA. The published report is Springfield v. Thame [1903] 89 LT 242.

154. Statement of Defense, 29 Apr. 1903, Springfield v. Thame, J54/1202, TNA.

155. Springfield v. Thame [1903] 89 LT 242.

156. Lauriat, "Walter v. Lane," 179–80; and "Death of Mr. Moberly Bell," *Times*, 6 Apr. 1911.

157. Copyright Act, 1911, 1 & 2 Geo. V, c. 46 [hereafter 1911 Act], § 5 (1)(b).

158. Bellido and Bowrey, "From the Author," 222–24.

159. 1911 Act, § 2 (1)(i), § 2 (1)(v), § 20.

160. Bently, "Electric Telegraph"; Michael D. Birnhack, *Colonial Copyright: Intellectual Property in Mandate Palestine* (Oxford: Oxford University Press, 2012), 212–38; and Bannerman, *International Copyright,* 92–94.

CHAPTER SIX

1. See also Leon Jackson, *The Business of Letters: Authorial Economies in Antebellum America* (Stanford, CA: Stanford University Press, 2008), 120–26, 140–41.

2. Jonathan Silberstein-Loeb, "Exclusivity and Cooperation in the Supply of News: The Example of the Associated Press, 1893–1945," *Journal of Policy History* 24, no. 3 (2012): 466–98; and Jonathan Silberstein-Loeb, *The International Distribution of News: The Associated Press, Press Association, and Reuters, 1848–1947* (New York: Cambridge University Press, 2014), 13–16. I am indebted to Silberstein-Loeb's pioneering work in this area.

3. Paul Starr, *The Creation of the Media: Political Origins of Modern Communications* (New York: Basic Books, 2004), 153–89; Richard R. John, *Network Nation: Inventing American Telecommunications* (Cambridge, MA: Harvard University Press, 2010); and Richard B. Kielbowicz, "Regulating Timeliness: Technologies, Laws, and the News, 1840–1970," *Journalism & Communication Monographs* 17, no. 1 (2015): 6–9, 12–13.

4. Victor Rosewater, *History of Cooperative News-Gathering in the United States* (New York: Appleton, 1930); and Richard A. Schwarzlose, *The Nation's Newsbrokers* (Evanston, IL: Northwestern University Press, 1989–1990), 1:1–78.

5. Richard R. John, "Private Enterprise, Public Good? Communications Deregulation as a National Political Issue, 1839–1851," in *Beyond the Founders: New Approaches to the Political History of the Early American Republic,* ed. Jeffrey Pasley, Andrew Robertson, and David Waldstreicher (Chapel Hill: University of North Carolina Press, 2004); and David Hochfelder, *The Telegraph in America, 1832–1920* (Baltimore: Johns Hopkins University Press, 2012), 32–72.

6. John, *Network Nation,* 77–82.

7. Menahem Blondheim, *News over the Wires: The Telegraph and the Flow of Public Information in America, 1844–1897* (Cambridge, MA: Harvard University Press, 1994), 44–45; Schwarzlose, *Nation's Newsbrokers,* 1:58–64; and Kielbowicz, "Regulating Timeliness," 21.

8. The present-day Associated Press traces its own origins to the ventures that began in 1846. "Our Story," About, Associated Press, accessed 29 Jan. 2018, https://www.ap.org/about/our-story/. As detailed later, the institutional history is rather complex.

9. Agreement, "Harbor News Association," 11 Jan. 1849, Henry J. Raymond Papers, NYPL. The six papers were the *Journal of Commerce,* the *Sun,* the *Herald,* the *Courier and Enquirer,* the *Express,* and the *Tribune.*

10. *New York Times,* 10 Mar. 1852.

11. Silberstein-Loeb, *International Distribution,* 14–15.

12. Ibid., 46–57. In the late 1850s, a few newspapers began attaching labels such as "By Telegraph to the Associated Press" or simply "To the Associated Press." The AP formed in Chicago in 1892 was a descendant of the Western Associated Press rather than the New York Associated Press.

13. Schwarzlose, *Nation's Newsbrokers,* 2:34–39; Blondheim, *News over the Wires,* 96–142; and Kielbowicz, "Regulating Timeliness," 29–32.

14. Robert J. Chandler, "The California News-Telegraph Monopoly, 1860–1870," *Southern California Quarterly* 58, no. 4 (Winter 1976): 459–84.

15. Schwarzlose, *Nation's Newsbrokers*, 2:58–59; and Daniel J. Czitrom, *Media and the American Mind: From Morse to McLuhan* (Chapel Hill: University of North Carolina Press, 1982), 23 (figures). Western Union reserved the right to collect and sell stock quotations and other market reports, which caused some trouble for the NYAP. Kielbowicz, "Regulating Timeliness," 22–23.

16. Quoted in John, *Network Nation*, 146–47.

17. John, *Network Nation*, 65–199.

18. Sen. Cmte. on Railroads, S. Rep. No. 805–45, at 51 (1879).

19. *Id.* at 50–51.

20. It was not until 1910 that Congress treated telegraph companies as common carriers, placing them under the jurisdiction of the Interstate Commerce Commission. Kielbowicz, "Regulating Timeliness," 15, 35.

21. S. Rep. 805-45, at 51 (1879).

22. *Id.* at 63–69.

23. Silberstein-Loeb, "Exclusivity," 468; and Kielbowicz, "Regulating Timeliness," 14, 18–19.

24. Schwarzlose, *Nation's Newsbrokers*, 2:132–35. Note that the United Press created in 1882 has no relationship to the agency by the same name started in 1907.

25. John, *Network Nation*, 172–75, 192–93.

26. A pioneering account of the 1884 campaign that pointed me to crucial sources is Barbara Cloud, "News: Public Service or Profitable Property?," *American Journalism* 13, no. 2 (Spring 1996): 141–56.

27. In the months preceding Watterson's visit to Washington, two other bills related to newspaper copyright were introduced, although both were criticized as ill-conceived in the press and both died in committee. The first bill represented an effort to protect the rights of contributors as distinct from those of publishers. 47th Cong., 2d Sess., H.R. 7341 (1883); reintroduced 48th Cong., 1st Sess., H.R. 62 (1883). The other bill sought to protect copyright in the titles of newspapers. 48th Cong., 1st Sess., H.R. 4160 (1884); and *Cong. Rec.*, 29 Jan. 1884: 734.

28. 48th Cong., 1st Sess., S. 1728 & H.R. 5850 (1884).

29. "Watterson Argues for the Copyright Bill," *Oregonian* (Portland), 15 Mar. 1884.

30. "Proposing to Copyright News," *New York Times*, 18 Feb. 1884.

31. *Louisville Courier-Journal*, 6 Mar. 1884, quoted in Cloud, "News," 148.

32. "Proposing to Copyright News."

33. See the exchanges reproduced in *Oregonian* (Portland), 16 Feb. 1884, 18 Feb. 1884, 25 Feb. 1884, and 10 Mar. 1884.

34. Memorial to Charles E. Boyle, 10 Mar. 1884, file HR48A-H21.3, RG 233, NARA; and Memorial to C. H. Morgan, 18 Feb. 1884, file HR48A-H12.5, RG 233, NARA.

35. William Toman to D. B. Henderson, 20 Feb. 1884, file HR48A-H21.3, RG 233, NARA.

36. The Iowa proprietor's statement seems to anticipate Justice Louis Brandeis's language in the INS case. See chapter 7.

37. Edgar L. Vincent to E. G. Lapham, 4 Apr. 1884, file S48A-H14, RG 46, NARA.

38. *Milwaukee Sentinel*, 22 Feb. 1884, quoted in Robert Brauneis, "The Transformation of Originality in the Progressive-Era Debate over Copyright in News," *Cardozo Arts & Entertainment Law Journal* 27, no. 2 (2009): 357.

39. "Curious Claim for Copyright," *The Printers' Circular and Stationers' and Publishers' Gazette* (Philadelphia) 18, no. 12 (Feb. 1884): 243.

40. Sen. Cmte. on Post-Offices and Post Roads, Postal Telegraph, S. Rep. No. 577-48, at 287–316 (1884).

41. "The News Copyright Bill. To the Members of the Senate and the House of Representatives" (1884). More than eighty copies of this petition have been found among the following file units at NARA: HR48A-H12.5, HR48A-H21.3, S48A-H14, and S48A-J6. A scan of one of the copies has been posted by Robert Brauneis on his faculty web page, http://docs.law.gwu.edu/facweb/rbrauneis/originality/petitions/The_News_Copyright_Bill.pdf.

42. Feist Publications, Inc. v. Rural Telephone Service Co., 499 U.S. 340 (1991); and Miriam Bitton, "Feist, Facts and Functions: Historical Perspective," in *Intellectual Property Protection for Fact-Based Works: Copyright and Its Alternatives*, ed. Robert F. Brauneis (Cheltenham, UK: Edward Elgar, 2009), 3–38.

43. See chapter 4.

44. Brauneis, "Transformation of Originality." An important contemporary case that dealt with the question of what constituted authorship was Burrow-Giles Lithographic Co. v. Sarony, 111 U.S. 53 (1884).

45. See also *Sacramento Daily Union*, 27 Feb. 1884, which argued that "the collection of news cannot, by any contortion of the copyright principle, be construed into an intellectual origination, and that alone do copyright laws protect."

46. "Stealing News," *The Nation*, 21 Feb. 1884: 159.

47. See chapter 2.

48. "Stealing News."

49. "The Copyright Law," *Oregonian* (Portland), 18 Mar. 1884 (credited to *New York World*).

50. *Oregonian* (Portland), 20 Mar. 1884 (endorsing views of the *Providence Journal*); and *Current* (Chicago) 1, no. 12 (8 Mar. 1884): 177.

51. "The Press Copyright," *Oregonian* (Portland), 26 Mar. 1884 (crediting *Inter Ocean* [Chicago]).

52. For earlier experiments with ready-print, see Elmo Scott Watson, *A History of Newspaper Syndicates in the United States 1865–1935* (Chicago, 1936), 1–6. Watson attributes the origins of the term *boilerplate* to a period when the American Press Association had its Chicago office in the same building as an iron foundry, and printers for the syndicate joked about working in "that boiler plate factory." Ibid., 36.

53. Barbara Cloud, *The Business of Newspapers on the Western Frontier* (Reno: University of Nevada Press, 1992), 140–45 (figures at 141). See also Eugene Harter, *Boilerplating America: The Hidden Newspaper*, ed. Dorothy Harter (Lanham, MD: University Press of America, 1991), 20–23; Charles Johanningsmeier, *Fiction and the American Literary Marketplace: The Role of Newspaper Syndicates, 1860–1900* (Cambridge: Cambridge University Press, 1997), 34–43; and Gerald J. Baldasty, *The Commercialization of News in the Nineteenth Century* (Madison: University of Wisconsin Press, 1992), 91–92.

54. Cloud, *Business of Newspapers*, 143–44.

55. "Press Copyright."

56. In the late 1890s, the Chicago-based AP reported that it was serving "two or three" publishers of patent 'sides but that the contracts required these clients to wait eight hours after news appeared in AP papers before using it. *The Associated Press. Seventh Annual Report* (Chicago, 1900), 60.

57. "Copyright in News," *Harper's Weekly*, 8 Mar. 1884: 151.

58. Thorvald Solberg, *Copyright in Congress, 1789–1904* (Washington: GPO, 1905), 228.

59. Henry Watterson, *"Marse Henry": An Autobiography* (New York: Beekman, 1974), 2:104–5.

60. *Boston Evening Journal*, 5 Dec. 1885.

61. *Inter Ocean* (Chicago), 28 Sept. 1890.

62. "Newspaper Copyright," *Philadelphia Inquirer*, 29 Apr. 1894.

63. "Washington Gossip," *Wheeling (WV) Sunday Register*, 18 July 1886.

64. Ibid.

65. Copyright Record Books, Southern District of New York, Rare Books Division, LOC, microfilm copy available in USCO. Record Books (recording registration applications) for after 1870 are held by USCO, with entries listed in the General Index, 1870–1896.

66. Melissa Homestead, *American Women Authors and Literary Property, 1822–1869* (Cambridge: Cambridge University Press, 2005), 184. For examples of notices, see *New York Ledger*, 19 Apr. 1856, 17 May 1856.

67. "The New Copyright Law," *New York Times*, 20 Nov. 1870.

68. General Index, 1870–1896, USCO; S. S. McClure, "Newspaper 'Syndicates,'" *The Critic: A Weekly Review of Literature and the Arts* 186 (23 July 1887): 42.

69. Graham Law, *Serializing Fiction in the Victorian Press* (Basingstoke, UK: Palgrave, 2000), 64–79.

70. McClure, "Newspaper 'Syndicates.'"

71. For more on how the syndicates operated and the degree of control enjoyed by newspaper editors, see Johanningsmeier, *Fiction*, 79–85, 147–54, 182.

72. Frederic Hudson, *Journalism in the United States from 1690 to 1872* (New York: Harper & Brothers, 1873), 727.

73. General Index, 1870–1897, USCO. Pinpointing who registered when is difficult given that the cards in the General Index are sometimes out of order and incomplete. For example, the earliest entry indexed for the *New York Times* is 1 June 1886, but the actual record books recording registration applications show entries going back to at least 23 Feb. 1886 (entry 4361 for 1886). In the case of the *Sun*, a copyright notice on a telegraphic dispatch appeared in the issue of 27 Dec. 1885, but this is not recorded in the index and I was unable to find it in the record books. The earliest registration for the *Sun* that I found was 23 Feb.1886 (no. 4362), the same day as the *Times*'s first entry. The record books are arranged chronologically and at time of writing are not available digitally, making systematic searches difficult. Sometimes the only way to locate unindexed entries is by chance.

74. For example, "Paris and Brussels Joined by Telephone," *Cincinnati Commercial Tribune*, 30 Jan. 1887 (labeled as "New York Herald Cable Service" and copyrighted by James Gordon Bennett Jr.); "The Negotiations Abroad," *Chicago Tribune*, 31 Oct. 1888 (labeled as "Special Cable Dispatch to the Tribune" but copyrighted in Bennett's name);

and "Statutes for Famous Men," *Idaho Statesman* (Boise), 22 Mar. 1890 (copyrighted in Bennett's name).

75. These included the North American Cable News Company, the International Cable Agency, and the California Associated Press. General Index, 1870–1896, USCO.

76. "Resort to the Scissors," *Leadville (CO) Herald Democrat*, 11 Sept. 1886. Other reports referred to a C. A. Colby who ran either the Western News Bureau or the Colorado News Bureau. "Telegraph," *Aspen (CO) Daily Times*, 28 July 1886; and *Solid Muldoon Weekly* (Ouray, CO), 25 Mar. 1887.

77. A. R. Spofford to Colorado News and Press Association, 17 Sep. 1886, quoted in *Leadville (CO) Herald Democrat*, 18 Sept. 1886. See also *Leadville (CO) Evening Chronicle*, 18 Sept. 1886.

78. An Act to Revise, Consolidate, and Amend the Statutes Relating to Patents and Copyrights, ch. 230, § 90, 16 Stat. 198, 213 (1870), available in *PSC*.

79. General Index, 1870–1897, USCO; and Record Books for 1886 and 1887, USCO.

80. Based on a perusal of the Record Books for the 1890s. The records are voluminous and currently unavailable digitally, making any attempt at statistical analysis impractical, although this should change.

81. Harper v. Shoppell, 28 F. 613 (S.D.N.Y. 1886). Note that this was a retrial of a suit that Harper & Brothers initially lost for complex reasons that cannot be discussed here. See Harper v. Shoppell, 26 F. 519 (S.D.N.Y. 1886).

82. Eric B. Easton, "Who Owns 'The First Rough Draft of History'?: Reconsidering Copyright in News," *Columbia Journal of Law & the Arts* 27 (2003–2004): 539–40. The delay between initial publication and reproduction, however, suggests that the value of the work was not fleeting.

83. *Aberdeen (SD) Daily News*, 20 Dec. 1886; *Rockford (IL) Daily Register*, 22 Dec. 1886; and *Bismarck (ND) Daily Tribune*, 26 Dec. 1886.

84. R. R. Bowker, *Copyright: Its Law and Its Literature* (New York: Publishers Weekly, 1886), 13.

85. Ibid.

86. Schwarzlose, *Nation's Newsbrokers*, 2:149–82; Silberstein-Loeb, *International Distribution*, 42–47; and Kielbowicz, "Regulating Timeliness," 31–32.

87. Schwarzlose, *Nation's Newsbrokers*, 2:173, 248; Silberstein-Loeb, *International Distribution*, 48–51; and *The Associated Press. Fourth Annual Report* (Chicago, 1897), 3–6.

88. General Index, 1870–1897, USCO; and Record Books for 1892 (entry 21684) and 1894 (entries 1–365), USCO.

89. General Index, 1870–1897, and Claimant Files, 1898–1937, USCO.

90. General Index, 1870–1897 (indexed under James Gordon Bennett), USCO.

91. In 1892–1893, a very small number of dispatches were entered, suggesting the desire to protect particular stories. Beginning in 1894, registration became more systematic, with around 200 entries in 1894, followed by about 160 entries in 1895 and approximately 400 entries in 1896. Estimates based on General Index, 1870–1897, USCO. Not all of these entries were perfected by deposit, however. *CTE* (see list of abbreviations) shows 17 titles deposited by the AP in 1894, compared to about 200 listed in the General Index. For 1896, *CTE* lists 251 deposited works, compared to almost 400 listed in the General Index. *CTE* lists 509 articles deposited by AP in 1898.

92. *The Associated Press. Sixth Annual Report* (Chicago, 1899), 137, 149. After the

AP reincorporated in New York in 1900, a similar resolution was passed. *The Associated Press. Second Annual Report* (New York, 1902), 80.

93. "Caught Pilfering," *The Newspaper Maker* 7, no. 169 (June 9, 1898): 1.

94. Melville E. Stone, *Fifty Years a Journalist* (New York: Doubleday, Page, 1921), 63–64.

95. For examples, see correspondence between A. S. Ochs and Wallach and Cook, 1896–1905, and correspondence between A. S. Ochs and the Short Story Publishing Company, 1896–1897, New York Times Company Records, Adolph S. Ochs Papers, NYPL.

96. See Kielbowicz, "Regulating Timeliness," 25.

97. Tribune Co. of Chicago v. Associated Press, 116 F. 126 (N.D. Ill. 1902).

98. "Answer of the Associated Press" at 3–4, Tribune Co. v. Associated Press, C.C.N.D. Ill., case no. 25443 (1900–1903), NARA Chicago.

99. *Tribune*, 116 F. at 128.

100. Quoted in *Tribune*, 116 F. at 127.

101. As Seaman noted, Thompson's opinion had been quoted with approval by the Supreme Court in *Baker v. Selden* (1879) and by the Court of Appeals for the Seventh Circuit in *J. L. Mott Iron Works v. Clow* (1897). *Tribune*, 116 F. at 127–28.

102. *Tribune*, 116 F. at 128.

103. Correspondence between C. F. Moberly Bell and A. S. Ochs, 1900–1907, and Frank B. Noyes to A. S. Ochs, 25 Mar. 1904 and 8 Apr. 1904, New York Times Company Records, Adolph S. Ochs Papers, NYPL.

104. *The Associated Press. Seventh Annual Report* (Chicago, 1900), 182.

105. "Is a Newspaper Entitled to Copyright?," *Central Law Journal* 57, no. 2 (10 July 1903): 21.

106. Ibid., 23.

107. See Oren Bracha, *Owning Ideas: The Intellectual Origins of American Intellectual Property, 1790–1909* (Cambridge: Cambridge University Press, 2016), 103–11.

108. Samuel J. Elder, "Our Archaic Copyright Laws," *American Law Review* 37 (Mar.–Apr. 1903): 221.

109. See E. Fulton Brylawski and Abe Goldman, eds., *Legislative History of the 1909 Copyright Act*, 6 vols. (South Hackensack, NJ: Fred B. Rothman, 1976); and Jessica Litman, *Digital Copyright* (Amherst, NY: Prometheus Books, 2006), 38–40.

110. "Thirty-One Years of Service by A.N.P.A.," *Editor and Publisher* 49, no. 45 (21 April 1917): 10–12.

111. Herbert Putnam to Melville E. Stone, 9 Mar. 1906; Stone to Putnam, 10 Mar. 1906; and Putnam to Stone, 12 Mar. 1906—all in uncatalogued papers related to 1909 act, USCO (copies on file with the author).

112. Stone to Putnam, 15 Mar. 1906, uncatalogued papers related to 1909 act, USCO (copy on file with the author).

113. Ibid.

114. "Stenographic Report of the Proceedings of the First Session of the Conference on Copyright," in Brylawski and Goldman, *Legislative History*, 1:22.

115. Ibid.

116. *Report of the Nineteenth Annual Meeting of the American Newspaper Publishers Association* (New York: ANPA, 1905), 25.

117. Ibid.

118. Leopold Wallach to A. S. Ochs, 28 Mar. 1904, New York Times Company Records, Adolph S. Ochs Papers, NYPL.

119. "Stenographic Report of the Proceedings of the Second Session of the Conference on Copyright," in Brylawski and Goldman, *Legislative History*, 2:202.

120. Ibid., 2:203.

121. Ibid., 2:205.

122. "Stenographic Report of the Proceedings at the Third Session of the Conference on Copyright," in Brylawski and Goldman, *Legislative History*, 3:163.

123. *Report of Proceedings of the Ninth Annual Convention of the American Newspaper Publishers Association* (New York: ANPA, 1895); and Act of March 2, 1895, ch. 194, 28 Stat. 965.

124. *Report of Proceedings of the Eleventh Annual Convention of the American Newspaper Publishers Association* (New York: ANPA, 1897), 39.

125. Ibid., 40; *Report of the Nineteenth Annual Meeting*, 26.

126. *Report of Proceedings of the Eleventh Annual Convention*, 39–41.

127. "To the Honorable [name of Representative]," printed memorial dated 1907, H.R. Cmte. Patents, files HR59A-H19.1, RG 233, NARA; and Sen. Cmte. Judiciary, files SEN59A-J79, NARA. Other petitions against the amendment can be found in the same files and in H.R. Cmte. Patents, HR60A-H27.9, RG 233, NARA.

128. On the development of privacy law in this context, see Samantha Barbas, *Laws of Image: Privacy and Publicity in America* (Stanford, CA: Stanford University Press, 2015).

129. Frank W. Medlar to William B. Allison, 11 Jan. 1907, file SEN59A-J79, NARA.

130. "Statement of Mr. Pirie Macdonald," in Brylawski and Goldman, *Legislative History* 5:159–61.

131. Underwood and Underwood to Joint Committee on Patents, c/o Librarian of Congress, 15 Dec. 1906, uncatalogued papers related to 1909 act, USCO (copy on file with the author).

132. "Statement of Copyright Committee of American Newspaper Publishers' Association," in Brylawski and Goldman, *Legislative History*, 5:156.

133. The new limit was two hundred dollars, whereas the maximum amount for damages in other cases was five thousand dollars. An Act to Amend and Consolidate the Acts Respecting Copyright, ch. 320, § 25 (b), 35 Stat. 1075 (1909) [hereafter 1909 Act].

134. R. R. Bowker to Thorvald Solberg, 11 Dec. 1905, and Charles Scribner II to R. R. Bowker, 6 Jan. 1909, R. R. Bowker Papers, NYPL; Solberg to Scribner, 16 Jan. 1906, and Scribner to Solberg, 27 Jan. 1906, uncatalogued papers related to 1909 act, USCO (copies on file with the author).

135. American Copyright League correspondence, 1905–1906, R. R. Bowker Papers, NYPL.

136. 1909 Act, § 5 (b).

137. Ibid., §§ 9, 12.

138. Solberg to Bowker, 29 Apr. 1905, R. R. Bowker Papers, NYPL.

139. Scribner to Solberg, 27 Jan. 1906, uncatalogued papers related to 1909 act, USCO (copy on file with the author).

140. Andrew Miller to Alfred B. Kittredge, 2 Feb. 1907, file SEN59A-J79, NARA.

141. 1909 Act, §§ 3, 12, 19.

142. R. R. Bowker, *Copyright: Its History and Its Law* (Boston: Houghton Mifflin, 1912), 76.

143. Ibid., 76–77.

144. Correspondence between R. R. Bowker and Charles Scribner II, 1908–1909, R. R. Bowker papers, NYPL (quote from Bowker to Scribner, 16 Jan. 1909).

145. Bowker, *Copyright*, 88–89.

CHAPTER SEVEN

1. In 1912, the *New York Times* failed to obtain an injunction because it filed court papers before registering and depositing the articles for copyright, and the statute clearly stated that a suit could only be brought after registration and deposit. The *Times* drew attention to the problem and complained to the copyright office that the procedures were confusing. See "Grave Danger in Copyright Decision," *New York Times*, 8 Apr. 1912; and Correspondence between C. V. Van Anda and Thorvald Solberg, 1 Apr. 1912–23 Apr. 1912, R. R. Bowker Papers, NYPL.

2. Chicago Record-Herald Co. v. Tribune Ass'n, 275 F. 797 (7th Cir. 1921).

3. Copyright Act of 1976, 17 U.S.C. § 102 (2016); and "Copyright Basics," US Copyright Office, revised Sept. 2017, https://www.copyright.gov/circs/circo1.pdf.

4. International News Service v. Associated Press, 248 U.S. 215 (1918) [hereafter *INS*].

5. *INS* is the subject of hundreds of law review articles. For an overview, see Victoria Smith Ekstrand, *Hot News in the Age of Big Data: A Legal History of the Hot News Doctrine and Implications for the Digital Age* (El Paso, TX: LFB Scholarly Publishing, 2015), which is an updated version of Victoria Smith Ekstrand, *News Piracy and the Hot News Doctrine: Origins in Law and Implications for the Digital Age* (New York: LFB Scholarly Publishing, 2005).

6. Examples include Exchange Tel. Co. v. Gregory, [1896] 1 Q.B. 147; Exchange Tel. Co. v. Central News, [1897] 2 Ch. 48; and Exchange Tel. Co. v. Howard, [1906] 22 T.L.R. 375. See Tanya Aplin et al., *Gurry on Breach of Confidence: The Protection of Confidential Information*, 2nd ed. (Oxford: Oxford University Press, 2012), 53–65 (section by Lionel Bently). Litigation along the lines of *INS* does not seem to have been tried in the United Kingdom. The reasons for that deserve further study, but there were a number of indications that such an approach was less likely to work in that jurisdiction. British courts declined to develop a broad principle of "unfair competition" apart from cases in which illegal acts had clearly been committed. There are parallels in the areas of privacy and unjust enrichment, suggesting that the common law in Britain and America was diverging during this period. See William Cornish, David Llewelyn, and Tanya Aplin, *Intellectual Property: Patents, Copyright, Trade Marks and Allied Rights*, 8th ed. (London: Sweet and Maxwell, 2013), 12–17.

7. Melville E. Stone, *Fifty Years a Journalist* (Garden City, NY: Doubleday, Page, 1921), 359.

8. David Hochfelder, "'Where the Common People Could Speculate': The Ticker, Bucket Shops, and the Origins of Popular Participation in Financial Markets, 1880–1920," *Journal of American History* 93, no. 2 (Sept. 2006): 335–58.

9. The *New York Stock Exchange Sales* was registered in July 1872 but not after that. The *New York Daily Price List of Stocks* entered six consecutive issues in 1874 and

then stopped. The Gold and Stock Telegraph Company and J. J. Kiernan also entered their quotations (as "prints") in 1873–1874. E. R. Powers, who also began to register his *New York Cotton Exchange Market Report* in 1873, was exceptional in that he continued to register until 1880. General Index, 1870–1897, USCO.

10. The NYAP should not be confused with the AP that sued INS in 1917. The NYAP had existed since the 1840s. In 1892, a new organization called the Associated Press, built on the foundations of the old Western Associated Press, was incorporated in Chicago. Then, in 1900, the Chicago-based AP was dissolved and a new AP was incorporated in New York. See chapter 6, text preceding notes 12 and 86.

11. Kiernan v. Manhattan Quotation Telegraph Co., 50 How. Pr. 194, 198 (N.Y. Sup. Ct. 1876).

12. *Id.* at 203.

13. David Hochfelder, *The Telegraph in America, 1832–1920* (Baltimore: Johns Hopkins University Press, 2012), 96.

14. Brief for Appellants, National Tel. News Co. v. Western Union Tel. Co., 119 F. 294 (7th Cir. 1902), posted by Robert Brauneis on his faculty web page, http://docs.law .gwu.edu/facweb/rbrauneis/originality/briefs/National_Telegraph_Brief_for_Appellants .pdf.

15. Brief for Appellee at 8, *National Tel.*, 119 F. 294, http://docs.law.gwu.edu /facweb/rbrauneis/originality/briefs/National_Telegraph_Brief_for_Appellee.pdf.

16. *Id.* at 10. On *Clayton v. Stone*, see chapter 4.

17. Stone, *Fifty Years*, 359–61; and Peter S. Grosscup, "Property in News," in *M.E.S. His Book* (New York: Harper & Brothers, 1918), 66–72.

18. *National Tel.*, 119 F. at 297–98.

19. See chapter 6.

20. Robert Brauneis, "The Transformation of Originality in the Progressive-Era Debate over Copyright in News," *Cardozo Arts & Entertainment Law Journal* 27, no. 2 (2009): 321–73.

21. *National Tel.*, 119 F. at 296.

22. "Decision Protects Newsgatherers," *The Fourth Estate*, 1 Nov. 1902: 2.

23. See Hochfelder, *Telegraph*, 94–96, which inspired me to use this image.

24. For 1830s bulletins, see chapter 3, text surrounding note 89. On electric displays, see Steven Wilf, "Making Intellectual Property Law in the Shadow of Law: *International News Service v. Associated Press*," *WIPO Journal* 5, no. 1 (2013): 93.

25. Richard A. Schwarzlose, *The Nation's Newsbrokers* (Evanston, IL: Northwestern University Press, 1989–1990), 2:226–34.

26. Ekstrand, *Hot News*, 58–62; and "International N.S. Barred from Britain," *Charleston (SC) News and Courier*, 11 Oct. 1916.

27. In the 1890s, the Chicago-based AP had been regularly entering titles for copyright (entries peaked in 1898 during the Spanish-American War). After the AP's reorganization in New York in 1900, there were no entries until 1916. CTE; and CCE.

28. John Byrne Cooke, *Reporting the War: Freedom of the Press from the American Revolution to the War on Terrorism* (New York: Palgrave MacMillan, 2007), 89–103.

29. Assoc. Press v. Int'l News Serv., 240 F. 983 (S.D.N.Y. 1917). The Transcripts of Record for the district court and Second Circuit Court of Appeals were printed by the AP as *Law of the Associated Press: Property in News* (New York, 1917).

30. *The Associated Press. Sixteenth Annual Report* (New York, 1916), 74.

31. Edwin T. Earl to Frank B. Noyes, 13 Oct. 1916, Administrative Records of the Early AP, Series IV: Membership Records, box 48, AP Archives.

32. *Assoc. Press*, 240 F. 983.

33. Richard B. Kielbowicz, "Regulating Timeliness: Technologies, Laws, and the News, 1840–1970," *Journalism & Communication Monographs* 17, no. 1 (2015): 14–15.

34. Douglas G. Baird, "The Story of *INS v. AP*: Property, Natural Monopoly, and the Uneasy Legacy of a Concocted Controversy," in *Intellectual Property Stories*, ed. Jane C. Ginsburg and Rochelle Cooper Dreyfuss (New York: Foundation Press, 2006), 9–35.

35. Jonathan Silberstein-Loeb, *The International Distribution of News: The Associated Press, Press Association, and Reuters, 1848–1947* (New York: Cambridge University Press, 2014), 64, 69.

36. Assoc. Press v. Int'l News Serv., 245 F. 244, 245 (2d Cir. 1917). INS also contested (unsuccessfully) the two injunctions issued by the district court.

37. Brief for Defendant, printed in *Law of the Associated Press* (1917), 551–99.

38. Brief for Complainant, printed in *Law of the Associated Press* (1917), 435–510 (quote at 443).

39. Board of Trade v. Christie Grain & Stock Co., 198 U.S. 236, 251 (1905).

40. Brief for Complainant, printed in *Law of the Associated Press* (1917), 468.

41. For an interpretation that stresses the collective action problem, see Shyamkrishna Balganesh, "'Hot News': The Enduring Myth of Property in News," *Columbia Law Review* 111, no. 3 (Apr. 2011): 419–97.

42. Argument, printed in *Law of the Associated Press* (1917), 671–72.

43. *Assoc. Press*, 245 F. at 247–53.

44. *Id.*, at 254.

45. *Id.*, at 253.

46. *The Associated Press. Eighteenth Annual Report* (New York, 1918), 66.

47. The Transcript of Record [hereafter TR], held by NARA (Oct. Term 1918, No. 221), is also available through Gale's "Making of Modern Law" collection. The oral arguments were printed by the AP in *Law of the Associated Press: Property in News* (New York, 1919), 2:749–811. A copy of this book is held by the AP Archives.

48. Argument of Mr. Samuel Untermyer, printed in *Law of the Associated Press* (1919), 2:752–79; and Inter-Ocean Pub. Co. v. Assoc. Press, 184 Ill. 438 (1900). On the background and significance of this case, see Silberstein-Loeb, *International Distribution*, 51–58.

49. Argument of Mr. Samuel Untermyer, 754. As explained later in the chapter, the AP would not relax its restrictive bylaws until forced to by the Supreme Court in 1945. Before that, the system of protest rights was actually expanded. Gene Allen, "News as Property: The Case of Associated Press, 1942–1945" (paper presented to the International Communication Association, Seattle, 25 May 2014).

50. Cooke, *Reporting the War*, 100.

51. Argument of Hiram W. Johnson, printed in *Law of the Associated Press* (1919), 2:798, 809.

52. Ibid., 798–810.

53. TR, Brief for Respondent-Complainant Below, at 36.

54. Ibid.

55. TR, Brief for Respondent-Complainant Below, at 35.

56. Davies v. Bowes, 209 F. 53 (S.D.N.Y. 1913). The *Sun*, which was registered for copyright daily, had assigned the rights over this piece back to the author.

57. *Davies*, 209 F. at 56, cited in Brief for Defendant, printed in *Law of the Associated Press* (1917), 569.

58. TR, Brief for Respondent-Complainant Below, at 36.

59. Hochfelder, *Telegraph*, 74–82; and Baird, "Story of *INS*," 14–15.

60. Argument of Mr. Samuel Untermyer, 772.

61. See Schwarzlose, *Nation's Newsbrokers*, 2:112–14, 122.

62. Oren Bracha, *Owning Ideas: The Intellectual Origins of American Intellectual Property, 1790–1909* (Cambridge: Cambridge University Press, 2016), 54–123.

63. Bleistein v. Donaldson Lithographing Co., 188 U.S. 239 (1903); and Bracha, *Owning Ideas*, 105–8.

64. Supplemental Brief for Complainant, printed in *Law of the Associated Press* (1917), 514–15.

65. Argument of Mr. F. W. Lehmann, printed in *Law of the Associated Press* (1919), 2:788.

66. TR, Brief for Respondent-Claimant Below, 35.

67. TR, Petitioner's Brief, 49.

68. *INS*, 248 U.S. at 234.

69. Titles entered daily include the *New York Times, New York World, New York Tribune, New York American* (a Hearst paper and AP member), *Boston Globe*, and *Philadelphia Inquirer*. Claimant File, 1898–1937, USCO.

70. Walter v. Steinkopff [1892] 3 Ch. 489. See chapter 5.

71. *INS*, 248 U.S. at 234–35.

72. See David L. Lange and H. Jefferson Powell, *No Law: Intellectual Property in the Image of an Absolute First Amendment* (Stanford, CA: Stanford Law Books, 2009), 149–67; and Wendy J. Gordon, "On Owning Information: Intellectual Property and the Restitutionary Impulse," *Virginia Law Review* 78 (1992): 149–281.

73. *INS*, 248 U.S. at 248.

74. Abrams v. United States, 250 U.S. 616, 630 (1919). See Sam Lebovic, *Free Speech and Unfree News: The Paradox of Press Freedom in America* (Cambridge, MA: Harvard University Press, 2016), 16–18.

75. *INS*, 248 U.S. at 250.

76. *Id.* at 263.

77. *INS*, 248 U.S. at 265–67. The Pan-American Convention allowed for newspaper articles to be reproduced with acknowledgment unless expressly prohibited, and it denied protection for "news and miscellaneous items published merely for general information." 38 Stat. 1785 (1910), art. 11.

78. *The Associated Press. Nineteenth Annual Report* (New York, 1919), 5.

79. "Supreme Court Recognizes Property Rights in News by Gathering Associations," *Editor & Publisher*, 28 Dec. 1918: 5.

80. "News Is Property," *New York Times*, 24 Dec. 1918.

81. "News Piracy Defined," *Oregonian* (Portland), 25 Dec. 1918.

82. Scholars have begun to use such tools to study patterns of text reuse in nineteenth-century newspapers (see chapter 3, note 7). The available digital corpus for the twentieth century is much more limited, in part because of copyright restrictions. Such

a study would have to take into account the institutional arrangements among newspapers—such as who was a member of the AP—in order to distinguish between licit and illicit publication. Moreover, in cases where non-AP papers ran the same story in a different form, it would often be impossible to verify whether independent sources had been consulted, in which case the second paper could not be said to have relied entirely on the first.

83. Silberstein-Loeb, *International Distribution*, 66.

84. Cf. Richard A. Epstein, "*International News Service v. Associated Press*: Custom and Law as Sources of Property Rights in News," *Virginia Law Review* 78 (Feb. 1992): 85–129. There is no evidence that copying was not widespread before 1916, as Epstein claims, and every reason to think otherwise.

85. Quoted in Silberstein-Loeb, *International Distribution*, 207. On Stone's fears about accusations of monopoly, see Ibid., 77.

86. Silberstein-Loeb, *International Distribution*, 207.

87. Heidi J. S. Tworek, "Journalistic Statesmanship: Protecting the Press in Weimar Germany and Abroad," *German History* 32, no. 4 (Dec. 2014): 559–78.

88. "Declaration and Resolutions Adopted by the Conference of Press Experts" (1927), quoted in Silberstein-Loeb, *International Distribution*, 210.

89. Ibid. See also Heidi J. S. Tworek, "Protecting News," in *MN*, 211–12.

90. 1932 proposal, quoted in Tworek, "Protecting News," 214.

91. Roderick Jones, "Property in News," quoted in Tworek, "Protecting News," 213.

92. Tworek, "Protecting News," 214.

93. See also Sam Ricketson and Jane Ginsburg, "Intellectual Property in News? Why Not?" in *Research Handbook on Intellectual Property in Media and Entertainment*, ed. Megan Richardson and Sam Ricketson (Cheltenham, UK: Edward Elgar, 2017), 10–46.

94. William Cannon to Jackson Elliot, 15 Aug. 1927; Kent Cooper to William Cannon, 21 Dec. 1927; and Davis, Polk, Wardwell, Gardiner, and Reed to Kent Cooper, 23 Jan. 1928—all in Subject Files, Series I, boxes 24–25, AP Archives.

95. Cooper to Bickel, 9 June 1925, 13 Oct. 1926, and 14 Dec. 1926; Bickel to Cooper, 30 Oct. 1926; and [Cooper?] to Bickel, 16 Feb. 1928—all in Subject Files, Series I, boxes 24–25, AP Archives.

96. On informal agreements and other aspects of Cooper's strategy, see Gene Allen, "An American Newsman: Kent Cooper, Associated Press, and the 20th-Century World of News" (unpublished manuscript, forthcoming). I am grateful to Allen for sharing his research, including the correspondence cited in the two preceding notes.

97. See CCE.

98. Solberg's remarks in Byron Price to Kent Cooper, 16 July 1926, Subject Files, Series I, box 6, AP Archives.

99. Byron Price to Kent Cooper, 10 Aug. 1926, Subject Files, Series I, box 6, AP Archives.

100. Crediting AP Dispatches (and Use of Logo) 1925–1929, Subject Files, Series I, box 6, folders 11–12, AP Archives; Price to Cooper, 23 July 1931; and Cooper to Price, 24 July 1931—Subject Files, Series I, box 6, AP Archives. Under the 1909 act, copyright was secured by publication with notice; registration was only required to bring a suit. 1909 Act, §§ 9, 12.

101. J. S. Elliott to Grafton Wilcox, 22 June 1928, Subject Files, Series I, box 6, AP Archives; and [Kent Cooper?] to T. M. Storke, 18 Feb. 1941, Subject Files, Series I, box 53, AP Archives.

102. Correspondence related to 1932 dispute between Elmer E. Meadows and the AP over an article in the *Milwaukee Sentinel*, Subject Files, Series I, box 6, folder 9, AP Archives. The policy memo by Jackson S. Elliott dated 19 Sept. 1932 is in the same folder.

103. Stuart Banner, *American Property: A History of How, Why, and What We Own* (Cambridge, MA: Harvard University Press, 2011), 90.

104. Cheney Bros. v. Doris Silk Corporation, 35 F. 2d 279, 280 (2d Cir. 1929).

105. For a full account of the case law, see Ekstrand, *Hot News*, chapters 4–5.

106. Gwenyth L. Jackaway stresses the different ways that newspapers attempted to block radio. *Media at War: Radio's Challenge to the Newspapers, 1924–1939* (Westport, CT: Praeger, 1995). By contrast, Michael Stamm shows that many newspapers incorporated radio into multimedia businesses. *Sound Business: Newspapers, Radio, and the Politics of New Media* (Philadelphia: University of Pennsylvania Press, 2011).

107. For a fuller account of radio regulations, see Paul Starr, *The Creation of the Media: Political Origins of Modern Communications* (New York: Basic Books, 2004), 327–84.

108. Michael Stamm, "Broadcasting News in the Interwar Period," in *MN*, 133–63.

109. Ibid., 143–46.

110. Stamm, *Sound Business*, 62–63.

111. Jackaway, *Media at War*, 23–27.

112. Ibid., 27–30; Stamm, "Broadcasting News," 150.

113. In addition to action by the AP discussed here, some newspapers also filed suits. See "Radio Piracy Hearing Set for Monday," *Editor & Publisher*, 17 June 1933: 10; and "New Orleans Dailies Win Injunction," *Editor & Publisher*, 1 July 1933: 12.

114. "A.P. Gets Injunction against Station," *Editor & Publisher*, 18 Mar. 1933: 8; "News Injunction Affirmed," *Editor & Publisher*, 8 Apr. 1933: 8; and "Unfair Competition—Broadcasting News Dispatches—Injunction," *Air Law Review* 4, no. 3 (July 1933): 323–24.

115. "KSOO Appeals Action in A.P. Radio Suit," *Editor & Publisher*, 15 Apr. 1933: 10; and "Drops News Ban Appeal," *New York Times*, 24 Sept. 1933.

116. Assoc. Press v. KVOS, 9 F. Supp. 279, 288 (W.D. Wa. 1934).

117. "Between You and Me," *Washington Post*, 31 Dec. 1934.

118. Assoc. Press v. KVOS, 80 F. 2d 575, 584 (9th Cir. 1935).

119. KVOS v. Assoc. Press, 299 U.S. 269 (1936).

120. "Fight against Radio News 'Pirating' Lost by Associated Press," *Chicago Tribune*, 15 Dec. 1936.

121. Stamm, *Sound Business*, 37–39, 73–74.

122. Jackaway, *Media at War*, 30–33. On the number of newspaper-owned stations, see Stamm, *Sound Business*, 60, 195.

123. Stamm, *Sound Business*, 76.

124. Erie Railroad Co. v. Tompkins, 304 U.S. 64 (1938).

125. Pottstown D.N. Pub. Co. v. Potts. Broad. Co., 411 Pa. 383 (1963).

126. Copyright Act of 1976, 17 U.S.C. § 301 (2016).

127. National Basketball Association v. Sports Team Analysis and Tracking Systems, Inc., and Motorola, 939 F. Supp. 1071, 1075 (S.D.N.Y. 1996).

128. National Basketball Association v. Motorola, 105 F. 3d 841, 845 (2d Cir. 1997).

129. *NBA v. Motorola*, 105 F. at 854.

130. Ekstrand, *Hot News*, 158–59.

131. Associated Press v. U.S., 326 U.S. 1 (1945).

132. Lebovic, *Free Speech*, 76–84.

133. Robert W. McChesney and John Nichols, *The Death and Life of American Journalism: The Media Revolution That Will Begin the World Again* (New York: Nation Books, 2011); James L. Baughman, "The Decline of Journalism since 1945," in *MN*, 164–95; and Robert G. Picard, "Protecting News Today," in *MN*, 223–37.

134. Associated Press v. All Headline News Corp., 608 F. Supp. 2d 454 (S.D.N.Y. 2009).

135. David Kravets, "AP Defeats Online Aggregator That Rewrote Its News," *Wired*, 13 July 2009, https://www.wired.com/2009/07/hot-news-doctrine-defeats-aggregator-site/.

136. Barclays Capital Inc. v. Theflyonthewall.com Inc., 700 F. Supp. 2d 310 (S.D.N.Y. 2010).

137. Quoted in Shawn Moynihan, "AP Joins Brief in Potentially Groundbreaking Legal Case," *Editor & Publisher*, 23 June 2010, http://www.editorandpublisher.com/news/ap-joins-brief-in-potentially-groundbreaking-legal-case/.

138. James Boyle, "Hot News: The Next Bad Thing," *Financial Times*, 1 Apr. 2010, https://www.ft.com/content/0c1efcf4-3d11-11df-b81b-00144feabdco.

139. Quoted in Melissa Lipman, "Google, Twitter Back Removal of 'Hot News' Injunction," *Law360*, 22 June 2010, http://www.law360.com/articles/176629/google-twitter-back-removal-of-hot-news-injunction.

140. "Hot News Doctrine Could Stifle Online Commentary and Criticism," press release with link to amicus brief, 22 June 2010, http://www.eff.org/press/archives/2010/06/22.

141. Barclays Capital Inc. v. Theflyonthewall.com Inc., 650 F. 3d 876, 907 (2d Cir. 2011).

142. Jacqueline Bell, "2nd Circ. Favors Fly in Wall Street 'Hot News' Fight," *Law360*, 20 June 2011, http://www.law360.com/articles/252433/2nd-circ-favors-fly-in-wall-street-hot-news-fight?article_related_content=1.

143. Clay Calvert and Matthew D. Bunker, "Framing a Semantic Hot-News Quagmire in Barclays Capital v. Theflyonthewall.com: Of Missed Opportunities and Unresolved First Amendment Issues," *Virginia Journal of Law and Technology* 17, no. 1 (Spring 2012): 50–74.

144. See Ekstrand, *Hot News*, 197–98, and references therein.

145. Compare Balganesh, "Hot News," and Silberstein-Loeb, *International Distribution*, 63–64.

EPILOGUE

1. Kenneth J. Arrow, "Economic Welfare and the Allocation of Resources for Invention," in *The Rate and Direction of Inventive Activity: Economic and Social Factors* (Princeton, NJ: Princeton University Press, 1962), 615. See also Gerben Bakker, "Trading Facts: Arrow's Fundamental Paradox and the Origins of Global News Networks," in *International Communication and Global News Networks: Historical Perspectives*, ed.

Peter Putnis, Chandrika Kaul, and Jürgen Wilke (New York: Hampton Press / International Association for Media and Communication Research, 2011), 9–54.

2. In the case of works for hire in the United States, copyright lasts for 95 years after publication or 120 years after creation, whichever comes first. 17 U.S.C. § 302 (c) (2016). The UK statute specifies different durations for films, sound recordings, broadcasts, and typographical arrangements. See Copyright, Designs and Patents Act 1988, c. 48, §§ 12–15, https://www.legislation.gov.uk/ukpga/1988/48/contents [hereafter CDPA 1988].

3. Berne Convention, amended 28 Sept. 1979, art. 2 (8), http://www.wipo.int /treaties/en/text.jsp?file_id=283698; and Sam Ricketson and Jane Ginsburg, "Intellectual Property in News? Why Not?," in *Research Handbook on Intellectual Property in Media and Entertainment,* ed. Megan Richardson and Sam Ricketson (Cheltenham, UK: Edward Elgar, 2017), 10–46.

4. Berne Convention, 1979, art. 10 (1).

5. Note that in the UK there is an additional copyright in the typographical arrangement of a published edition, which lasts for twenty-five years. CDPA 1988, §§ 8, 15.

6. There are differences between the UK and the US. In 1991, the US Supreme Court rejected the "sweat of the brow" doctrine and said that protection for fact-based compilations would be limited to original elements of selection and arrangement. Feist Publications, Inc. v. Rural Telephone Service Co., 499 U.S. 340 (1991). In the UK, courts have been more likely to provide some kind of protection in cases in which the collection of facts involves significant labor, skill, and judgment. Notably, the UK has a separate sui-generis-database right that protects "substantial investment in obtaining, verifying, or presenting the content." Copyright and Rights in Databases Regulations 1997, no. 3032, § 13 (1), https://www.legislation.gov.uk/uksi/1997/3032/contents/made. See also Lionel Bently and Brad Sherman, *Intellectual Property Law,* 4th ed. (Oxford: Oxford University Press, 2014), 96–105, 212–15.

7. I borrow the idea of flexibilities from Patricia Aufderheide and Peter Jaszi, *Reclaiming Fair Use: How to Put the Balance Back in Copyright* (Chicago: University of Chicago Press, 2011).

8. CDPA 1988, § 30 (2); Bently and Sherman, *Intellectual Property,* 244–47.

9. Patricia Aufderheide and Peter Jaszi, "Copyright, Free Speech, and the Public's Right to Know: How Journalists Think about Fair Use" (Feb. 2012), Center for Media and Social Impact, School of Communication, American University, http://cmsimpact .org/resource/copyright-free-speech-publics-right/; and Jaszi and Aufderheide, "Set of Principles in Fair Use for Journalism" (June 2013), http://cmsimpact.org/code/set -principles-fair-use-journalism/.

10. 17 U.S.C. § 107 (2016).

11. CDPA 1988, § 30 (1), § 30 (1ZA).

12. Melville B. Nimmer used the example of photos of the My Lai massacre and the Zapruder film of the Kennedy assassination. Melville B. Nimmer, "Does Copyright Abridge the First Amendment Guarantees of Free Speech and Press?," *UCLA Law Review* 17 (1970): 1197–99.

13. For a starting point, see Eric Barendt, *Freedom of Speech,* 2nd ed. (Oxford: Oxford University Press, 2005), 247–67; and Jonathan Griffiths and Uma Suthersanen, eds., *Copyright and Free Speech: Comparative and International Analyses* (Oxford: Oxford University Press, 2005).

14. In the UK, the potential tension between copyright and freedom of expression

became more relevant after the passage of the Human Rights Act 1998, which incorporated the European Convention on Human Rights (ECHR) into UK law. Article 10 of the ECHR defines freedom of expression to include the freedom "to hold opinions and to receive and impart information and ideas without interference by public authority and regardless of frontiers." But this is subject to respect of other laws, including copyright. See Kevin Garnett, "The Impact of the Human Rights Act 1998 on UK Copyright Law," in Griffiths and Suthersanen, *Copyright and Free Speech*, 171–209.

15. AFP 2005 court filing, quoted in Shannon Henson, "Google Settles Suit over News Content," *Law360*, 9 Apr. 2007, http://www.law360.com/articles/22235/.

16. Eric Auchard, "AFP, Google News Settle Lawsuit over Google News," Reuters, 7 Apr. 2007, http://www.reuters.com/.

17. Associated Press v. Meltwater US Holdings, 931 F. Supp. 2d 537 (S.D.N.Y. 2013).

18. Rosalind Jane Schonwold, "*Associated Press v. Meltwater US Holdings, Inc.*: Fair Use, a Changing News Industry, and the Influence of Judicial Discretion and Custom," *Berkeley Technology Law Journal* 29 (2014): 801.

19. Case C-5/08, Infopaq Int'l A/S v. Danske Dagblades Forening, 2009 E.C.R. I-06569. See Eleonora Rosati, *Originality in EU Copyright: Full Harmonization through Case Law* (Cheltenham, UK: Edward Elgar, 2013), 97–118.

20. Case C-360/13, Public Relations Consultants Association Ltd. v. Newspaper Licensing Agency Ltd. and Others [5 June 2014] ECLI:EU:C:2014:1195.

21. Newspaper Licensing Agency Ltd. and Others v. Meltwater Holding BV and Others [2010] EWHC (Ch.) 3099 [70].

22. Bently and Sherman, *Intellectual Property*, 110–12; and Rosati, *Originality*, 114.

23. Quoted in Dominic Ponsford, "Independent Declines to Pay for Court Story 'Lifted' from Wales Online Telling Freelance: 'There Is No Copyright in News,'" *Press Gazette*, 10 July 2017, http://www.pressgazette.co.uk/.

24. Dominic Ponsford, "Freelance Claims Victory in Dispute with Independent over Payment for Court Story from Wales Online," *Press Gazette*, 9 Aug. 2017, http://www.pressgazette.co.uk/.

25. Quoted in Dominic Ponsford, "'David and Goliath' Legal Battle Sees Rochdale Online Win Payout from Manchester Evening News over Danczuk Expenses Story," *Press Gazette*, 12 July 2017, http://www.pressgazette.co.uk/.

26. Heidi J. S. Tworek and Christopher Buschow, "Changing the Rules of the Game: Strategic Institutionalization and Legacy Companies' Resistance to New Media," *International Journal of Communication* 10 (2016): 2126.

27. Joe Mullin, "New Study Shows Spain's 'Google Tax' Has Been a Disaster for Publishers," *ArsTechnica*, 30 July 2015, https://arstechnica.com/. See also Eleonora Rosati, "Ancillary Rights for News Content: The State of Play in Europe," 29 Jan. 2016, Commsrisk, http://commsrisk.com/.

28. European Commission, "Proposal for a Directive of the European Parliament and of the Council on Copyright in the Digital Single Market," COM(2016) 593, 14 Sept. 2016, art. 11, https://ec.europa.eu/digital-single-market/en/news/proposal-directive-european-parliament-and-council-copyright-digital-single-market.

29. Richard Danbury, "Is an EU Publishers' Right a Good Idea? Final Report on the AHRC Project: Evaluating Potential Legal Responses to Threats to the Production

of News in a Digital Era" (2016), Centre for Intellectual Property and Information Law, University of Cambridge, https://www.cipil.law.cam.ac.uk/projectscopyright-and-news-research-project-2014-16/working-papers (see "Paper 4: Report Submitted to the Commission") See also European Copyright Society, "General Opinion on the EU Copyright Reform Package," 24 Jan. 2017, Opinions, https://europeancopyrightsocietydotorg.files.wordpress.com/.

30. This idea is expressed eloquently in Aufderheide and Jaszi, *Reclaiming Fair Use*, 25–26.

31. In the United States, works of US origin still need to be registered in order to bring an infringement suit. 17 U.S.C. §§ 411–12 (2016).

32. L. Ray Patterson and Stanley W. Lindberg, *The Nature of Copyright: A Law of Users' Rights* (Athens: University of Georgia Press, 1991), 138.

33. See Paul Fyfe, "Access, Computational Analysis, and Fair Use in the Digitized Nineteenth-Century Press," *Victorian Periodicals Review* 51, no. 4 (forthcoming).

34. *Times* (London), 6 Feb. 1852.

35. James Mussell, "Elemental Forms: The Newspaper as Popular Genre in the Nineteenth Century," *Media History* 20, no. 1 (2014): 4–20.

36. In England and Wales Cricket Board Ltd. v Tixdaq Ltd. [2016] EWHC (Ch.) 575, the court acknowledged that members of the public might qualify for the fair-dealing exception for the purposes of reporting current events. In the case at hand, however, the court found that cricket fans who used a mobile phone application to reproduce and share short clips of protected broadcasts did not engage in fair dealing, even if they accompanied the clips with their own comments.

37. *Reynolds's Weekly Newspaper* (London), 25 Mar. 1855.

38. "Stealing News," *The Nation*, 21 Feb. 1884: 159.

39. Express Newspapers Plc. v. News (U.K.) Ltd. [1990] 1 WLR 1320, 1325.

40. Ibid.

41. But attitudes and practices vary. See Norman P. Lewis and Bu Zhong, "The Root of Journalistic Plagiarism: Contested Attribution Beliefs," *Journalism and Mass Communication Quarterly* 90, no. 1 (2012): 148–66.

42. Reuters, "Why Google and Facebook Prove the Digital Ad Market Is a Duopoly," *Fortune*, 28 July 2017, http://fortune.com/2017/07/28/google-facebook-digital-advertising/.

43. See Ben Thompson, "The Local News Business Model," 9 May 2017, *Stratechery* (blog), https://stratechery.com/2017/the-local-news-business-model/.

44. See, for example, Leonard Downie Jr. and Michael Schudson, "The Reconstruction of American Journalism," *Columbia Journalism Review*, Nov./Dec. 2009, http://archives.cjr.org/reconstruction/; and Robert W. McChesney and John Nichols, *The Death and Life of American Journalism: The Media Revolution That Will Begin the World Again* (New York: Nation Books, 2011).

45. See the essays in *MN*. Sam Lebovic argues that the development of a particular vision of press freedom in America helped to foreclose the possibility of significant state funding for journalism. *Free Speech and Unfree News: The Paradox of Press Freedom in America* (Cambridge, MA: Harvard University Press, 2016).

Index

Page numbers in italic indicate material in figures.

CPSIA information can be obtained
at www.ICGtesting.com
Printed in the USA
BVHW031929070920
588252BV00003B/4